General view of the agriculture of the county of Caithness, etc.

Anonymous

General view of the agriculture of the county of Caithness, etc.

Anonymous
British Library, Historical Print Editions
British Library
1812
2 pt. ; 8º.
287.e.6.

[illegible] 24. [illegible]

Vol. I. to face the Title

GENERAL VIEW

OF THE

AGRICULTURE

OF THE

COUNTY OF CAITHNESS,

WITH

OBSERVATIONS ON THE MEANS OF ITS IMPROVEMENT.

DRAWN UP FOR THE CONSIDERATION OF

THE BOARD OF AGRICULTURE

AND INTERNAL IMPROVEMENT.

BY CAPT. JOHN HENDERSON.

WITH AN APPENDIX,

INCLUDING

AN ACCOUNT OF THE IMPROVEMENTS CARRIED ON,
BY SIR JOHN SINCLAIR, BART.
(FOUNDER, AND FIRST PRESIDENT, OF THE BOARD OF AGRICULTURE),
ON HIS ESTATES IN SCOTLAND.

LONDON:

PRINTED BY B. McMILLAN, BOW-STREET, COVENT-GARDEN:
SOLD BY G. AND W. NICOL, BOOKSELLERS TO HIS MAJESTY,
PALL-MALL; LONGMAN, REES & CO., AND SHERWOOD,
NEELY & JONES, PATERNOSTER-ROW; ARCHIBALD
CONSTABLE & CO. EDINBURGH; AND
J. YOUNG, INVERNESS.

1812.

[Price Fifteen Shillings.]

ADVERTISEMENT.

THE desire that has been generally expressed, to have the AGRICULTURAL SURVEYS of the KINGDOM reprinted, with the additional Communications which have been received since the ORIGINAL REPORTS were circulated, has induced the BOARD OF AGRICULTURE, to come to a resolution, to reprint such as appear on the whole fit for publication.

It is proper at the same time to add, that the Board does not consider itself responsible for every statement contained in the Reports thus reprinted, and that it will thankfully acknowledge any additional information which may still be communicated.

CONTENTS.

DIRECTIONS TO THE BINDER,

FOR PLACING THE PLATES.

IN THE APPENDIX.

CONTENTS.

CHAP. I. GEOGRAPHICAL STATE AND CIRCUMSTANCES.

CHAP. II. STATE OF PROPERTY.

CHAP. III. BUILDINGS.

CHAP. IV. OCCUPATION.

CHAP. V. IMPLEMENTS.

CHAP. VI. INCLOSING.

CHAP. VII. ARABLE LAND.

CHAP. XI. WASTES.

CHAP. XII. IMPROVEMENTS.

CHAP. XIII. EMBANKMENTS.

CHAP. XIV. LIVE STOCK.

CHAP. XV. RURAL ECONOMY.

CHAP. XVI. POLITICAL ECONOMY;

CIRCUMSTANCES DEPENDENT ON LEGISLATIVE AUTHORITY.

CHAP. XVII. OBSTACLES TO IMPROVEMENT.

CHAP. XVIII. MISCELLANEOUS ARTICLES.

CONCLUSION.

ADDENDA.

Obser-

No. XVIII.

APPENDIX.

No. II.

AGRICULTURAL SURVEY

OF THE

COUNTY OF CAITHNESS.

CHAP. I.

GEOGRAPHICAL STATE AND CIRCUMSTANCES.

SECT. I.—SITUATION AND EXTENT.

CAITHNESS is the most remote and northern county on the main-land of Scotland. It is situated between 58° 20″ and 59° of north latitude, and between 2° 50″ and 3° 27″ west longitude. It is divided from the county of Sutherland on the S.W. and W. by a range of mountains and high moory hills, from the Ord of Caithness on the south, to the shores of the North Sea at Drumholasten. It is bounded on the S. E. and E. by the Murray Frith and German Ocean, and on the north from Duncansbay-head to a line with Holburn-head, by the Pentland Frith, dividing it from the Southern Isles of Orkney, and westward from Holburn-head, it is bounded by the North Sea.

The estates of this county not having been, in general, measured, its extent is not exactly ascertained. From the best calculation that can be made by the usual modes of estimating extent, it may be stated, on a medium, at 616 square miles,

	English Acres.		Scotch Acres.
Which is equal to	394,240,	or	315,932
To which add the island of Stroma, $2\frac{1}{4}$ square miles, or	1440,	or	1152
Total of the county, $618\frac{1}{4}$ square miles, or	395,680	=	316,544

The whole consists of nearly the following divisions:

	English. Acres.	Scotch. Acres.
1. Arable land of every description and quality, about	50,000	40,000
2. Meadows, and haughs near rivers, &c. &c.	2500	2000
3. Green pasture, common downs, and partly of a moory surface, ...	77,500	62,000
4. Under brushwood and small plantations, about	1062	850
5. Sand, of Dunnet-bay, Keise-bay, &c. &c.	3750	3000
6. Mountains and high moory hills in the parishes of Latheron, Wick, Cannisbay, Reay, and Halkirk, ...	89,000	71,200
7. Deep mosses and flat moors covered with heather, &c.	163,454	130,763
8. Fresh-water lakes 7680, rivers and burns 734 acres, or about	8414	6731
Total, ...	395,680	316,544

From this calculation of the superficial extent of this county, it will appear, that in subdividing these denominations, the parts bear to the whole extent, thus: arable land near $\frac{1}{8}$th, meadow about $\frac{1}{158}$th, green pasture about $\frac{1}{5}$th, brushwood, &c. about $\frac{1}{372}$d, sand about $\frac{1}{105}$th, mountains about $\frac{1}{4}$th, deep mosses about $\frac{2}{5}$ths, and lakes, rivers, &c. about $\frac{1}{48}$th of the whole.

Templeman, in his Survey of the Globe, made this county 690 square miles; but the Reporter is convinced, from

from his own knowledge of the length of the several lines of road which have been surveyed in the county, that such a calculation is far beyond the truth.

SECT. II.—DIVISIONS.

1. *Political.*—This county, and the shire of Sutherland, were, from 1756, until the year 1807, considered as one Sheriffdom, but there is now a Sheriff-depute for each county. The Sheriff-depute of the county of Caithness appoints a substitute, who acts in his absence, and for whom he is responsible in his judicial conduct. The Commissioners of Supply have divided this county into five districts, for the purpose of levying and expending the commutation-money for the statute labour on the public roads, and for holding meetings for adjusting the rolls, previous to ballotting for the militia. There is no other political subdivision in the county.

Caithness is the only county in Great Britain, of any fertility, population, and extent, which has not the right of a perpetual representation in the British Parliament. It is coupled with the Isle of Bute on the S.W. coast of Scotland, and each county returns a Representative alternately to the House of Commons, to represent them both. This half species of franchise is very much felt in the county of Caithness, as a grievance that ought to be remedied. In fact, Bute and Caithness are so distant from each other, that no common interest can be supposed to exist between them, more than between Cornwall and Caithness, at the two extremities of the British Isle. The only other instances of of such political representation in Scotland, are, 1. Kinross and Clackmannan; and, 2. Nairn and Cromarty; but the case is very different in these, as they are contiguous districts, which have a common interest in every local political occurrence, and which might easily be incorporated together.

2. *Ecclesiastical.*—The county of Caithness is divided into ten parishes, forming one Presbytery. The two Presbyteries of Caithness and Sutherland are erected into one Synod. In ancient times the two counties formed one Bishopric, known under the name of the Bishopric of Caithness. The following is the Ecclesiastical state at present.

Parishes.	*Patrons.*	*Remarks.*
Bower	Sir John Sinclair, Bart.	
Cannisbay	W. Sinclair, Esq. of Freswick	
Dunnet	Sir John Sinclair	
Latheron	Ditto	And a missionary at Berridale
Halkirk	Ditto	A ditto at Achrenie
Olrig	Ditto	
Thurso	Ditto	
Reay	The Crown	One-fourth of this parish in Sutherlandshire
Watten	Sir John Sinclair	An occasional missionary
Wick	Sir B. Dunbar, Bart.	Ditto

Besides the established church, there are in the town and parish of Wick, a Haldian chapel, and a Seceder meeting-house; and in the town of Thurso, a Haldian chapel, and a Seceder chapel, also a few Anabaptists, who hold their meetings in a private house, because they are too few, to afford an establishment for their preacher (a ci-devant Haldian), who also follows the trade of a baker. There are no individuals of any other religious persuasion in the county.

SECT.

SECT. III.—CLIMATE.

1. *Prevailing Winds.*—For three-fourths of the year the wind blows from the W. or N. W., and in the winter, spring, and autumn, there are frequent hard gales from that quarter. There being no mountains or high land on the north side of this county where it bounds with the Northern Ocean, the inclemency of the weather in the winter and spring, is felt more severely here, than in the neighbouring counties of Sutherland and Ross. From the beginning of May to the middle of June, the prevailing wind is usually from the N. W. with a bleak cloudy sky, which checks vegetation much, and is said to nourish that destructive insect called the grub caterpillar, so injurious to bear (or barley), and to potatoe oats, in the early stages of vegetation. From the end of June to September, the wind is variable from the S. W. to the S. E., and but seldom northerly; during this season, vegetation makes, perhaps, a more rapid progress, than it does in counties enjoying, on the whole, a better climate. This, perhaps, may be partly accounted for, by the check given to vegetation in May, and the beginning of June.

2. *Quantity of Rain that falls.*—Although no instrument has been made use of, to ascertain the quantity of rain that annually falls in this county, it is the general opinion, that no county in Scotland has more frequent and heavy rains, than the county of Caithness, the county of Argyle, and the western parts of Inverness, Ross, and Sutherland excepted. During the months of October, November, and December, rain

is generally so frequent and heavy, as to overflow the land adjoining to the streams (provincially burns) and rivers. Generally about the end of December, and sometimes earlier, snow and hard frost commence; and there are instances of a fall of snow commencing about the end of December, and continuing two to three feet deep on the ground, until the beginning, and even the 25th of March; but more frequently the weather, during that season, is variable and squally; a few days of intense frost and snow, then a thaw, with rain from the S.W. or from the East for some days; then the same scene of falls of snow are renewed, until about the 20th February, when the weather, occasionally, becomes more mild; and for some years past the weather, from the 15th February to the 20th March, has been more favourable, than from that period to the middle of April. In 1810, snow and frost were frequent to the 9th of April, so that little progress was made before that time, in field-work. When the season is moderate, the seed-time for oats, is from the 1st of March to the middle, and even the end of April; and the seed-time for bear or bigg, is from the latter end of April to the 12th of June, and sometimes to the 20th June, along the north coast.

Potatoes are planted the first week of May, but some in April. Turnip sowing commences about the 10th of June, and thence to the 10th of July. The earlier sown the better, because the cold weather, in the latter end of autumn, prevents the plants shooting to seed. The bear harvest commences about the end of August, or beginning of September; and the oat harvest, with a favourable season, soon after. Since the introduction of red oats, there are many instances of the harvest being concluded by the 30th of September, but in general

neral not before the 20th of October, and even to the 1st of November.

3. *Other Meteorological Tables.*—I have not found that any meteorological tables have been made up in this county. We have in it some thunder and lightning, followed by heavy falls of rain, in the months of June and July. In July 1808, a thunder hail-shower destroyed a whole field of corn in the parish of Bower, the hailstones being of great size. There have been instances of people and cattle being killed by lightning, in this county; also of houses being struck and much damaged by that powerful fluid. When flashes of lightning are seen during the winter months, it indicates a severe gale of wind, commonly from the N.W. quarter, accompanied by rain or snow. The country people remark, that when with a clear night, they observe the descent of a meteor, called a falling star, it indicates an approaching storm.

The aurora borealis (provincially *merry dancers*), is seen frequently during the winter season, and sometimes at other periods of the year. When seen low in the horizon towards the north, it indicates stormy weather, and when extended across our zenith, calm easy weather.

SECT. IV.—SOIL.

We shall endeavour briefly to describe the soils of the county.

1. *Clay.*—The soil of the arable land, and green pasture, in that district of the county, from the east bank of the water of Forss, on the north coast, to Assery, and thence across by the loch of Calder, and Halkirk,

 on

on the river of Thurso, and thence along that river to Dale, thence eastward by Achatibster, Toftingal, Bylbster, Bilbster, Thurster, &c. to the German Ocean at Hempriggs, then along the east coast to the Water of Wester, and along that rivulet, by Bower, Alterwall, and Thurdistoft, to the sea at Castle-hill, on the north coast, abounds with clay, incumbent on a horizontal rock, in the western part of that district, and hard till, schistus, or gravel, on the eastern part of it; comprehending the whole of the parishes of Thurso, Olrig, and Bower, the lower or northern parts of the parishes of Halkirk, Watten, and Wick, with a part of the parish of Dunnet.

2. *Loam.*—There is a mixture of various kinds of vegetative earth, to which the name of *loam* may be given, in various parts of the county. In the parish of Reay, westward from the banks of the Water of Forss, the arable land and green pasture is in general composed of a dark earth, mixed with a crystally sand, which may be denominated a black loam, incumbent, in general, on a grey freestone, &c. not so tenacious of moisture, as the clay district incumbent on a horizontal rock. This species of soil is productive of corn and grass, both natural and artificial. The same kind of soil, namely, a dark loam, abounds, in the parishes of Dunnet and Cannisbay, and a part of the parish of Wick, to the water or river of Wester, on the east coast. Near the shore it is incumbent on a red freestone, in many cases with perpendicular seams, which carry off the moisture; and at a greater distance from the shore, towards the peat mosses and moors, the loam is incumbent on a gritty red gravel or schistus. The soil along the shore is deep, and capable of producing

ducing good crops. Along the sea shore, from Hempriggs to the Ord of Caithness at the S. W. which is bold and rocky, comprehending the coast-side of part of the parish of Wick, and the parish of Latheron, the arable land and green pasture, is chiefly composed of a dark earth, mixed with gritty sand and fragments of rock: it may be termed a stony hazel loam, sharp and productive, incumbent on a blue whin, or gritty rock of vertical seams, or seams of considerable declivity, and dry.

Upon the straths or vallies of the remaining district of the county, comprehending the Highland parts of the parishes of Latheron, Halkirk, and Watten, the soil is variable; near the banks of rivers and burns, there is some haugh or meadow-ground, composed of sand and clay, or soil that may be called alluvial. Farther back, the soil is a dark loam, of peat-earth and gravel, and in some partial spots consists of clay.

3. *Sand.*—The sea coast of Caithness, with the exception of the bays of Sandside, Dunnet, Duncansbay, and Keiss, is a bold rocky shore, from the Ord at the S. W. all along to the coast, till you reach the point of Drumholasten, bounding with Strath-halladale (part of Sutherland) at the N. W. Sandside-bay is about half a mile broad, with some sandy links a little above flood-mark, about the Kirk of Reay, abounding with rabbits, and producing excellent pasture. Dunnet-bay is about three miles across, from the Castle-hill to the Hill of Dunnet on the east side, and it extends about a mile of sandy links up the country to Greenland. This tract may be computed at three square miles, principally a bare barren sand, which produces nothing but tufts of bent grass; a plant which spreads, and thus prevents the usual drifting of the sand, if it is preserved,

preserved, as has been the case for some years in that neighbourhood. Reits, or Keiss-bay, is a low sandy shore, for four miles from Keiss to Ackergill, and in some parts, the sand has drifted half a mile up the country. There is also a small extent of sandy *links* at Freswick-bay, also at Duncansbay, where there are great quantities of various kinds of sea-shells driven in every stormy tide. These shells are carried away for manure, as will be afterwards noticed.

4. *Chalk.*—There is no soil of this description in this county.

5. *Peat.*—The principal attempt made in this county, to convert peat to arable soil, was made by the President of the Board of Agriculture (Sir John Sinclair), on the estate of Langwell, where a number of acres of a coaly black peat, covered with heath, were, by the paring and burning system, enabled to produce corn and grass, and if there had been lime, to give the soil consistency, and to destroy its natural acidity, or tanning principle in the peat, the improvement would have answered effectually; but without calcareous matter, it is problematical, whether it is not as useful under its native crop of heather. Small patches of low peat mosses have been improved in various parts of the county, by planting potatoes, but after one or two succeeding corn crops, the soil is covered with sorrel (*Acetoga.* Lin.), unless calcareous matter is mixed with the peat earth.

General State.—From the account already given of the extent of the county, it is evident, that about three-fourths of the whole surface, is either deep peat moss, or high barren mountains covered with peat earth and heather, or a barren rock; the highest of which are the Morven mountains, on the Langwell estate: these mountains are, from 1500 to 2500 feet above the level of the sea; they are chiefly puddingstone, a bare, gritty, whin rock. After ascending a little distance from their base, which is peat moss covered with heather. The estate of Langwell contains 27,302 English acres, of which, 25,236 acres are either peat moss, gritty moor, or barren mountains; and yet it is an excellent sheep farm, as will be afterwards stated.

From the Morven mountains, there is a ridge of high moory hills, of considerable height, which divides Sutherland and Caithness, from the Ord to the North Sea at Drumholasten, and a similar ridge runs eastward from the Ord along the south-east, or parish of Latheron coast, to within two miles of the town of Wick, having a stripe of coast of arable land and green pasture, of from a quarter to a mile broad, between their base and the rocky precipices of the sea shore. The remainder of the county is rather flat than otherwise, of course much of it is a deep flat peat bog, or moor, of easy declivity, with a great number of lakes of small extent in the highland part, and a few larger lakes in the lower parts of the county.

6. *Acres of each.*—The 107,000 Scotch acres, already stated, of arable land, straths, or sandy meadows, and downy green pastures, either of divided or undivided commons, may be thus classed:

	Scotch Acres.
Clay loam, about	77,000
Dark loam or earth,	20,000
Sharp hazel loam,	7910
Alluvial land on straths,	2000
Cultivated peat, about	90
Total,	107,000

7. *Acres of Waste.*—The amount has been already stated.

SECT.

SECT. VI.—MINERALS.

In the Appendix, will be found the Minutes of a Mineralogical Survey of a considerable part of this county, by Mr. John Busby, which may furnish some hints to any individual, who may be employed, at some future period, to make a similar Survey, with more minuteness, and on a more extensive scale. The following observations on the subject are derived from other sources.

1. *Coal.*—In a common near the crown lands of Scrabster, in the vicinity of the town of Thurso, some fragments of a coaly nature were discovered; and the Barons of Exchequer, a few years ago, sent the Rev. Mr Headrick, as a man of science, and some hands, to bore and explore for coal in that ground. After working a whole season, they returned without success, though it is imagined, that with some perseverance, they might have effected their object.

On the Earl of Caithness's estate, near Barrogil Castle, a thin stratum of coaly black stone is found, on a level with the sea, which burns with a clear flame for some time, but does not consume to ashes. A small seam of coal, resembling small English coal, was lately found in a stone quarry, at the Spittle-hill, in the parish of Halkirk; about a hundred weight was collected of it, which caked in the fire, and burnt exactly like Sunderland coal.

2. *Copper.*—None discovered.

3. *Lead.*—About 40 years ago an English company employed two men for a season at the hill of Achinnarrass, near the Spittle-hill, working pits or shafts for lead

lead ore. They dug up several tons of it, and although it was allowed to be of good quality, the work was discontinued, and no other trial has since been made there.

In the year 1807, some ditchers in the employ of Sir John Sinclair, found pieces of a few solid inches of lead ore, in the bottom of a three-feet ditch which they were making on his estate on the east side of the hill of Skinnet. These pieces having been sent to London to be analysed, the ore was found to contain 70 parts in 100 of pure lead. Some time after, some men (about six), came to Caithness, from Derbyshire, to make a trial for lead ore at Skinnet; they proceeded in digging down a pit or shaft to the depth of about six feet, and had collected about 1 cwt. of ore, when they were ordered back to England; and that effort was also given up without a fair trial being made. The miners declared, that while they wrought there, the appearances were favourable.

Some veins of mundic were also discovered, near the same part of the Skinnet-hill, about 30 years ago, by some workmen employed by the proprietor, Sir John Sinclair, who is well disposed to give every necessary accommodation to any respectable individuals, who may be inclined to give these mines a fair trial.

4. *Tin.*—None.

5. *Iron.*—None.

6. *Marl.*—There is shell marl in many bogs and lakes in the parishes of Halkirk, Olrig, Bower, Wick, Watten, Latheron, and Reay; and clay marl in the parishes of Cannisbay, Latheron, and Thurso, of excellent quality. The greatest quantity of shell marl, and the most easy of access, is in the lake or loch of Westfield, in the parish

parish of Halkirk, near a tract of country capable of improvements. The lake is about 100 acres of surface; the general depth of water in summer, is from one and a half to two feet over, from nine to sixteen feet deep of excellent shell marl, in at least three quarters of its extent; and by a level taken, it is found, that about 400 guineas would drain it to the depth of twelve feet. It is calculated, that it contains about 2,800,000 cubic yards of marl, which, at *6d.* per cubic yard, would be worth about 70,000*l.* sterling. In the lochs of Duren, Stempster, Watten, and several other lakes and bogs throughout this county, the quantity of marl is great, but is often difficult of access; and what is more extraordinary, the loch of Stempster, in Bencheil, and Loch Yarrows, in the hills of Yarrows, though both are surrounded by high moory hills, yet contain excellent shell marl. There are also some veins of limestone in the Stempster loch. This hidden treasure for improving the county, has hitherto been but little used, from the want of roads. It is to be hoped, however, that when the great lines of road are completed, at the mutual expense of the public and of the county, the annual commutation for the statute labour, will be effectually applied to the making of bye-roads of communication to these marl repositories, &c. which will induce the proprietors to drain these lakes and bogs, and open sources of wealth for the improvement of the county.

7. *Freestone.*—This article is found in the greatest perfection in Caithness. The following is an extract of a letter from Mr. James Scott, builder in Edinburgh, who had an opportunity of ascertaining the qualities of the freestone quarry at Scrabster, near Thurso, having built several houses with it in the New Town

Town of Thurso, and who is well acquainted with the principal freestone quarries in Scotland.

"My opinion is, that the freestone quarry of Scrabster, near Thurso, is superior to any in Scotland, for quality, durability, or beauty. It will furnish blocks 150 feet long, and of any breadth required. The depth of the rock in the quarry was ascertained by Mr. Headrick, at the south-west end of the quarry, when sinking for coals, and was found to be 35 feet.

"My knowledge of freestone is from much experience, having had an opportunity of examining most of the quarries, both public and private, in Scotland, and having built some of the largest and most magnificent houses, and other edifices in that part of the island.

"I think it would be a great pity to cut up and waste so fine and valuable a rock into clumsy blocks for docks or bridges, as it would fully answer any building of the largest magnitude, and from its fine quality, is well calculated for the embellishment of a palace, or to be converted into the finest ornaments that ever suggested themselves to the fancy of a Roman or Grecian architect."

8. *Various Articles.*—There are some thin stratas of blue limestone in various parts of this county, but in general of indifferent quality, ill to work, or in inaccessible places, of course of little benefit to the general improvement of the county.

The hills of Morven and Scarabin consist principally of silicious spar on quartz. Mr. Headrick, who examined those hills, states, that this substance is called *petunse;* reduced to impalpable powder, and mixed with white clay, it obtains the name of *kaolin*, and is formed into that beautiful earthenware for which China

China is so much celebrated. What a pity it is, that so valuable an article should remain useless in those barren mountains.

SECT. VI.—WATER.

1. *Rivers and Streams.*—There are no navigable rivers in this county. The principal river, is the Water of Thurso, which originates from springs in the mountains bounding with Sutherland, and partly from the Latheron hills; thence it passes through several lakes and small lochs, 24 of which are in one flat bog in Strath-more, in the parish of Halkirk; all send their tributary streams to this river, and after traversing a distance of about 30 miles, discharges itself into the Pentland Frith at Thurso-bay. Its ancient name, in the Gaelic language, is *Avon-Horsa*, (Horsa's river), and the town of Thurso *Bal-inver-Horsa*, (the town of Horsa's harbour). Tradition says, that this Horsa was a Danish general, who landed an army here; perhaps the same with the Scandinavian god *Thor*, the son of Odin, the Supreme Father, or Jupiter, of the Northern Nations.

There is a valuable salmon-fishing on the river of Thurso, let at present by Sir John Sinclair, to an Aberdeen Company, for a very moderate sum, only about 400*l.* per ann. It will soon be out of lease, when it will bring a considerable additional rent.

At the village of Halkirk, this river is so rapid, that a fall of 14 feet could be commanded for machinery, or two falls of seven feet each, in the course of 200 yards; but, in general, the river is not rapid enough for falls, or deep enough for navigation, although, with floods of of rain it rises from five to seven feet above its natural level; yet, as the country on each side rises gradually from its banks, it does not overflow much ground in the low country. Its Highland branches, however, frequently overflow their banks, and spoil the hay in its meandering haughs.

The next river in point of size, is the Water of Wick, originating from the lochs of Watten, Toftingal, Scarmclate, or Stempster, and from various springs in the moors of the parish of Watten, whence it runs eastward, until it falls into the sea, in the sandy bay of Wick. The tide flows up this small river for two miles, but of little depth.

The third river is the Water of Forss, which originates from springs in the mountains between Sutherland and Caithness, and coming through Loch Kelm, Loch Shurary, &c. it runs due north to Cross Kirk-bay, where it enters the Northern Ocean, dividing the parishes of Reay and Thurso. In general, it is rather flat, than rapid and shallow, in its meandering course through Strath-glaston. There is here a small salmon-fishery.

The fourth river is the Water of Wester, a stream which runs through the parish of Bower, from lochs and springs, eastward to the Loch of Wester, and thence becomes a deep stream for a short distance, to Keiss-bay, on the German Ocean.

There are various *burns*, or small streams, beside those above mentioned, in the northern and eastern part of this county; and on the south side of the county, there are the waters of Dunbeath, Berriedale, and Langwell, with a number of small burns, running from springs in the mountains, which have a rapid, rugged, and shallow course to the Murray Frith. There are salmon-fishings, besides the great one on the river Thurso, in the waters of Wick, Dunbeath, and Langwell; the fish of the latter is considered the firmest and best in Scotland.

2. *Lakes.*—The principal lake, is the Loch of Calder, in Halkirk parish, being two miles long, and from a mile to a quarter of a mile broad; in the north end, it is about 12 fathom deep.

The second is Loch-More, in the Highland part of the same parish; it is about one mile and a half long by about half a mile broad, and deep.

The third is the Loch of Watten, about one mile and a half long, and from one-half, to a quarter of a mile broad, but in general rather shallow. Then in order, are the Lochs of Hempriggs, Westfield, Stempster (Bower), Rangag, Stempster, (Latheron), Alterwall, Harland, Dunnet, Mey, Duren, Kelm, Shurary, Rheard, Yarrows, and about 24 smaller lakes in a flat bog in Strath-more, in the parish of Halkirk.

All these lakes, rivers, and burns, or rivulets, abound with trout and eels, and in the Loch of Calder, there are char, (a fish called in Gaelic *tardearg*, or red, belly), about six inches long.

3. *Springs.*—The county of Caithness abounds with springs of excellent water, not apparently impregnated with any mineral.

A spring at Buckies, in the parish of Thurso, and at Borg, in the parish of Latheron, are remarked for their purity and lightness when compared to other springs. There are other springs in the county, which form a reddish scum on their surface, and colour the grass in the course of their streams; and at Scarscerry, (a ferry place in the parish of Dunnet), there is a

spring

spring near the ferry-house, of clear water, but when spirits are mixed with it, the compound becomes as black as if gall had been infused in it. This spring seems to be of a chalybeate quality. The Reporter was not informed of any springs in this county peculiarly famed for any medicinal virtues.

Near the ruins of Roman catholic chapels, there are generally springs of pure water, still esteemed as holy by the peasantry; and some of them, when feverish, will send for water from these springs, of which they drink, and wash their hands, &c. and from which they believe that great benefit is derived. It is customary, that those who take the water from the spring on such occasions, must leave something at the spring—a bit of cloth, &c. This species of superstition is now much discontinued.

CHAP. II.

STATE OF PROPERTY.

SECT. I.—ESTATES, AND THEIR MANAGEMENT.

THE following table will point the number of Estates in the county, with the ancient value of each, according to which the land tax is paid.

Names of Estates.	Valued Rent in 1702, Scotch Money. £	s.	d.	Tenures.	Remarks.
1. Ulbster estate	7813	1	0	Principally of the Crown	Part entailed
2. Freswick ditto	4259	4	4	Partly ditto	Entailed
3. Hempriggs ditto	3624	16	10	Ditto	Ditto
4. Murkle ditto	3300	17	5	Ditto	Ditto
5. Castlehill, &c. do.	2630	12	8	Ditto	Not entailed
6. Watten, &c. ditto	1136	18	0	Ditto	Partly entailed
7. Mey ditto	1225	3	4	Of the Crown	Entailed
8. Stircock ditto	786	17	0	Ditto	Not entailed
9. Sandside ditto	900	0	0	Ditto	Ditto
10. Standstill ditto	999	17	2	Partly ditto	Entailed
11. Toftingal ditto	729	12	4	Of the Crown	Ditto
12. Forss, &c. ditto	907	7	0	Partly ditto	Not entailed
13. Barrock ditto	742	19	6	Ditto	Entailed
14. Calder ditto	676	0	0	Of a subject superior	Not entailed
15. Crown Lands, including tiends	1800	6	8	—	—
16. Banniskirk, &c. ditto	704	12	1	Blanch of the Crown	Ditto
17. Forse ditto	650	0	0	Ditto of ditto	Ditto
18. Olrig ditto	381	2	2	Of the Crown	Ditto
19. Wester Watten, &c. ditto	316	17	0	—	Ditto
Carry forward	33,636	4	6		

Names of Estates.	*Valued Rent in 170[illegible], Scotch Money.* £	s.	d.	*Tenures.*	*Remarks.*
Brought forward	33,636	4	6		
20. Swinzie ditto ..	400	0	0	Of the Crown	Not entailed
21. Duren ditto ..	483	14	2	Ditto	Ditto
22. Hopeville ditto ..	412	10	0	Ditto	Ditto
23. Stempster ditto	248	0	0	Ditto	Ditto
24. Brabster Myre do.	34[illegible]	18	8	Ditto	Ditto
25. Achingale ditto	62	2	0	Subject Superior ..	Ditto
26. Latheron ditto ..	248	6	8	Ditto	Ditto
27. Shebster ditto ..	216	2	6	Ditto	Ditto
28. Lynager ditto ..	62	3	0	Ditto	Ditto
29. Lybster ditto ..	124	0	0	Ditto	Ditto
30. Wester Dale do.	74	10	5	Ditto	Ditto
31. Campster ditto ..	22	19	4	Ditto	Ditto
32. Harry Bain Wick	6	0	0	—	Ditto
33. B.Water's feu do.	4	0	0	—	Ditto
34. Bridgend's Heirs ditto ..	2	13	4	—	Ditto
Town of Wick	166	13	4	—	Royal Burgh
Town of Thurso	666	13	4	—	Burgh of regality
	37,179	11	3	—	—
Feu-duties of Lynager	76	1	6	—	—
Total valued rent ..	37,255	12	9	—	—

Abstract.

			£	s.	d.
No. 1.	8 Estates, at or above 1000*l.* Scotch, of valued rent		£24,327	10	7
2.	11 ditto, at or above 500*l.*		8808	13	11
3.	10 ditto, from 100*l.* to 450*l.*		2600	7	0
4.	5 ditto, from 1*l.* to 50*l.*		110	3	1
5.	The two Towns		333	6	8
Total	34 Estates				
	Feu-duties of Lynager, ...		76	1	6
			£37,256	2	9
	The 37,256*l.* 2*s.* 9*d.* Scotch, in sterling is		£3104	10	2¼

 The

The number of proprietors of land constantly resident in the county, is	19
Occasionally resident,	10
Not resident,	5
Total,	34

Every resident land proprietor, has usually a farm attached to his residence, which is managed under his own direction, by a *grieve* or manager, who has the superintendance of the farm servants. The remainder of the estate is let in farms, of various extent, from five to one hundred acres, and there are a few farms of still greater extent of arable land, besides common pasturage, &c.; but the principal part of this county is let to tenants paying from 5*l.* to 20*l.* annual rent, including money, farm, &c. The most considerable proprietors employ a factor or chamberlain, to collect the rents, &c. from their tenants, at a stipulated salary, and during pleasure. The resident owners of small estates, generally collect their rents themselves.

SECT. II.—TENURES.

1. *Freehold.*—All the estates in this county are held either under the Crown, or of a Subject Superior, in perpetuity, upon paying a trifle, such as a penny Scots, if demanded. When held under a Subject Superior, in some cases a few pounds are payable annually, by way of feu duty. Those who hold their lands immediately of the Crown, have a right to vote for, or be elected Member of Parliament for the County, in case their lands

lands were valued in 1702 at, or above 400*l.* Scotch. Those whose properties did not then amount to 400*l.* Scots of valued rent, have no vote, even though they hold directly of the Crown.

In ancient times, all the lands of the county were the property of the Earls and Thanes, and in progress of time, these Earls sold lots of their estate to their friends or vassals, at an agreed price, for which a charter was granted to the vassal, to hold such land in perpetuity of the Earl and his successors, and in general, the Earl retained the superiority of such land in his own family, though he sold the property to the vassal, who paid him an annual sum, by way of feu, or acknowledgment of his being a vassal. This annual payment is still called the feu-duty, payable to the Superior, and is frequently sold with the superiority, for political motives, to a different person, who, by such transfer, becomes the superior of the land, and has a right to vote at an election of a Member of Parliament (if amounting to 400*l.* Scots of valued rent). The vassal, though he enjoys the *dominium utile* of his land, has no vote at such elections. About one-third of this county is held by persons not enjoying the *dominium directum*, from the cause above stated.

2. *Copyhold.*—There is no such manner of holding of land in Scotland.

3. *Church Leases.*—When episcopacy was abolished in Scotland, the church lands were annexed to the Crown. The lands of that description, in this county, have been generally let to one person, on a lease of 19 to 21 years, at a rent commonly moderate. By

a late measurement, the crown lands in Caithness amount to 756 acres arable, 1537 acres of green pasture, and 4500 acres of moss and moor. They were let on a lease of 21 years, which terminated in 1809, at the yearly rent of 80*l*. sterling. Government having then determined to let them to the highest bidder, the former holder has now got a new lease of them for 21 years, at 630*l*. sterling of rent. The tenant is allowed meliorations for building and other improvements, to the extent of 3000*l*. out of the surplus rent, as it is expended.

4. *Entails.*—There are nine estates within this county, under strict entail, a measure intended to perpetuate particular families; but which is very inimical to the improvement of its soil.

CHAP. III.

BUILDINGS.

SECT. I.—HOUSES OF PROPRIETORS.

1. *Advantageously situated.*—In ancient feudal times, when one Clan was constantly at war with another, and committed mutual depredations, the Proprietors of land, and Heads of Clans, built their castles or strong-holds on precipices, or necks of land, on the sea shore, with a fosse or draw-bridge on the land side, which bridge was drawn up, and guarded at night, or on the approach of an enemy. The most ancient of these in this county, are castles Girnegoe and Sinclair, erected by the Thanes and Earls of Caithness, on a bold rock, on the north side of Noss-head, near Wick, the ruins of which still point out their former strength and magnitude.

Ackergill tower, half a mile west from castle Girnegoe, is very strong and ancient, was built by the Keiths, Earls Marshal, and is now the property of Sir Benjamin Dunbar, of Hempriggs. There are also Mowat's Castle of Freswick, Castle Sinclair of Keiss, the Castle of Old Wick, or Oliphant's Castle, two miles south from Wick; all ruins on the east coast of Caithness. Forse Castle in ruins, the Castle of Dunbeath, habitable; Berridale Castle in ruins; all on the south-east coast, on similar rocks on the sea shore.

Upon

Upon the north coast is 1. Barrogil Castle, the Earl of Caithness's residence, at a small distance from the shore. 2. Thurso Castle, the seat of Sir John Sinclair, Bart. built in 1616, and by him repaired in 1808; the ruins of a castle at Scrabster, a mile west of Thurso, once the residence of the Bishops of Caithness; a small castle at Erims, habitable; and the ruins of a castle at Dowureay, all on the north coast of Caithness. There are also the ruins of Brawl Castle, and Durlet Castle, on the river Thurso, in the interior of the county.

2. *Well planned for Country Gentlemen of moderate Fortunes.*—The modern houses of Sandside, Westfield, Castlehill, Freswick, Keiss, Hempriggs, Stircock, Lybster, Swinzie, and Nottingham, along the coast, or near it, and of Barrock-house, Standstill, Watten, Bilbster, Hopeville, Stempster, Tister, Dale, and Calder, in the interior of the county, are all the houses of land proprietors, commodiously built, and in some cases handsomely finished. Among these, the house of Stircock is, perhaps, the most showy and commodious. The house of Thrumster, erected by Captain Brodie on Sir John Sinclair's Estate, is also well planned. In both these houses, they suspend their window-sashes by *springs*, in place of weights and pulleys. The springs are made of steel, about nine inches long by one inch broad, and a quarter of an inch thick, having a small curvature; they are counter sunk in the sides of the sashes, and one end being fixed by two screw nails, the other end, or rather the middle, projects out beyond the wood, and when the sash is put in its casement, this projecting part of the spring presses so to the casement, that it suspends

suspends the sash in any position to which it is elevated or depressed. In short, it has all the effect of the rope and pulley, without being visible, and of course neater and warmer, and not so liable to decay. Care, however, must be taken, to make the strength or elasticity of the springs, conformable to the weight of the sash, because, if made too strong, it will be difficult to move the sash up or down, and if too weak, it will not support the sash in any given position.

SECT. II.—FARM-HOUSES AND OFFICES.

There are a number of farm-houses in this county, slate-roofed, and having from five to nine fire-rooms each, commodiously built and well finished, with squares of farm-offices, substantially constructed, and generally slate-roofed; though in some cases thatch-roofed, with divots, or thin turf, 1000 of which are cut and prepared at the expense of 4*s.* which will thatch one rood and a half. These are secured on the houses with ropes made of heath, or straw (provincially *simmons*), and if a covering of straw is laid over the divots, the roof or thatch will last from three to four years, when it is either repaired, or the whole of the old thatch turned off for the dunghill, and new thatch as before laid on. In a country where timber is both scarce and high priced, such roofs are the only ones within the ability of the general run of tenants, who cannot afford to make or erect better houses.

A farmer who rents from 100 to 150 acres of arable land, requires a stable of 24 feet by 14 feet, for six horses,

horses, with a loft for hay, &c. over them. Another stable of 15 feet by 12 feet, to hold four *garrons*, or small horses for the harrows, and perhaps to work a thrashing machine in winter; a byre of 18 feet by 15 feet, for six cart oxen; another byre of 60 feet by 16 feet, for about 40 head of small black cattle; a thrashing barn 50 feet by 14 feet, and a kiln barn 30 feet by 14 feet, with a kiln 14 feet diameter. This barn to have a loft for grain; and the kiln to be arched and tiled, is the safest mode of drying corn, to prevent accidents by fire; also a cart-shed, 40 feet by 13 feet, with a loft over it for grain, because generally the crop lays on the farmer's hands until June, when, sometimes, there is a demand to export oats and bear to the Leith and London markets. The expense of such office-houses, with a suitable dwelling-house, will cost about 1500*l*. in this county; but if the roofs are thatched, in place of slated, the first cost will be much less, but the annual repairs will be considerable.

SECT. III.—REPAIRS.

In all bargains betwixt landlord and tenant in this county, the latter is bound to repair the dwelling-house and farm-offices which he receives on the farm at his entry. Such houses are commonly valued at the tenant's entry, by tradesmen mutually chosen by the landlord and tenant; and it is stipulated, that he will, at the expiration of his lease, be allowed meliorations to a certain extent, and is bound to repair, or to pay for any deterioration.

In cases where a farmer takes a tract of land formerly occupied

occupied by small tenants, the modes of allowing for building and enclosures are various: in some cases the farmer stipulates, that he is to be allowed the first one, two, or three years' rent, for building a house and offices, he being bound to leave houses on the land at the expiration of his lease, at least equal to the sum allowed, and perhaps be allowed a certain sum more, should such buildings, at his removal, be worth it. The appreciated value of fences made of stone or hedge and ditch, is also in general allowed to the tenant, at the issue of his lease. In other cases, some farmers in Caithness have inconsiderately taken a similar tract of land, and engaged to erect a house and farm-offices on the farm, and to enclose and subdivide the same, upon the landlord becoming bound to pay a stipulated sum at the issue of a lease of 21 years; they being bound to leave buildings, &c. on the farm, equal to the promised allowance; and should such buildings be worth treble the sum agreed on, (which is sometimes the case), all of it becomes the landlord's property, without any further allowance. No farmer who undertakes to build and improve on these terms, can expect to be remunerated by the produce of his farm, and indeed such outlays cramp his future ability to improve, and to provide extraneous manure for the land. In no case, so far as I could discover, does the proprietor build houses, &c. for the farmer, and charge him 7½ per cent. for such outlay in this county, as is the case in the southern districts of Scotland. That seems, indeed, to be the most equitable mode for both parties.

The smaller tenants, or the occupiers of farms from *5l.* to *20l.* or even *30l.* rent, usually reside in low thatched houses, with their horses and cattle in the one end of them,

them, and a fire on the hearth, placed on the floor equi-distant from each wall, the whole fabric erected and repaired by themselves; and as, at the first erection, the landlord found timber for the roof, at the removal of each tenant, the timber on the roof is valued, and meliorations, if any, paid by the incoming to the outgoing tenant; and if deterioration, it must be paid to the landlord, or to the incoming tenant, on the landlord's account; the tenant being always bound to uphold the original value of the *master wood*, as it is termed. In all such cases, the tenant has a written note from the landlord, certifying the amount of wood belonging to the proprietor on the premises, this master wood therefore must be given, or its value to the incoming tenant, by the outgoing tenant. The walls and gables of such house are seldom if ever valued.

SECT. IV.—PRICE OF BUILDING, MATERIALS, AND ARTISANS' LABOUR.

PREVIOUS to my stating the price of building, &c., it is necessary to observe, that in this county, masons do not only charge for girth-measure, or the superficial content of the building in square yards, (36 of which make a rood of work); but they also charge what they term "*work and half*," for doors and windows, *i. e.* the superficial content of the doors and windows is ascertained, and the half of it is added to the girth measure; then they charge a foot in height for levelling they have to make for joisting, &c. in the course of the building, then the outside and inside squares of the gables are measured, and every three feet in length of these

these is computed a square yard; all this is added to the girth-measure; and according as the doors and windows, squares and levelling, are extensive, or otherwise, it adds from one-fourth to one-third more to the real girth-measure of the building, in their charge of roods and square yards; such being understood to be the measure, from long custom, within the county.

The mason charges for building work, that requires but one scaffolding, from 36*s*. to 2*l*. per rood; and if it requires two or more scaffolding, they charge from 45*s*. to 55*s*. per rood of rubble-work, the materials of stone, and clay or mortar, being laid near them. For quarrying the stone, from 15*s*. to 26*s*. per rood is given, as the quarry may be easy wrought, or otherwise, the thickness of the wall being understood to be from 27 inches to 2½ feet; the carriage of the materials of stone, mortar, and water, depends on the distance and season of the year. The mason charges 8*d*. per foot for freestone rigging, 10*d*. per foot for freestone lintels of doors and windows, 4*d*. per yard for squaring, and laying flags for pavement, or tabling, 7*s*. 6*d*. per rood for harling walls, &c., 36*s*. per rood for slating with Eisdale slate, and from 26*s*. to 30*s*. per rood of slating with grey or Caithness slate. There is also a separate charge for flankers, and laying on scaffolding. All job-work done by a mason is charged by the day, now at from 2*s*. 9*d*. to 3*s*. per day-wages. About 25 years ago, a mason charged 26*s*. per rood for building, 18*s*. for slating, &c., and the mason's wages per day was from 10*d*. to 1*s*. 3*d*. When freestone is furnished by the mason for corners, doors, and windows, the charge is from 8*d*. to 10*d*. per superficial or square foot, for quarrying, and dressing or hewing the stone. When a mason is employed to build any circular work, his charge

charge is double that of square work of the same dimensions.

Timber for Building.—About 20 years ago, foreign fir timber was purchased in Caithness, at from 8*d.* to 1*s.* per solid foot; now, Scotch fir is from 2*s.* 6*d.* to 3*s.* per solid foot, and foreign fir log, at from 4*s.* to 4*s.* 6*d.* Sawyers' charge 3*s.* per 100 square feet for sawing.

The house-carpenter charges from 1*s.* 6*d.* to 2*s.* 4*d.* for making a couple; from 1*s.* 1½*d.* to 1*s.* for every square yard of flooring, the deals being about seven inches broad; and 1*s.* 4*d.* per square yard for baton flooring, of four inches broad; from 3*d.* to 4*d.* per foot for wash-boards and architraves; 2*s.* 6*d.* per square yard for panneling, or bound-work; 10*d.* per square for lath and plaister, and 6*d.* per square yard for wall-plaister; 1*s.* per square foot for making windows without glass, and from 2*s.* 6*d.* to 3*s.* 6*d.* per square foot, including glass and putty, wood in every case excepted; preparing and laying on the roof, the sacking 3*d.* to 4*d.* per square yard; and for job-work, a house-carpenter charges from 2*s.* 6*d.* to 3*s.* per day.

Iron.—About 25 years ago the stone of 16 lb. Dutch, of Swedish iron, cost, by retail, 1*s.* 6*d.*; and now it costs from 4*s.* 6*d.* to 5*s.* 6*d.* per stone. Single nail 6*d.*, double 1*s.*, and double double 1*s.* 4*d.* per 100. When the blacksmith furnishes iron and coal, he charges 8*d.* per hundred for farm-work or utensils; 3*s.* per set for shoeing horses. When iron and coal are furnished to him, the smith charges from 2*s.* to 2*s.* 6*d.* per day's work at the forge.

Lime for Building, &c.—The cheapest mode of furnishing

nishing lime is, to import it from Sunderland, which can be done at the rate of 5*s*. per Sunderland boll of shells: this boll contains about 63 English gallons, and will make about five herring barrels full of slacked lime; which may be reckoned at 1*s*. per barrel on landing from the vessel. It is whiter than the lime from the Frith of Forth, or that burnt in the county, and takes more sand for plaister than either of the others; of course it is much cheaper for building. In plaister, it is apt to blow, owing to sulphureous and metallic particles in it. To cure this defect, the lime is previously run in a liquid state, through a wire riddle, and allowed some time to sour, and these particles will probably have disappeared before it is used as plaister. The Scotch lime is more durable and adhesive than the Sunderland, for harling houses, or any work exposed to the weather.

SECT. V.—COTTAGES.

There are few cottages to be met with here, of any improved construction. Sometimes a mechanic who resides in the country, and has a lease of some land for a garden, or for feeding a cow, &c. builds a cottage, consisting of two rooms, for himself and family, each room about 15 feet long by 12 feet broad; the walls about six feet high, built with stone and clay, with gable tops of feal (turf) or stones, as the case may be, with one couple in each room, and rafters from the gables resting on the couples, upon which small timber is placed across, to support the thatch, which is divots, as before described. The inside of the walls are plaistered with clay, and whitewashed with lime; some of them even plaistered with lime, and harled outside, with a glazed window in each room, 2½ feet by two feet, and a chimney in one of the rooms: the whole has a warm, compact appearance, with a cow-house built at one end of the house.

The cabins in which the cottagers reside, are of a mean construction; where stone is easily had, perhaps about two feet high of the walls and gables are of stone, and earth thrown in, to fill up the crevices, *vice* mortar; above that, the whole walls and gables are built of feal or sods of two feet long, and seven inches in the side of the square. Of these materials the walls and gables are made ready for the roof, which is a Highland semicircular couple, made of birch, with rafters, to support the thatch of divots, &c. Each cabin has generally two apartments, nine or ten feet broad by twelve feet long, with the hearth or fire-place in the centre of one of them, and the smoke goes out at a hole of about a foot diameter, on the roof just above the fire. These cabins are warm, but they are very smoky, and dirty.

Expenses.—The artisan's cottage, as above described, will cost as follows:

To building the walls, &c. gable tops, feal,	£3	12	0
Timber for the roof, say	2	14	0
Divots and simmons for thatch, ...	0	8	0
Two windows, each 7*s*.	0	14	0
Door, lock, and jambs, ...	0	15	0
Plastering the inside, ...	0	8	0
Total, ...	£8	11	0

The

The cabin for a cottager will cost—walls and gable 20*s*., timber 30*s*., divots, &c. 6*s*., a door and lock 9*s*. 6*d*., ... } £3 5 6*

SECT. VI.—BRIDGES.

The largest bridge in this county is on the river Wick, at the Burgh of Wick. It consists of three arches, built with whin stone, at an expense of about 1700*l*. The second bridge is at Thurso, on the river there, three arches, erected by subscription in 1800; the expense about 1200*l*.; the arches are of freestone, and the remainder rubble-work. The parapet, which is three feet high, is coped with freestone. The third bridge, in point of magnitude, is on the Thurso river, at the village of Halkirk, seven miles south from Thurso. It was built of rubble-work, anno 1731, by John Sinclair, Esq. then of Ulbster. It consists of three arches, and could not now be erected for less than 1000*l*. It was erected at the sole expense of the Ulbster family.

There are various bridges of one arch on several rivers and burns throughout the county, as over the rivers of Dunbeath, Berriedale, Langwell, and Forss, which cost from 100*l*. to 500*l*. each, and several burns or rivulets, which cost from 25*l*. to 100*l*. each. These were chiefly erected out of the bridge assessment annually collected with the cess of the county, and from the commutation for statute labour annually charged and collected, at the rate of 30*s*. for every 100*l*. Scots of valued rent.

* An old corporal, who was laying the foundation of one of these cabins, was asked by a person passing by, what kind of house he would make of it? "I am determined to have a good room in it, (he said), if "it should cost me *twa pounds*."—Such cabins are the best nurseries for hardy soldiers.

CHAP. IV.

OCCUPATION.

SECT. I.—SIZE OF FARMS.

IT has been a practice in this county, from time immemorial, that people of opulence took a lease for 19 or 21 years of a town-land, occupied by from 10 to 40 small tenants, at a rent, commonly paid in money, and not partly in kind, as was the case with smaller tenants. These *tacksmen*, as they are called, generally occupied a part of the land themselves, and they sub-let the remainder to the small farmers, for a certain money-rent, payments in grain, customs, and services, (the latter, in many cases, unlimited), so as to have, upon the whole, a surplus rent for the trouble and risk of recovering their rack-rent from their sub-tenants. This practice, in a few cases, still exists in the county. There are some tacksmen who pay a rent of from 200*l.* to 800*l.* per annum, and these cultivate from one-half, to one-fourth of the land so let, the remainder being occupied by their sub-tenants. There is one arable farm of 600 acres, (Murkle), one of 400, two of 300, six of 200, five of 150, and seven farms of about 100 arable acres each. Some of these farms have sub-tenants, and others have none, but all have a certain extent of pasture ground. The greater part of the landholders have farms of from 100 to 300 arable acres in their own occupancy. The remainder of the arable land of the county, is divided into farms of from 10 to 20, and

even

even 40 Scotch acres. The greater number, however, is from 10 to 20 acres; a few of them are still on the run-rig system. Besides these, there are many cottagers, who occupy from one to five acres each of arable land, much of it recent improvements.

SECT. II.—FARMERS.

A few young men from the South of Scotland have been brought to this county, to superintend the Proprietors' farms or domains, for the purpose of introducing the practice of modern husbandry: these, from time to time, have taken farms in this county; but whether their agricultural skill was superficial, or, that they did not understand the mode of farming best adapted to this cold and moist climate, they have neither increased the crops, on the landlords' farms placed under their direction, nor has their industry or skill produced better crops on their own farms, than what is raised by a similar class of the county farmers, who have never been out of it.

The principal Farmers in the county under review, are intelligent Gentlemen, who have been for some time in the army, or followed other avocations, either in the southern counties of Scotland, or in England, who work up their farms upon the principles of modern agriculture, as practised in the southern counties of Scotland, as far as the state of the county, as to climate, the roads, the means of improvement, markets, &c. will admit, but at a much greater expense than is done to the southward, and of course much less benefit to themselves. In general, they have other sources of income, which enable them to live in a sociable and comfortable state in society: they are better educated than farmers paying a similar rent in England; agricultural knowledge, therefore, is soon circulated amongst them.

The smaller class of farmers, with but few exceptions, are industrious, sober, sagacious, and moral in their behaviour. They have, unfortunately, a turn for litigation, and expend more money than they ought to do in law, by which their circumstances are often injured.

The old custom of run-rig and crooked ridges, is now much in disuse, as the Proprietors in general are gradually getting their land divided into distinct lots or farms; and the tenants then find it for their own interest, to plough their land straight, and to raise turnips, potatoes, and artificial grasses.

SECT. III.—RENT.

Along the coast of this county, the arable land, on recent leases, lets at from 15s. to 25s. per acre, partly in money-rent, and partly in grain, (bear and oatmeal), allowing any pasture ground attached to the farm, to the bargain. In the immediate vicinity of the towns of Thurso, and Wick, land lets at from 3*l.* to 5*l.* by the acre, chiefly for potatoes. Farmers in the interior of the county, in short, all those who have not the advantages of the neighbourhood of the sea, for manure, &c. pay at the rate of from 12*s.* to 20*s.* per Scotch acre for their *stock*, or *infield land*, or such as will produce bear or oats; but for land called *outfield*, which is occasionally under a poor crop of oats, and then pasture,

ture, the rent may be averaged at from 3*s*. to 5*s*. per acre; their pasture ground and hay meadows being allowed as a necessary appendage. This rent is paid in money in the Highland part of the county, and in the Lowland districts, partly money, and partly grain, and in some instances, with customs, casualties, and services.

All the estates are not actually measured, they commonly therefore reckon the arable land, by the boll of bear's sowing, which is about a Scotch acre. Good meadow ground, on the straths of rivers, &c. may be rent d at 12*s*. per acre, considering the quantity of hay it produces, as well as pasture, with little trouble or expense. I shall here give some specimens of rent, &c. formerly paid, and of the rent as now paid by the tenants.

1. The town-land of Weydale, including Todholes, four miles inland from the town of Thurso, the property of Sir John Sinclair, contained what was called twenty-penny land, was occupied by 18 tenants, and paid anno 1762, the following money-rent, customs, casualties, &c.

Weydale, and Todholes, Twentypenny-Land, or 160 Acres, 18 Tenants.	Scotch Money, anno 1762.		
	£	s.	d.
1. They paid in money-rent, ...	277	19	6
2. Victual, 109 bolls 1 firlot 1 peck 2 lippies in kind, or at 5*l.* Scotch, per boll, ...	546	14	$4\frac{1}{2}$
3. Fowls, 90 in kind, or at 3*d.* each, ...	13	10	0
4. Eggs, 720 ditto, or at 1*s.* Scotch, per dozen, ...	3	0	0
5. Custom peats, $80\frac{1}{2}$ feet in kind, or at 1*l.* per foot, N. B. The foot of peats is 12 feet broad and 12 feet high.	80	10	0
6. To 21 geese in kind, or at 9*s.* Scotch, each, ...	9	9	0
7. To swine, the 10th pig, as it might happen. Services unlimited.			
Total, ...	931	2	$10\frac{1}{2}$
The above 931*l.* 2*s.* $10\frac{1}{2}$*d.* Scotch, was the rent, exclusive of services and swine, which in sterling is	£77	11	$6\frac{19}{17}$

Weydale, and Todholes,	Rent in 1809.		
	£	s.	d.
Are now occupied by 11 tenants, paying from 8*l.* to 35*l.* sterling each; all customs, &c. are converted, and the total money in sterling is ...	132	7	4

2. *Glut, a Highland Farm, on the same Estate.*	Scotch Money, anno 1762.		
	£	s.	d.
In anno 1762, paid a rent of	66	13	4
Which in sterling amounts to	5	11	$1\frac{1}{3}$

Glut,	Sterling, anno 1809.		
	£	s.	d.
As a sheep farm, now pays	40	0	0

3. Upon some estates in the parish of Latheron, on the S. E. coast of this county, customs, casualties, and limited services, are still paid by the tenants *in kind.* In the rental they are valued rather high, to induce the people to pay the articles in kind. I annex a state of

of the rent, &c. paid from a farm of about 10 arable acres in that parish, viz.

				Sterling. £	s.	d.
To money-rent due at Martinmas, 1809, ...				3	0	0
Farm, one boll oatmeal for crop 1808, or	£1	0	0			
6 feet of custom peats in kind, or at 2*s*.	0	12	0			
A meat lamb, or	0	2	6			
A wedder, or	0	10	0			
Wintering four head of cattle, or	0	12	0			
7 fowls and 2 dozen of eggs, or	0	3	8			
Spinning 4 lb. of lint or flax, or	0	2	0			
Vicarage, or	0	2	0			
A load of heather simmons, or	0	1	0			
2 days' ploughing of 1 plough, or	0	6	0			
10 days' services of one person, or	0	10	0			
				4	1	2
Total rent, &c.				£7	1	2

A tenant occupying land near the sea shore, if a fisherman, pays a pint of oil, or 2*s*.; and some of those occupying a farm near the Laird's ancient residence, or castle, are still charged with two, three, or four pecks of *feudal* oats at the current price. This originated from a practice in old times, that the Laird's tenants, vassals, or clan, contributed a quantity of oats to feed their Chief's horses. The tenants residing near a lake, paid a given number of trout annually, and if there was any wood or shrubbery on the farms, they paid so many *nasks*

nasks (binders made of birch twigs), to secure the Laird's cattle in the byre. In general, these customs and casualties are now converted to money-rent.

SECT. IV.—TITHES.

TITHES were abolished in Scotland, when the presbyterian form of religion was established. The tithe of corn, however, was collected by a lay proprietor, in a part of the parish of Cannisbay, in this county, about 20 years ago; and, in the parish of Olrig, the small tithes or vicarage, are still payable to the incumbent clergyman.

SECT. V.—POOR'S-RATES, AND OTHER PAROCHIAL TAXES.

THERE are no poor's-rates, or any other parochial tax in this county, if we except the commutation tax of statute labour on the roads; the minister and elders of each parish also, commonly appoint an exemplary devout man, to teach the Catechism of the Church of Scotland, to the illiterate part of the parishioners, in their dwelling houses: he goes frequent rounds on this duty, from house to house, where he is for the time maintained, and he commonly receives annually from a peck to two pecks of oatmeal from each family where he officiates. These catechists, repeat and teach the questions (as they call them), to the illiterate persons in each family, sing psalms, pray, and on Sundays they

they explain portions of the New Testament, to such as collect to hear them. In the more remote parts of the parishes, this no doubt has a good effect, tending to impress the principles of religion and morality on the minds of that class of society, and these religious duties being explained, and inculcated to them at their fire-sides, have as great an effect on their minds, as the sermons they hear at church on Sundays, though delivered in a more learned and fluent language.

SECT. VI.—LEASES.

Some estates in this county, are so strictly entailed, that the proprietors can grant leases only for 14 years: but the proprietors of other entailed estates, may grant leases of 19 or 21, and even 31 years, on certain conditions of enclosing the farm, &c. Until about the year 1798, landlords did not grant, to the general run of their tenants, more than five, seven, or nine years lease; but from time immemorial, the tacksmen who leased a corner of a parish, had from 19 to 21 years lease from the landlord, &c. they gave leases of from three to five years to their sub-tenants and cottagers.

It has often occurred, indeed, that the tenant would not take a lease of his land, at the rent demanded by the proprietor, but he would promise the rent, rather than remove, and occupy his land from year to year. I recollect one instance, where the proprietor measured and divided a town, occupied by about eight tenants, in run-rig, into distinct farms; having done this, he offered to give the land to these tenants, under the new plan, on a lease of fifteen years, at a small additional rent; they unanimously refused to take so long a lease,

because

because they were sure that they should be ruined before the end of it, at so great a rent, and when they were thus obliged to change their mode of occupying it.

The landlord then told them, that he wished to give them the preference, and that he would oblige himself by the lease, to continue them for 15 years, in their farms, if they made good payments; but that he would leave it optional to them, to remove at the end of three, six, or nine years, in case they then found it not a bargain. They readily acknowledged the fairness of this offer, and took their farms on these terms. The result was, the improvement of their farms, and the bettering of their circumstances; of course they did not consider the 15 years too long a term, and they have since often thanked their landlord for his humanity and kindness to them, in inducing them, by such an offer, to benefit themselves and their families.

Agricultural improvements made rapid progress in this county, during the latter end of the last, and beginning of this century, partly owing to the indefatigable exertions of Sir John Sinclair, Bart. the President of the Board of Agriculture, who shewed to others what could be done by improving waste land, even in the climate of Caithness, by cultivating also the old arable land on a better system, and by granting leases of from 19 to 21, and even 31 years to deserving tenants. His example was soon followed by the Earl of Caithness, the Lord Lieutenant of the County, James Traill, Esq. of Hobbister, the Sheriff of the County, whose improvements have been carried on, not only successfully, but on a great scale; and several other respectable Proprietors and Farmers, whose names shall be afterwards mentioned.

The

The circulation of paper currency also, in consequence of the establishment of a branch of the Bank of Scotland in the town of Thurso, enabled the industrious farmer to pay his rent, &c. without disposing of his effects at an under value; but the withdrawing of that branch, has almost destroyed that spirit for agricultural improvement, which then pervaded every class of society in the county. There is at present no means of accommodation to assist the industrious farmer, or mechanic, nearer than Tain in Ross-shire, a distance of about 75 miles.

In regard to leases, several Heritors in the county now grant them for the space of from 19 to 21 years, and sometimes even for 31 years, to tenants paying about 20*l*. rent and upwards, stipulating certain conditions for improvement, such as raising turnips, sowing grass-seeds, &c.; to those paying less than 20*l*. rent, the leases usually given are from nine to twelve years; and to cottagers, leases are commonly for seven years. Since the year 1795, many lots of one, two, and three acres of barren ground, have been improved by cottagers, the ground being let to them upon the following conditions.

1. The lot is given for seven years, rent-free, upon condition, that certain stipulated portions of the lot be annually improved, and that what was improved, is kept in good condition. 2. At the end of the seven years, a rent is to be put upon the lot, by two men, mutually chosen by the landlord and cottager, which regulates what he was to pay for seven years more; and, in case the improver failed to execute the annual improvements prescribed to him, he was bound to pay a rent, say 10*s*. per acre, for what he neglected to cultivate the first year; double that for the second year's neglect;

lect; and should he not fulfil his engagements at the end of the third year, he gets a fair value for what improvements he had made, and may be removed by a legal process.

These conditions made it doubly their interest to improve, and benefit themselves. Their mode of improvement is, generally, trenching the ground with the spade, and the pick where it is rocky. The first crop, potatoes with manure; the second, oats; the third, bear, manured, then oats, &c.

These lots being commonly in the vicinity of a moor, or common pasturage, the cottager is enabled to keep some stock on it.

The Proprietor, in some instances, gives the improver a spade and pick to begin with, gratis.

Where landlords wish to improve their property by means of the cottage system, it is absolutely necessary, to secure to the improver an interest in the soil, by a lease of reasonable duration.

The entry and the termination of every lease in this county, is at the term of Whitsunday, or 15th May, old style, as to the houses and pastures; and to the arable land, when the crop is removed off the ground. The tenant pays no public burden with his rent, except the income-tax, when the rent is above 50*l*. This, in many cases is an unfair tax upon the improving farmer, as he must pay five per cent. for the amount of his yearly rent, although he is ready to prove, that he derived no profit from his farm, but rather an expense without adequate return. It is to such a tenant, therefore, a tax upon *supposed income;* whether real or not, he has no redress; yet all the other classes of society, are taxed only according to the amount of

their

their real income. The landlord pays the land-tax or cess, say about 1*l.* 3*s.* 2*d.* for every 100*l.* Scotch, of valued rent, also the stipend to the Clergy, which is often augmented, and loudly complained of; yet it is preferable to the system of tithes exacted in kind, as it does not check the spirit, or interfere with the industry of the farmer, and improver of the soil.

SECT. VII.—EXPENSE AND PROFIT.

In a county where there is no regular market for the produce of the soil, and neither a population nor resources to consume it where it is grown, it is difficult to ascertain the proportion between expense and profit. Upon farms that are taken on an improving lease of from 21 to 31 years, with a rise of rent at certain periods, the farmer must be considerably the loser for the first 10 years of the lease, when he has to make regular fields of land interspersed with cairns of stones, and green pasture, &c. to make crooked ridges straight, also to marl or lime his farm, in order to fertilize it, and to destroy the acidity in the outfield land, to clear the old croft land of weeds, &c. &c. &c. even admitting that the Proprietor builds a house and farm-offices for the tenants. But in order to form an idea of the expense and profit on farming, in the county under review, let us suppose, a farm of 102 arable acres, Scotch measure, six miles distant from the sea, and from either of the towns of Thurso or Wick, and suppose the farm to have been already brought under a regular rotation of a six years' shift—say, 1st year, turnips; 2d, bear, with grass-

seeds;

seeds; 3d, hay; 4th, pasture; 5th, potatoe oats; and 6th, black oats: there will be about 17 acres in each species of crop annually.

Expenses.

		£	s.	d.
1. Four plough-horses, at 30*l.*		120	0	0
Six oxen, at 12*l.*		72	0	0
Two ponies for harrowing, &c. at 12*l.*		24	0	0
Two ploughs, with their furniture, at 4*l.* 10*s.*		9	0	0
Two horse-carts, ditto, at 18*l.*		36	0	0
Three oxen ditto, ditto, at 15*l.*		45	0	0
One break-harrow,		5	5	0
Three pair of harrows, ditto, at 50*s.*		7	10	0
A turnip-sowing machine,		6	6	0
Small utensils, spades, mattocks, &c. &c.		3	0	0
A fanner 6*l.*, sacks 5*l.*, sundries 10*l.*		21	0	0
Stock supposed to last 10 years, including the loss on horses and utensils,		349	1	0
To 16 bolls seed-bear for 17 acres, at 20*s.*	£16 0 0			
17 ditto potatoe-oats, 17 ditto, at 20*s.*	17 0 0			
26 ditto black ditto, 17 ditto, at 16*s.*	20 16 0			
51 lb. turnip-seed for 17 ditto, at 1*s.*	2 11 0			
Grass-seeds for the 17 do. in bear, 25*s.*	21 5 0			
68	77 12 0			
In hay 17, in pasture 17, 34				
102				
To 10 milch-cows, at 8*l.*	80 0 0			
10 winterers, to eat the straw, &c. at 4*l.*	40 0 0			
One year's cost and wages for servants and hirers,	105 0 0			
The farmer's family expenses, 1 year,	100 0 0			
		402	12	0
The capital required to stock 102 acres, is		£751	13	0

Exclusive of a year's rent, which is often paid in advance; say about 80*l.*, or 16*s.* per acre.

2. The

2. The annual expense per acre, may be calculated thus:

	£	s.	d.
Farm stock and utensils, about 350*l.*; 10 per cent. is	35	0	0
The amount of the seed annually required, as above, ..	77	12	0
The annual maintenance and wages of servants, &c. ..	105	0	0
The price of the cows and winterers 120*l.*; 5 per cent. on this, supposing no loss or accidents to happen,	6	0	0
Total expense on culture, exclusive of house expense, and rent, is	£223	12	0
Or the said expense of culture per acre is	£2	4	8½
Add house expense for the farmer, ...	1	0	0
	£3	4	8½

3. The produce on the above estimate, on a six-years' shift, may be taken as follows:

	£	s.	d.
To 85 bolls bear, or bigg, from 17 acres, or 5 bolls per acre, at 20*s.*	85	0	0
119 ditto potatoe oats, from 17 ditto, or 7 bolls per ditto, at 18*s.*	107	0	0
119 ditto black oats, from 17 ditto, or 7 bolls per ditto.			
15 ditto of which, for horse corn, &c.			
104 ditto remain, and will produce 67 bolls oatmeal (and multure), at 20*s.*	67	0	0
10 acres of the 17 in turnips, for feeding off winterers, &c. at 4*l.*	40	0	0
1200 stone of hay to be sold, of the produce of 17 acres, at 8*d.*, ...	40	16	8
(The remainder being required for food for the horses).			
The profit from 10 milch cows annually, at 4*l.* ..	40	0	0
Total produce per annum is	£379	16	8

So that the average annual produce, per acre, is about 3*l.* 15*s.* 11½*d.*

	Per Acre.			Per 102 Acres.		
	£	s.	d.	£	s.	d.
From the said calculation, the produce is	3	15	$11\frac{8}{10}$	379	16	8
Deduct the expense of culture, exclusive of the rent, the farmer's family expenses, taxes, &c.	2	4	$8\frac{1}{2}$	223	12	0
There remains to pay rent, &c.	1	11	3	156	4	8
Deduct the proprietor's rent per 100 acres,	0	16	0	80	0	0
And there remains to meet household expenses, taxes, &c.	0	15	3	76	4	8

The above estimate is as near the truth as could be made up, regarding the expense and returns of farms of that description. The prices of the farm-stock, and implements, are high, as well as the wages of servants and day-labourers.

The climate is *in general* too cold for the culture of wheat, in so far as any experiments have been hitherto made, though it has been found to answer near the shore when the land is in good condition. The produce of the crops commonly cultivated, is unfortunately uncertain. These circumstances leave but little to the farmer, for his toil and expenses. In the above estimate, I have not included any expense for lime, marl, or any manure, beyond what the farm will produce, because such expense would yield adequate profits, and the practice is not general; neither have I taken notice of the expense of building houses and offices, as the Farmer, in some cases, receives a stipulated allowance out of the first rents; and in others, melioration to a certain extent is allowed for buildings, at the issue of their leases. The latter do not expect that the farm will remunerate their outlays, the interest in some cases being equal to the rent of the farm.

In

In the vicinity of the town of Thurso, a few acres of turnips will sell on the ground, at from 7*l.* to 9*l.* per acre, to cow-feeders in the town. A few acres of hay, may give the same price there; but that is no general rule, in regard to the profit of land in a county where there are no regular markets.

Where land is marled or limed, the produce, in some cases, may be about ten bolls of bear, or potatoe oats, per Scotch acre; but that is the case only on the best arable land. A farm of 200 acres, will be wrought up at less comparative expense, than one of 100 acres, and of course yield more profit; on that account, farms should be at or above 200 arable acres, with some pasture, or, they should be small farms of from 12 to 30 arable acres and pasture. In a remote district, like the county under review, there should be a much greater proportion of small, than of large farms. Indeed, in the Highland part of the county, it must be so, because the arable land is in small patches, and much detached.

In order to show that in this county, people cultivating small farms, have more profit than those occupying large ones, with expensive cattle and implements, I shall, as nearly as possible, state the expenses and returns on a farm of 16 arable acres, with a proportion of hill, or common pasture, at a rent of 14*l.* sterling.

Stock required.

	£	s.	d.	£	s.	d.
o two horses, or garrons, six years old, at 8*l.*				16	0	0
Two oxen, five years old, at 5*l.*				10	0	0
A plough, with iron, and gears, ...	£1	5	0			
A pair of harrows, with iron teeth, ..	1	1	0			
An oxen-cart, second-hand wheels, ..	5	5	0			
Small implements, as spades, &c. ..	0	15	0			
Various articles, ...	1	0	0			
				9	6	0
Stock, suppose renewable in eight years,				£35	6	0
Two milch cows, at 4*l.*	£8	0	0			
Five cattle for working during winter, at 2*l.*	10	0	0			
				18	0	0
14½ bolls black-oat seed for 9 acres, at 14*s.*	6	13	0			
5 bolls seed bear for 5 ditto, at 20*s.*	5	0	0			
1 boll potatoe-seed, 2 lb. turnip-seed, for 1 ditto, ...	0	14	0			
Grass-seeds annually for one ditto, ...	1	0	0			
Total seeds, ...	£13	7	0			
Maintenance and wages for one female servant for one year, 2*l.* and 4 bolls, or	6	0	0			
Household expense for the tenant, his wife, and say 3 children, for 1 year,	15	0	0			
				34	7	0
Total capital required, ...				87	13	0
And one year's rent, say				14	0	0
				£101	13	0

The tenant, in most cases, commences on such a farm with no more than one-fourth of the above capital. They often beg for seed-corn, and buy cattle on credit.

Abstract

Abstract of the preceding Expenses.

	£	s.	d.
To stock, 35*l.* 6*s.*, renewable every eight years, say 12½ per cent., is	4	8	0
5 per cent. on the price of the cows and winterers, say 18*l.*, is	0	18	0
Amount of seeds,	13	7	0
Household expense 15*l.*, servant 6*l.*	21	0	0
Total annual expense is about 2*l.* 9*s.* 7*d.* per acre, or	£39	13	0
Add one year's rent,	14	0	0
Total expense is	£53	13	0

Per Contra.

	£	s.	d.
By 54 bolls oats, produce of 9 acres, at 14*s.*	37	16	0
20 bolls bear, ditto of 5 ditto, at 20*s.*	20	0	0
12 bolls potatoes, at 10*s.*	6	0	0
Butter, &c. from the two cows, at 3*l.*	6	0	0
Profit on the five winterers, say about 30*s.*	7	10	0
Total produce is	£77	6	0
Deduct the above rent and expenses,	53	13	0
Balance is the profit on the 16 acres, with pasture,	£22	13	0

Equal to nearly 1*l.* 10*s.* per acre. This proceeds from the small expense of farm-stock, implements, and servants' maintenance and wages.

The tenant makes sacks for his corn of straw, and ropes of rushes; also collars for his horses and oxen, of the same materials. He makes side-ropes for his plough (namely, chains or traces), of the horses' hair, and sometimes of raw hides, made into twisted thongs for that purpose. These circumstances I know from personal inspection and observation.

Some of this class of tenants, now sow a boll or so of

 red

red oats, and find the crop earlier by three weeks, but the returns not more profitable than from black oats, if the seed oats are changed every third year.

Even in the above statement, if an adequate allowance is made for the tenant's personal labour, little will remain, as real profit, on the capital employed, and the Legislature therefore, has most justly, as well as humanely exempted, such tenants from the tax on income.

CHAP. V.

IMPLEMENTS.

SECT. I.—PLOUGHS.

THE modern plough used in the county, by farmers occupying 100 acres and upwards, is the improved Scotch plough, the mould-board, head, and sole or heel of cast-metal, with a chain or iron rod from the coulter-hole to the muzzle below the beam, or a plate of hammered iron along the beam to strengthen it. Its expense is as follows, viz.

				£	s.	d.
To wood for the beam and stilts, and fitting, ...				1	1	0
75lb. cast-metal for the mould-board, &c. at 3*d*.				0	18	9
50lb. of hammered iron for coulter, sock, muzzle, chain, &c. at 8*d*.				1	13	4
Fitting the irons, and painting the wood, ...				0	5	6
Cost of the plough is, ...				3	18	7
The amble and trees mounted, ..	£0	12	0			
Two pair of hearns, ...	0	7	0			
Traces for a pair of horses, 19lb. at 9*d*.	0	15	0			
Two back bands, at 6*s*.; two pads, at 5*s*.	0	17	0			
Two horse-collars, at 8*s*.	0	16	0			
Two hearn-straps, leather 1*s*. 4*d*.; two bridles, at 8*s*.	0	17	4			
				4	4	4
Total expense of plough and harness for a pair of horses, ...				£8	2	11

There are very few, if any wheel-ploughs, and no trenching, draining, or road-ploughs, in this county.

About 120 years ago, the only plough known or used in Caithness, was called the thraple-plough. The Reporter saw one of these ploughs, kept as a curiosity by his grandfather. The beam was more bent, and nearly the same length with that of the modern plough, with a head or sole, key, land and mould-boards, all of wood; the mould-board having its convex side outwards, and ribbed, so as to break the mould, as the furrow passed off it; it had only one stilt, projecting from the centre of the head or sole, an iron coulter and sock, with or without a feather, as the land was grassy or stony, with a piece of wood fixed on the end of the beam by means of two wooden pegs, which served as a muzzle, and a band made of birch-twigs, or thongs of raw leather, embraced the notch of the muzzles, and an iron hook in the centre of the amble, by which the plough was pulled along. The person who held the plough, had a sheep's-skin tied round his right thigh, to which he held the stilt, to keep the plough steady in its course. Four *garrons*, (small horses), or oxen, were yoked abreast, and the driver went backwards between the two centre beasts, leaning his arms on their necks, which often saved his falling. He regulated the breadth of the furrow, by applying his whip, made of birch-twigs or thongs, to the laziest beast, in order to make the four pull as equal as possible. A third person pressed his weight and strength on the middle of the beam, to keep the plough in the soil. The gears or harness consisted of a main amble, with a little amble fixed to each end of it, by means of two iron links, and to each end of the little ambles was fixed a swingle-tree, by means of a rope made of twigs or raw hide, with side-ropes made of hair or thongs: a collar of straw,

straw, and two beams for each of the four beasts. Thus three persons, with four horses or oxen, were employed about this rude plough, which would not plough much above a quarter of an acre per day. I have heard old people however declare, that the soil yielded better crops, after these ploughs, than after the modern plough, because, as they averred, the mould-board broke the land better; but the real cause must have been, that they had much more command of manure for their small extent of arable land, owing to the extent of pasture for rearing cattle. The price of the thraple-plough was *2s. 6d.*, the ambles, &c. about *1s. 6d.*, in all about *4s.*

The modern plough used by the small tenants, is pretty much of the same construction with the improved Scotch plough, only that the sole, and mould, and land-boards are of wood, with thin plates of iron nailed on each side of the sole, to prevent its wearing, by the friction of the soil. They yoke the horses or ponies in the plough, two or four abreast, as their cattle are strong or weak; when four are yoked abreast, there must be a driver, who walks backwards, according to the ancient system.

SECT. II.—HARROWS.

	£	s.	d.
The best four-barred harrows, made of ash, wood, and making, cost	£1	1	0
Iron teeth, about 31½ lb. at 8*d.*	1	1	0
Amount of a pair is	£2	2	0

A six-barred break-harrow, moving on swivels in the middle, costs about *5l. 5s.* Such a harrow requires four

four horses to work it, in strong land, being too heavy for two.

In the Highland part of the county, they make light four-barred harrows of birch, with teeth of the same materials, which answer well enough for a light moory tender soil, where, they allege, that harrows with iron teeth, would sink the seed too deep in the earth.

SECT. III.—ROLLERS.

1. *Of Wood*—are made five feet long, and from 16 to 18 inches diameter, having an iron gudgeon in each end, to attach it to a frame or trams for one horse, with an oblong box on the trams, or frame above the roller, where stones are put to increase the weight when working.

2. *Of Freestone*—five feet long, and from 11 to 13 inches diameter, with an iron gudgeon in each end, as in the wooden one, and fixed in a three-barred frame, having two iron rings, to which the horse traces are fixed. The price of either the wooden or stone roller, is about 2*l.* 2*s.* The wooden roller, from its greater diameter, does better on ploughed land, but the stone roller does equally well on grass land.

There are neither fluted, concave, or convex rollers in this county, except the roller of turnip-sowing machines, which is both concave and convex, to suit the drills.

There are two cast-iron cylindrical rollers, of two feet diameter, and divided in the middle, upon two farms near Wick. They are allowed to be superior to wooden or stone rollers, for every purpose, and in particular,

ticular, for rolling land, after the young grain has vegetated. They are also of use, either to roll in grass-seeds, or to destroy the grub and slug, by rolling in the night time.

SECT. IV.—HORSE-HOES.

The principal and most general horse-hoo used in this county, is a small plough, with a double mould-board of wood, mounted with thin plates of iron, which may be widened or otherwise, by means of an iron swivel and pin behind the stilts, with a small coulter and sock, having a feather on each side. By taking off the left mould-board, (which is hooked on), this plough does for the first operation of taking down the earth from the drills, and cutting the weeds; and in due time, by putting on the said board, it serves to put up the earth to the drill of turnips or potatoes, as a last operation. Some farmers use a sharp thin plate of iron, commonly made of an old scythe, formed as a semicircle, both ends being fixed to a small iron bar, which is fixed to the beam above the coulter, and the middle of the semicircle fixed to the lower end of the coulter. The plough thus accoutred, and without mould-boards, is wrought by one horse, to cut the weeds between the drills, which it does effectually on land not very stony.

There is also a triangular harrow, drawn by one horse, which serves as an excellent horse-hoe: it consists of three beams, the two outer beams move on a swivel, which passes through the front end of the middle beam; and to the top of the rear end of the middle beam or bar, there are two stilts, attached by screw-bolts,

bolts, by which the ploughman directs the machine; a rod of iron passes through the rear end of the middle bar, upon which the outer bars are extended from, or drawn near to, the centre one, according to the breadth between the drills, and kept in that position by means of pins and holes in the said iron rod. Each of the bars are about three feet long, the centre bar has four teeth, and each of the other two, three teeth, like that of a break-harrow; to the lower end of the front tooth of the centre bar is attached a triangular piece of iron, of about six inches on the sides of the angle, and sharp on the side edges, with the point foremost like a sock; a swivel is fixed to the front of the centre bar, to which the swingle-tree is attached by a hook; the harrow is thus pulled along by one horse, directed by the driver, who holds the stilts. The triangular plate of iron fixed on the lower end of the front tooth, cuts the weeds under ground in the bottom of the drill, like a sock, and the teeth of the three bars act so, that all the earth between the drills is stirred, and the weeds torn by the roots. By repeating this operation twice through the season, the weeds are kept down and destroyed, and the top of the drills being hand-weeded, the crop, in due time, is ready to be earthed up by the double mould-board plough; which is the last hoeing operation of our turnip and potatoe crops, being the only drilled crops used in this county.

SECT. VI.—SCARIFIERS, SCUFFLERS, SKIMS, &c.

The only instruments of this kind used in this county, were brought from England, by Sir John Sinclair,

clair, along with a few Cambridge-shire men, in order to make an experiment of the fen husbandry, on the high moors of Caithness. The scarifier was wrought with two horses, its movement being regulated by the course of a pair of wheels, of about four feet diameter, a cross bar of wood being attached to the axle of the wheels, by iron rods. In this cross bar was fixed six coulters, at equal distances, and a pair of stilts is attached to the bar, by which the ploughman directs the machine, and drives the horses. After the operation of scarifying is over, a pair of horses are yoked in the paring-plough, with the cutting-wheel of 16 inches diameter (*vice* a coulter), and a broad sock; the course of the paring operation is at right angles with that of the scarifier. The sod is thus pared off from one to two inches thick, according to the uniformity of the surface, and the length of the sods is equal to the distance between the cuts of the scarifier. These machines are more adapted to low level fenny land or moss, than to the Highland moors or mosses of Caithness.

Sir John also imported the breast-plough, or paring-spade, and had five Westmoreland men busy with these instruments in 1802 and 1803, when they pared and burnt about 150 acres of a divided common, in the low part of the county, within a few miles of Thurso; at the expense of 28*s.* per acre, for paring, and 9*s.* for burning.

SECT. VII.—THRASHING-MACHINES.

MR. TRAILL of Hobbister, Sheriff-depute of the county, had a thrashing-mill erected at Castle-hill, as far

far back as the year 1790. The machine was first wrought by two horses, and afterwards by water. It has since undergone many alterations and improvements, and now answers the purpose effectually.

There are now above 11 thrashing-mills in this county, wrought by water, nine by horses, all of a four-horse power, and four machines of a two-horse power; the drum of the former is from four and an half to five feet long, and of the latter three feet long and three feet diameter, including the wings. The water machines of the four-horse mills, will thrash from six to eight bolls of oats per hour, and the two-horse machines from three to five bolls in the same space of time. Winnowing-machines are attached to almost the whole of these mills. When thrashing bear or bigg, if the roller-straps is put upon a larger shieve than that for oats, so as to make the motion of the feeding-rollers a little slower, they separate the bear pretty well from the straw; but it requires to be afterwards beat by the flail to clear it from the awns.

The price of the machinery of a four-horse machine, is from 80*l.* to 100*l.* and of a two-horse thrashing-machine, about 69*l.* winnowing-machine included. In both cases, the beams which support the horse-wheel is excepted, as that is not considered a part of the machinery, and of course not found by the millwright. These beams cost from 5*l.* to 7*l.* sterling.

A thrashing-mill of a two-horse power, is sufficient for a farm of 100 to 150 arable acres; and as such machines are not as yet in general use, I will here state its dimensions. The circle in which the horses move, is 26 feet diameter, the very tract of the horses is 24 feet diameter.

1. The

	Teeth.
1. The horse-wheel is 10 feet diameter, having cast-metal sections screwed on it, containing	216
2. The laying shaft 13 feet long, its metal pinion has	20
3. The spur-wheel of cast-metal, four feet diameter, has	96
4. The drum pinion of cast-metal, has	11

5. The drum is three feet long, and three feet diameter over the wings.

The horses move $2\frac{1}{4}$th times round the circle in a minute, to give the necessary velocity, or at the rate of about 1040 strokes in the minute. The fanners are wrought by a leather strap, on a shieve upon the drum axle and fanners' axle, and the metal rollers or feeders, move by means of a leather strap, over a shieve or cradle on the laying shaft behind the spur-wheel, and a smaller shieve upon the axle of the upper roller. The shaker is also put in motion by a similar strap from the laying shaft to a shieve on its axle.

SECT. VIII.—CHAFF-CUTTERS.

THERE were two of these machines brought to the county, but not much used.

SECT. IX. X. XI.—BRUISERS, WAGGONS.

THERE are one or two bruisers for crushing horse-corn, but no waggon in this county, nor roads to bear them.

SECT.

SECT. XII.—ONE-HORSE CARTS.

In general, every farmer has a cart for every pair of plough-horses, which cart is occasionally used for one horse, or two horses, one being in the shafts and the other in the traces. The present price of such a cart is as follows, viz.

					£	s.	d.
To wood and workmanship of a cart, box, trams, and shelvings,					3	10	0
Iron-mounting on the box and trams,					1	12	6
A pair of wheels, ash, 4½ feet high,	£2	5	0				
Rings on ditto, 8¼ stone of iron, at 6s.	2	9	6				
Nave-hoops, 17 lb. at 7d.	0	9	11				
Pipe-bushes, 23 lb. at 3d.	0	5	9				
					5	10	2
An iron axle, 66 lb., at 7d.					1	18	6
Painting the cart and wheels,					0	7	6
Total for the cart,					£12	18	8
A cart-saddle,	£0	14	0				
A good double-breeching,	1	8	0				
A mounted stretcher for the traces,	0	1	6				
A cart-whip,	0	4	0				
					2	7	6
Total,					£15	6	2

The above is the medium price of the farm-carts, to serve either for one or two horses, as the draught may be distant or not. And by good management, with some repair, such a cart should last seven years. A cart, for a pair of ordinary oxen, with an iron axle, will cost about 12*l.* sterling.

The shopkeepers of Thurso and Wick import second-hand carriage wheels from the Edinburgh market, which they sell to the small tenants through the county,

county, at from 15*s*. to 2*l*. 2*s*. per pair. The tenant buys some birch-wood for an axle and shafts, and fir for a box, and a country cart-wright will finish the cart at his house. The box, shafts, and axle may cost from 40*s*. to 50*s*. These carts serve for their ponies, or garrons, or when furnished with a pole and yoke, *vice* shafts, they are fitted for a pair of small oxen.

About 60 or 70 years ago, there were no carts in this county. Manure was carried to the land, and corn from it, in creels (baskets) or crubbans (a triangular wooden machine) upon their horses' backs. The first carts imported, were from Moray-shire, the wheels, three feet diameter, and not shod with iron, of course of little value or benefit. About the year 1780, a better kind of carts became more general; and there might be about 40 carts, with iron shod wheels in the county. In 1784, there were only six carts of this description in the parish of Olrig; but such was the rapid progress in agricultural improvement, that in 1792 there were 200 carts within that parish, yet the parish is not above three miles square. It is principally, however, a corn district.

SECT. XIII. AND XIV.—DRAINING-MILLS, SLUICES.

THERE are none in this county.

SECT. XV.—RAKES, HOES, SPADES, PARING-SHOVELS.

1. *The Common Hay-rake*.—The head is three feet long, having 16 wooden pegs as teeth, about two

inches and a half long, and a handle about five feet long; each end of a semicircular plate of iron, thus  is nailed on the head, and the middle nailed on the handle, to secure it more firmly in the head.

2. *Hoes*—Both common and Dutch, are imported from England for hand-weeding.

3. *Spades*.—The only spades now used in this county, are the iron spades and shovels, imported from the southern markets, commonly called English spades, though manufactured in Scotland. Their price at the shops, is from 3*s*. 6*d*. to 4*s*. per spade, and 3*s*. to 3*s*. 6*d*. for a shovel. About 25 years ago, when cargoes of oatmeal were exported to the ports of Bergen, and Drontheim, in Norway, fir planks, deals, and *fir shovels*, &c. were imported. These shovels were sold to the country people at from 4*d*. to 6*d*. each; they got them shod with a thin plate of iron, and they then served the purpose of the present iron spade at much less expense; but they were not so handy or effectual in farm-work.

4. *Paring-Shovels*.—The only paring-shovels or spades in use here, is what is called the divot-spade, *i. e.* a breast-spade for casting or cutting divots, or thin sods for thatch to their houses. The metal part of the spade has a semicircular edge, and a socket to receive the wooden handle, about four feet and a half long, and a little bent, having a cross wooden head; the workman, by pressing his belly to this head, pushes the spade into the ground, nearly in a horizon-

tal direction, in order to cut the sods thin. The shape of the spade is thus 

The mouth, or edge of this spade is steeled, and kept very sharp. A man, having a sheep's skin tied round his waist, will earn from 2*s*. to 2*s*. 6*d*. per day, by casting divots with this spade, at the rate of 3*s*. for every 1000 divots.

SECT. XVI.—WINNOWING-MACHINES.

THE most ancient, and still most general winnowing-machine in this county, is the fan (provincially called a *waight*), being a sheep's skin freed from the wool, and stretched on a wooden hoop of about 18 inches diameter, and fixed on it by thongs of the same skin, stitched through it, and holes in the hoop; when dry, the skin is as firmly stretched as a drum-head. With these, men are employed to separate the corn from the chaff, &c. by exposing them to the wind. Riddles are also used; too well known to require any description of them here. These are the only implements used by the small tenants for dressing their corn; but the more opulent farmers have winnowing-machines for dressing their corn for market, which now cost about 7*l*. 7*s*. a pair in this county. The fans or *waights* above described, are useful for bringing the corn to the fanners, filling sacks, &c.

SECT. XVII. AND XVIII.—BORERS AND DRAINING-TOOLS.

There are none of these used here; they are much wanted, to bore and carry off our numerous springs.

SECT. XIX.—SOWING-MACHINES.

There is one of Cooke's sowing-machines at Thurso Castle, with which a 20 acre field of bear was sown in 1805. The distance between the drills being too narrow to admit the horse-hoe, and hand-hoeing being too expensive, the weeds became so predominant, that the crop was very inferior to that sown broad-cast, or what that field would have produced in the usual mode. The machine, therefore, has not since been used.

There are a few turnip sowing-machines in this county, wrought by one man and a horse. They sow and roll two drills at a time; are of much benefit, in sowing the seed expeditiously after the drill is formed, while the soil is fresh and moist, which saves labour, and insures a crop. The largest roller, in front of the sowing-machine, is six feet long, being concave and convex, to suit the drills, and a divided small roller follows the sowing tubes and coulters, to cover the seed. One person will do more work, with this machine, than three men with hand-barrows. The expense of this machine is about 7*l.* 7*s.* and it may last 20 years.

SECT. XX.—MISCELLANEOUS ARTICLES.

The only other farming implements used in this county, are, 1. Wheel-barrows; very useful in driving out manure from stables to dunghills. 2. Grapes; a three-pronged instrument, stouter than a pitch-fork, with a handle of three feet long; useful in filling carts with long litter or manure, through which the spade or shovel will not easily penetrate. 3. Mattocks, or small picks, to one side of the eye only, with a handle three feet long; used to loosen dunghills that have been packed, to ease the labour of filling the cart with the grape or spade.

The smaller class of tenants still use the straw *cassie*, instead of sacks, for their corn. These *cassies* are made of oat-straw, and small ropes made of prepared rushes, like a mat. The *cassie* is of an oblong form, about three feet long at bottom, and two feet and a half at the top, and about 20 inches deep; it will hold half a boll of bear or oats.

Each *cassie* has a fettle or handle in each side and end, to carry it by, and two straw ropes to tie the mouth of it when full.

These are generally made during the winter nights, either by the tenant or his male servants, if he has any. A *cassie* will last two years, if taken care of, and the materials of which it is made, may be valued at 2*d.* The tenant has also a mat made of the same materials, three feet long, and two feet broad, for each of his horses or ponies; and, if he has not a cart, or that the road he has to travel to market, is unfit for wheel-carriages, he accoutres his ponies with these straw mats and wooden saddles (called *a clubber*) with a deep notch in the top of it, to hold a rope. A horse thus mounted, will carry a cassie on each side of his back, containing half a boll of meal, or six pecks of bear each, through the most rugged or worst roads, to any part of the county. The cassies being of equal weight, are held on the horse's back by a rope of straw or rushes, laid across the horse's back, turned up about each cassie; and after both the ends are fixed tight, that part of the ropes which pass over the saddle or *clubber*, is put into the said notch, in the top of the clubber, which keeps the whole steady.

I have been rather diffuse in the description of this part of rural economy, because I believe it is a practice peculiar to the Northern Districts. The horses thus loaded, are each tied by the halter to the other's tail; in some cases there may be about six or seven of them thus going in a kind of Indian file, a person leading the front horse, and each of the others pulled forward by the tail of the one before him. After the driver arrives at the destined place, the horses are unloaded, and the halter of the front horse is tied to the tail of the rear horse; by that means they cannot run away, as they can only move in a circle where they stand.

Odd as all this may appear, there is still a more barbarous custom in the Highlands. On a farm in Badenoch, in the month of May, 1795, the Reporter saw a servant, with a pair of stout good horses, harrowing a barley field, having the harrows fixed by ropes to the tails of the horses, in place of the common mode of pulling by the shoulders. The servant assured me, that it was a common practice in that district, and considered to be the best mode of breaking young horses to work.

There are no weighing-machines.

CHAP.

CHAP. VI.

INCLOSING.

SECT. I.—MODE OF DIVISION.

There are no inclosures by Act of Parliament in this county. The Land Proprietors have, in several instances, agreed to divide very extensive tracts of common, consisting of green pasture and moor, in the parishes of Thurso, Halkirk, Olrig, &c. Upwards of 7000 Scotch acres of land of this description, have been already divided by arbitration, according to the proportion of valued rent belonging to each Proprietor. A considerable part of these commons are capable of improvement, but the pressure of the war and taxation, retard the beneficial effects which might naturally follow so desirable a measure; and "a common is still no uncommon spectacle in Caithness."

1. *Effect on Produce, Population, Poor.*—The progress made in the improvement of these commons, is as yet too limited, to show any evident effect on produce; but in a county where there are very few villages, nor any manufactures to employ the small tenants, who are usually removed, previous to the inclosure of a large farm, the effect will tend to decrease the population, because many of these people go with their families to the manufacturing towns, in the south-west of Scotland, rather than attempt to improve a lot of these divided commons, perhaps in view of the old arable land, which they, and their forefathers, occu-

 pied,

pied, and now in the hands of farmers of greater capital. In some cases, it tends to increase the number of the poor; but that is not so generally felt, where no poor's-rates are collected.

2. *Expenses.*—The expenses of dividing a common, either by reference or arbitration, are, 1. The charge made by the Land Surveyor, for ascertaining the extent, and making a plan of the ground, which is commonly about 20*s*. per 100 acres; and, 2. The expense of extending the decreet-arbitral regarding the division.

3. *Rise of Rent.*—These commons having formerly yielded no rent, as they were merely appendages to the neighbouring farms, and as these farms now pay a greater rent, without the commons, than formerly with them, whatever is received from lots of divided commons let to cottagers or others, may fairly be considered as an additional rent to the Proprietor. There is one instance, on the estate of Sir John Sinclair, of a farmer having 200 acres of these divided commons, on a lease of 31 years, at the rent of 40*l*. sterling: he is allowed certain meliorations for buildings and inclosures at the end of his lease. He commenced his improvements in 1804, and crop 1810 will produce to him about 100 bolls of oatmeal, and bear; but his outlays are considerable in buildings, &c. and in collecting extraneous manure.

Lots of from five to twenty-five acres, have been let to small tenants, who were removed from the old land, upon the following terms, namely, for the first seven years, at a rent of from 2*s*. to 3*s*. per acre, according to the quality of the soil; for the next seven years, at double that sum; and for the third seven years, of

a lease

a lease of 21 years, at treble the first rent. The result has been, that where such lots were near the sea, and occupied by fishermen, or mechanics, and the lots small, the plan answered very well: they were industrious, and improved their little occupations. In cases where the lots were large, say about 20 acres, in the interior of the county, the occupier having nothing to depend on for his support, but the produce of his new soil, struggled with difficulties and disappointments in the crop, &c. for a few years, and then left the possession little better than he found it, and perhaps ruined by the experiment!

In all cases where lots are given to cottagers, some aid is given to build a house, and meliorations for inclosures, if he continues to carry on such improvements.

SECT. II.—FENCES.

1. *Sort.*—The most general kind of fences in this county, particularly on new ground, or upon new enlarged farms, is a ditch five feet wide at top, and 18 inches at the bottom; three feet in perpendicular depth, with three feals or sods set on edge about nine inches from the ditch, with the green sward outwards, or towards the ditch, and the earth, &c. thrown out of the ditch, is cast behind these sods. In the course of the first year, these green sods grow firm together, where it is not much exposed to the meridian sun. This kind of fence, properly directed, tends much to dry a spongy wet soil, with a rock or tilly bottom, such as the Caithness soil in general is; but it is not a sufficient fence against

against cattle, without a stone coping on the earth so thrown out of the ditch.

2. *Expenses.*—The expense of making or excavating a ditch of the above dimensions, is about *3d.* per yard of the ditch, or per cubic yard, because a yard of ditch, of the above description, is very near a cubic yard.

After the earth thus thrown out, consolidates for a year or two, it will bear about 15 inches high of a stone dyke, 18 inches broad, and a rough coping. This stone-work will cost about *4d.* per running yard, quarrying and building. The carriage must depend on the distance.

3. *Duration.*—The duration of ditches depends upon the nature of the soil: if it is stiff and grassy, and the front of the feal or sods is towards the north, or from the rays of the sun, and of course grows firm together, so as to sustain the weight of the stone coping, it may last 20 years, with some occasional cleaning or scouring of the ditch, from mud collected by the winter storms; but if the soil is of a friable nature, or calcareous clay, the sods should be placed 15 inches from the verge of the ditch, because such soil is apt to expand with the winter frost, and the faces of the ditch crumble down with the thaw. The back of such ditches should be towards the east, or south-east; broom and whin-seed should be sown on the earth thrown out of the ditch; and even hawthorn would thrive in such soil, if kept clean, and planted with some manure: a row of broom between the hawthorn plant and the top of the earth, would shelter it until it grew

strong

strong enough to stand the winter; and were such a ditch faced with stone, it would be very durable. There is one instance of a ditch faced with stone, and the earth thrown out fronting the east, and a hawthorn hedge in the east face of it, made and planted 60 years ago in this county, and the hedge still in vigour.

Upon ground where hawthorn will not thrive, and where draining is not necessary, the best and most durable fence is, a dyke, built of stone, without mortar, called a dry stone dyke, two feet four inches broad in the base, and 18 inches broad at the top, four feet high, and a rough coping. Such a dyke, properly built, may last a century, with little repair, and no animal will attempt to leap over it. Such a dyke will now cost, in this county, for quarrying and building, about 1*s.* per square yard, besides carriage of the materials. Several fields are inclosed with this kind of fence, on many farms through the county.

Upon the farm of Thurso East, in the possession of Sir John Sinclair, there are about 300 acres of arable land, inclosed and subdivided with stone dykes, principally erected from 40 to 50 years ago. The dyke is two feet and a half broad at bottom, two feet at top, and five feet high, with a double row of feal or sods on the top. These dykes have been built too broad in the top; and owing to their being top-heavy, (a great error in the building), they burst asunder in many places, which incurs an annual expense for repairs. A four-feet wall, with rough coping, and a regular batter from each side, and thorough bands, would be more durable, and equally serviceable, as a fence. This rough, or snap coping, was introduced into this county, about 20 years ago, and it is found to answer well, where the stone is weather-proof; but in case the stone yields to

the

the weather, the old mode of covering the top with sods, is preferable. The expense of these stone dykes, about 50 years ago, in this county, was 7*s*. 6*d*. per rood of 30 square yards for building, and 6*s*. per rood for quarrying: the stone was carried commonly by the farm servants and cattle.

The fences generally used by the tenantry about their arable land, commonly called the head-dykes, were built with *feal* or turf, from three to four feet broad in the base, two feet in the top, and from four to five feet high, seldom any distance in a straight line, and of course *zig-zag*, and much longer than necessary. Annually, after the crop was sown, the tenant and his servants were employed for two weeks in repairing the breaches made by the cattle in these dykes, during the preceding season. The peat-cutting then commenced, and afterwards they cut feal or turf on the commons, to be carried home for compost dunghills to their land. These operations gave them employment until the end of July, when they cut their bog or meadow hay.

These old head-dykes are now generally trenched up for bedding to cattle, and for compost dunghills, and the more modern plan of ditches made beyond the said dykes, is a new species of fence, which answers the double purpose of draining and of fencing the arable land.

In the Appendix, (A), will be found the opinions of several of the most intelligent Proprietors and Farmers in the county, on the subject of fences.

4. *Gates*.—Upon Gentlemen's farms, where the fences are stone dykes or walls, the gates are commonly formed by two circular pillars, eight feet asunder, each about three feet diameter, and six feet high, below a

tabling of flag, and above that, about two feet high of a cope, tapering to a point. These pillars are built with stone and lime, or mortar, and harled with lime, having either freestone or wooden posts built in them, for the iron batts upon which the hinges of the five barred wooden gate moves. The gate should move upon an iron pivot, in a free or whinstone socket, because hinges are apt to yield with the weight of a heavy gate, when the whole weight rests upon them. The expense of building these pillars, is by the square yard, *i. e.* at double the price of square mason-work.

SECT. III.—NEW FARMS.

In the parishes of Thurso, Olrig, Dunnet, and Cannisbay, there are several new farms formed, by converting a town-land, formerly occupied by from five or more tenants, into one farm of from 120 to 400 acres, where the modern system of husbandry is to be followed, by straighting ridges, squaring fields, sowing green crops, &c. There are also some new farms in those parishes formed from the divided common, one of which, in the parish of Thurso, I have already mentioned. Several other farms of less extent have been improved from common, in the parishes of Halkirk, Thurso, Olrig, Dunnet, and Cannisbay, principally by the paring and burning system; they are not hitherto productive of corn or grass, owing to want of that abundant supply of manure, which is necessary for a soil whose vegetative earth has been consumed by fire.

Any tolerable soil that is pared and burned, and the

ashes spread and lightly ploughed in, will produce one crop of oats, which should be sown with rye-grass, to give the soil a new sward, and afterwards pastured for one year. In the course of the autumn following, let it get a top-dressing of lime or marl, and if it can be manured with dung next spring, and ploughed, it will produce another crop of oats, which ought to be followed by a green crop or fallow, as circumstances require. If it is then manured, and laid down with bear and grass-seeds, the improvement will be completed, and the soil brought into an arable state; but if a second crop is attempted, after burning, without manure or calcareous matter, the soil becomes more difficult to improve, than it was in its original state of sterility.

Where the plan is adopted of reducing new ground, by repeated ploughings at certain intervals, to give time to the sod to moulder and putrify; the vegetative earth in that case is not consumed, and less manure will prove effectual; but in either case, calcareous matter is necessary to decompose the sterile acidity of the soil in its natural state.

SECT. IV.—ACCOUNT OF THE MANNER IN WHICH THE SMALLER DESCRIPTION OF TENANTS FORMERLY COMMENCED FARMING.

About the year 1775, a good farm-servant, in the county of Caithness, had no more than 26*s.* 8*d.* of wages per ann.; yet, out of this small pittance, he would make an annual saving; in a few years he would purchase a three or four year old cow, and give

give her to a small farmer, who agreed to maintain her for half the profits of her calf, &c. By the time he had saved about 5*l.* and owned one or two head of cattle, he would take a small farm, of from six to ten acres arable, and some pasture; the rent, including customs and casualities, might be from 3*l.* 10*s.* to 5*l.* He entered to this farm at Whitsunday; got married; the husband and wife would have some meal saved of their former wages in meal or grain, to assist in maintaining them until their fuel was collected; and they hired themselves to work at the ensuing harvest. In winter, the new beginner received the out-going tenant's crop on a proof, as is customary in the county; by the month of February he went among all the neighbouring tenants, &c. requesting some aid of oats and bear, to assist him for seed, &c. for his new farm, (this species of begging is called provincially *thegging*). If he was on good terms with his acquaintance, he would collect in this manner, a sufficient quantity to sow the land, and even to subsist him. At the previous Martinmas he would get four small oxen, to winter, for their spring work; these would plough the land to him; he could furnish his plough, ambles, and swingle trees, hems, &c. for about 20*s.*, and a pair of barrows about 2*s.* 6*d.*; he would buy an old poney for about 10*s.*, a pair of creels and clubbar for the poney, cost about 1*s.* 4*d.*; and the wife, with the poney thus accoutred, drove the manure to the bear (barley) land.

By these means the first crop was put in the ground, which, in time, enabled him to rear some cattle on his farm, and neighbouring common; but having very little when he commenced, and the increase of his family depriving him of a part of the wife's labour; though he had the name of being his own master, he

remained

remained in indigent circumstances, at least until his family was able to assist him.

In this county he had no alternative, but either to remain unmarried, or take this method, as there were then but very few married servants employed*, the general run of farms being small; but in a county where there were large farms, when he could get his cottage and a few acres, and engage as a farm servant, in the character of a *hind*, he and his family would be more comfortable, than in the above ideal state of starving independence; and it seems not only more patriotic, but more humane, to the families of many small tenants, still in the old course of management, to take the plough from their hands, and to employ them in other parts of manual labour necessary for improved cultivation; placing persons amongst them who can give them such employment, and who will set an example to those who appear most able, and best inclined to follow it.

The same class of servants have now from 6*l.* to 7*l.* per ann. and they can hardly save any of it, owing to their wearing better clothes, &c.; this, in many cases, is not so much from choice, as from necessity, because

* In a district where farms contain only from 70 to 100 arable acres, population must decrease, as such farmers must employ unmarried servants, with the exception of one as grieve or overseer; but in a country that abounds with coal, at an easy rate, farms of from 250 to 1000 acres of arable land, will not decrease the population; as it is the farmer's interest to have married servants, and the extent of his farm will admit of his giving each the means of maintaining a cow, and the carriage of a limited quantity of coal, to each can easily be done. But were the farmer to have a number of married servants in separate houses, where the only fuel is peat or turf, to be brought from a distance, the very labour of furnishing their fuel would be a greater burden on him than their wages. Hence, the very article of fuel determines the case, regarding married or unmarried servants.

now the farmers' wives do not make those coarse low-priced clothes for the market, as they did formerly, owing to their having no sheep, and the price of wool being high. In 1775, a servant purchased a pair of shoes for 1*s*. 6*d*.; now they cost from 9*s*. to 10*s*.; and other articles necessary for their wear, are high-priced in the same proportion.

CHAP. VII.

ARABLE LAND.

SECT. I.—TILLAGE.

1. *Ploughing*—Is performed, on the larger farms, with the two-horse improved Scotch plough; and the smaller tenants use four ponies or four oxen abreast, in their light plough, with a driver, who walks backwards, a custom of great antiquity in this county. Some of them, within these 12 or 15 years last past, work two stout garrons without a driver, in their plough, which is improved, in regard to the beam and stilts, but with a wooden mould-board in place of a metal one, strengthened by thin plates of iron on the boards, both on the mould and land side, to preserve the wood from wearing by the friction of the earth. This improved practice commonly prevails where the tenants' land have been divided into regular lots, and a condition made in their lease, that their ridges are to be made straight, and a proportion laid down in green crops. The ancient custom of tenants occupying a town-land in run-rigg, or, as it is called, *rigg* and *rennel*, is now in a great degree abolished, though, in some parts of this county, it still exists. It is not only a great bar to improvements, but a source of perpetual dissention between neighbours, the one complaining that the other has taken a furrow too many from his ridge, &c.

2. *Harrow-*

2. *Harrowing*—Is performed with one, two, or three, horses or oxen abreast, having a harrow attached to each. The harrow is drawn by one corner in an oblique direction, and the ropes which attach the swingle-tree of each beast to the harrows, are of such unequal length, as to allow the one harrow to continue in an oblique position behind the other, that of the harrow of the left hand horse, *i.e.* the one next the driver, being the shortest. The cattle are yoked to the harrows by collars and heams, as in the plough.

3. *Rolling.*—The land is seldom rolled in this county, except in preparing it for a green crop, or on strong soils during a summer-fallow; or lastly, when grass-seeds are sown with bear or oats; the land is then rolled, to give it a smooth surface for the scythe, when mowing the hay crop.

4. *Ribbing.*—In some cases farmers scarify strong land at Martinmas, (the beginning of November), *i.e.* they half plough it, by leaving as much land between each furrow, as that the turned up soil from each will nearly touch. They say that this plan meliorates the soil, by exposing it to the winter frosts, and destroys the roots of perennial weeds. What is properly called scarifying with the instrument called the scuffler, is not known in this county.

5. *Ridges.*—Where modern husbandry is practised, and the land straighted, the ridges in general are about fifteen feet broad; but in the old practice of crooked riggs and run-riggs, the ridges are generally of the shape of the letter (S) perhaps 30 feet broad in the middle, and more than from four to six feet at each end;

end; yet such is the effect of prejudices, that old people will yet affirm, that these broad, crooked, and high ridges, produced a better crop than the modern straight and narrow ridges; and that they could plough them better. It is found by experience, that in newly improved land, the ridges should be made from 20 to 30 feet broad, and raised high in the middle, in order the more effectually to carry off the superabundant moisture, particularly where the subsoil is till, or otherwise tenacious of moisture, more especially where the land cannot be trench-ploughed.

6. *Putting in Crops without Ploughing.*—It was formerly the practice merely to harrow the land after a potatoe crop, and then to sow oats in spring; but of late it is more common to plough the potatoe or turnip land once, and, if the soil is strong, twice, before sowing it in spring with oats or bear and grass-seeds.

7, 8, 9. *Drilling, Horse-hoeing, Hand-hoeing.*—No corn crop is drilled, horse, or hand-hoed, in this county, excepting a few experiments with wheat, which shall be noticed afterwards.

10. *Weeding.*—Previous to the introduction of green crops, and of summer-fallow, into this county, the arable land was much infested with various weeds, as the thistle *(cardus)*, the mugwort *(artemesia)*, dove-dock *(tusilago)*, &c. &c. &c. Thistles and mugworts were pulled by the roots, out of the oat crop only, in the month of July; and in order to defend the hand from the thistles, an oblong piece of sheep-skin was tied round the wrist of the right hand, which enabled the persons employed to pull them out with

with ease. The bear crop was not hand-weeded, but the tenants' sheep and cattle followed the plough in spring, and ate the mugwort roots, of which they are very fond, and basket-fulls of them would be collected to feed calved cows in the house. Notwithstanding these practices, weeds were very abundant in all the stock land, or old croft land, excepting such small spots as were cleaned by a potatoe crop. They had no means by which the tusilago, so prejudicial to the oat crop, from the early ploughing, could be destroyed; but bear land, being ploughed about the latter end of May, the crop commonly checked the growth of that weed.

In every case where large farms are formed of town-lands, formerly occupied as small farms, containing croft land and out-field land, the farmer is obliged to summer-fallow the croft land, before he can attempt a green crop in it, owing to the great quantity of roots of these perennial weeds, which he had to collect by hand-weeding between each ploughing, and burn them. Tusilago can be destroyed only by deep ploughing and summer-fallow.

SECT. II.—FALLOWING.

After clearing the land from weeds, in the manner above described, it is better to raise green crops, than to summer-fallow the land, in a county where wheat has not hitherto much succeeded. On this subject Mr. Sutherland of Brabster very justly observes, that in a rainy season, which Caithness so often experiences, fallowing is the occasion of losing a crop, without benefiting a light soil. When under a green crop, the

the ground may, in a favourable year, be thoroughly cleaned; and in an unfavourable one, the grain crop of the farmer who adopts the non-fallowing system, is certainly preferable to the luxuriant crop of weeds which will infallibly cover the fields of the fallower. As few farmers in Caithness, however, can command enough of manure to lay down a turnip or potatoe crop, in the whole of that part of the farm intended for those crops, they must content themselves with sowing turnips and potatoes, as far as their manure extends, and summer-fallow the remainder of that lot, to be manured in the course of the season, so that the whole may be prepared for the succeeding crop of bear with grass-seeds.

SECT. III.—COURSE OF CROPS.

Upon farms cultivated according to the improved system, the course of crops is as follows, viz.

1. Turnips, potatoes, or fallow, well manured.
2. Bear or bigg, with grass-seeds.
3. Hay.
4. Pasture.
5. Oats.

When manure is not easily procurable, some take a second crop of oats; but upon all farms near to sea-weed, or to calcareous clay or marl, for manure, the five years' shift is accounted the best, and most profitable, because, although land, after being two years more in grass, will produce a second crop of oats, the soil is more exhausted, and requires a greater proportion of manure, with the succeeding crop of turnips,

turnips, or potatoes, &c. This is the mode of managing the best arable land; but fields, of inferior quality, are allowed to remain three or four years in pasture, before they are broken up for oats; and by that time, such land begins to fog, or to produce moss, which is the signal for ploughing it up. Two successive crops of oats are then sometimes taken, the first red, and the second black oats.

The course of crops, formerly, and even still practised by the generality of the small tenants in this county, is this: Every farm has a proportion of in-field, or rich croft land, and of out-field, or inferior arable land. The former being old stock land, will produce bear and oats alternately; the latter only yields an inferior sort of oats, called grey oats.

In the best land, bear and oats are raised alternately, without any change, some small patches for potatoes excepted: the manure is applied every second year with the bear crop. The outfield land (provincially *afterwald)*, commonly a light sour kind of soil, over-run with knot-grass *(polegonium)*, sorrel *(acetosa)*, yellow gollan, wild marigold *(chrysanthemum legetum)*, after being kept in pasture for four or five years, is sown with black or grey oats; which crop is repeated for two, three, or even four years, without any manure, until it becomes quite sterile, and will produce no more corn: it is then allowed to lie ley, until it acquires a sward of its native grasses, which are pastured, until it gathers moss again, when the same miserable mode of cropping is repeated. The returns, it may easily be supposed, are very scanty. Two bolls of grey oats are sown per Scotch acre, and the return is only about five bolls. The straw, however, is valuable for cattle. This kind of soil is commonly dry,

 and

and capable of improvement by means of lime or marl. If 90 cubic yards of marl were spread per acre, in autumn, and if next autumn it were ploughed in, and sown with oats next spring, the second year the land might be dressed, manured, and sown with bear, or oats; the next season, the soil would probably work fine enough for a turnip crop, to be fallowed with bear and grass-seeds. In the course of these operations, the calcareous matter will have so acted on the soil, that its native acidity will be overcome, and the mould will have a dark fertile hue, which may still be improved by a proper rotation of crops, and an adequate quantity of manure.

On the subject of rotations of crops, a number of observations have been communicated from various intelligent quarters, which will be found in Appendix, B.

SECT. IV.—WHEAT.

A GREAT diversity of opinion is entertained regarding the practicability of cultivating wheat, in Caithness, with advantage. As that is a point of great importance to the agriculture of that district, it may be proper to state, 1. The instances where trials of winter-sown wheat have failed; 2. Where they have succeeded; and 3. Any trials that have been made with the bearded or spring wheat.

1. Sir Robert Anstruther, on his farm of Wattin, situated in the interior of the county, sowed 18¼ acres of fallow with wheat, early in October; and it had at first a most promising appearance; but whether from over anxiety, he had pulverised the ground too

too much, though sown under fur, the alternate frosts and thaws spewed it so entirely out, that, after waiting till May, it was obliged to be sown with bear and grass-seeds, of which there was a most luxuriant crop. This failure made Sir Robert conclude, that it was not a grain suitable to Caithness. This trial, however, was made in the interior, and does not prove the impracticability of raising winter wheat on the coast side.

General Sinclair, of Lybster, tried winter wheat for two seasons. It was sown in September, and in November, but its success has not encouraged a third trial.

Major Innes of Sandside, states, that for 12 or 14 years past, winter wheat has been grown for family use at Sandside, which is on the coast side, with a good and early soil; but though it answers well to appearance, it never fully ripens, and does not make good bread alone. It is sown the first week in September; he thinks the red wheat answers better than white wheat.

Major Williamson has sown winter wheat in October: it started well, and stood the winter and spring, but was unfortunately destroyed by a north-west storm on the third of May. Excepting in very sheltered situations, the spring storms will have the same effect six years in seven.

It is contended by others, that winter wheat is not likely to prove an advantageous concern, the winters in Caithness being too long, and the climate too uncertain and variable, and the springs too severe; and, that in order to give it any chance of success, it ought to be sown much earlier than is practised in the southern parts of the island; perhaps not later than August, or the

the beginning of September. This opinion is sanctioned by an experiment made by Captain Henderson, of Stempster, in the interior of the county, who, about the 12th of August, sowed half a boll after fallow well dunged; and on the 1st September, half a boll more was sowed in like manner, and contiguous to the former; about the 12th September, two bolls more were sowed in the same ground. The two former were, on the 12th August following, quite full. The last, being sowed immediately before heavy rains, perished almost entirely in the ground.

2. On the other hand, it is the opinion of some intelligent farmers in Caithness, that winter wheat would answer very well, in many places in the county, especially where the soil is strong, and inclining to clay or deep loam, provided the land is well manured, had been well fallowed the preceding summer, and is sown in August, or early in September. On the coast side at Clyth, Dr. Henderson sowed some winter wheat about the 18th September, and had from eight to nine bolls per acre; and Mr. Sinclair of Barrack, has sown winter wheat in October, and as late as the 24th January, and has had ten returns. It succeeds best after potatoes and fallow.

Mr. Traill, the Sheriff of the County, had some winter wheat sown at Castlehill, in September 1809, the land being well prepared and manured; the one-half of it was drilled, as if for turnip, and the wheat sown broad-cast on it; (as is done in the King's County in Ireland, upon wet land near the Bog of Allen;) the other part was prepared in ridges of 15 feet, in the common manner, both being well harrowed. The appearance of the young wheat was nearly equal, on the drilled and undrilled land, in November;

but

but in April 1810, the crop on the drilled land looked well, and that on the other part, on the broad ridges, had almost all disappeared and perished. The seed sown was steeped in pickle, and dried with quick-lime. The crop of the drilled land was about 10 bolls per acre, and the crop of the plain land very scanty.

On the whole, there are certainly difficulties in the way of cultivating winter wheat in Caithness; at the same time it is too important an object to be relinquished, without farther experiments. The land should be of a strong quality, in good heart, manured with lime as well as dung, properly drained, and perhaps ridged in the manner above described, and if sown in August, an adequate return may be expected. There is, at present, no flour-mill in the county; but some of the wheat produced, has been ground on grist mills, as fine as possible, and the meal or flour produced, made good bread, and as palatable, as if done of the flour of the southern markets.

3. Some of the bearded, or spring wheat, sent to the county by the President of the Board of Agriculture, in spring 1809, was sown at Thurso East, and on some other farms in that vicinity, about the 7th of May, 1809, without being pickled; and the crop, a thin one, was hardly ripe, when cut down, about the 21st October, 1809.

About the 17th April, 1810, some small quantities of this grain were sown on several farms in this county; and it was ready to cut down about the 17th October, 1810, which shews that it takes six months, in this climate, to bring it to maturity; perhaps, if it were pickled, and sown in March, in land well manured, it might become a general crop in all the lower part of the county, and tolerably productive.

SECT.

SECT. V.—RYE.

Some partial experiments have been made with rye, sown in spring, in this county; one in particular, on the farm of Thurso East. The crop was very close, and the straw luxuriant, but from the difficulty in procuring proper seed in so remote a part of the kingdom, and the want of a market for the grain, when produced, the trial has not been repeated.

SECT. VI.—BARLEY, AND BEAR OR BIGG.

1. *Tillage.*—The land intended for barley, or rather bear, is ploughed through the winter, or at least before the 15th of March, and in that state it remains till the beginning of May, when it is harrowed smooth, and about 25 to 30 cart-loads of manure spread per acre, which is immediately ploughed in, and sown broad-cast, with from five to six bushels of bear per acre. If the land is intended for grass, the rye-grass and clover is sown after the first tine of harrowing is given it, after sowing the bear. In some cases, the land intended for bear is manured before the first ploughing is given, and the second ploughing brings the manure to the surface, to mix with the seed; this, on dry land, does well enough for the bear crop, but not so well for the succeeding oat crop, where these crops are alternate. The principal benefit of this mode of manuring is, that it gains time, because much time is lost in manuring the land in the bear seed-time. Norfolk barley has been sown in various parts of the county; and on good land, a heavy

crop

crop has been produced, but too late, owing to the backwardness of the climate, to answer well; of course, bear or bigg is the general crop: it has four rows of grain on the ear, and not two rows, as barley.

There is no barley or bear put in the ground without ploughing, in this county. The only instance of drilling in, bear or barley, was at Thurso East, in 1804, by Cooke's sowing machine, as stated in Chap. V. Owing to the quantity of weeds that got up, the crop was very poor, and the experiment was not repeated.

The proper time for sowing bear, is from the 1st of May, to the 20th of June, as the land can be prepared and manured. Where green crops are practised, bear should be sown the first week in May, after turnips, and if the land is previously twice ploughed, so much the better; but where bear and oats are alternately sown from time immemorial, the tenants do not wish to sow bear until the 15th of May, because, say they, if we sow it earlier, the crop is choaked with *shiolag* (wild mustard), and other weeds. In a dry season, if any bear is not sown against the end of May, the seed is steeped in cold water for a night, before sowing it, and if they can collect soot enough to sprinkle on the wet grain, previous to sowing it, the produce is the more early and abundant, and the grain of superior quality: this points out in the clearest light, the benefit which might be derived from pickling bear, and even oats; and the advantages that might be derived by making salt, used for agricultural purposes, *duty-free*, as is the case in regard to the fisheries, are too evident to require being dwelt upon.

2. *Harvesting.*—The commencement of the bear harvest, in this county, depends much upon the season.

son. Some years it is as early as the 12th of August, and in other seasons as late as the end of September; but it generally takes place about the first week in September.

3. *Produce.*—The produce, upon land not under a rotation of green crops, may be averaged at about four bolls per Scotch acre; and on land cleared from weeds, and after a green crop, from six to 10 bolls per acre, according to the quality of the soil.

4. *Straw.*—The bear crop is commonly thrashed in spring, and the straw used for food to black cattle. When fodder is abundant, horse-litter is made of the bear straw; but this is seldom the case. I have not found, that any experiments have been made, to ascertain the weight of straw produced per acre, there being no market for straw in the county.

5. *Awns.*—The awns of bear are usually given dry to black cattle, but when scalded, or boiled with turnips, horses and cattle are fond of them. The awns of bear, sown on the surface of land after the seed is harrowed in, checks the progress of the grub, slug, or caterpillar, because it annoys these insects, during their nocturnal depredation, insomuch that they cannot move over them. Several experiments have been made, by sowing awns in this manner, and uniformly attended with success.

6. *Mode of Consumption.*—Malt is made of bear for the distilleries and the breweries. When the distillers were permitted to use grain, a great proportion of the bear crop was consumed by them in the north, or cargoes of it sent to the southern markets for the

the same purpose. Some bear is manufactured into meal for family use, and the farm-servants receiving *cost*, or wages in kind, are bound to take it, one-half bear-meal, and one-half oat-meal: a boll of bear weighing 16 to 17 stone Dutch, will yield 12 from to 14 stone of meal.

7. *Price.*—The price of bear, like that of all other grain, is very fluctuating, according to the demand. Previous to the year 1800, it seldom exceeded 13*s*. 4*d*. per boll, of six bushels and twelve quarts Winchester, but since then it has varied from 16*s*. to 30*s*. per boll, and in the summer 1808, it sold so high as 40*s*. owing to the deficiency of crop 1807. At this time, (April 1810), there is no demand for it at any price, owing to the distillers being prohibited from using grain; this measure is severely felt by the farmer, in districts where wheat cannot be produced, and where bear must be raised, in order to keep the soil under a proper rotation of crops.

8. *Bread, and mode of making it.*—Bear is kiln-dried, twice shilled, or hulled, dressed, and ground as fine as possible, on a grist-mill, into what is termed fine bear-meal, for family use: it is then baked into thin cakes, or *scones*, with cold water, and fired on a gridiron, and in this state it eats as palatable as flour *scones*, and has much of that appearance, only a little darker: 1 lb. of such meal yields just 1 lb. of cakes or *scones*, of about 1 oz. each. When bear-meal is prepared for farm-servants, it is sometimes, but not always, once shilled and dressed, before grinding into coarse meal, and they bake it into flexible cakes, as above described, but of a coarser appearance.

It is admitted, that cakes of bear-meal are not such substan-

substantial food as oat-meal cakes, for work-people, but equally wholesome.

On the general subject of cultivating barley or bear, it may not be improper to state the sentiments of some intelligent Proprietors and Farmers in the county.

Sir Robert Anstruther is of opinion, with the exception of the Carses, and a very few spots of the Lothians, and southern shires, that the soil of Scotland, and also the high grounds of Yorkshire, and other northern parts of England, are much better adapted for bear or bigg, than for barley; and Mr. Mackid, who rents a valuable farm from Sir Robert, is convinced, that bear is much better adapted for the soil and climate of Caithness, though he has found that Lincolnshire barley, sown on his best lands, sometimes answers well, producing from eight to ten bolls per acre.

It is a great advantage in favour of bear, that it ripens from two to three weeks earlier than the two rowed barley. It also yields on the whole a weightier crop, though it is not so saleable an article. It is remarked, that a change of seed is desirable, and that bear taken from the shore side answers particularly well in the interior of the country.

Mr. Leith is of opinion, that what is called in some parts of Scotland, *rammel barley*, that is, one third barley, and two thirds rough bear, might answer in Caithness, when the land is in good order, and the season favourable. It may be had from the Carse of Falkirk, and produces plentiful crops.

It may be proper to add, that the old mode of preserving bear, in what were called *bykes*, is now almost totally, if not altogether, in disuse.*

* *Bykes* are mentioned by Pennant, vol. i. p. 202. They were stacks in the shape of bee-hives, thatched quite round.

SECT.

SECT. VIII.—OATS.

1.—*Tillage.* Either infield or outfield land is only once ploughed for any species of oats, except in the case where oats is sown on land previously fallowed, to clear it from weeds. When clover ley is ploughed for oats, it is generally done in winter, and the land thus ploughed, gets one tine of harrowing before it is sown. The grain is sown broad-cast, and the land afterwards gets two or three tine of harrowing, as the soil is strong or weak, until the seed is well covered. The land is not rolled for the oat crop, unless grass-seeds are sown with it, when oats are sown, instead of bear, after turnips or potatoes.

No oats are sown on unploughed land, nor is scarifying practised for an oat crop in this county.

2. *Manuring.*—In some cases, where the outfield land, abounding with knot-grass, sorrel, or wild marigold, and with too much acid in it to produce bear or bigg, unless calcareous matter is previously applied, is intended to be continued for some years under repeated crops of grey oats, some compost of earth or dung is spread on it, every second spring, previous to ploughing it, to make it yield a scanty crop of grain and straw. But infield land, which is always manured for the previous bear crop, is never manured for the succeeding oat crop, where bear and oats are alternate crops, (which has been the practice in regard to the good land in this county, from time immemorial), and even in many cases, two oat crops are taken between every bear crop.

3, 4. *Drilling—Dibbling*—Not practised in this county.

5. *Time.*—The time of sowing oats is from the middle of March to the middle or end of April, according to the season.

6. *Sort.*—There are various sorts of oats cultivated in this county. As 1. the grey, 2. the black, 3. the red, 4. the dun, 5. the potatoe, and 6. the Polish. Partial experiments have been made with the Blainsley, and the white Burley oat. But the former was found to be too late a grain for this climate, and the latter so ready to shake, that half the crop could not be saved; so that the cultivation of both has been almost entirely given up.

1. The grey oat is generally sown in the outfield land, (afterwald), where only occasional crops are taken after natural grass; and though very unproductive, particularly in regard to meal, yet that sort is frequently sown by small farmers, as it will grow almost in any land, though much run out. Mr. Trotter of Duncansbay, states, that he has sown oats of this kind, the produce of which was only at the rate of five bolls per acre, and it required three bolls of these oats to make one boll of meal. This did not pay the expense of labour. This kind of oat, however, must be frequently sown, wherever the wretched system of bear and oats alternately, is persevered in.

2. The black oat was formerly much cultivated, and is still strongly recommended as a useful grain, where the finer sorts cannot well be cultivated. It has less awn than the grey one, and is more productive in meal; but requires better soil. Black oats were formerly

merly sown in the best land after bear, as grey oats were on inferior soils. The black oat is the hardiest of any of the species, which *tells* in bad seasons, and it is said that it will produce more meal per acre, but it will not sell so readily in the state of oats.

3. About the year 1791, red oats were introduced into this county by Sir John Sinclair, and they still continue to be of much benefit to the farmer; they are about three weeks earlier in harvest than the black, and are sooner ripe than any other sort of oat. Many farmers, however, now complain, that red oats are not so productive as when they were first introduced, and that their crops have been very thin for the last few years. This is probably owing to their not changing the seed once every three years, or sowing that species of grain in light dry land, whereas it answers best in a deep damp soil, either clay or dark loam, and then even without a change of seed. One instance of this can be stated on the farm of Nottingham, in Latheron parish, the property of Major Sutherland of Forse, where the soil is a deep dark mould, and rather damp: *red* oats have been sown there, for the last seven years, without changing the seed, and this season (1810) these oats produced 14¾ bolls of meal, at 8½ stone, from 16 bolls of oats. In every case where red oats is imported from the port of Leith for seed, it is productive for the first two or three years. The red oat is not only peculiarly well calculated for damp soils, but for every place where the crop is late in ripening, which is much in their favour in so northern a climate. They are also not apt to shake. Some contend that the straw is sapless, but that can only be owing to a defect in the soil. Red oats, when well dressed, have been known to give meal for oats, a sure sign of their good quality. From its

 ripening

ripening so fast, the red oat has been sown so late as the beginning of May, and it has been harvested about the end of October.

4. The dun oat was also first introduced by Sir John Sinclair. The vessel in which this sort of oat was sent, was unfortunately wrecked on the Wick coast, but the grain, though damaged, vegetated. This oat should be sown in a good soil, and in the course of a proper rotation of crops, otherwise it does not answer. Major Williamson considers the advantages of dun oats to be, that they give abundance of straw and corn, and it is admitted by the farm servants, who are very competent judges, that the meal is of a superior quality. They are certainly an excellent substitute for the grey and even the black oat. The dun oat produces from seven to eight bolls per acre, and has sometimes yielded eighteen bolls of meal, from twenty bolls of oats. It is ten days later in ripening than the red.

5. Within these last ten or twelve years, the cultivation of the potatoe oat has become general in the lower part of the county. It is a short white oat, and stout bodied. It thrives well in a clover ley, or on strong soils, in good heart, but is very subject to the depredations of the grub and slugs in spring, and to be shaken by the equinoxial gales in harvest. It is about three weeks later in ripening than the red oat; and is seldom ready for the sickle before the beginning of October. It produces from eight to ten bolls per Scotch acre, and generally yields nearly a boll of meal from a boll of oats, (six bushels and twelve quarts Winchester); it weighs from 14½ to 15 stone Dutch. It produces strong bulky straw, and is always saleable either in grain or meal.

6. Mr. Donald Miller of Noss, considers the Polish

oat

oat to be the best adapted for Caithness. It is from twelve to sixteen days earlier than potatoe, and but little inferior in quality, the difference being only from 1*s.* to 1*s.* 6*d.* per quarter, in the London market. However, though cheaper, yet as it produces more per acre, it is contended that on the whole it should be preferred.

On the subject of oats in general, Captain Sutherland of Brabster very justly observes, that, although the black Murkle oat, which is indigenous to the county, will in the average of years, produce the greatest quantity of meal, yet that it is attended with this disadvantage, that it must be mealed before finding a market, which occasions considerable labour and expense. The red and potatoe oats have, for some years past, met with a surer sale than meal, and consequently have been much cultivated. In bad seasons, their produce is far below that of our indigenous oat, and for raising them the land must be in a high state of cultivation. In an unfavourable autumn, both red and potatoe oats are apt to vegetate in the stook, as was experienced, greatly to the loss of the farmer, in the harvest of 1807. The damage sustained, by the common oat, at the same period, was comparatively small.

It may not be improper here to state, the result of an experiment made by Mr. Traill, the Sheriff of the county, with several kinds of oats. In summer 1792, that respectable agriculturist, caused fallow a field of good arable land, on a farm in his own possession, and in the month of October following, he limed it at the rate of 80 bolls (barrels of 32 gallons) per Scotch acre; the lime was left upon the surface, and the land water-furrowed through the winter. It was ploughed down in spring 1793, and sown with oats, *i. e.* six ridges of the field, each being a quarter of an acre, were sown with six different kinds of oats, and the produce was as follows:

Acres.	Quantity of Oats sown in each Lot.				Name of each Kind of Oats sown.	Quantity of Oats produced by each Lot.				Weight of each per Boll.	Quantity of Meal produced by each Lot, at $8\frac{1}{2}$ Stone per Boll.			
	B.	F.	P.	L.		B.	F.	P.	L.	Stone.	B.	F.	P.	lb.
$\frac{1}{4}$	—	1	2	—	Black Murkle oats	4	2	2	—	$11\frac{1}{2}$	2	1	3	6
$\frac{1}{4}$	—	1	1	2	Blainsley oats	2	2	2	$2\frac{1}{2}$	$10\frac{1}{4}$	1	3	—	—
$\frac{1}{4}$	—	1	1	$3\frac{1}{4}$	Red oats	2	2	2	—	$12\frac{7}{8}$	2	—	—	2
$\frac{1}{4}$	—	2	—	—	Common grey oats	4	1	2	—	$9\frac{3}{4}$	2	1	—	—
$\frac{1}{4}$	—	1	2	—	Black Burley oats	3	2	1	—	$11\frac{1}{8}$	2	1	1	5
$\frac{1}{4}$	—	1	2	—	Tartarian oats	3	1	1	—	$9\frac{1}{4}$	1	1	1	—
$1\frac{1}{2}$	2	1	1	$1\frac{1}{4}$	Total produce	21	—	2	$2\frac{1}{2}$	—	12	—	2	$4\frac{1}{2}$

The

The red oats being ready for the hook three weeks before the other kinds, it suffered much by the depredation of sparrows, &c., otherwise its produce would have been more considerable, and as all the small corn was included, the weight of course appears less, than had the oats been dressed for market.

The several kinds of oats before described, in general weigh, and produce in meal, when cultivated in good soils, and more especially after artificial grasses, nearly as follows:

		Weight.	*Produce in Meal.*	
1. One boll	of grey oats, about	10 stone,	½ boll, at 8½ st. per boll.	
2. Ditto	black do. about	12 do.	¾ ditto,	ditto.
3. Ditto	red do.	13 to 14 do.	¾ ditto,	ditto.
4. Ditto	potatoe do.	14 to 15 do.	⅞ to $\frac{8}{8}$ ditto,	ditto.
5. Ditto	dun do.	14 to 14½ do.	⅞ to $\frac{8}{8}$ ditto,	ditto.
6. Ditto	Polish do.	14 to 15 do.	⅞ to $\frac{8}{8}$ ditto,	ditto.

On poorer soils, under a bad state of cultivation, the returns are necessarily inferior.

One remark is uniformly made,—that wherever oats are not of the sort that may be called indigenous, a frequent change of seed is essential; and that the returns, after such a change, are uniformly very great.

As the oat, after all, is the species of grain, the most likely to be generally productive, and to be the most profitable to the Caithness farmers, since the sale and culture of bear is so much discouraged, by the disproportioned duty of malt to which it is now subjected, it was thought necessary, to enter into a full detail of the various sorts that might be cultivated in the county, and to explain their several advantages and defects.

7. *Seed.*—The quantity of seed sown in a Scotch acre is as follows:

Of grey oats, about two bolls.
Black oats, about $1\frac{1}{2}$ to $1\frac{3}{4}$ ditto.
Potatoe oats, about one ditto.
Dun oats, about $1\frac{1}{8}$ ditto.
Red oats, about $1\frac{1}{2}$ ditto.

Thus it appears, that the sorts which are the least productive, require the greatest quantity of seed; an additional material objection to their cultivation.

8. *Depth.*—When sown broad-cast, the depth depends on the length of the harrow teeth.

9. *Rolling*—Is only practised when grass-seeds are sown.

10. *Weeding.*—Formerly the farmer's sheep and cows followed the plough in the spring time, feeding on the roots of mugwort, (the most abundant weed in the Caithness soil); and in the month of July, after the farmer had taken home his feal and fuel, he, with his domestics, traversed the oat land, after the corn was about two feet long, pulling out mugworts and thistles by the root. But notwithstanding these practices, mugwort continued to increase in the best land, until fallow or green crops destroyed them. During the fallow, or in preparing the soil for a green crop, much labour is required, to hand-weed, and to gather these roots, more especially for the two first rotations, it being extremely difficult to clear land from weeds, that has been for centuries under crops of bear and oats alternately.

11. *Harvesting.*—The oat crop ripens at different periods, according as the season is dry or wet, warm or cold: much also depends on the kind of oats, red oats being

being generally ripe three weeks before the other sorts. The harvest usually is from the beginning of September to the end of October. When cut down, the crop is bound in sheaves, and stooked; in a dry season, in whole stooks; consisting of 12 sheaves each, but in wet seasons in half stooks, or rather eight sheaves each, in which state it remains until it is *win*, *i. e.* dry enough to be carried off stacked, and in the corn yard. During a wet late season, when corn must be cut down wet, the bands are tied near the head of the sheaves, and then the straw so spread, that each sheaf will stand by itself. This is called gating, or goating it, so that a few hours of dry windy weather has a great effect upon it; and as soon as it is dry, the sheaves are tied in the usual manner, and secured from rain in small ricks. This gating has another advantage, that corn so set up, can be preserved during rain, for a long time, without vegetating, whereas in stooks it would spoil in the course of a week of rainy warm weather. Those who occupy land in a good climate, and of course enjoy the advantages of an early harvest, may ridicule this plan; but in a cold and wet climate, the farmer cannot, in some seasons, preserve his crop, without such troublesome, but essential practices.

12. *Produce.*—The produce, as has already been observed, is very variable, as much must depend upon the soil, and the mode of cultivating it. Under the old plan of bear and oats alternately, the produce can only be stated at the rate of from three to six bolls per acre: under the modern system of green crops, the produce on an average is as follows:

Black oats, from four to seven bolls per acre.

Red ditto, four to six ditto, and even eight bolls.

Potatoe

Potatoe oats, from five to eight bolls per acre.
Dun ditto, five to seven ditto.

On the best soils, when well cultivated, the produce of potatoe oats, on clover ley, (if they have escaped the grub in spring, and gales of wind in harvest), may amount to from eight to ten bolls; and even nine bolls of red oats have been produced from an acre, but this is by no means general.

13. *Straw*.—The oat straw in this county, is consumed by the horses and black cattle on the farm, it being their food, from the month of October, till March, and even April. There is no market for straw in this remote corner, whereas the farmers near great towns, will make more of the straw of an acre, than a Caithness farmer will make both of his straw and corn. The average weight of oat straw produced on a Scotch acre in this county, may be stated at about 60 stone, of 24lb. Amsterdam each. Besides feeding his cattle, the farmer employs his oat straw for various other purposes. He makes *cassies* with it, to hold his corn; ropes to secure his corn-ricks in the yard, and with it he dries his corn on the kiln. The plan may be thus described: About six feet above the bottom of the kiln, there are four or five beams set across, parallel to each other, and upon these there are small sticks or laths laid one or two inches asunder; upon these there is a quantity of oat-straw spread, about one inch thick; and lastly, oats or bear is spread upon the straw, a few inches thick; then the *ingle* (fire) is kindled, and the fire is kept up, and the corn frequently turned on the straw, until it is thoroughly kiln-dried, say about 12 hours for each quantity the kiln can dry. This is the most general mode of kiln-drying corn in this county, but

is

is a very bad one, and many accidents happen, owing to the straw taking fire, and burning the whole building to the ground. Some tile-kilns are now erected, which is a much safer, and more expeditious mode of kiln-drying corn.

14. *Application.*—Black, grey, and dun oats, are commonly kiln-dried, and made into oat-meal, except what is used for seed and horse corn; red and potatoe oats are exported to the Leith and London markets, except in cases when, owing to a rainy harvest, it is too soft to bear sea-carriage. Both the red and the potatoe oats are then mealed, and it is admitted that they produce meal of better quality than either the grey or the black.

15. *Modes of consuming Oat-meal.*—The mode of making oat cakes, as practised in Caithness, is as follows: a quantity of meal is put into one end of a wooden trough, and the house-maid or cook, mixes a part of the meal with cold water, so as to make it a thick paste or *leaven*, and meal is added, until the leaven is so dry and firm as just to adhere together; then she takes about a handful of this leaven, and kneads it out with her knuckles, on a board, into a round cake of about nine inches diameter, and from one-eighth to one-fourth of an inch thick. The cake thus formed, is gently laid on a gridiron over live coals of peat, where it is occasionally turned, until firm enough to stand on edge to the face of a flat stone or plate of cast metal, close to the fire, till completely hard and firm, when it is laid by for use; this operation goes on until her quantity of meal is made up in cakes, *i. e.* till there is a suf-

a sufficient quantity to serve the family for 24 hours, or perhaps two days.

Pottage, (hasty-pudding), is made of oat-meal, for the breakfasts of servants and children which they eat with milk, small beer, or butter. *Brochan*, (water-gruel), is made of oat-meal, mixed with a little milk or butter, and is given to servants for supper, with bear or oaten bread or cakes.

Lastly, the seeds (bran) of oat-meal are steeped in warm water; and after laying for some days to sour, the liquor is strained off, and kept for use. Farm-servants drink it raw, or it is made into boiled sowans, (flummery). It is also boiled, or rather par-boiled, pretty thick, for work people, and is reckoned a substantial meal. Some housewives also, add a little oat-meal, milk, and eggs, to a quantity of this liquor or sowans, and of the mixture they make scones (pancakes), upon a hot gridiron, which is a palatable light food.

16. *Price.*—About 60 years ago, the boll of Caithness oat-meal; (136 lb.), was sold as low as 5*s.*; the price increased gradually to from 10*s.* to 13*s.* 4*d.* per boll, and was even higher in bad seasons. Crop 1781 having failed, owing to frost, mildews, and a rainy harvest, in 1782 the boll of oat-meal rose to 21*s.* and thence to 25*s.* Such was the general scarcity throughout Scotland, that several poor people died from want. From that period, till the year 1806, the price of oat-meal varied from 13*s.* 4*d.* to 20*s.*

Crop 1807 in a great degree failed, so that the price of oat-meal, in summer 1808, was at from 30*s.* to 40*s.* per boll: yet such was the abundance of circulating medium among every class of society, that none suffered

fered from want that season. Crops 1808 and 1809 sold at from 26*s.* to 30*s.* per boll, but the price of labour and other commodities, having increased in a similar proportion, no inconvenience was felt by the labouring classes in consequence of these prices.

From the augmented land rent, the high price of labour, and of farming utensils, if the price of Caithness victual, (bear and oatmeal), fall below 20*s.* per boll, the farmer will not be able to carry on his business, if he has nothing to depend upon but the profits of his farm, and failures and bankruptcy will be the natural result; an event not very distant, should the distilleries continue to use sugar in place of grain.

SECT. IX.—PEASE.

The climate of Caithness is too wet for the production and bringing to maturity a good crop of pease, and of course that species of grain is seldom sown: a few farmers near the coast, however, occasionally sow an acre or two, and, when the land is free from weeds, there is generally an abundant crop of straw; but frequently the rains in harvest prevent the pods filling, and even when cut down, the crop, owing to the wetness of the season, is sometimes spoilt on the field. The pea usually sown, is the common grey pea, brought from the Leith market. It is sown broad-cast, on land once ploughed, after an oat crop, and then harrowed in. Upon light dry land, pease are sown on the stubble land, and afterwards ploughed in with a shallow furrow. The time of sowing is from the middle of March to the middle of April, as the seasons will admit.

admit. The quantity sown on an acre, is about four bushels; and the returns, when the crop is saved, may be from 16 to 20 bushels Winchester; the pease-straw is given to the plough-horses in spring. The early white pea of Norfolk, if it did not produce ripened grain, would at least furnish straw in abundance.

SECT. X.—BEANS.

Few beans are sown in this county. Several experiments have been made with drilled beans, on a good loam, well manured, but they generally turned out a late crop. I have not found any account of the quantity sown, or the returns per acre.

SECT. XI.—TARES.

A few farmers in this county, sow spring tares for food to their work horses, in July and August, until the clover foggage is ready, but it is by no means so general a crop as it might be, partly owing to the high price of seed, and the uncertainty of a supply from the Leith market; and partly because, when the land is not well manured, and cleared from weeds, the crop becomes stinted, and the produce trifling. The few experiments which have been made upon clean land, well manured, shew, that an abundant crop of tares may be raised annually by the Caithness farmers, which might prove of much benefit in soiling their horses

horses and cattle, in July and August, in place of feeding the former with the dry hay of the preceding year's crop. At the same time, the farmer naturally considers, that he must pay 15*s*. per bushel for seed; that three bushels are required per acre, and that a good deal of manure must be laid on the land for that crop; he then calculates, that he can feed his horses cheaper on old hay, for this reason, that there is seldom any market for hay in the county, and of course that he must use it on the farm.

No attempt has been made to raise a crop of tares for seed, nor has the quantity of food per acre for soiling, been ascertained.

SECT. XII.—LENTILS.

None.

SECT. XIII.—BUCK WHEAT.

It is not understood that any fair trial has been made with this grain in Caithness. I saw one or two instances where about half an acre was sown with this article, but the crop was so choaked with weeds, that the produce was very trifling.

SECT. XIV.—TURNIPS.

About 20 years ago very few turnips were raised in this county, except in gardens for kitchen use. Now that useful root has become almost a general crop; even small

small tenants and cottagers raise field turnip for their cattle; and among farmers who have adopted a regular rotation of crops, turnips is almost the only green crop used in the course of the rotation.

1. *Soil.*—The Caithness soil in general produces good crops of turnips. The best soil for this crop is a light dry loam; even a loam with a mixture of clay, will produce turnips, if made dry; but a light soil is the best.

2. *Tillage.*—Land intended for turnips is commonly ploughed in November, and again cross-ploughed in March or April, when it is harrowed, the weeds collected, and carried off. About the latter end of May, or beginning of June, the land is again twice ploughed, with a deep furrow each time, harrowing and collecting all the weeds that may appear on the surface; and about the 10th of June, the season for sowing turnip commences, which is executed in this manner. A plough with a pair of horses is set to work, to open drills for the manure, and carts are run down the centre one, of each three drills; the manure is then deposited in small heaps, at regular intervals, and as soon as a few rows are thus manured, women or boys are employed to spread the dung in the drills, either with forks, or spades, as it is long or short manure. That operation being done to as many drills as can be manured at one yoking, the same plough is employed to close *in* the drills, and as soon afterwards as possible, after the turnip seed is sown, either by a hand-barrow, (the drills having been first flattened with a light roller); or what is more expeditious, and effectual, the seed is sown by a machine, drawn by one horse, which sows and

and rolls two drills at a time, having a roller before, and behind the sowing coulters. This machine is managed by one man, and will sow more ground, than four men with hand-barrows can do in the same period of time. The price is about seven guineas, and it will last 20 years. At all events, it is of the greatest consequence to close in the drills, &c. and sow the seed, immediately after spreading the manure, *i. e.* the forenoon and the afternoon yokings, should be completed in all their operations before quitting it at each time. Experience has often shewn, that where drills have been manured and closed in, and the sowing of these drills neglected or delayed for even one day, that the crop of such drills was always thin and stunted.

6. *Sort.*—The sort most generally sown in this county is the red topped Norfolk turnip, because it stands the winter better than the green topped, or the white globe kinds. Yellow turnip is now become a more general crop than formerly, and farmers, who pay proper attention to this valuable crop, sow one third of the turnip field with white globe, one third with red topped, and the remaining third with yellow turnip. The white turnip grows to a considerable size, and should be consumed by the middle of January; next the red topped, which will be in good condition until the middle or even end of March; the yellow turnip will keep, in a dry soil, until early in May. Should the season be so mild, that they are likely to spring to seed, if they are pulled about the end of March or first of April, and the tops and tails cut off, they will preserve in heaps for a month or six weeks.

7. *Seed.*—About two pounds of turnip seed, with a

proper sowing machine, will saw an acre. More is generally used, because people think that thick sowing gives the best chance for a regular crop.

8. *Rolling.*—The drills, as before stated, are rolled before and after sowing the seed, so as to press the soil, that the first shoots of the plant may speedily reach the manure, and of course promote and expedite its growth in a dry season. Mr. James Anderson strongly recommends passing a heavy roller over the drills, as soon as they are formed by the plough, as an excellent practice for retaining moisture in the soil.

9. *Weeding.*—Various kinds of harrows are used to destroy the weeds between the drills, but the most effectual kind is that with three beams or bars, the two outer beams moving on a swivel which passes through the front end of the middle beam, and close to it, with two stilts on the rear end of the middle beam, &c. as already explained in the Section, on *Horse-hoes.* By running this harrow or triangle twice between the drills, in the course of the season, the weeds are completely checked. The tops of the drills are hand-weeded, and hoed, in due time; the turnip thinned to regular distances; and lastly, when at a proper size, the drills are earthed up with a double mould-board plough, drawn by one horse, which finishes the weeding operation, commonly about the end of August, when the turnip tops nearly cover the ground.

10. *Fly Preventatives.*—Some farmers of my acquaintance, have, for several years past, sprinkled water on the seed, and then mixed it with flour of sulphur previous to sowing it. Some sulphur is also put in

in the drill boxes of the sowing machine, that each grain of the seed may have a coat of sulphur, as it falls into the earth. The sulphur has not injured the plant, and they believe that it defends it from the depredation of vermin, (as the fly, the grub, and slug), for their turnip crops have suffered no injury from these insects, since they have been in the habit of using sulphur. Some experiments have been tried, by strewing bear chaff, (the rough awns of bear), on the top of the drills, after sowing the turnip seed, and that practice tends to prevent the progress of the grub, and grey slug, in preying on the young plants in the night time. These are the only artificial means of prevention practised in this county. Warm weather, with frequent, but moderate showers, soon after the turnip is sown, promotes a rapid vegetation, and soon puts the young plant beyond the power of the destructive fly.

11. *Hoeing.*—Already mentioned.

12. *Consumption.*—Almost the only mode used in this county is pulling, and carrying them home, as food to the black cattle and horses; for the latter, in some cases they are boiled with chaff or small corn; and on a few farms, turnips are consumed on the field by sheep.

13. *Value—Price.*—In a remote district like Caithness, the value of the turnip crop cannot well be ascertained, as there is no market for them, except a few acres that are annually disposed of to cow-feeders in the towns of Thurso and Wick, by farmers in the immediate vicinity of these towns, and the price given depends much upon the closeness of the crop; it is generally from 7*l.* to 10*l.* per acre.

I 2 The

The common farmers, who have for several years past cultivated turnip crops, allow, that in consequence of turnip feeding, their two years old cattle, are now as fit for the market, as similar cattle used to be at three years old; that their whole stock is kept in better condition through the winter, by means of this esculent root; and that their quantity of manure is also increased. There is no market within 100 miles of this county for the consumption of fat beef, should the farmer direct his attention to the feeding of cattle for the butcher: keeping his young stock in condition therefore, in the winter and spring, is the most profitable mode of consumption.

14. *Modes of Preservation.*—I have not found that any artificial mode, to preserve turnips, has been practised in this county. The people will sometimes tear them out of the ground with picks during frost and snow, which is certainly injurious both to the cattle, and the soil. During the first light frost, on the approach of a snow storm, I have taken as many turnips from the field, as would serve the ordinary consumption of the cattle for a fortnight, and put them into a house, where they kept well until the whole was used. A house with a thatched roof, the top of the walls and gables being of sod, large enough to hold the produce of an acre of turnip, may be erected for about 4*l.*: by that means the farmer may always have it in his power, to carry his turnip off the field, either with dry weather, or light frosts, so as not to poach his land, and may have a regular supply of turnip for his stock at all times, whatever may be the state of the weather.

15. *General Remarks.*—There is no part of the kingdom, where turnips can be raised in greater perfection, nor crops of a greater weight, than in Caithness, though

the value is not so high, owing to the want of a market. They do not succeed in new lands, from the spunginess and wetness of their nature. The mode of consumption so general in England, and the southern parts of Scotland, that of eating them on the ground by sheep, which prevents the expense of digging them up, carting them off, and carrying back the manure, has its advantages; but on the other hand, when they are consumed in a fold-yard or feeding-house, they are the means of converting a great quantity of straw into dung, and the dung is completely at the command of the farmer; whereas, when the dung is spread on the surface of the ground, the consequence of the folding system, a certain portion of it must be washed away or evaporated. Hence, on the whole, the latter system, though the most expensive, may be the most advantageous.

SECT. XV.—COLESEED, OR RAPE.

About eighty years ago, from twenty to thirty acres of a deep black mould, bordering on peat earth, on the estates of Forse, and Toftingall, were pared and burnt by the proprietors, ploughed, and sown with rape. I have been informed by old people who had seen it, that the crops produced were close and good; that they were thrashed out on the field; and that the seed sold at a guinea per barrel. That ground has ever since been used as pasture only; it was then inclosed, and subdivided with ditches, to carry off the moisture, as it lay low and wet.

Some recent experiments were made with coleseed,

in the new improvements, on Sir John Sinclair's estate, after paring and burning; but the soil being thin, shallow, and gritty, the crop proved but indifferent. There are several low-lying peat-mosses in this county, however, on which coleseed might be produced to good account, by the paring and burning system. I have inclosed about half an acre of such peat-moss, and mean to make the experiment of preparing and sowing it with coleseed in July 1811, and the result will be communicated to the Board of Agriculture. The only dread is, that the severity of our winter frosts may blow the plants out of the ground, by the expansion of the wet peat earth.

SECT XVI.—CABBAGES.

1. *Soil.*—Cabbage will thrive in any good soil, provided it is deep and well manured. A few experiments have been made in this county, of planting Dutch cabbage in the field, as a green crop for cattle; but it was found, that a greater quantity of food, could be produced on the same ground, with less manure, by sowing turnip.

2. *Cabbage Nursery.*—Previous to the introduction of potatoes into this county, which took place about 40 years ago, every farmer and cottager had a good cabbage garden, principally of the red and white Dutch species. Nurseries for raising cabbage plants were thus made, in the lower part of the county: cottagers on the border of commons, in the course of the month of June, inclosed a piece of common, about $\frac{1}{8}$ or $\frac{1}{10}$ of an acre, with a dyke or wall of sod about six feet high, to keep off

off sheep. In the month of July, they pared and burnt the surface of the inclosed spot; they then dug the soil a spade deep, and broke the earth with a rake or small harrow, and having spread the ashes made on the ground, with a compost of dung, &c. from the cottage, upon the surface of the soil so prepared, the cabbage seed was sown and raked in. There was no other trouble attending it until next spring; about the end of March commonly, every farmer had his cabbage garden manured, and prepared for the young plants, which they purchased from these cottagers at *3d.* to *8d.* per 100 plants, as they were plentiful or otherwise, and in proportion to the demand. They made these nurseries or *plant tofts* of small extent, that the dykes might shelter the young plants from the severity of the winter, and in the course of the ensuing spring and summer a new nursery was formed, so that the dyke of one side of the former plant toft, served as a side to the new, and the old toft was delved and sown with oats, as soon as the plants were sold. This mode of having nurseries for plants, served as a slow mode of improving a part of these commons.

SECT. XVII.—RUTA BAGA, OR SWEDES.

SWEDISH turnips were introduced into this county, about 20 years ago, by the President of the Board of Agriculture.

Soil.—Swedish turnips require a deep soil, in good condition, and double the quantity of manure necessary for common turnip, to produce a close good crop. Where the soil abounds with acidity, or in other words,

 requires

requires calcareous matter, the Swedish turnip are full of threads or fibres, of course of little size or value. The not attending to this circumstance, is the principal cause of the culture of this root not being more general and successful than it is, or deserves to be; but in a good rich loam, well manured, they grow to a considerable size, and stand the climate better than any other turnip, and being more solid, they are more nourishing than the common kinds.

2. *Tillage*—The same as for common turnip.

3. *Manure*—Double the quantity used for common turnip.

4. *Seed*—About two pound per acre, where the drill husbandry is practised.

5. *Sort*—The only sort of Swedish turnip sown or known in this county is the yellow.

6. *Time of Sowing*—Swedish turnip, if not transplanted, should be sown about the 20th of May.

7. *Transplanting*—About the middle of July, or when the plant is of a proper size for that operation; but, (I presume owing to bad management), the transplanted turnips seldom root so well, as those not transplanted. This may be owing to the root of the plant, when put into the ground, being doubled, as I have found those, whose fibry roots were put down straight into the soil, soon took root, and grew to a good size: but as the operation must be performed by hirelings, it is seldom done well. When they are to be transplanted, the

the seed should be sown about the 20th of April, and thence to the 10th of May, in a bed; and when they are about the same size with cabbage plants, or about eight or ten weeks old, (about the middle of July), they should be transplanted in dampish weather. They should be put into drills about a foot asunder, and each plant from eight to twelve inches apart.

8, 9, 10, 11.—The same as for common turnip.

12. *Value.*—The Swedish turnip is undoubtedly a valuable root for a cold climate; because storms of frost or snow, and alternate thaws, do not injure them in the smallest degree, and they have been known to grow, though buried under ten feet of snow. In the month of May also, though vegetating, yet they are fresh and eatable. It is said that the tops may be cut from August to April, without injury to the turnip, and they make excellent greens for the table.

13. *Comparison with the common Turnip*—It is presumed that 1 cwt. of Swedish turnip will yield more nourishment in feeding cattle or horses than 2 cwt. of either the white, green topped, or red topped turnip, but then, an acre of our soil in general will not produce half the quantity of Swedes, that it does of the common turnip. The great consideration is, that the Swedish turnip will keep in good condition for cattle even till the month of May, when the other kinds are quite useless; but as the Caithness farmer finds that he can raise double the quantity of yellow turnip, with less manure, on the same extent of land, and that the yellow turnip stands the winter and spring, much better than the red topped, he will be less anxious about the cultivation of the ruta baga, as it does not thrive on a shallow soil of inferior quality.

SECT. XVIII.—TURNIP CABBAGE.

None of these are cultivated in the county.

SECT. XIX.—KHOLL RABIE.

None.

SECT. XX.—BOORCOLE KALE, THOUSAND-HEADED ANJOU, JERUSALEM, BRUSSELS, &c.

In gardens only.

A few plants of the thousand-headed cabbage, were raised from the seed by the gardener at Thurso Castle in 1810, and some of them transplanted by a few farmers in that vicinity: they informed me in December 1810, that the plants do not appear larger or better than common greens, and are stunted in their growth.

SECT. XXI.—CARROTS.

Sown in gardens only.

SECT. XXII.—PARSNIPS.

Sown in gardens only.

SECT. XXIII.—BEET.

Red and white, sown in gardens only.

SECT. XXIV.—POTATOES.

This best of all roots, was introduced into the county of Caithness about the year 1754, and for some years after, they were only cultivated in the gardens of landed gentlemen. From 1760 to 1786, the tenantry of the county planted a few of them annually in new ground, in the lazy-bed fashion. In those days, the idea of losing the straw, prevented their planting potatoes, instead of raising grain. Since that period, the tenants by degrees began to plant them in arable land, and increased the quantity, finding that much benefit might be derived therefrom. Of late years, every farmer, both small and great, plants potatoes with the plough in their arable land, in drills, as for turnip. And even the farm servants must have a few drills of potatoes each, planted for them, for which they stipulate when they engage.

1. *Soil.*—The best soil for every species of potatoe, is a light dry loam. They do not produce well in a wet or a clay soil. If the soil is dry, though acid and deficient of calcareous earth, if well manured, potatoes will grow in it, if cultivated in the lazy-bed way: such soil would be too grassy for the drill husbandry, and in such soil, turnips would become stunted, fibrous, and forky.

2. *Manuring.*

2. *Manuring*.—People commonly prefer horse-dung litter to cattle dung, for the potatoe crop, as they contend that it makes them drier and more farinaceous than the other; and in particular, it is found, that if potatoes are planted in land recently marled or limed, the crop will be soft and of indifferent quality; marl, on the other hand, makes turnips grow very luxuriant, and to a great size. Indeed the more calcareous earth, the better for turnips.

When potatoes are planted in lazy-beds, in a strong new soil, a layer or stratum of white moss, collected in furzy peat-bogs, put under and over the slip, below the sods, will answer in place of other manure, and will produce a tolerable crop of dry mealy potatoes. It has been found that cut whins will do as manure, and perhaps cut heather might also answer.

When potatoes are planted in a good old loam, without manure, the crop, though less abundant, will be of better quality, than if the land was manured for them.

3. *Mode*.—1. Cultivating potatoes in lazy-beds was the original mode, and is still used in new ground. Indeed, were it not owing to the additional labour attending that mode, it would tend more to the improvement of the soil, and the increase of the produce, if they were planted in lazy-beds, even in the arable land; because in laying down two crops of potatoes in the same land, taking care that the bed was formed in the second rotation of the part that was the trench the first crop, thus the land would be completely trenched by the two potatoe crops. This is the custom in Ireland, where the crops are very abundant, namely, from 50 to 70 barrels per Irish acre. 2. Drills.—The most general

general mode in this county, of planting potatoes, is in drills, after the plough, the land being manured, as for turnips. 3. Dibbling.—None are dibbled. Those cottagers who have no plough, plant them with the spade, by digging a drill across the ridge, spreading manure in it, then dropping the potatoe slips on the manure, at six inches distance, and the earth taken up with the spade in opening the next parallel furrow, is thrown in the planted drill, and so on, until their lot is all planted.

4, and 5. *Preparation, Tillage.*—The land is prepared for the potatoe crop, intended to be planted in drills, in the same manner as for turnips, already described. And for those planted with the spade, there is no previous preparation of the soil; of course there is more labour in weeding and hand-hoeing.

6. *Sets.*—The potatoes intended for seed, are cut in two, three, or four slips, according to the size of the potatoe, and the number of eyes, so that each slip or cutting may have two eyes. It is beneficial to perform this operation a week or two previous to the time of planting, so that a crust will be formed on the parts cut with a knife; practical farmers likewise say, that the plant will vegetate the sooner. Several years ago, experiments had been made, by scooping out small pieces of potatoe with the eye, by means of a semicircular iron; these pieces to be planted in place of the slips; but the returns were found to be inferior to the crop produced by slips cut with the knife, and the experiment was not repeated.

7. *Sort.*—In general, it may be observed, that the best

best sort of potatoe for a cold district, is that which stands best wet and frosty weather, and has the strongest shaws, or haulm, to cover the soil. There are many sorts of potatoes in this county; viz. the long white kidney, round white, round red with white eyes, round red with black or dark eyes, and the pale red, or apple-potatoe, and frequently, from inattention, all these mixed perhaps in one drill. The most general kind is the white or pale yellow long kidney; but the driest and most farinaceous, is the round red with dark eyes, called *black potatoe*, and the apple-potatoe, or pale round red. Some prefer what in Glasgow is called the *calico* potatoe, which is hardy, prolific, and good for the table. Others recommend what are called *dons*. When any of these sorts are for several years repeated in the same soil, they degenerate in quality and quantity: it it is therefore essential to procure seed from a different soil, once in two or three years.

The yam potatoe is also cultivated for horses or cattle in spring, and should be raised for improving waste land.

8. *Planting*—Is performed between the 1st of April and the 15th of May, and even as late as the 25th of May. In planting potatoes in the drill-husbandry, by the plough, after the manure is spread in the drills, as described for turnips, the potatoe-slips are dropped on the manure in the drill, at about six inches distance, so that a drill of ten chains long, will take about 1½ peck of these slips, or about 36lb. weight of potatoes previous to cutting them; and by calculating 25 such drills to an acre, it will take 37½ pecks to plant an acre. As soon as a few drills are thus planted, the drills are again closed in with the plough.

9. *Horse*

9. *Horse and Hand-hoeing.*—As soon as a coat of weeds appear on the drills, a double tine of harrowing is given to them lengthways, which checks the growth of the weeds, and flattens the drills, so that the haulm of the potatoe gets the sooner to the surface, and whenever the weeds make fresh progress, the horse-hoe, or harrow, is run between the drills, and the top of the drills hand-hoed, and weeded between the plants. When the haulm is about a foot high, and the weeds destroyed, the drills are afterwards earthed up by the double mould-board plough, and one horse, which completes the weeding operation in the drill system. Potatoes planted by cottagers with the spade, are hand-weeded and hoed; this being done by manual labour, is troublesome, but more productive.

10. *Tops.*—I have witnessed some experiments, and have been informed of others, in which the tops of the shaws, (haulm), were taken off when in flower. This has been done in alternate drills, in the same field. No difference, however, was discovered between the produce of the topped or the untopped drills.

11. *Taking up.*—When potatoes are laid down with the plough, it is usual to open up the drills in harvest, and the produce is collected with the hand, aided by hand-hoes and muck-hacks, to stir the soil. Those planted with the spade are taken up with the same tool.

12. *Storing.*—*Heaps*, or *Pies.*—Those kept in the house, for immediate use, are set up in heaps, in a cellar, or close place, and protected as much as possible from frost.

Pits.

Pits.—The best, and most secure mode of keeping potatoes from frost, &c. is in pits, made in any dry soil, the bottom and sides of the pits being lined with dry divots, (thin sods), then the potatoes are poured in until it is quite full, and even heaped; the top is then to be covered with dry divots, or drawn straw, and the earth excavated out of the pits put over the whole, so that a foot deep of earth will be over the whole of the pit. The heap is brought to a narrow ridge on the top, like the roof of a house, which is to be beat smooth with spades, to make the rain run easily off; the potatoes will thus be kept in good condition until April or May, when they are generally taken up for seed or food.

13. *Buildings.*—Unless buildings erected to hold potatoes, are very warm and tight, they are apt to be frost-bit and spoilt.

14. *Produce.*—Potatoes being chiefly, if not totally cultivated in this county for family use, from the want of markets, such as may be had in more populous districts, little attention is paid to keep any accurate account of the produce per acre. That produce must necessarily vary, according to the soil, the manner of planting, manuring, weeding, &c. but where the land is of a good quality, and well manured, where a field is 10 chains long, 25 drills in breadth makes an acre, and these 25 drills will produce, in a favourable season, from 36 to 40 bolls per acre, each boll being 16 pecks of 24 lb. each, or 384 lb. Dutch per boll, equal to 15,360 lb. per Scotch acre. From 16 to 20 bolls per acre, however, is a more general crop.

15. *Price.*—The price of potatoes, through the winter

winter months, is from 7*s*. to 10*s*. per boll, and in the latter end of spring, seed potatoes are sometimes sold as high as 20*s*. per boll.

16. *Application.*—The most general application of this crop is as human food, and the mode of cooking potatoes, is as various as the fancy of those who use them may desire. It is only necessary here to observe, that boiling them with as little water as possible, is the best rule for cooking them well. Some farmers give an occasional feed of potatoes to their farm-horses through the spring; and cottagers, who rear a few small hogs, give them the smaller potatoes. But there is no good system among the people of this county, for feeding either hogs or cattle, with this valuable esculent; that may be owing to the want of a market for fat beasts.

Steaming.—This plan has not hitherto been practised in this county; but some farmers are on the eve of providing boilers, &c. to prepare potatoes by steam, either for food to cattle, or family use.

Drying to keep.—No experiment of that kind has yet been tried in this county.

Starch.—Some active housewives make potatoe starch thus:—The potatoes are washed clean, and grated down in a tub, when the mass remains for twelve hours; then, the red water on the surface is poured off, and fresh water put on, and in twelve hours after, the whole is filtered through a coarse cloth, and the liquor which passed through, having settled, the surface water is poured off, and fresh water put on: this watering operation is repeated daily for a week, or until the water poured off is clear as when put on. The last water that is put on this farinaceous sediment, is mixed with a little prussian blue; the starchy sediment is afterwards dried in the sun, or by fire, when it is ready for use. Some people contend, that from 16 to 20 lb. of potatoes will make one pound of starch; others aver, that it will take 24 lb. of potatoes. It is said that potatoe starch, is much inferior to wheaten starch, the former being apt to cut and damage linen.

Bread.—I have not found that any experiments have been made in this county, to make bread of potatoes. Some housewives direct a quantity of potatoes to be boiled in the evening; the skins being then peeled off, they are mashed down in a wooden vessel, and laid by until next morning, when the mass is sliced down and toasted on a gridiron, and eaten to breakfast, as a substitute for bread. I have also seen oat-meal mixed among potatoes so mashed and kneaded, like oaten cakes, and toasted to the fire in the same manner, and this compound ate very well while warm; but when the mashed potatoes is mixed with fine bear-meal, and baked into thin cakes, it eats more palatable than with the oatmeal.

17. *Exhaust or Improve.*—It is the general opinion in this county, that the potatoe crop exhausts the soil more than the turnip crop, and of course that it requires more manure, to make the succeeding crop after potatoes, equally productive, as if after turnips; yet it must be allowed, that weeding the ground under a potatoe crop, must be of advantage to the soil.

18. *What succeeds.*—Some farmers affirm, that

land

land will not produce a good crop of bear, after a potatoe crop, and that oats do better; others again say, that their land, after a potatoe crop, will produce bear better than oats. Both these opinions may thus be reconciled: if the soil is light, and abounds with acidity, from want of calcareous earth, though, with manure, it may produce a crop of potatoes, it will not yield a crop of bear, but it may produce a tolerable crop of oats; again, a good rich dry loam, not deficient of calcareous earth, will produce a crop of bear, or oats, after a previous potatoe crop, either manured for the potatoe crop, or the succeeding grain crop. In general, where artificial grass is raised, grass-seed is sown with the crop of bear, or oats, succeeding the potatoe crop.

In the Highland part of the county, the potatoe crop is frequently injured by frost and mildew, in the months of July or August. When the sky is clear, if a hoar-frost comes on at night, if it is not succeeded by rain before the morning sun darts his rays on the earth, the haulm, or shaws of the potatoe crop, droop down in the course of a few hours after, as if parboiled, and become by degrees quite black. The crop then makes no further progress. A smaller degree of frost and mildew, injures the potatoe crop, than what is commonly pernicious to the corn crops.

19. *Yams.*—Some farmers plant a few drills with yams, as food for their horses the ensuing spring. The mode of culture is the same as for potatoes.

20. *Importance of Potatoes.*—It is said to have been ascertained, that an acre of land planted with potatoes, will produce sufficient food for 16,875 healthy men

men for one meal, while an acre of wheat, will not feed more than 2745. The expense of cultivating the potatoe, is estimated at 12*l.* 1*s.* and that of wheat at 11*l.* 16*s.*; hence, in regard to produce, compared to expense, there can be no comparison between the two articles.

SECT. XXV.—CLOVER.

1. *With what Crops sown.*—Red and white clover-seed is most commonly sown with the bear crop, after a green crop, or fallow; but upon land of inferior quality, oats follow the green crop, and clover and rye-grass seeds are sown with it.

2. *Manuring.*—After a green crop that had been manured, no manure is applied with the succeeding bear or oat crop, or the clover; but if after a fallow, the land is manured at the rate of about 30 cubic yards per acre, with any compost of earth and dung, such as the farmer can collect.

3. *Seed.*—Upon good strong land, from 10 to 12 lb. of red, and 4 lb. of white clover seed, and about two bushels of rye-grass, is sown per acre, at any time during the month of May, when the night frosts are gone, or as soon as the land is well harrowed. After sowing the grain, it is then lightly harrowed, and rolled, and the stones collected off the surface.

4. *Use.*—The crop of the first year is commonly cut for hay, and the foggage, by the first of September,

is

is ready to be cut for soiling the farm-horses and milch cows at night.

The climate of this county is too cold, to bring clover-seed to maturity: at least I have not found that any attempt has been made to raise clover-seed.

5. *Is the Land tired of Clover?*—It is only within the last twenty years, that clover crops have been produced in this county, of course the number of rotations are too few, to ascertain how long the land will continue to yield clover; but it is ascertained, that the crop of clover and rye-grass, produced in the first rotation, on land that had previously, from time immemorial, been under alternate crops of bear and oats, is much more weighty, than that produced during the succeeding rotations.

It is believed, that red clover extracts more calcareous matter out of the soil, than any other crop; it is therefore presumed, that repeated applications of lime or marl is necessary, to keep the land in a state fit to produce crops of clover in abundance. I have seen repeated experiments made, of sowing red clover on land that wanted calcareous earth, and of course was full of acid; but no clover was produced, until the nature of the soil was changed by a good dose of marl or lime. The best clover crops are produced on a well-manured clay loam.

SECT. XXVI.—TREFOIL.

None sown in the county.

SECT. XXVII.—RYE-GRASS.

This is the grass most generally sown in this county. Soil which will not produce clover, owing to its lightness or sterility, will yield a light crop of rye-grass, after a turnip crop; but in such a soil, it commonly disappears, or degenerates into Yorkshire fog, the second year.

Rye-grass, as has been already observed, is commonly sown with the bear or oat crop, mixed with clover. If the soil is light, and deficient in regard to clay or calcareous earth, about three bushels of rye-grass is sown, without any other grass-seeds.

Application.—In general, the first crop is mowed for hay; and, if the rye-grass is not of the annual kind, the land is pastured for one or two years after, when it is ploughed up for oats.

Those who use the four years' shift, sow annual rye-grass, because it produces a heavier crop than the perennial; but the more general practice is, the five or six years' shift, and of course the perennial rye-grass is preferred, from its duration, and the superior quality of the hay.

There are instances of cutting a hay crop of clover and rye-grass, for three successive years, before breaking up the land for a corn crop. This practice, however, scourges the soil too much, and the better plan is, to cut the first crop for hay, and pasture the land the second year, then break up for oats.

Several of the Caithness farmers now preserve rye-grass seed on their own farms, by leaving a ridge or more uncut until about the end of July; then they cut

it

it down with the sickle, and tie it up in small sheaves, like corn: when dry, it is made into a small rick, until next spring, when it is thrashed, and ready for sowing. By preserving it thus from the second year's crop, they are certain of having real perennial seed, of much better quality than they can procure from the Leith or Aberdeen markets. The expense also is much less, the price of what is imported being from *4s. 6d.* to *6s.* per bushel.

Good old cultivated land in Caithness, when well manured, will produce as heavy crops of clover and rye-grass, as any county in Scotland. Such land will yield from 250 to 300 stone of hay per Scotch acre, at 24lb. per stone, which, at *1s.* per stone, is a valuable produce.

SECT. XXVIII. XXIX.—SAINFOIN, LUCERN.

Some years ago, two or three Gentlemen in this county tried the sowing of sainfoin and lucern in their gardens, and even on a small scale in the field, under the drill system; but they found that it required so much attention in weeding, that the returns were too small to encourage a perseverance in such experiments.

SECT. XXX. XXXI.—CHICORY, BURNET.

Some chicory and burnet were sown, in the year 1803, in a piece of moory ground, that had been pared and burned. The crop, however, was very thin and indifferent. I have not heard of any other experiments made with these articles in this county.

SECT. XXXII.—HOPS.

A FEW hop plants have been reared to garden walls, but they do not flower in this county.

SECT. XXXIII.—HEMP.

SOME experiments have been made, of sowing hemp, but the result was not such as to encourage any trial upon a larger scale.

SECT. XXXIV.—FLAX.

SMALL quantities of flax have been annually sown by the small tenantry of this county, from time immemorial, and in every instance, where the land is in good condition, and cleared from weeds, the crop is abundant; but frequently damaged in the watering process.

1. *Soil.*—The best soil for Dutch flax-seed, is a clay loam; and for American seed, a light dark loam.

2. *Tillage.*—The best plan is, to plough up clover ley. It should be once ploughed, and then well harrowed, both before and after sowing the seed. No manure is necessary.

3. *Seed.*—The quantity of seed is from eight to ten pecks per acre, sown broad-cast, in calm weather.

4. *Time.*—It cannot with safety be sown before the

12th of May, in this county, because the night frosts in April are apt to destroy the germinal seed. Where the land is foul, it is hand-weeded when the crop is about nine inches high.

5. *Pulling.*—When the seed-pods are full, and the stalks assume a brown colour, the flax is pulled by the hand, and tied in small sheaves, the seed ripped off, and then it is ready to be watered.

6. *Watering.*—It should be put in moss water, and if impregnated with marl, so much the better. River water, or any current water, is reckoned prejudicial to the flax; soft, pond, or stagnant water, are much better.

7. *Time.*—The time required to water flax, depends upon the warmth of the weather, and the quality of the water. In marl-pits, with warm weather, the flax will be sufficiently watered in five or six days. If soft, stagnant water-ponds are used, from ten days to a fortnight is necessary; and in deep peat-banks, from 14 to 21 days in autumn. Were the Caithness farmers to keep their flax unwatered until the month of June, it would then be done more effectually; and the grassing operation would be executed without any risk from frost.

8. *Grassing.*—This is performed by spreading the flax thin upon grass land, immediately after it is taken out of the water; the more foggage at the time the better, as it will keep up the flax from the ground, and the quicker the vegetation at the time, the more effect the oxygen gas will have to separate the flax from the stalk. A frosty night, after it is spread on the grass, will completely spoil the flax, and this of itself is a sufficient

sufficient reason for postponing the watering process until the summer season, in this cold climate.

9. *Binding.*—When the flax comes freely from the bone, or stalk, it is tied up in small parcels, of about a handful each when dry, and kept in a dry, airy place, until it is manufactured, either by manual labour, such as breaking, beetling, scutching, &c. &c. or it is sent to a lint or flax mill, to be prepared for the hackle.

There are three flax mills in this county, but the trifling quantities of flax raised by the small tenantry and cottagers, are manufactured by their own manual labour, and heckles are borrowed for the purpose of dressing. By this process, they say, that they will have double the quantity of dressed flax and tow, they would receive from the same quantity of flax sent to the mill. The Irish are of the same opinion; they would not send their flax to a mill; of course, though a country where great quantities of flax are produced and manufactured, there is not, it is said, one flax mill in that kingdom.

10. *Price, broken, heckled, &c.*—I could obtain no satisfactory account of these particulars, because, what is produced on each farm, or lot, is only for family use, and not for sale. The soil of Caithness produces good crops of flax, but it is frequently damaged in the course of the watering, &c. in autumn; and it is owing to the difficulty of obtaining good seed, its high price, and disappointments in manufacturing it, from want of skill, that there is not so much flax raised in this county, as was formerly the case when labour was cheap. In the year 1793, an English acre of clover-

ley was ploughed at Castle-hill, and sown with nine pecks of Dutch flax-seed, and the produce was as follows:

Forty-three stone of milled flax, which yielded

	£	s.	d.
85 lb. of 5 hank lint, then worth 1s. 6d. per lb.	6	7	6
43 lb. of 3 hank ditto ditto 1s. 0d. per do.	2	3	0
72 lb. of 2 hank ditto ditto 0s. 9d. per do.	2	14	0
200 lb. of lint, or dressed flax, equal to	£11	4	6
And 25 stone of tow, worth, at that time 5s. per stone, (now 10s.)	6	5	0
Total	£17	9	6

The expenses of milling the flax, and heckling it, are to be deducted.

11. *Repetition in the same Soil.*—Flax is considered a scourging crop; it is not therefore repeated on the same spot. Those who understand it best, sow flax-seed on clover ley, and after the crop is pulled, about the end of August, the land is manured with some compost, and ploughed, and it is next spring in good condition for any other crop.

It is admitted, that if the seed is allowed to ripen, it will serve for next year; but foreign seed is more productive. The seed of the flax in Caithness is therefore of little value, as there is no market for it in this county for making oil; were it preserved until their cows calved in the spring, and were it then boiled, and equal quantities given of the mother's milk and of the linseed decoction, to the calf, it would improve them much. This is attended to in Perthshire, and they attribute to this practice, the glossy appearance of their cattle, and their good condition.

CHAP. VIII.

GRASS LAND.

SECT. I.—MEADOWS.

1. THE only meadows in this county, are those formed along the winding banks of the various streams and rivers which abound in it. The size and fertility of these meadows, depend upon the nature of the ground, and the traversing course of the streams, which occasionally overflow, and, where not rapid, tend to enrich or manure them. With the exception of patches of green ground, at the lower end of corn-fields, which are fertilised by the winter rains washing down some rich mould from the arable land above them, these meadows, when level, are kept for meadow hay, and generally produce a tolerable crop. They are preserved from cattle, from the 1st of May, until about the end of July, when the hay crop is mown by the farmer and his family, aided occasionally by hired persons, who are now paid at the rate of 1*s.* 6*d.* per day, and two meals. The hay, as soon as cut, is carried from the meadows, which are liable to be overflowed, to eminences in the vicinity. With dry weather, the hay, in the course of five or six days, is ready to be put up in tramp cocks, where it remains until the corn-harvest is over, and then it is carried to the stack-yard, and built into stacks, or ricks, according to the quantity.

Mr. John Manson, overseer on the farm of Thurso East,

East, has a peculiar mode of making hay, which it may not be improper to insert in this place.

When the weather is likely to be rainy, he puts the hay into tramp cocks, a turn, or perhaps two, sooner than usual, observing to make them very small; and after standing some few days in the tramp cocks, he takes the first fair opportunity of bringing it to the stack-yard, and puts it up in small square ricks, or gilts, in three rows, the centre row of which is intended for building the hay-stack upon it at last. For that purpose, he studies to make the length of the small stacks in the centre row, to answer the breadth of the principal one, at the last building, which the following rough sketch will explain:

The row on each side of the centre row is for filling up the vacancies, and forming it into a long stack at rebuilding.

2. *Produce.*—As these natural meadows are generally occupied by small tenants, few have any more hay than what may be necessary to feed their horses during the spring labour; little attention therefore is paid to ascertain the quantity produced per acre. Indeed the crop is very variable, depending upon the level, depth, moisture, or fertility of the meadow, and on the moisture of the season, but it may be averaged at from 50 to 100, or even 200 stone per Scotch acre, of 24lb. per stone. It is said that Mr. Smith of Olrig, has a meadow, which has produced even 300 stone per Scotch acre, but this is

a very

a very uncommon circumstance*. Great crops of natural hay have also been produced at Ackergil.

3. *Rent.*—These meadows, or patches of hay-ground, are generally appendages to arable land, and included in the cumulo rent of the farm; but in cases where detached pieces of meadow are rented per acre, the rent varies from 4*s*. to 12*s*.

4. *Half-year Meadows.*—None.

5. *Expense.—Mowing, Making, and Stacking.*—From what is already stated, these expenses are not exactly to be ascertained in this county. Cutting an acre of good meadow, may cost 4*s*., making and stacking, about 3*s*., in all 7*s*. per acre. This I consider equal to the expense of making hay, even in good meadows.

6. *Manuring.*—The meadows are not top-dressed, or manured in this county. They are commonly pastured by horses and black cattle, from the time the hay crop is taken off the ground, until next May, when they are again preserved for the succeeding crop.

Were such meadows as are not subject to be overflowed by rivers or streams, manured with a compost of earth and dung, as soon as the hay crop is carried off, and not pastured for some time after, they would become much more valuable, by yielding a good foggage crop in October, and a better hay crop next season.

* It is stated by an intelligent farmer, that a sack of natural hay, will weigh a sack and a half of artificial hay, of the first crop.

In

In this case, inclosure would be necessary, that the ground might not be poached in wet weather.

SECT. II.—PASTURES.

This county, was originally divided into small farms, of from eight to twenty acres of arable land, and each tenant, where there were several, had his arable land in run-rigg, (which was commonly the case in the low part of the county), and the whole community had the arable land, and some pasture ground with it, inclosed with a ring fence of feal, or sods, not very remarkable for regularity or straightness. This fence was called *The Loaning Dyke*. It divided the in-town pasturage from the common pasturage, which generally bounded it, at least on one side.

When seed-time was over, *i. e.* when the oats and bear were sown, for in those days there were no green crops in the fields, the tenant and his domestics began to repair the loaning dykes, and the cattle, horses, sheep, geese, and swine, were driven off to the common pasture-ground, where they are herded during the summer, and housed at night. Thus the green ground within the loaning dyke, was preserved for the milch cow, or cows, and all the green borders round the arable land, not fit to produce hay, was the pasture of the milch cows, until the corn was cut down and ingathered, when all became common again.

About the middle of August, their horses were *tethered* on coarse borders within the loaning dyke. These tethers were made of heather, *(erica)*, twisted like a rope; they were about 25 feet long, with a noose, or eye, at each end, and were sold at 1*d*. each. In the

one

one noose was fixed a stake of wood, about 12 inches long, and tapering to a point, called a *backie*, and to the other noose was attached the horse's halter. The backie being drove into the ground by a mallet, or stone, the horse pastured in a circle formed by this tether as a radius; and thus they were shifted occasionally, as the ground became bare, through the autumn, both night and day, until the corn was ingathered, when every beast was set at liberty till the return of April.

Wherever a town land is occupied by these small tenants, this practice is still continued, with the exception of winter herding, where they are near a farm on which the modern system of husbandry is practised.

There is no rich feeding land preserved inclosed in this county, except some arable land in the course of the rotation of crops, because there is no market to consume the meat that would be produced by occupying rich land as pasture. In one or two instances, a tract of green ground, of about 200 acres, interspersed with crofts of old arable land, has been inclosed with a stone fence, and in the summer months, cattle and horses taken in to graze, for one, two, or even four months, at about 11*s*. 6*d*. per month for plough horses, and 8*s*. per month for full-grown black cattle, and at these prices the land thus occupied will not pay above 4*s*. per acre of rent, after deducting interest of the expense of inclosing it.

Mr. Sinclair of Barrock, is of opinion, that if the natural meadows were always kept, from the 1st of March, and the ground drained, and top-dressed, the crop of hay would be abundant.

General Sinclair, of Lybster, states, that four acres of

of clover and rye grass yielded, *in bulk*, equal to what was cut on twelve acres of old pasture, reserved for hay; but the cattle fed on the natural hay, looked by far in the best plight*.

2. *Dairy Grounds.*—In former times, the dairy, and dairy grounds, were chiefly confined to the Highland Straths, in the parishes of Reay, Halkirk and Latheron, where each tenant had a considerable extent of pasture ground of moor and dale, attached to his limited portion of arable land. In many cases the farm was stocked with cattle by the proprietor; they were valued, and delivered over to the tenant on *steelbow*, *i. e.* he received the stock at an appreciated value, and became bound to pay a certain yearly rent, for the stock delivered, and the land he occupied, during a lease of seven, or nine years; and at the end of the lease, he was bound to deliver over, (in case of removal), a stock of cattle, of similar value, to the proprietor of the land, or to pay for any deficiency. This manner of farming was called a *steelbow tack*, but it is now in disuse. The Highland tenant had, in common with the Lowland, his loaning dyke, his in-town pasture and hay meadow, or haughs, along the river or burns, of considerable extent; some of them had also their (*airie*), shealings, in distant and remote glens. These shealings were preserved from cattle, &c. from the 15th of April,

* Mr. John Manson considers natural hay to be only one half as valuable as artificial grasses; and an intelligent farmer is of opinion, that it would be much more profitable, to drain and plough these natural meadows, as the hay is commonly of a bad quality, unless very carefully made, consequently not much better than straw, and that the ground does not pay one sixth part of what it would do, under crops of corn, properly managed.

until about the 20th of June, when the housewife and maid, set out with the milch cows, perhaps from 10 to 20 in number, to the shealings, where a booth or cabin was previously prepared for their reception, another for the milk vessels, and a small fold to keep the calves from the cows, during the night. There they passed a complete pastoral life, making butter and cheese, and living on curds and cream, or a mixture of oat-meal and cream stirred together cold, seasoned with a glass of whisky before and after meals, dancing on the green, and singing Gaelic songs, to the music of which, at milking time, morning and evening, the cows listened with apparent attention and pleasure. Here they remained for a month or six weeks, at least while there was good pasture for the cows; that being consumed, they removed to the homestead and the in-town grass. The rule among the Highlanders was, to rear a calf between every two cows, and after serving the family, there generally was from 24 to 30 lb. of butter, and as much cheese for sale, from each cow. About 40 years ago, butter, in lumps of a stone, or 24 lb. each, sold at five shillings, and cheese at from two shillings to two shillings and sixpence per stone.

When the housewife and milch cows left the shealing for the homestead, the yeld, or young cattle, and the horses, who were until then herded on the outskirts of the moors, had the freedom of the shealing, until the winter storms drove them home. What these ancient dairies would produce per acre, cannot be ascertained, because land was not subject to measurement in those days.

In the Highland part of this county, there is still more attention paid to rearing cattle, than to the making of butter and cheese.

In

In the lower parts of the county, several proprietors and farmers, have from 10 to 20 milch cows in dairies, principally pastured on arable land, laid down with white and red clover and rye-grass. A dairy-woman, hired on cost and wages, has the charge of them; a few calves are reared, and as much butter and cheese made as the milk will furnish. Some farmers informed me, that when they rear a calf between every two cows, they value the calf at Martinmas, (about the 11th of November), at 2*l.* and that the butter and cheese produced from each cow, will bring about 3*l.* When butter gives 22*s.* per stone of 24 lb., and cheese 6*s.* to 8*s.* per stone, (being the average price for several years past), that is equal to 4*l.* per cow. Others again say, that the produce of each cow brings them 5*l.* per annum; but these cows are fed on clover in the byre, with warm weather, and are larger than the generality of Caithness cows.

Mr. Traill of Hobbister, the Sheriff of the county, for several years past has had a dairy of Dunlop or Ayrshire cows, on a farm he has appropriated for trying the dairy system, and he brought a dairy-woman from Ayrshire, for the purpose of making of *Dunlop cheese* alone, no butter being made at this dairy. The cheese is annually sent to the Edinburgh market, where it is sold at 14*s.* per stone of 24 lb. and is much in vogue. I am informed that each cow in that dairy produces annually about 7*l.* 10*s.* by the Dunlop mode of management; but the Ayrshire dairy-woman, who manages 20 cows, has 20*l.* per annum, besides the cost and wages of a maid, who assists her. These cows are allowed about two acres each of artificial grass, for summer pasture, and the calves reared are included in the above average produce of 7*l.* 10*s.*

 each.

each. Upon the whole, however, tho making of Dunlop cheese, is the most profitable mode of conducting a dairy, that has as yet been tried in this county.

2. *Produce per Acre.*—There are instances of good land, under a crop of clover and rye-grass, feeding a milch cow per acre, through the summer months; but in general, it will take two acres of land under artificial grass, to feed a cow through the season. The extent of natural grass required to pasture a milch cow, depends much upon its luxuriance, &c. &c.

3. *Sheep Pasture.*—There are no down or green pasture entirely allotted for sheep in this county. Several extensive commons, partly green pasture, when undivided, were pastured by horses, cattle, sheep, swine, and geese promiscuously. The sheep pasture, for a breeding stock, will be treated of, in the Chapter for sheep.

4. *Laying Land to Grass.*—This subject has been already dwelt on, in treating of arable land, under a rotation of crops. The mode of managing outfield land also, scourging it with repeated crops of grey oats, and then letting it lie for years, to gather a new sward of sorrel, knot-grass, &c., in which state it remains in pasture, until overrun with moss or fog, when it is again broken up for oats, has been likewise explained. In the vicinity of marl, several fields of this kind of land, have been brought into a state of fertility, by using about 30 cart-loads of marl per acre.

Fiorin Grass.—Before the subject of grass land is closed, it may be proper to observe, that fiorin grass grows

grows naturally in Caithness in great abundance. In Gaelic, it is called *rhionoghin*, that is, the running or creeping grass. It is the earliest of grasses, and seems productive. How far it will answer in this county, equal to what has been said regarding its produce in Ireland, remains to be ascertained.

Importance of Grazing.—There is every reason to believe, that more attention should be paid to grazing, in this county, than hitherto has been the case. Sir Robert Anstruther, a most intelligent practical farmer, who bought an estate in Caithness, with a view of improving it, states, that, with the help of a grazing, supposed to contain about 2000 acres, formerly let at 16*l.* 13*s.* 4*d.*, he reared work-horses, garrons, and cattle from Fife bulls, and Assynt cows, which, when he gave up farming, amply repaid every expense he had laid out, on the whole estate he had purchased.

CHAP. IX.

GARDENS AND ORCHARDS.

SECT. I.—GARDENS.

THE only garden that is let at a rent per acre, is one belonging to Sir John Sinclair's estate, in the vicinity of the town of Thurso, which was formed with a view of supplying the inhabitants of that town with roots, and other vegetables for the kitchen, also with small fruit, such as black, red, and white currants, gooseberries, and strawberries. About seven Scotch acres have been inclosed for that purpose, and let at a rent of 4*l.* per acre.

The land proprietors have gardens at their own residences, in particular, those of Sandside, Westfield, Brawll, Castle-hill, Barogill Castle, Ackergill, Nottingham, Dunbeath, Langwell, &c. have a variety of small fruit, and in some of them, wall trees, and orchard trees, of apples, pears, and cherries, which bear good crops; cherries in particular are produced, in full maturity and flavour. Every farmer has a garden for roots and vegetables, to serve his family, producing turnips, carrots, parsnips, early potatoes, beet, onions, leeks, celery, lettuces, cresses, pease, beans, greens, cabbages, &c. &c.

Cottagers.—The cottagers gardens produce only cab-

bages,

bages, potatoes and in some cases a few turnips, all for their own use, there being no market for them.

Destruction of Insects, Grub, and other Vermin.— The small fruit is frequently injured in the Caithness gardens, by the caterpillar and white moth, while in the grub state.

Several experiments have been made, by washing the bushes with tobacco juice, burning sulphur under them, and washing the bushes with soot and water: all these tend to retard the progress of these destructive insects, who devour the foliage, but none of them prove completely effectual for their destruction: others again, keep the stem of the bushes, for six or eight inches above ground, clear of branches, put a ring of tar round the middle of the stem, and put some soot and salt on the ground round the root of the bush, which in a great degree prevent the grub from crawling up to the branches; they also frequently look at the bushes, and pick off any of the insects, which have got to the branches.

The grub destroys many of the cabbage plants, in the course of the first month after they are transplanted. To prevent this, some farmers make a ley of stale urine and peat-ashes, and dip the roots and stems of the plants in it, immediately before they are planted, which completely preserves them from the grub.

SECT. II.—ORCHARDS.

THERE are no orchards in the county under review, the climate is too cold for them. There are a few orchard trees planted in the gardens of the proprietors already mentioned, which bear fruit, as well as some wall trees.

CHAP. X.

WOODS AND PLANTATIONS.

SECT. I.—COPSE WOOD.

THERE is no oak, or copse wood, of any size, in this county. Upon the two straths of Berriedale, a part of Sir John Sinclair's Estate, there are about 680 acres of copse, chiefly birch, and some aller, hazel, roan, or mountain-ash, and willow, the remains of woods, which, half a century ago, produced large trees, sufficient for building highland houses, and being converted to agricultural purposes in general, but now, no better than brushwood. There is a similar kind of shrubbery on the strath of Dunbeath, and at Rumsdale, in the Strathmore; and about sixty years ago, that kind of wood, skirted all the straths of rivers and burns in the parishes of Latheron and Halkirk, which have decayed, owing to neglect, the peasantry of the country being permitted to cut it down, and to take the bark for illicit tanning of leather, to make shoes, or rather *brogues*, for themselves and their families; a practice now in disuse, from the want of bark.

The principal useful purposes to which these woods of Berriedale &c. were applied, was by the people in their vicinity, cutting down the largest trees, for plough beams, and other agricultural instruments, such as were then in general use; and which are still used by the smaller tenants in the highland parishes, as *crub-bans*,

bans, for carrying corn or peats on horses' backs, and *criells*, or baskets, for carrying the manure to the land on horseback. The tenantry of these straths, having generally a mechanical turn, made these implements of husbandry, and carried them for sale to the country fairs. That species of industry, with the profit of their black cattle, and the produce of the small lots of arable land they occupied, supported their families, and enabled them to pay their rents. These woods afford them now only some twigs for making criells or baskets, and *supples*, or flails, for thrashing their corn.

There is no vestige of oak, beech, or any other hard wood being natural in this county. In almost all the low-lying peat-mosses, the remains of wood found, is principally willow, aller or alder, hazel, and in some Highland mosses, on the borders of the county, toward Sutherlandshire, *fir* has been found, both roots and trunks of considerable size, fresh and sound, under from three to six or seven feet of peat-moss. These the Highlanders use for the roofs of their houses, or they split them into small slips, for light, in place of candles, during the winter nights. Wherever the root of a fir tree is found, it has the appearance of having been burnt, the surface being charred.

No attempt has ever been made by the proprietors, to cut or char these woods; and of course their value by the acre, or otherwise, cannot be ascertained; the only advantage arising to the landlords from the woods was this, that their tenants in their vicinity, were enabled to pay a higher rent for their small farms, owing to the money they annually made by the sale of the rural implements manufactured by them, as before stated. The woods were also a shelter to their cattle during the winter months; they browsed on its branches during a

snow

snow storm; the spring grass appeared earlier among the woody banks, than in less sheltered places, and it was in greater abundance in summer.

It is the general opinion, that on the straths or vallies, where these woods have entirely decayed within these forty or fifty years past, there is not now above one-fourth of the pasture produced, that was to be found while the woods flourished, and of course they cannot rear the same number of black cattle as they formerly did, on the same pasturage; but it is also remarked, that they lose fewer by disease; because cattle pastured on the luxuriant grass produced among these shady bushes, were liable to a disease they called the *heasty* (murrain), which will afterwards be explained.

SECT. II.—PLANTATIONS.

Several plantations of Scotch fir have been tried in various parts of this county, within these last forty years; but in general they have failed, partly owing to inattention, in keeping the fences to preserve them from sheep and black cattle, but it may be principally ascribed to the nature of the soil, as fir grows spontaneously in a colder climate than Caithness. The soil in which I have seen experiments made, is a gritty close gravel, of little depth, and incumbent on a horizontal flaggy rock, which keeps the rain water near the surface, and of course is inimical to the growth of any timber. As an exception to these remarks, there is a thriving plantation of larch and Scotch fir, at Langwell, a part of Sir John Sinclair's Estate, about twenty acres having been planted with these trees, about eigh-

teen

teen to twenty years ago, on a declivity in the strath of Langwell, having a southern exposure, and being well sheltered from the north and north west, by the Berriedale mountains. The soil is a gritty open gravel, (with rocks occasionally breaking out), and not tenacious of moisture. About two acres of this soil had been trenched many years ago, for agricultural purposes; and the trees growing on the trenched ground, are now double the size of those planted, at the same time, on the untrenched ground. Some of the larches, are now about twelve feet high, and at four feet above the ground, are about from nine to fourteen inches in circumference. Sir John Sinclair has had an experienced gardener and planter at Langwell for several years past, who has planted many thousand larches and Scotch firs, on the moory banks and among the native brushwood, of the Langwell estate; and, wherever the soil is favourable, the plants are in good condition.

There are a few very large ash trees in a glen near the garden of Langwell. At the garden of Brawll, in the parish of Halkirk, there is an old plantation of ash, elm, beech, mountain-ash, and Scotch fir, planted by Sir John Sinclair's grandfather. By his directions, the tenants of several town-lands in that vicinity, were bound to carry a certain quantity of compost manure to that plantation, in the month of October annually, each tenant raising a mound of the compost around the root of a prescribed number of trees, for seven years after they were planted, which preserved their roots from the severe winter frosts, and undoubtedly was the cause of the plantation growing so vigorously. This plan ought certainly to be adopted, wherever

wherever there is any difficulty, from the situation or climate, to raise trees. The soil is a sandy loam, near the banks of the river Thurso.

There are small plantations of ash, elm, beech, roan, and willow, at Westfield, sheltered by a bank from the north, and doing well. At Cathell, now much neglected; at Sandside, in a thriving state; and a few trees, about garden walls, in various parts of the county. There are about two acres of ground planted on the north bank of a burn near Castle-hill, on Mr. Traill's estate, within 200 yards of Dunnet-bay. The trees grew very well, until their branches were above the level of the stone wall which inclosed the ground; but now they seem stunted, their branches taking a horizontal direction towards the south from the stem, as if bending for shelter from the inclemency of the northern blast, the place being on the north coast of the county.—There was a plantation of various kinds of trees, in one of the inclosures at Thurso East, which has a stunted and declining aspect, partly from its being exposed to the north-west gales from the North Sea, and perhaps partly owing to the ground being choked by a reedy strong kind of grass, which hinders the growth of trees. The Earl of Caithness has been at considerable trouble and expense in rearing a plantation at Barrogil Castle, near the Pentland Frith: there are ash, elm, plane, beech, &c. in a thriving state, under the shelter of a high wall, which as yet defends them from the northern blast; but when the trees get above the level of that wall, in all probability they will become stunted.

At Barrack-house, in the parish of Bower, there is a small plantation of ash, &c. on the south side of a

garden

garden wall, which has grown to a considerable size. The soil is deep, dry, and at a distance from the north coast*.

All these plantations are only to the extent of a few acres contiguous to gentlemen's gardens. No plantation of any considerable extent has been tried in this county, because the soil is in general not favourable to the growth of trees; and it is remarked, that the branches of trees, on the north coast of the county, if tasted after a gale of north wind, are found as salt as if they had been steeped in brine.

SECT. III.—TIMBER.

TIMBER is very scarce in this district, there being none of the produce of the county for sale. About 25 years ago, there was a trade carried on between this county and the ports of Norway: oat-meal was exported from Caithness to Bergen, &c. and timber imported in return. At that time, fir logs and deals, could be purchased from the importer, at from 7*d.* to 9*d.* per solid foot; afterwards a duty was imposed on tim-

* Mr. Mackid has no doubt, that trees would answer in the more inland parts of the county. About fifteen years ago Sir Robert Anstruther planted firs and larches at Scoriclet, a part of the estate of Wattin, which were in a thriving way for some time, but from the carelessness of the tenant of that farm, the plants were destroyed by his sheep and cattle, and even the country people cut off their tops, not knowing their value. As a proof that trees will grow in the county, some of a large size are still thriving at Achingale and Bilbster. If the proprietors therefore were to encourage planting, and grant protection to the plants, they may reasonably expect profit to themselves, and advantage to the county. The pine, the larch, the ash, and the beech, in Mr. Mackid's opinion, are the best adapted to the soil of the county.

ber

ber imported, the good policy of which is questionable, as there was no timber to be had of the produce of the county, or the neighbouring districts. When meal was exported to Norway, it was purchased in the county at from 10*s*. to 12*s*. per boll of 136 lb.; but the price having advanced here, beyond what the exporter could afford for the Norway trade, that, and other causes, put an end to that branch of commerce, and the only supply, at present, is from Strathspey in Moray-shire, and Beauly in Inverness-shire. Fir wood, of small scantling, is now sold in Caithness at 3*s*. 6*d*. to 4*s*. per solid foot; and hard wood in the same proportion.

The only tree that could be considered as extraordinary in this county, was an ash in the garden of Brawll, called "The Ladies' Tree." It was from 30 to 40 feet high, exclusive of the branches, and at nine feet above the ground, it was three feet diameter. It was blown down by a gale of wind many years ago, but owing to its uncommon size, the Proprietor allowed it to remain on the ground, as a specimen of Caithness timber.

As the roan tree, or mountain ash, is supposed to be of short duration, it may be worthy of notice to state, that there are two trees of that sort at Brawll, 80 years old, and still in vigour. There are a few trees of the same species in the garden of the manse of Halkirk, near Brawll, 50 years old; but some of them are now shewing symptoms of decay.

CHAP.

CHAP. XI.

WASTES.

SECT. I.—MOORS.

UNDER this head may be considered such sterile ground, in the vicinity of the green pasturage, as is covered with a stunted heather, mixed with a similar sort of burry grass: the upper stratum of the soil, is commonly a kind of gravelly clay, or it consists of a stratum, or a thin coat of peat earth, incumbent on till or schistus. Sometimes this kind of soil lies low, and at other times it may be found on eminences, on the declivity of hills. It is uniformly the case, that where the soil is either a dry gravel, or hard till or schistus, it only yields that stunted heather and burry grass. It is of very little value, and difficult to bring to a fertile state. Of this kind of ground, there is probably, in the county, about 18,000 acres.

SECT. II.—MOUNTAINS.

OF this description there are, 1. The Morven, or Berriedale mountains, along the Latheron coast, to the boundary of the parish of Wick. 2. Another range of high hills, reaching from the Morven mountains, by the boundary with Sutherland, through the parishes of Reay and Halkirk on the west, to the North Sea. These may contain in all, about 71,200 acres.

1. Their

1. Their present value cannot be computed at above *3d.* per acre.

2. *Application.*—The Morven, or Berriedale mountains, are principally occupied in sheep pasture, *i. e.* such part of them as are accessible to sheep. Morven, Scariben, and the Maiden Pap mountains, are very high and steep, and towards their summit, which is from 1500 to 3000 feet above the level of the sea, there is nothing but bare rock. The other mountains are clothed with heather, with some ling, and deer-hair, rather spongy and wet for sheep, and more suitable for pasturing black cattle, and Highland horses or garrons. In former times, herds of goats were kept in those mountains, but very few now remain. At their base, there is a stratum of coaly peat-moss, of from one foot to three feet deep, incumbent either on moor-stone rock, or till (schistus), and incapable of any effectual improvement.

3. *Improvements.*—The most considerable experiment ever made to improve high moory ground, of the above description, was by Sir John Sinclair, on the Langwell Estate. In the years 1802 to 1805, about 150 acres of high moor, at the base of the mountains, and not far distant from the sea shore, were pared and burnt. It is necessary to describe this kind of moor, because it was more of the mountain coaly nature, than of the low peat-mosses. It had a coat of thick heather, incumbent, on from one foot to two feet deep, of a coaly hard peat earth, the subsoil a hard till, or moorstone rock, and the elevation about 400 feet above the level of the sea. The mode of culture was as follows: 1. The heather was burnt; 2. The surface cut across by a scarificator wrought by two horses; 3. It was then

then pared with a fen plough and two horses; the sods thus turned, might be about two to three inches thick, and from one foot to two feet long. 4. These sods were set up on end in heaps to dry, and afterwards burnt. The ashes of this kind of peat-earth, being white and light, much of it was carried off by the wind, in the act of spreading it. 5. It was lightly ploughed down, with an English plough, well harrowed, and broke with hoes, and sown with red and white turnip seed, partly broad-cast, and partly drill, in June; the whole of the operation being performed in May, June, and July. The first show of turnips looked well, but they soon became stunted in their growth. In the more moist parts of this moor, the crop was tolerably close, by the beginning of September, and the size of the turnip, from that of a pigeon, to that of a common hen's egg. The turnip was ate off by sheep, and the next crop was bear, laid down in the month of May, partly with a little manure, and part without manure; some rye-grass, white clover, and Yorkshire fog-seeds, were sown with the bear crop. The crop of bear was very indifferent, from two to three seeds. The grass crop was light, say about 60 stone per acre; the Yorkshire fog continued in the soil for a few years, but the second year sorrel spread much on the surface; and now the native heather is re-appearing. That ground, however, is now let to a sheep farmer at 40*l.* rent, and if lime, or calcareous clay, could be had for a top-dressing, that improved moor would continue to produce grass, and the sorrel and heather would be destroyed; but unfortunately, neither of these sorts of manure can be had at any adequate expense.

Perhaps this is the only experiment ever made to improve a high moor, of a hard coaly peat-mosss, and to convert it to agricultural purposes: the result has shown, that if calcareous manure could be got to complete the process, the improvement would be durable, and beneficial, especially in a district, where the raising artificial grasses, for winter food to a stock of sheep, is so essentially necessary. This experiment was executed at a very considerable expense. Some hands skilled in the fen husbandry, were brought from Cambridgeshire, to Caithness, for that purpose, with such implements as they judged necessary, as fen ploughs, scarificators, &c. With these instruments, low flat mosses, of an uniform surface, may be pared and burnt, at the expense of 25*s*. per acre.

Several small lots of elevated moor, with less peat-earth above the gravel, were about that time improved, by fishermen on the Langwell and Dunbeath Estates, either by planting potatoes with manure in lazy-beds, or by trenching the ground 14 inches deep, turning off the stones, manuring the surface with compost of dung, peat-earth, and ashes, and sowing it with bear or bigg, as a first crop; the second, oats; both of which proved abundant. These people have their lots rent-free for the first 3, 4, 5, or 7 years, according to the difficulty of improving the soil; and they agree to pay afterwards a small rent per acre. They are near a tract of moor or heathery mountain, where they feed a milch cow each. This mode of improving wastes, is encouraged on the various estates along the parish of Latheron coast, where that class of people are employed in the season, at the herring fishing, and it is the cheapest and most effectual mode of improvement that can be adopted, on a property so situated, near a fishing station. The cottagers will raise from three to five bolls of bear or oats from an acre of improved waste, either

by

by trenching, or after a potatoe crop with compost manure; whereas, not above half that produce will be brought forth upon the improving a similar soil, by burning, ploughing, &c. at the expense of the man of capital, because the soil will not be so thoroughly wrought and manured, as is done by the cottager and his family, on their small spot.

Several experiments have been made, upon a large scale, by Sir John Sinclair, and other proprietors in the county, in improving the low moory ground first described in this Chapter; but hitherto it has not been found a profitable concern.

In the year 1802, Sir John Sinclair directed five acres of a moory ridge on his property near Thurso East, to be ploughed, and as the soil was a coarse gravelly yellow clay, incumbent on a horizontal rock, he directed that the burry soil turned up by the plough, should be burnt by means of coal and turf. This operation was effected by much labour and expense; the ashes lay in heaps on the ground until next spring, 1803, when it was spread, and a light ploughing ensued. The field was then sown with oats, which yielded a very indifferent crop, and did not average $2\frac{1}{2}$ bolls per acre. This ground was in 1805 let to cottagers in small lots, and it still continues unproductive, principally owing to the thinness of the clay soil over the rock. It is contended that such soil would, in the end, be more effectually improved without the aid of fire.

Upon a farm which I occupy, there was a barren moory knoll, of about four acres, in the angle of a field; I was therefore determined to attempt its improvement. In November 1806, after a very heavy fall of rain, I got it ploughed, and the moor-stones collected off it, as much as could be effected. It lay

 thus

thus until November 1807, when it was cross-ploughed, break-barrowed, and more stones collected. In February and May 1808, it was twice ploughed and barrowed, and such of the heather roots, &c. as did not yield to the plough or the weather, were collected and burnt. It was then so much reduced, as to enable me to lay it down with turnips in June 1808, having manured it with above 40 cart-loads of compost of earth and dung, per acre. As there were no weeds in the soil, the drills were not thinned, and the turnip leaves covered the ground effectually in August. The turnips were but small, as they were too thick to grow to a large size. Upon the whole, I considered the crop as equal to half a crop of red topped turnip, in a good soil. In April 1809, it was sown with red oats and rye-grass seeds. Five bolls and a half of seed oats to the four acres; the return was, four bolls per acre, or sixteen bolls, and there was more than a seed lost by a gale of wind, before it was cut down. The young grass looks well, and will make good pasture next summer: I intend giving it a top-dressing of marl and clay next October, and if the rye-grass keeps the ground, will pasture it another year, and then break it up for oats.

When I commenced improving it, the surface was half covered with roots of heather, the subsoil a gritty dry gravel, incumbent on hard till or schistus, mixed with moor-stone, not worth 2*s*. per acre. I have now thirty acres of a similar moor, ploughed up, and preparing for a similar mode of improvement, which is preferable to paring and burning a shallow soil, though not so expeditious.

SECT. III.—BOGS.

THE extent of deep peat-bogs in this county, including the peat moors of every description, is very considerable; it is estimated at 128,763 Scotch acres, or nearly one-half the extent of the county. Large tracts of this soil are flat and level, between the base of hills or high ground, in the interior of the county; and in the parish of Canisbay, not far even from the sea-shore, they are of great depth, and so swampy, that cattle cannot travel over some parts of them: these may be generally termed quick or growing moss. There is also a great extent of deep peat-moss, of considerable declivity, and of a firm texture; the depth from two to six feet, of a coaly black peat, incumbent on a hard till, and clothed with heather, and some heath, ling, and deer-hair. If the surface of these moors is not much intersected with mires, &c. they afford good pasture for young stock, both in summer and in winter. No attempt has hitherto been made, to improve any part of these bogs or deep moors, upon any scale worthy of notice, with the exception of what was done at Langwell, as already stated; and about ten acres of deep peat-bog at Weydale, within three miles of Thurso, which was pared and burned, the ashes spread and ploughed, some rye-grass and chicory were sown in it, neither of which succeeded well, as the severity of the winter frosts expands the porey moss earth, so that the roots of vegetables are blown out of the soil, unless the surface got a dressing of clay, to give it consistency.

In the parish of Canisbay, and in particular at Mey, there is a peat-bog, not thirty feet above the level of the sea, and not 300 yards from it, and in the vicinity of

 deep

deep banks of blue calcareous clay, by which that bog might be thus improved: In the winter season, during frost, cut parallel ditches, at about twelve yards distance, to drain the bog; let these be two feet broad, and three feet deep, with declivity enough to carry off the water. Let the intermediate ridges be pared, deep or shallow, as the moss may be quick, or dead; and in the following month of May, it can be burnt, and the ashes spread on the ground: plough it lightly, and give it a good dressing of calcareous clay; then, about the middle of June, sow it broad-cast with turnip and rye-grass: the leaves of the turnip will shelter the young rye-grass; the turnip may be carried off for cattle in winter, and there is no doubt of a good crop of rye-grass next summer, or even for two seasons; when it should be ploughed up for oats, giving it a top-dressing of the same calcareous clay, mixed with sea-weed as a compost: it will then yield good pasture for several years, after a good oat crop.

SECT. IV.—FENS AND MARSHES.

THERE is very little extent of this description of soil in the county, except the deep flat peat-bogs already described. The other parts of the county, (though, upon the whole flat), have many ridges of hills, or high ground, with a gentle declivity to each side; the soil not deep, but where cultivated, it is productive; and in the bottom of each valley, there is either a river, rivulet, or burn.

Mr. Traill, having partly drained the loch of Durran, has recovered about forty acres of a fenny meadow, affording bog hay, which has also given him access to marl in that lake.

SECT.

SECT. V.—FORESTS.

The only ground known by the name of forest, is the ridge of mountains dividing Caithness from Sutherland, terminating at the Ord of Caithness, which is a part of the Langwell estate. In this district, red deer, and roe, as well as black cattle, were formerly maintained; but it is now occupied as a sheep farm, and stocked with the Cheviot breed of sheep. Its extent may be about 15,000 acres of mountain, covered with heather, heath, ling, deer-hair, and wild cotton, capable of no other improvement than its present use as a sheep farm.

SECT. VI.—HEATHS AND DOWNS.

The ridges of hills, or high ground, in the parishes of Wick, Bower, Watten, Dunnet, Olrig, Thurso, Reay, and Halkirk, are principally green pasture, except the summits of some hills and knolls, covered with stunted heather, which have been, from time immemorial, used as common pasture for the horses, cattle, sheep, geese, and swine, of the town-lands in their vicinity. This is the only ground applicable to the denomination of downs, in this county; the extent may be presumed to be about 44,000 acres. Considerable tracts of these commons have, within these last ten years, been divided among the neighbouring proprietors, by arbiters mutually chosen; and such as have been divided, have been valued at from *1s.* to *2s. 6d.* per acre. Several of these downy hills were, about a century ago, covered with long heather, and abounding with grouse; but as population, sheep, and cattle in-

 creased,

creased, the heather decayed, and has now almost entirely vanished. The soil of most of these commons, is a gravelly yellow clay, under a thin stratum of black earth, formed by the decayed heather, &c. The depth from four inches to a foot, and even two feet in some hollows, or low ground; incumbent upon a horizontal flag rock, or very hard till or schistus.

Improvements.—Several tracts of these divided commons, were improved by the paring and burning system, &c. on the Earl of Caithness's estate, Sir John Sinclair's, Mr. Traill's, &c. &c.; but by far the greater part remain in their natural state, and even where such ground was pared and burnt, if not improved by good doses of manure, and calcareous matter, it was as valuable in its natural state, as after the fiery trial. The arable land in this county, being almost all formerly, and still principally, occupied by small tenants, paying from 5*l.* to 20*l.* rent, each tenant had a small flock of sheep on these commons, (on an average from 12 to 40 head), of the old native breed, and also their flock of geese, pastured with their cows and horses; the ground always over-stocked, and constantly kept bare, as vegetation had no time to make any progress before it was eaten by a set of hungry animals of different species, and the most fertile spots of these commons, were generally peeled by cutting feal, or sods, for manure to the old arable land. A tenant paying about 10*l.* rent, would peel from $\frac{1}{8}$ to $\frac{1}{6}$th of an acre annually, for compost to his land. This shameful practice is now almost entirely abolished, by the resolutions entered into by the Landed Proprietors, who make it a stipulation in the tenant's lease, that he is not to cut or use any midden feal, (sods), from the adjoining commons, &c. In

In winter 1807, a disease among the native flocks of sheep, carried them all off, so that very few of these tenants have sheep at present; and indeed the progressive division of the commons, prevents their taking any steps to renew their flocks. Many of them, from want of leases, or those of short duration, have not due encouragement to improve new ground, and, from the effect of prejudice, and old habits, are averse to any new experiment, as they term it; but the want of capital among them, is, on the whole, the greatest bar to improvement.

On that most important subject, the improvement of wastes, much additional information has been transmitted, from a number of intelligent correspondents, which will be found detailed in Appendix C.

CHAP.

CHAP. XII.

IMPROVEMENTS.

SECT. I.—DRAINING.

1. *Elkington's System.*—The mode of boring, to find the spring, is undoubtedly the cheapest, and most effectual mode of draining, not only new ground, but also the old arable land, in many parts of this county, where the subsoil is a flag rock, with horizontal beds. It points out where the water, in ground of some declivity, issues out at the level of each stratum. The principle is just, but it has not hitherto been practised, except in very few instances, principally owing to the want of persons skilled in that mode of draining.

2. *Open Cuts.*—Either old land, or new ground intended for improvements, is generally inclosed and subdivided by open cuts, or ditches, of various breadths and depths, to carry off the superabundant moisture, and to receive the water of oblique cuts from springs in any parts of the field, as described in Chap. VI.

3. *Hollow Drains.*—1. The depth is commonly about two feet, the breadth at top two feet, and sixteen inches at the bottom. 2. How filled? Where the ground has a considerable declivity, and the quantity of water not great, thin flags are laid in the bottom, and small round stones, collected off grass land, &c. are thrown in; the drain is filled with these, nine inches deep,

deep, the stones being covered with divots, (sods), or straw; the remainder of the drain is filled with the earth that was taken out of it, and it is then ready for the plough. This kind is called *rumble drains*, and are found very useful. In cases where the declivity is small, and the spring to be carried off is strong, the drain is excavated, as above stated, thin flag stones laid in the bottom, and the two sides built up with stone, six inches high; the cavity in the middle is from three to four inches broad: this is then covered with flag stones, and their top covered with sods, to prevent the earth falling into the covered cavity. The earth is afterwards thrown in, as in the rumble drain. The thin flag stones in the bottom of the drain, prevent it from choaking, otherwise worms would throw up mud, &c. to stop the passage of the water.

4. *Expenses.*—As this kind of drain is generally required in soft deep ground, the expense of excavating the drain is about 1*d.* per yard, or ell, running measure; the expense of filling the rumble drain, may be valued at 1*d.* per yard, where the stone is at hand, and that of building and filling the hollow-drain, and finding stone for the purpose, may be computed at 1½*d.* to 2*d.* per yard; the carriage of the stone is to be added, which must depend upon the distance. Any ingenious farm servant, may build these hollow-drains, and in many cases, the filling of them is done by the farm servants, at spare hours.

5. *Effect.*—When these drains are properly directed, and substantially made, the effect is very great, because the soil, formerly so wet and cold, that no artificial crop would grow thereon, will thus be made perhaps the

the most productive part of the field, and if made at a proper depth from the plough, is not subject to decay, and of course requires no repair.

6. *General Benefit.*—The draining of springs, or stagnant water, from arable land, makes the soil produce a better crop of corn, and artificial grasses, &c., than could be expected in its wet state; and new ground, intended for agricultural improvement, if spongy or wet, must be thus drained, otherwise all attempts at improving it, will prove abortive. In a county like Caithness, abounding with springs in almost every hollow, no regular arable fields could be formed, on a large scale, in many parts, without the aid of one or more of these drains, to give uniformity to the land, and make the whole field productive; and again, where spongy land is thus properly drained, the crop comes sooner to maturity than in its former state; a consideration not to be lost sight of in a cold and wet climate.

Some additional observations on the subject of draining, will be found in Appendix D.

SECT. II.—PARING AND BURNING.

1. *Soil.*—Paring and burning old land, has not been practised in this county, and this system seems to be best calculated for new land, where the soil is deep, with a rough surface*.

* Mr. Innes, of Isauld, improved 20 acres of *moss ground*, by paring and burning, at an expense of 30*s*. per acre. The best plan for improving such ground, he thinks is, to take one crop of oats, to lay it down with grass-seeds, and to let it remain for some years in pasture, by which means the ground acquires strength of itself.

In

In spring 1802, Sir John Sinclair brought five men from Westmoreland, accustomed to paring with the breast-plough, or spade. They commenced paring a tract of green common, of about 80 English acres, on Sir John's property, upon the 5th April, and in the course of that season, they pared the whole of it; the ground was at the same time inclosed with a ditch, and subdivided into four equal fields; a sufficient number of hands were employed to burn the sods, and a great part of it was ready by the end of July; the ashes spread, and lightly ploughed in, and it was sown partly with common turnip-seed, and partly with cole-seed. That season was so rainy, that the country people could with difficulty make peat enough for fuel, and of course this new improvement was not well laid down; the crops of turnip and of cole-seed were therefore light. This new land, however, being within a mile of the town of Thurso, then in a thriving state, with a branch of the Bank of Scotland accommodating all classes of society with the medium of circulation, and inspiring them with an ardent spirit for improvement, set on foot and encouraged by the active zeal and patriotic example of the proprietor, the four fields were let, in the month of September, 1802, on a lease of 21 years, at the rent of 21*s*. per acre.

The expense of this improvement may thus be estimated:

	£	s.	d.
1. Paring and burning, per English acre	1	17	0
2. Spreading the ashes	0	3	0
3. Ploughing for the seed	0	10	0
4. Harrowing ditto	0	3	0
5. Inclosing and subdividing the fields with a ditch, 5 ft. by 3 ft. deep, about	0	15	0
Total	3	8	0
Add ⅕ more, to ascertain the expense per Scotch acre	0	13	6
Total expense per Scotch acre	£4	1	6

The ground thus improved, might, in its natural state, let at 2*s*. 6*d*. per acre per annum, for pasture.

In the course of the year 1803, these five men pared about 70 English acres, in the hills of Thurso East and Skinnet, on the same estate; the whole was burnt in the course of that season, and the ashes remained in heaps until April 1804, when it was spread, the ground lightly ploughed, and sown with red oats. The result was a good regular crop of about five bolls per acre, which nearly paid the expense of paring and burning, and inclosing the land with a common ditch. The soil was formerly green pasture, on the declivity of a hill, rather damp, but not springy. This improvement was let to cottagers, or rather small tenants, who were removed from the old arable land in that vicinity, which was formed into large farms. It was given to them in lots of about 12 acres each, on a lease of 15 years, at 3*s*. per acre, for the first five years, 6*s*. the second five years, and 9*s*. the third five years of the lease. These poor people, however, owing to their want of industry, and

want

want of capital, were unable to do justice to the plan laid down to them.

Depth.—The depth of the sod pared off by the Westmoreland breast-plough, is from one to two inches thick, as the surface is burry grass, or of a finer quality. The greater part of the improved ground above alluded to, was of a friable clay, below a stratum of two inches deep of brown earth, formed by the decayed leaves and roots of grass, &c. The soil of these commons, is too shallow for the fen husbandry system, and the horizontal flag rock being near the surface, it becomes spongy and wet, soon after the surface is pared and burnt; of course the succeeding crops have not been so productive as was expected. This in a great measure may be owing to mismanagement, and want of manure, or calcareous matter, to meliorate the new turned up soil. The burning system will serve only for one crop; and if a second crop is taken, without manure, the land becomes sterile, and covered with sorrel.

The fen husbandry will answer well, even upon a shallow soil, provided, 1. The ground is well drained; 2. That there is calcareous and other extraneous manure, made up with earth as a compost, ready to lay on the ground preparative to a second crop; and 3. That no more be pared or burnt, than what can be ready by the 10th July annually, to be sown with turnip, to be eat off on the ground by sheep, in the winter and spring following. The second crop may be bear, or red oats, with grass-seeds, according to the quantity of extraneous manure laid on.

In cases where the surface is burry, but of such uniformity as to admit of paring and burning it thin, either with the breast, or fen-plough, the operation of paring

paring might continue to the end of August; the sods to be set up by pairs on edge to dry, and when sufficiently dry to keep firm through the winter, they might be collected into parallel dykes, 18 feet distant from each other; then let them stand until the first dry weather in April or May; the ridges between the dykes 15 feet broad, ought then to be ploughed and harrowed, then alternate cuts of the sod dykes ought to be taken and burnt in heaps upon the ploughed ridges, and when burnt, the ashes should be spread, and the ground sown with red oats, or bear, as the season may suit. The remaining parts of the sod dykes should then be carried off the unploughed land, and laid on the ploughed ridges, until the spaces they occupied are ploughed and harrowed: the sods or turf should then be burned in the manner above stated, on these new ploughed ridges, &c.

If there is no prospect of manure to be prepared for the succeeding year's crop, sow grass-seeds with the first crop, and as it will thus receive all the benefit of the ashes, there is little doubt of a good crop of corn, and the succeeding crop of grass will be tolerable for pasture, upon the foggage of which, a compost of lime or marl, earth and dung, should be spread in October, the second year, and should the rye-grass still keep the ground, it may be pastured for another season, then broken up for oats, and the land will thus be ready in future for a regular rotation of crops.

James Traill, Esq. of Hobbister, has improved a great extent of these green and moory commons, on his property in the parishes of Dunnet and Olrig, within these last ten years. 1. By paring and burning the surface, and previous to a second crop, manuring it with compost and marl from the loch of Durran, or sea shells, carried

carried from the shores of Duncansbay, in the parish of Canisbay, for which he pays a guinea per boat-load, of about six tons burden; and, after landing it on his own property, the shells are burned with peat-moss, yielding heavy red ashes. This mixture of burnt shells and ashes, is spread upon the new improved land, after the first crop of oats, and sown with either bear, or red oats, and rye-grass seed, which produces a tolerable crop.

The Earl of Caithness has improved a considerable tract of the same kind of common, upon the estate of Mey, by the paring and burning system; but as there was no calcareous manure laid on that land, it has hitherto produced very little corn or artificial grasses. His Lordship, however, having discovered several banks of an excellent blue clay marl, at a small distance from this pared ground, it is intended to give it a top-dressing of that calcareous clay, which, with proper management, will make the soil productive. It is afterwards to be let out in lots, of about three acres each, to fishermen, (it being within one mile of the shore of Mey); it may thus, in a few years, become a valuable acquisition to that property, being also near peat-moss for fuel, which can be procured at a moderate expense.

Ground of the above description, if of a tolerable depth, may be brought to a state of improvement by paring and burning; but experience has pointed out a more durable, although a slower process, of improving such waste land as is above described. The following plan is recommended for that purpose: 1. The ground intended for improvement being drained, and brought into a regular shape, it ought to be ploughed in the course of the winter months, and left in that state for eighteen months. 2. It should then be cross-ploughed, and, with the first dry weather, break-harrowed, as the sod will then be rotten enough to yield to the breack. Let it then have two more ploughings and harrowings, in the course of the next twelve months; the soil will then be perfectly reduced for a drilled turnip crop, with manure. Let the turnips be eaten off by sheep, during the ensuing winter and spring, and let the land be then laid down with red oats and grass-seeds; the oat crop, and succeeding hay crop, will pay all the expenses. 3. In September, after the hay crop is either cut or pastured, let a good top-dressing of either lime, marl, or any other calcareous substance, be laid on the foggage, to remain in that state through the winter, and in spring plough it up for oats. The succeeding crop to be drilled turnips, with manure; and the next bear, with rye-grass, and white and red clover seeds. The improvement may then be considered as completed; because the soil, thus managed, is ready for any rotation of crops that is practised in the county.

By this mode, the vegetative earth, and roots of grass, &c. in the original surface of the ground, is not destroyed, as by the process of paring and burning; the calcareous matter applied to the soil, will act principally, upon the decayed roots and vegetative earth, and will bring the soil to a more permanent state of fertility, than can be expected from the fiery trial; for, in the latter case, there are no decayed vegetable substances in the burnt soil, for the calcareous matter to act upon, and all that can be expected from it, is the decomposition of the natural acidity of the subsoil, turned up by the plough, which is no more than half the benefit to be derived from its action, in the slower process of putrefaction; and although some more time

is

is lost, the saving of expense, acquisition of soil, and durability of effect, more than compensates for it, particularly with such a shallow soil as is generally the case with the commons in Caithness.

The quantity of calcareous matter usually laid on such a soil is, of shell-marl, 60 cubic yards; of clay-marl, 80 cubic yards; or if slacked lime, about 70 barrels, of 32 gallons each, per Scotch acre; and should the grass foggage shew an appearance of vegetation next spring, after applying the marl, &c., I would prefer pasturing the ground for another season, and ploughing it down the succeeding spring for oats. In either case, the manure used with the first crop, after the oats, should be a compost of rich earth, and stable dung; but should the improved land be chiefly of a clay nature, a compost of peat-earth, fermented with stable dung, or sea-weed, will answer very well. On this subject I have only to add one remark more, that marl, &c., will not act upon a spongy wet soil, and every exertion should previously be used, by draining, to make the land free from the effects either of springs or stagnant water.

SECT. III.—MANURING.

1. *Marl.*—Considerable quantities of shell-marl are found in various lakes and bogs throughout this county, but owing to the want of roads, this valuable manure has hitherto been only used by farmers in the vicinity of the places where it has been discovered. Shell-marl acts well on any dry soil, but its effects are most evident on a sandy, or light dry loam. The quantity applied is from 25 to 30 cart-loads, or from 50 to 60 cubic

 yards

yards per Scotch acre, and, if the soil is deep, more especially if it be clay, even 80 cubic yards is not too much.

2. *Chalk.*—None in this county.

3. *Lime.*—There are thin veins of blue limestone in several parts of the county, but generally of inferior quality, and difficult of access; so that very little of it has hitherto been burned for manure. The best limestone, and the most abundant, is in some parts of the parish of Reay. Upon the whole, lime may be imported from Sunderland, at less expense than it can be manufactured in the county. Lime-shells may be landed, in any part of Caithness, from Sunderland, at the rate of 5*s*. per Sunderland boll of shells. This boll of shells is equal to 10 cubic feet, and it will produce from 25 to 30 cubic feet of slacked lime, which is equal to at least five barrels of the Caithness measure, (namely, 32 gallons); this would make the barrels of slacked lime at from 10*d*. to 1*s*. on the shore.

4. *Limestone broken*—Has not been used as a manure in this county.

5. *Limestone Gravel.*—There is no pebbly limestone gravel found in this county.

6. *Clay.*—Not used as a manure, except in cases of using clay feal, or turf, in compost with dung.

7. *Gypsum.*—None in the county.

8. *Shells.*—There are banks of shells, and shell sand, in

in various creeks and bays along the coast, as at Brims, in Thurso-bay; Murkle-bay, Mey-bay; and above all, at Duncans-bay in Canisbay parish, where there is an extensive bank of sea-shells, thrown in, and supplied almost every tide, many of the shells whole, and others in various stages of decay. The predominant shell or *buckie*, in these banks, is a white spiral kind of shell, of various sizes, from that of a pigeon's egg, to the size of a goose egg. A few cockle-shells, shells of spout-fish, a smooth brown shell, about the size of the cockle, various kinds of the wilk, and lastly, a small shell, of the size of a large pea, called *John O'Groat's buckies.*

The only attempt hitherto made to use these Duncansbay shells as manure, to any extent, is by Mr. Traill of Hobbister. The shell land in Thurso-bay, is used as litter or bedding for the farm-horses at Thurso-castle, and as these half-decayed shells, imbibe the horses' urine, they make a valuable addition to the stable dung.

There is also a small powdery kind of grey sand, in the bays of Sandside, Thurso, Murkle, Dunnet and Keiss, which, upon minute inspection, is found to contain a mixture of broken shells, and hence, it effervesces in diluted marine acid. Though this sand has not hitherto been used for any purpose, except mixing with lime for plaister, I am convinced, it would prove an excellent top-dressing for grass land, and increase the vegetation considerably. A similar small sand, along the shores of the Cove of Cork, and Youghall-bay, in Ireland, is carried by the peasantry of that district, in cars, for 10 miles up the country, in the spring time, and they sow it with oats on the light black mountain land, (as they term the light black soil in their up-lands); and their perseverance in this practice, is a convincing proof, that they find adequate benefit from it, in the produce of their land.

9. *Sea-Weed.*—Sea-weed or sea-ware, as it is called in this county, is driven in, after stormy weather, in the various bays and creeks in the North and East Coast of this county, and it is carried off by the neighbouring farmers for manure. During the winter months. it is collected and formed into compost dunghills, with earth; and in the spring season, when great quantities of it is driven on the shores, it is carried away, and spread upon the land, and ploughed in fresh, as manure for the bear crop, In this manner it produces a good crop of bear, but the succeeding oat crop is not so good as it would have been, had the previous bear crop been manured with a compost of earth and stable dung. The most general kind of sea-weed driven on the shore of this county is, the great tangle-weed, (*alga fucus marinus*). This weed shrinks much when reduced to a putrid state in the dunghill; six carts of it fresh, will not make above one cart from the dunghill. But the sea-weed, or bell-ware, which grows about low water mark, (*zostera marina*), is firm and fibry, with many hollow balls on its leaves: this is the *kelp* weed along the Scotch shores, and when collected through the winter into dunghills, the farmers, who use it, say, that it does not shrink; that they will have as many cart-loads to spread on the land in May, as they collected through the winter and spring; and this weed is considered to be better manure than the great tangle. Fresh sea-weed has been used as manure for turnips, but the crop failed; and it was supposed that

that the maggots collected in the putrid weed, destroyed the turnip seed, or that it was eaten by birds attracted by those maggots.

It is now perfectly ascertained, that, by the following process, sea-weed will heat and ferment peat-earth, upon the Meadow-bank system, as well as stable dung. Make a layer of peat-moss, about 15 feet broad, eight feet long, and six inches thick, then cover it with a layer or stratum of fresh sea-weed, six inches thick, and so on, stratum super stratum, until the heap is about five feet high, and tapering to a narrow ridge on the summit, like the roof of a house. The first cut being thus finished, commence another cut of six, seven, or eight feet long, at the one end of it, and so on, piece after piece, as the weed and peat-moss can be collected, until the heap is of any convenient length, and all of the same shape and height. The peat-earth used, should be of the dead moss kind, and not the quick or vegetative. It should be allowed to dry a little, after it is collected, before it is mixed in the compost. It should be just moist enough to adhere together when pressed in the hand, and to be previously cut very small, so that the heat and fermentation, occasioned by the mixture with the sea-weed, may be the more general, and operate more effectually, in decomposing the acidity of the peat-earth. A heap thus formed during the harvest and winter months, will be found in a state of heat and fermentation, in the course of a month after it is put together, and in the months of March or April, it should be completely turned over, and made up in the same shape, taking care to throw the outside of the old heap into the centre of the new, so that the whole will be ready for manure to the bear land in May, or for the turnip in June; for either it proves a very good manure, if the soil is of any other kind than peat-moss. Care should be taken, that no part of the heap or ridge of this compost, is pressed, because pressure prevents the necessary heat, and consequent fermentation, that prepares it as a manure.

To farmers who have the command of sea-weed, and of peat-moss, this discovery is of great value, as they may prepare these composts throughout the year, and thus may have abundance of manure, that essential article for raising good crops, at their command.

11. *Pond and River Weeds.*—There is no quantity of these in the ponds or rivers of this county.

12. *Burnt Earth.*—Some of the smaller tenants cut and collect the surface of commons, which they form into heaps and burn, and spread the ashes on land for a bear crop. It generally promotes acidity, and consequently the growth of sorrel in the soil; but were such ashes spread on the surface of grass land in August, it would tend to increase the growth of the after-grass or foggage. Were sea-shells, marl, or any other calcareous material burnt in these heaps, it would make good manure for any soil.

13. *Refuse of Fish.*—This manure is used on the farm of Thurso East, collected from the sheds where cod, &c. are cured, at the port of Thurso. The refuse of fish thus collected, is mixed with double its quantity of pitted earth, formed into dunghills, where it ferments, and makes excellent manure for turnips, bear, or indeed any crop produced in the county.

During the season for the herring-fishing along the coast of the parishes of Wick and Latheron, where from

from 20,000 to 50,000 barrels of herrings are annually cured, some of the farmers in that vicinity, collect the refuse of fish, salt, brine, &c., and mixing it with earth into compost dunghills, it makes excellent manure, either for old land, or new improved ground; and were the refuse of fish applied in making compost with peat-earth, in that part of the county, the quantity and value of the manure would be greatly increased, from the rapid tendency of animal substances to heat and ferment in peat-earth made up according to the Meadowbank system.

14. *Ashes.*—See above, 12.

15. *Soot.*—In a district where there are no populous towns, or villages, the quantity of soot which can be collected must be small; but in every experiment made with soot as a manure, its effects are found to be very beneficial, both in the field and in the garden. Among the small tenants in this county, when their stock of manure is done, ere their bear seed is finished, they brush the inside of the roof of their thatched houses, where the fire is commonly on the centre of the floor, and the smoke diffused through the whole building; the soot thus collected, is used in the following manner: After the seed bear is steeped for a few hours in a tub with water, it is spread on the barn floor, and soot sifted or riddled over it, until, by mixing, every grain has got a coat of soot; it is then sown in land newly ploughed, and without any other manure: the seed thus prepared, produces better returns, and even earlier, than what is laid down with manure from their dunghills, and the grub will not injure the soot-dressed bear seed.

16. *Malt-Dust.*—There is no quantity of it collected for manure in this county.

17. *Salt.*—The only instance of using salt as a manure, is in the case already stated, of the refuse salt, and fish collected from the sheds of the cod and herring fishery, which is very productive as a manure.

18. *Hair, Hoofs, Bones, Feathers.*—The only place where any quantity of these could be collected here, is at the Thurso tannery; where hair, hoofs, &c. and the dregs of the lime-pits, are put together, and prepared as manure, by the owner of the tannery. It is well known to be a powerful manure; but as these are not used separately, I can give no account of any experiments with any particular sort, unmixed with the rest.

19. *Ploughing-in Green Crops.*—Some experiments have been made, of ploughing-in a pease crop for manure, and the result proved equal to expectation. The crop was ploughed when the pods begin to form, *i. e.* when the straw is most bulky and juicy.

20. *Town Dung.*—Town dung is generally of a more fertilizing nature than stable-yard dung, and of course a smaller quantity of it will serve an acre of land. It is also very useful in making up composts, as it promotes fermentation, if it has not been already heated.

21. *Yard Dung.*—1. Long or fresh dung will answer well, either for a corn or turnip crop, on strong land, if ploughed in immediately after it is spread, because it promotes heat, fermentation, and consequent putrefaction in the soil, the effluvia from which, ascending

ascending to the roots of the young plants, assist vegetation.

2. Rotten dung, in which the heat and fermentation is on the decline, suits a light soil, because it is not so apt to blow it up by heat, and loosen the roots of the young plants of either corn or turnips, during the summer months and dry weather.

3. Comparison. In making a comparison between fresh and rotten yard-dung, I have already observed, that the one suits a strong, and the other a light soil; but it is admitted, that the quantity of fresh dung necessary to manure an acre, would not excite the same degree of fertility, had it been previously rotted, and brought to a complete state of putrefaction; of course, that it is more economical to use fresh yard-dung. It is well known that, by packing or pressure, the process of fermentation may be prevented in a heap of yard-dung, and thus it may be preserved nearly in a fresh state, until the seed-time. I consider it, however, still more beneficial to the farmer, to make up his stable dung into compost heaps with earth, because the earth, thus mixed with the dung, will, in the course of the heat and fermentation, imbibe all the fertilizing particles which might otherwise exhale from the dung. By this means the farmer may at least double his quantity of manure, and of course keep a greater extent of his arable land in good condition for agricultural purposes.

22. *Composts, and various Manures.*—Many farmers throughout this county, mix pitted earth, feal or turf, from the surface of the neighbouring commons, with their stable dung, during the harvest and winter months, but in so careless a manner, that the compost

very

very rarely heats or ferments; because they drive their cattle and carts over the heaps thus formed for manure, of course the turf, or earth mixed in the heap, imbibe very little of the fertilizing quality of the dung, and when it is spread upon their land, it tends more to increase weeds and acidity in the soil, than to fertilize it. Whereas if they formed their compost as above described, (see 9, of this Section, as to sea-weed and peat-moss), the heap would ferment, and in due time become an uniform mass of rich manure. It is well known, that if peat-earth is applied to arable land, in its natural state from the bog, it is very prejudicial to the vegetation of any plant but sorrel. Let it, however, be previously prepared, in a compost heap, with stable dung, town dung, sea-weed, or any other animal or vegetable matter to ferment, and it becomes a valuable manure for turnip, and its succeeding rotation of crops.

While the small farmers had their little flocks of sheep, feeding on the commons all day, and which they housed at night, they were daily littered with earth, heather, ferns, or whatever else could be procured to keep them dry; and during the bear-seed time, the sheep-cot was cleared out, and one cart-load of this manure, was considered equal to two cart-loads of stable or cattle dung.

For other remarks on the subject of Manures, the reader is referred to Appendix, E.

SECT. IV.—IRRIGATION.

THIS mode of improving grass land, has not been practised in this county, excepting in one instance by Mr. Traill; yet from its numerous springs, rivers, and rills of fresh water, it might be done to advantage in many parts of it. A Mr. Stephens was sent to Caithness by Sir John Sinclair, to ascertain to what extent irrigation was practicable. His report on the whole was favourable, and in particular, he was of opinion, that a number of acres might be irrigated in the neighbourhood of Brawll.

CHAP. XIII.

EMBANKMENTS.

SECT. I.—AGAINST THE SEA.

THIS county, being in general surrounded by a bold rocky shore, and having no inlets of the sea, of any extent, excepting the bays of Sandside, Dunnet, and Keiss, which are wide, exposed, sandy bays, of little depth inland, there is no opportunity of embanking, with any prospect of profit.

SECT. II.—AGAINST RIVERS.

THESE are shallow; and although they traverse, sometimes considerably in the more inland straths, and of course overflow the haughs in these angular points during rain, yet no attempt of any moment has been made, either to make their course straight, or to construct any embankment, though both might be done, in many cases, with much advantage.

CHAP. XIV.

LIVE STOCK.

SECT. I.—CATTLE.

1. *Breed.*—Until within these last 20 or 30 years, the Caithness breed of cattle were considered inferior, in proportion to their size, to the cattle of almost any other county of Scotland, being of a thin, lank make, and though hardy enough in driving to the southern markets, they did not fatten there to that advantage that better shaped cattle did. This was principally owing to their distance from market, which made their owners careless about them, and their sale depending on the integrity of a few adventurers, who annually purchased the cattle on credit; and who, if the market turned out a bad one, demanded, and commonly obtained, a considerable discount at the time of payment. The farmers also, were too much inclined to keep as many cattle throughout the winter, as the fodder they had was likely to maintain with a mild season; and, as the winter is commonly severe in this county, these animals were not fed, but merely kept alive, by a little straw, given them twice a-day, from the end of December, until the hill-pasture would recover them in May and June; it was till the end of July, they had so far recovered their strength, as to stand a journey to the southern markets. Being thus starved one half of the year, the animal necessarily acquired a thin, lank shape; yet when fattened, the beef was well mixed, and palatable.

palatable. Their weight, sinking offal, would in general be about from 50 to 70lb. per quarter.

Within these last 20 years, Sir John Sinclair imported the Galloway breed of cattle, and a cross between a Galloway bull, and the native cows, improved the breed of working cattle, but the cross was not so well calculated for droving, or for milch cows. A few years ago, Sir John imported 20 cows and a bull of the real Skye breed, and he gave them, at prime cost, to two farmers on his estate, the one occupying a Highland, and the other a Lowland farm, situated within four miles of the town of Thurso. It was supposed at the time, that the pasture and climate of this county would not suit them; but, the result of four years experience has proved the contrary, and, although the cows were not young, they have rather improved, on both farms, and the young stock from them are very promising, both in regard to pile, size, and cylindrical shape. They are housed in winter, and, on the Lowland farm, fed with straw and turnip.

Several other Proprietors have imported bulls of the Argyle, Skye, and Assynt breeds of cattle. A cross between the Argyle and the native cows, improves the breed, as to pile, size, shape, and quantity of milk, where the pasture is good, and when they are well fed in winter. A cross from Skye and Assynt bulls, produces a well-shaped breed, and being hardier, they suit better the more Highland parts of the county. Dunlop and Buchan cows have likewise been imported, principally as being excellent milkers. In short, by a perseverance on the part of the landholders, to increase the breed of the Argyle, Skye, and Assynt cattle, among their tenants in this county, with the aid of turnip-feeding during the winter, the Caithness breed of black

cattle,

cattle, have already improved, and will still continue to improve, in value and appearance, so as not to be inferior to those of the neighbouring counties of Sutherland, Ross, and Inverness, either in size, pile, or shape.

The cross with the Argyle bull, is reckoned the best for beef and milk; and both the Argyle and the Skye breeds are quicker, and hardier for work, than the Galloways, who are slow in their pace, soft, and heavy.

2. *Rules pursued in Breeding.*—In dairies of from 20 to 30 cows, a calf is reared between every two cows; the calf is allowed to suck the cows, and is then turned off to a separate inclosure, or apartment, until it is about three months old, when its allowance of milk is discontinued.

In smaller dairies, the proportion of calves which the farmer chooses to keep, are hand-fed with milk, not being allowed to suck the cows, so that they may be turned to pasture along with them; but it is admitted, that an equal quantity of milk, sucked by the calf from its mother, does it more benefit, than when given in a vessel. Much depends, however, upon giving them, while young, the milk quite warm, and furnishing them with plenty of pasture, and water, as they grow up.

3. *Size, Constitution, Form.*—In regard to these particulars, much depends upon the breed, and mode of feeding, &c. The Galloways fatten to the greatest size, say from five to six hundred weight, sinking offal; the Argyle next. The Argyle, Skye, and Assynt breeds, have, in general, the best constitution, and are preferred by drovers accustomed to Highland stock.

The Galloways are polled; the other breeds have horns, well shaped, and pointing upwards.

4. *Colour.*—The prevailing colour, among the Galloway breed, is branded; that of the Argyle, Skye, and Assynt breeds, is black.

5. *Food—Winter.* During the winter months, the black cattle are fed on straw, in houses or byres, built for that purpose; and on farms where the turnip husbandry is carried on, turnips are given them morning and evening, and a little straw, after the feed of turnips, to chew their cud upon. In general, they are allowed to wander over the fields or commons, during the middle of the day, in easy weather. It is not reckoned safe to feed cows in calf with turnips, as they are said to be apt to cast their calves, if turnip-fed. They are fed with straw only until they calve, and for a few days after, with an occasional feed of bear or oat chaff, scalded with boiling water. A few sheaves of bear are sometimes boiled, both corn and straw, and given to new-calved cows, and the water in which the bear was boiled, is given them luke-warm, to drink; or warm water, with some oat-meal or seeds in it, given them for the first two or three days after calving. At the end of a week, they are fed with turnip, either boiled or raw, and with hay or straw occasionally, as it can be spared; also cabbage, or any other green food out of the garden. There is no oil-cake used in this county for feeding cattle.

Summer.—From the severity of our climate, and having no water-meadows, there is very little pasture

for

for cattle in the fields, before the end of May, except rye-grass, which starts early, and is commonly as luxuriant about the end of April, as it is through the month of May.

Upon extensive farms, where rye-grass is sown for pasture, cattle get a good bite in April, which puts them early in good condition for the market; and the young cattle, turnip-fed in winter, who get rye-grass in April, are as fit for the market at two years old, as those, straw-fed in winter, with the chance of common pasturage in summer, are at three years old. It is too often the case in this county, that the farmer keeps too many cattle, both in summer and winter, for the quantity of food provided for them.

6. *Soiling Cattle.*—This is not a general practice in this county. A few farmers in the vicinity of the towns of Thurso and Wick, soil milch cows of a large breed, in order to increase the quantity of milk for the market. If these cows were fed in open stalls, or sheds, in summer, in place of close houses, and combed and brushed, their milk would be of a better quality, and the cows more healthy, than they are at present.

7. *Water.*—Milch cows, or other cattle, pastured in the field, are driven to water, (either a river, burn, or pond kept for that purpose), twice a-day, if there is no water in the pasture ground itself; and soiled cattle, either get water in the house, or they are driven to it in the same manner.

8. *Salt.*—Very few farmers use salt in feeding cattle, either in summer or winter, although its benefit to cattle is well known: the high price of that article prevents

vents the use of it in feeding cattle. If Government would permit salt, duty free, for agricultural purposes, as well as for the fisheries, it would prevent disease in cattle, and increase the produce of bear and oats, by pickling the seed-corn.

9. *Management.*—In such a remote district as the county of Caithness, much attention to the management of black cattle is not studied, beyond the rearing of a few for sale, to drovers who annually visit the county, from the end of May to the end of September, and drive such as they purchase to the southern markets.

The next care is, to make as much butter and cheese as can be done, from their milch cows. Upon extensive farms, when the farmer can contrive to give abundance of artificial and natural pasture to about 20 milch cows, he makes a bargain with a dairy-woman, to deliver to him a certain quantity of butter and cheese, and a well-reared calf between every two cows, at the end of the season, at an average, about two stone of butter, and two stone of cheese, of 24lb. Dutch per stone, for each cow, according to the breed of cows, and the quantity and quality of the pasture. Where these are good, the farmer reckons from 4*l.* to 5*l.* from the produce of each cow, including the value of the calves. The butter, for some years past, has sold at from 21*s.* to 24*s.* per stone, and the cheese at from 6*s.* to 8*s.* per stone. About thirty years ago, the common price of butter was 5*s.*, and cheese 2*s.* 6*d.* to 3*s.* per stone. In those days, butter was made up in conical lumps, of 24lb. each, but now it is packed in casks, containing from 72 to 84lb. each.

The usual time of milking the cows, is at nine o'clock

o'clock in the morning and eight o'clock at night, when they are brought from the field to byres, or folds, for that purpose; but where they are fed on artificial grasses, they are milked thrice a-day, in June and July, and of course yield much more milk, than when they are milked only twice a-day. Much, however, depends upon the pasture, and the sort of cattle.

10. *Fattening.*—The few cattle fed here, either for family use, or for the consumption of the two small towns of Wick and Thurso, are generally aged cattle. A few head are fed in March, April, and May, but in general, they commence feeding them in the house, in November, by giving them, for the first month, as many turnips as they can eat, with oat-straw: water is given them twice a-day, but, from the quantity of turnips used, little water serves them. They are combed and brushed morning and evening, and kept clean. When they become in good condition, and their appetite fails, a sheaf of bear is boiled, and given them, which they eat greedily, and it sharpens their appetite for turnips and straw; and latterly, some feeds of oats are given them, to make the beef firm. Thus, in about two months, as the beast was in good condition when stall-feeding commenced, it is ready for the butcher, who sells the beef at from 5*d.* to 6*d.* per pound, and the tallow at 8*d.* to 10*d.* per pound.

A better mode of feeding, though little practised in this county, is to feed them with boiled potatoes, and cut straw, or boiled yellow turnip with straw, and giving occasionally a boiled sheaf of bear, to sharpen their appetite. They would, by this mode, be sooner ready for the butcher, than by feeding with raw turnip.

A farmer in the parish of Thurso, fed an ox of the

Devonshire breed, (one he had worked in the plough), in spring 1811, and when slaughtered, the ox produced 136lb. of melted tallow, and the four quarters exceeded 9cwt. He was fed in the common mode, with turnip, straw, hay, and corn. The beef sold at 6*d*. per lb.

11. *Dairy.*—The only exception, to the mode of dairying already stated to be the practice in this county, is on a farm belonging to James Traill, Esq. Sheriff of the county, which has been already described, in Sect. 2, Chap. VIII.

12. *Stalls, Yards, Sheds.*—During the summer months, cattle are, in some cases, kept all night in yards, or folds, but the more general practice is, to house them both summer and winter. Open sheds are very seldom used, though I am convinced that, cold as our climate is, if cattle were kept all night in open sheds, in place of close byres, they would be more hardy, keep a better pile of hair, and of course, would be of greater value to drovers, who send them to the markets in the south of Scotland, and even to England.

In close *byres*, the best mode of binding cattle is, by iron collars round the neck, which are attached to a short chain and ring of the same metal, to stakes fixed parallel to, and two feet from, the wall, or gable; the ring moving up or down upon the stake, as the animal raises or depresses its head. Whenever cattle are fed with turnips, this ring should be kept down low on the stake, by means of a pin fixed in the stake for that purpose, (to be taken out at pleasure). By thus keeping down the cattle's head, while eating turnip, they are not apt to choak, by swallowing large pieces of turnip,

as

as they are apt to do, when they can raise their heads above the level of the carcass.

Before the introduction of iron binders, the only mode of binding them in their byres, was, by a collar and shank, made, (like a rope), of twisted green birch, *waddies*, or twigs. These were purchased at from 6*d*. to 18*d*. per dozen of binders, (called *nasks*); and in old times, the tenants on whose farms any birch-shrubbery grew, paid a given number of these binders annually, to their landlords, as part of their rent. These binders served only for one season; and the poorer tenants made similar binders of rushes or straw. Cattle frequently broke these in the night-time, and would gore the beast next to them, before any person could come to relieve them. This often brought on a decay, and the gored beast, after lingering perhaps for several months, would die. The lungs and viscera would then be found grown together in one mass.

13. *Ascertaining, by weighing alive, the Meat gained by Food in a given time, &c.*—Owing to want of machines for weighing the animal alive, I have not found that any experiment of this kind has been made, or ascertained in this county. It is generally understood, that the weight alive, of a beast in good condition, is double the weight of the four quarters when killed.

14. *Distempers.*—In this county, black cattle are subject to various distempers, and although some of these are pretended to be cured by superstitious charms, by old women, &c., yet there are none in the county, who professionally know the cure of those distempers to which cattle are subject.

The most formidable of these distempers is called the

murrain, (provincially, *hasty*), because the animal dies soon after it is seized with it. The symptoms are these: the animal swells, breathes hard, a great flow of tears from its eyes, it lies down, and in some cases, is dead in the course of a few hours. The carcass should be buried in the earth, as soon as possible, for the contagion is apt to spread among the cattle on the same ground or pasture.

About 25 or 30 years ago, this distemper was frequent and general, on the Highland straths, when the pasture ground was in many places covered with a thick shrubbery of birch, &c., which shaded the luxuriant grass about their roots, from the rays of the sun, and consequently made it noxious to the cattle pasturing there. Those shrubberies are now entirely gone, and the recurrence of this distemper is not so frequent.

In those days, when the stock of any considerable farmer was seized with the murrain, he would send for one of the charm-doctors, to superintend the raising of a *need-fire*. It was done by friction, thus: upon any small island, where the stream of a river or burn run on each side, a circular booth was erected, of stone and turf, as it could be had, in which a semicircular, or highland couple of birch, or other hard wood, was set; and, in short, a roof closed in on it. A straight pole was set up in the centre of this building, the upper end fixed by a wooden pin to the top of the couple, and the lower end in an oblong trink in the earth or floor; and lastly, another pole was set across horizontally, having both ends tapered, one end of which was supported in a hole in the side of the perpendicular pole, and the other end in a similar hole in the couple leg. The horizontal stick was called the auger, having four short arms or levers fixed in its centre, to work it by: the building

having

having been thus finished, as many men as could be collected in the vicinity, (being divested of all kinds of *metal* in their clothes, &c.), would set to work with the said auger, two after two, constantly turning it round by the arms or levers, and others occasionally driving wedges of wood or stone behind the lower end of the upright pole, so as to press it the more on the end of the auger: by this constant friction and pressure, the ends of the auger would take fire, from which a fire would be instantly kindled, and thus the *need-fire*, would be accomplished. The fire in the farmer's house, &c. was immediately quenched with water, a fire kindled from this *need-fire*, both in the farm house and offices, and the cattle brought to feel the smoke of this new and sacred fire, which preserved them from the murrain. So much for superstition.—In order to expedite the raising this need-fire, several gimblet-holes, in the ends of the auger, were previously filled with bruised gunpowder and tinder. It is handed down by tradition, that the ancient Druids superintended a similar ceremony of raising a sacred fire, annually, on the first day of May. That day is still, both in the Gaelic, and Irish dialects, called *La-beal-tin*, *i. e.* the day of Baal's fire, or the fire dedicated to Baal, or the Sun.

I have seen another mode of cure prove effectual, which may be thus described: A few pieces of sooty divots, (turf), from a thatched roof, are put in a metal pot, with a coal of fire, to cause a sooty smoke to ascend: the diseased animal would then be brought, and with its tongue held in a person's hand, its nostrils were held in the smoke for about 15 minutes, causing much saliva to run from its mouth and nostrils; then, about two English pints of ale, mixed with an equal quantity of the decoction of fresh plantain roots, would be, by

means

means of a horn, poured down the animal's throat, in a lukewarm state; and in the course of a few hours, this dose, if necessary to be repeated. An animal thus treated, on the first symptoms of the distemper, is generally cured *.

A distemper, called the black quarter, or *spaul*, prevails among young cattle of one or two years old.—*Symptoms*: The animal looks languid, refuses its meat, and upon examining the carcass, some quarter of it sounds as if there were feathers, or chaff, below the skin. In the course of a day or two, he dies, and

---

* I recollect, in the year 1798, being quartered in a small village in the county of Cork, (Ireland), one afternoon as I was conversing with my landlord, his maid informed him, that one of his milch cows was sick, and had fallen down in an adjoining inclosure. Curiosity led me to accompany him to see what was the matter with the cow; she appeared much swelled, breathed very hard, and tears running from her eyes; in short, every symptom indicative of the distemper called in Scotland, the murrain, or *basty*. A cow-doctor was instantly sent for from the village. When he arrived, he said the cow had the *blisters*, and having got two men to open the animal's mouth, he pulled out the tongue, and showed two blisters or bags under it, each about the size of an apple, of one inch and a half diameter; he then put a needle through them, and cut them with a knife, when air and some reddish water issued out of them; he rubbed the tongue with salt. In a few minutes the swelling, or inflation, subsided, the cow got on her legs, and ate some hay given to her.

This man informed me, that unless these blisters were cut, the cow would in a few hours die from suffocation, as she could not breathe, and that her flesh would soon become putrid. He showed me the plant that caused blisters to cattle, growing in that inclosure. It grows in springy ground, and if bruised, will blister the human skin sooner than cantharides; the common name of it in Scotland, is the *water-coal*. I could not find out the Linnean name of it. In July, it bears a light-coloured purple flower on a slender stalk. I know the plant very well, in the fields.

The symptoms of the blisters, and that of the murrain, among cattle, in Scotland, are so similar, that I am induced to think that both originate from the same cause, and that the after-contagion proceeds from the putrid effluvia of the dead animal.

upon

upon taking off the hide, the diseased quarter looks black, or livid, as if the flesh and blood had been congealed together.

The only rational cure, or rather preventive for it, known in this county, is to take some blood from the calves in July. It is generally the stoutest, and fattest beasts, that die of this distemper.

In former times, superstition pointed out the following singular mode of preventing the spreading of this distemper: When a beast was seized with the *black-quarter*, it was taken to a house where *no cattle were ever after to enter*, and there the animal's heart was taken out while alive, to be hung up in the house or byre where the farmer kept his cattle; and while it was there, it was believed, that none of his cattle would be seized with that distemper.

The *sturdy*, (water in the head), is a distemper affecting young cattle of one, two, or three years old. The symptoms of this disease are, that the animal moves in a circular course, and cannot move in a straight line for any distance. The only cure known here, is, to cut out the watery bag, formed within the skull, and when properly managed, it effects a cure.

Blood-gruss, (bloody urine), is another complaint that black cattle is subject to in the summer season, on a change of pasture, particularly from a lowland to highland pasturage. The Highlanders pretend to point out the plant which causes this complaint. It is a brown plant, with three or four short stalks, from the same root. It grows in wet moors or bogs, among heather, and during the hottest and driest summer weather, its beardy stalks are covered with dew. When the Highlanders find a beast troubled with this complaint, they search for either a *trout*, or a *frog*, and put

put it alive down the animal's throat, as a cure: others consider warm milk, poured down the beast's throat, a specific for the bloody urine.

Elfshot, is another disease to which black cattle are liable. The *symptoms* are, that the beast refuses its food, looks languid, and breathes hard. The old knowing women, rub and search the hide of the beast, where they pretend to find holes, not in the hide, but in the membrane under it. These they rub well with their fingers, and bathe them with salt and water. When all the holes are thus found out, and rubbed, two table spoonfuls of salt, are dissolved in half a Scotch pint of cold water, a little of it poured in the ears, and the remainder poured down its throat; and after some time is thus spent, in going through this process, the animal generally recovers. Some silver is put in the water while the salt is dissolving in it. I do not pretend to account for this distemper or cure, but I have felt what they termed holes, and have seen all the ceremonies performed.

Working oxen, and even other cattle, are sometimes subject to costiveness, which occasions a great heat in their stomach and intestines; they refuse their food, and generally lie down, and soon get lean from want of nourishment. The cure commonly recommended is, to take about one ounce of gunpowder; mix it with about two ounces of salt butter, made into balls, and put them down the animal's throat: repeat the dose, at the end of twelve hours, if necessary. The second dose usually relieves the animal, as physic, and he soon afterwards returns to his food.

WORKING OXEN.

The number of oxen kept on each farm, depends upon its extent; that is, a pair of oxen is necessary for every cart used on the farm. The smaller class of tenants work four oxen a-breast in their ploughs, with a driver who goes backwards, between the two centre oxen. In some cases, two oxen and two ponies are yoked together a-breast in the plough, with a driver, as above described. This is generally the case with poor tenants, who cannot afford to have four of either species, and whose cattle are too small and weak for working two in a plough.

A few farmers in this county have purchased large oxen from the southern markets, and work them by pairs in the plough, without a driver. These, when properly broke to a long pace at first, will plough, in the course of the day, as much as an ordinary pair of horses; but not so much in the same space of time. They require to be better fed than the ordinary kind of oxen, and during the hard work of spring, they ought to get corn, as horses do, to enable them to stand the labour. From the difficulty of getting a supply of these oxen, (none of that large size being reared in the county), their price is as high as from *40l.* to *50l.* per pair. From the slowness of their pace, and the consequent unwillingness of ploughmen to work them, the farmers in this county generally prefer horses for the plough, notwithstanding their original cost, the expense of keeping them, and the heavy tax imposed upon them by the Legislature.

Age.—Oxen are wrought at three years old, but they are not fit for regular work until they are five; they are then wrought in the cart until they are ten, and even, twelve years, if their teeth stand. They are, about that

that age, fed with turnips, straw, and corn, for the butcher, or sold to drovers, who purchase them under the designation of *runts*, and drive them to the southern markets.

Food.—The food for oxen in winter, is straw, chaff, and turnips, where that esculent is raised. In the months of April and May, they are occasionally fed with hay, but get no corn, except large oxen for the plough, as already stated. During the summer months, when out of yoke, they commonly feed on the same pasture with the milch cows. There may be a few instances of their being soiled with artificial grass in summer, but the practice is by no means general in the county.

Shoeing.—Oxen are not shod in this county: when good roads are made, the farmer may find it necessary to shoe his oxen.

SECT. II.—SHEEP.

I. *Breed.*—Until about eighteen, or twenty years ago, the only breed of sheep in this county, was the old native horned; their fleece was generally white, but in every flock, there were some with black wool and some with grey, and some of them were polled. The quality of their wool was good; though inferior to the Shetland wool, yet superior to the wool of the black-faced sheep. The weight of their carcass was from 7 lb. to 10 lb. per quarter. In those days every tenant, and even cottager, had a small flock of sheep; they pastured on the extensive commons and moors, both summer and winter, and they commonly were housed at night; but unless during a very deep snow storm, they

they received no food in the house, and even then, only a little hay or straw was given them. They were not so subject to disease, as the black-faced, or the Cheviot breeds. The distemper to which they were most liable, was the rot, (dropsy), for which no cure was known. In the spring-time they followed the plough, and fed upon the roots of mugwort, which was considered wholesome for them; and it tended to diminish the quantity of that pernicious weed. Of their wool the tenants' wives made clothing for the family, and any surplus, was sold at the country fairs, either in yarn, blankets, scoorins, (a kind of flannel), or black greys, a kind of cloth made for the men's coats and great-coats. The wedders were sold in the summer and autumn, to butchers from Thurso and Wick, at from 4*s*. 6*d*. to 6*s*. each. In those days good mutton was sold at 1½*d*. to 2*d*. per pound.

In October 1792, the President of the Board of Agriculture, (Sir John Sinclair), ordered 500 old ewes, from the Cheviot hills, to the farm of Langwell, in order to try how the Cheviot breed of sheep would thrive on the soil, and in the climate of Caithness. The ground having been pastured by black cattle all that season, until the sheep arrived, of course the green pasture was bare; but there was abundance of heather, heath, ling, and deer-hair, on the hilly part of the farm.

The succeeding winter was stormy, with much snow. The flock, notwithstanding, did very well, very few casualties having happened from disease or want. The principal loss was owing to the depredation of foxes. No turnip had been provided for them, and they required very little hay. This flock increased rapidly, so that in 1800, they were about 3000; the

wedders

wedders and draught ewes, were annually driven to the southern markets, in the month of August, and the wool was packed up for the English market. The steep banks of the rivers of Langwell and Berriedale, being covered with a close shrubbery of birch, &c. &c. some wool from every fleece was torn off; hence it took about nine fleeces to make a stone of wool of 24 lb. Dutch; but many of these bushes being thinned, and others decaying fast, it now does less damage to the fleece. As the flocks increased, Sir John Sinclair removed the tenants, who occupied the inland parts of the Langwell estate, and placed them in new colonies near the sea shore, with small lots of land, where they were employed as fishermen or day-labourers.

The estate of Langwell contains about,

	English Acres,	*or*	*Scotch Acres.*
Arable land,	443	....	354
Good pasture,	775	....	620
Under brushwood and coppice,	848	....	678
Moor and moss,	25,236	....	20,189
Total contents,	27,302	....	21,841

In 1792, the gross rental of this estate was only 282*l.* 6*s.* 9*d.*, including the salmon fishery: the population was then 86 families, or about 516 souls. In 1805 the Proprietor let the principal part of the estate in two sheep-farms, at 1200*l.* per ann.: he had besides another sheep-farm, since let, and a considerable number of small tenants, and colonists near the sea-shore, who paid a small rent. The President of the Board of Agriculture has thus given the most undoubted proof, that the Cheviot breed of sheep, is as hardy as any other breed,

and

and much more valuable, from the superior quality of their wool.

Major Innes of Sandside, having seen how the Langwell flock succeeded, purchased a flock of the black-faced sheep to stock a farm on his estate, on the north coast of Caithness, which was formerly chiefly occupied as pasture for black cattle. He then was of opinion, that the black-faced was more hardy than the Cheviot. He is now so convinced of the superiority of the Cheviot breed, that he has changed his flock entirely to that breed, of which he has about 1000 on that farm, and finds them a profitable concern.

System.—The flock is smeared with a mixture of tar and butter annually, in the month of October, which enables them to stand the inclemency of the weather, on the heathy mountains, under the care and direction of the shepherd and his dog.

1. *Crosses.*—No cross was tried with the Cheviot breed until the year 1810, when two rams with Spanish blood, were brought to Caithness, to try the effect upon the fleece. The result will soon be ascertained.

2. *Food.*—*Winter.* Wherever it can be accomplished, the lambs and year-olds, are fed with turnips, during the months of October and November; which is considered a specific for the braxy. The remainder of the flock are brought from the higher grounds, nearer the sea-shore, during the winter months; but except with a very severe storm of snow, when a little hay is spread out to them, they receive no other food, in winter or summer, than what they pick up on their usual pasture ground.

Spring.—There is no water-meadow prepared in this county, nor is there any other artificial food provided for the flock, during the time of dropping their lambs. The ewes and their young lambs, require to be brought, therefore, at that trying season, to the best sheltered dry pasture that can be procured. It is contended, that the Cheviot lambs require more attention at this season, than those of the black-faced breed.

Summer.—During this season, the year-olds are kept on the highest and most heathy part of the sheep-walk, as the pasture, in low ground, is apt to purge them too much.

Salt.—I have not found that salt had been given to any of the flock throughout the year.

3. *Folding, or Housing*.—None of the flocks at Langwell or Sandside are folded, and of course no manure is collected from them.

The native breed of sheep were all housed at night by the country tenantry, and their dung was considered of much benefit as a manure for their arable land, particularly for a sandy soil. A cart-load of it was reckoned equal to two cart-loads from the cow-byres or stables, it being of a warm stimulating quality, and produced an early crop of bear.

I have not ascertained what extent of land could be manured from a given number of sheep, because no account of the kind has been kept by any farmer. Much depends upon the kind of litter with which they are bedded. Where fern can be procured to litter them, the manure is of a superior quality to that which is procured from straw or dry sods. Dried peat-earth is a good litter, because it absorbs their urine, and of course increases the quantity and quality of the manure.

Effect

Effect of Housing on the Flock.—The only effect on the flock was, that they did not require to be smeared, as is necessary for the flocks kept constantly in the fields. Thus an annual expense was saved, of from 6*d*. to 8*d*. per head. Their being kept in the house at night, preserved them also from the attacks of foxes and dogs.

Number kept.—Previous to the year 1792, and to the division of the commons, almost every farmer and cottager had his flock of sheep, from half a dozen to 40 head. The aggregate number in the county might be computed at about 20,000. Since that period, the number of small farms having been diminished, several extensive commons divided, and latterly, in spring 1807, almost all the native breed in the county having died of the scab and other distempers, hence there is not one-eighth of that number in the county, exclusive of the Cheviot flocks in Langwell and Sandside. Several attempts have since been made by the tenants to rear small flocks, by purchasing lambs from Lord Reay's county, or Strathnaver; but they commonly die the second year, owing, as is supposed, to the range of pasture being so much contracted, by the division of commons. This is a considerable loss to these people, as they must now purchase English cloth, &c. for their families, in place of the cheap and warm clothing formerly made by their wives from the wool of their little flocks.

4. *Management.*—1. *Breeding Stock.* This is the only species of stock that was formerly, or is now kept in this county, there being no consumption in it to encourage the farmer, in the low districts, to buy in a

 stock,

stock, at least to any extent, for fattening on turnips or otherwise.

The present stocks on the Langwell and Sandside estates, are managed by shepherds, hired from the southern counties of Scotland, near the Cheviot hills; and their mode of managing is of course the same as practised in those counties.

5. *Live and Dead Weight, and Meat gained by Food.*—As there are no feeding farms in this county, I have not found that any experiments have been made, to ascertain accurately the meat gained by food. The four quarters of a three year old Cheviot wedder, fattened for the butcher, weighs from 40 to 60 lb. Amsterdam, equal to, from 10 to 15 lb. per quarter, and even some are as high as 20 lb. per quarter. The general average of those slaughtered in this county, is about 12 lb. per quarter, and that of the native breed from 8 to 10 lb. Their weight alive, is commonly double the weight of the four quarters dead.

6. *Wool.*—*Weight.* The weight of a fleece of the native breed, would be about 2 lb.; that of the Cheviot breed will average about 3 lb. *i. e.* including the weight of the smearing materials. It takes, on an average, about eight fleeces to make a stone of 24 lb. Amsterdam.

Quality.—The quality of the wool from the Cheviot breed, is the best of the mountain breeds in Great Britain, though not equal to the Ryland, or South-down, and far less to the Spanish. Experience proves, that the Cheviot breed, reared in Caithness, retains the original quality of their wool. The wool of the

the native breed, would perhaps sell at half the price of the Cheviot wool, when that of the black-faced sheep would sell at only one third of what the Cheviot wool gives.

Price.—The only wool now for sale in this county, is the Cheviot, which in 1795, sold at about 27*s*. per stone, and this year (1810), it sold at 42*s*. per stone of 24 lb. The average price between these two periods, was about 30*s*. per stone. It is generally purchased by agents employed by the Leeds manufacturers, little or none of it being manufactured in this county.

7. *Distempers.*—The most predominant distemper, among the Cheviot breed, in this as well as other counties, is the *braxy*, as it is called, and no effectual remedy has as yet been discovered, to cure it. It is admitted by the sheep farmers, that feeding the lambs and hogs, or year olds, with turnips, in October and November, prevents this distemper, because this esculent purges them. Blindness is another complaint to which they are liable. When the shepherd discovers that a sheep is becoming blind, he rubs her eyes with salted butter, and keeps the animal in the house for a few days, the film forming on the eye then disappears, and the sheep recovers its sight, yet frequently this is only a prelude to other distempers, as blindness proceeds from the general unhealthy constitution of the animal.

The scab or leprosy, is a prevalent discasse among sheep. This prevails less among sheep that are smeared, than among the native breed, who do not undergo that operation. But smearing will not protect sheep from its contagion, in case a scabbed sheep comes near them, as their breath infects the sound animal.

animal. Smearing the scabbed sheep with butter, mixed with flour of sulphur, and putting some of it down their thoats, will cure them, by repeating the operation twice or thrice, as the case may require. Rubbing their skins with a decoction of tobacco, will have the same effect; but this can be done only on a small scale, or among small flocks.

8. *Number kept on different spaces of Land.*—The estate of Langwell, is by far the best for a sheep-walk in this county. Its superficial contents, as already stated, is

	English Acres.
Arable land	250
Under brushwood	500
Mountains, hills, or deep peat-bogs, covered with heather, ling, deer-hair, &c. &c.	22,250
Total	23,000

Experienced shepherds have informed me, that the whole of that estate, would maintain from 8000, to perhaps 9000 sheep of the Cheviot breed, which is equal to two acres and a half to a sheep. Throughout the other parts of the county, the native sheep are accustomed to pasture on the commons, along with black cattle, horses, swine and geese, so that no idea can be formed, what extent of such commons is necessary for the pasture of a sheep or flock.

SECT. III.—HORSES.

1. *Breed, and Breeding*.—About 40 years ago, the only breed of horses in this county, (except Gentlemen's saddle-horses), was small *garrons*, of from 11 to 14 hands high. These were reared by the farmers, and a considerable portion of the year-old colts, (provincially *staigs*), were sold to horse-dealers, who annually exported them, in the month of August, to the Orkney Isles, and in return, they brought back cargoes of garrons of from four to seven years old, which they sold at fairs, to such farmers as required a supply of horses for the plough. In those days, the horse-dealers purchased the colts at from 15*s*. to 30*s*., and they supplied the county farmers, with Orkney garrons, at from 3*l*. to 5*l*. each. Four of these horses were commonly yoked abreast in the plough. They were fed on straw in winter, a little hay in spring, and no corn at any season of the year. Their harness was simple, and the driver's wages was only about 5*s*. in the half year, besides victuals.

The few colts that are now reared in this county, are sold to the horse-dealers, at from 50*s*. to 4*l*. each, and the garrons which they import from Orkney, fetch, in the Caithness markets, from 10*l*. to 15*l*. sterling each, according to their age, size, and quality.

Within the last 20 years, as the size of farms increased, two-horse ploughs were introduced, and, of course, horses of a larger size were purchased, for that purpose, from the southern counties of Scotland, at a considerable expense. Notwithstanding, however, the increased price of horses, very few of that breed have as yet been reared in this county, principally owing

 to

to the want of proper stallions. This is a greater loss to the farmer, than people in general are aware of; because he has no means by which to supply his stock of farm-horses, but perhaps going, or sending to the distance of 200 miles, to purchase them. Another disadvantage attending this importation of horses, is, that during the first year, they require much care, as they are liable to colds and disease, from the change of climate, and even of food.

As the interest of the landlord and tenant, in this, as well as many other cases concur, it is a duty incumbent on the Caithness Proprietors, to remedy this evil, by contributing a fund, to purchase and maintain a stallion of a strong, hardy breed, to be kept in a centrical part of the county, that the farmers might have the use of him, at a reasonable hire or fee, say 15*s.* for each mare, and 2*s.* 6*d.* to the keeper. By this means, in the course of a few years, there would be a regular supply of plough-horses reared in the county, which would be more hardy and durable than the second-hand horses taken from a distant market. The farmer would of course be enabled to procure more extraneous manure to improve his farm, be more punctual in the payment of his rent, and latterly, be more able to give an increase of rent at the end of his lease.

2. *Number kept to Space of Land.*—This depends much upon the extent of the farm, and whether the soil is naturally dry or wet. The seasons here being more variable, and, (if I may use the expression), shorter, than in the southern counties, from the difference of climate, of course more cattle is required to work the same extent of land, in seven months, than in ten months of the year. In general, a plough and pair

pair of horses is required for every 35 or 40 Scotch acres of arable land, on a farm under a rotation of four or five years' shift, besides oxen for carts and harrows. But the greater the extent of the farm, the less stock proportionally will work it.

3. *Work performed.*—During the long days of summer, a pair of good horses, yoked twice a-day, will plough from one half to three quarters of an acre of land, with a narrow furrow, according as it may be clover-ley, stubble-land, or fallow.

4. *Food.—Price.* Farm-horses are fed on oat-straw, from the middle of October, till March, or April, with a feed of corn per day, when they can work in the field. From thence, to the month of July, they are fed on hay, and an occasional feed of oats; and from the beginning of July to October, they are fed on green hay, or foggage. In some cases, they are pastured in the field, but in general they are housed at night. It is found from experience, that horses, kept in the stable at night, will last longer than horses who are left in the field.

Price.—Plough-horses, from four to seven years of age, cost from 30*l.* to 40*l.* each, or from 60*l.* to 80*l.* per pair. If of the heavy, or draught kind, and above that age, the price is in proportion to age, size, &c.

	£	s.	d.
5. *Expenses.*—1. Food.—The average expense of food for one plough-horse per annum, is	20	0	0
2. Shoeing per annum, about	1	0	0
3. Decline in value per annum, about	2	10	0
And 4. Harness cost first 3*l*. 3*s*., may last six years, is per annum	0	10	6
Supposing the horse lives to 22 years, the annual expense is	24	0	6

6. *Distempers.*—This useful animal is liable to various distempers; among others, the following:

1. Glanders, or suppuration of the glands about the tongue, } Contagious.
2. Farcy, or leprosy of a virulent kind, } Contagious.
3. Scab, } Contagious.
4. Strangles, or common cold.
5. The gravel, or stoppage of urine.
6. Bees, or bots, in the head.—Incurable.
7. Bots in the stomach and intestines.—May be expelled by drastic purges.
8. Cholic.

The glanders is cured by cutting out the diseased glands, which adhere to the jaw-bone, and constant attention afterwards in washing the wound with sour urine, twice a-day, until it heals.

The farcy is cured by some external and internal medicines, given by quacks in the county.

The scab is cured by a decoction of a shrub, found in deep moors, or peat-bogs, called *wild myrtle*, mixed with fish-oil, and the sores frequently bathed with it.

The strangles, or common cold, is also a swelling and

and suppuration of the jugular glands, which at times subsides of itself, but frequently a suppuration takes place, the purulent matter is thrown out at the nostrils, and there is even danger of suffocation, unless the diseased gland is cut, and, by means of plasters, the matter drawn off, until it heal: in these cases it is also contagious.

A few years ago, I had a young horse, troubled with worms, or bots, in his stomach, and the horse-doctor continued, for ten days, giving him various drugs, to no effect. I was advised by a neighbouring farmer to give him a handful of a plant, (provincially called *creeping bur*), among his oats, and the next day I gave him 20 drops of *oil of savin*, in a bottle of warm ale. I repeated these doses the third day after. The worms were expelled, and the horse continues healthy. I now once a-year give a handful of that plant, cut small, in the oats, to all my horses. I cannot give the Linnæan name of the plant. It is generally found among short heather, on barren, heathy knolls, in this county; a creeping, burry, pea-green plant; and as it seems to be a most powerful medicine to expel worms in horses, its use should be more extended.

For the colic, I have seen from half a drachm to a drachm of laudanum, given in a bottle of warm ale, prove an effectual cure.

SECT. IV. V.—ASSES, MULES.

No asses are used in this county; but some mules have been brought to it, of too small a size, however, to be of any real service. If a well-sized jack-ass were

were imported, for the purpose of getting mules of a size fit for the plough, it would be very beneficial to farmers of every description, as they are very hardy, after they are seven years old, live to a great age, are easily fed, not subject to distempers, and bear a cold climate.

SECT. VI.—HOGS.

1. *Breed, and Breeding.*—The native breed of swine are small, short bodied, and generally of a reddish or grey colour. There are a few black, but the grey are reckoned the best. There are likewise some crosses with the English and Chinese breeds.

2. *System.*—Hitherto no regular system has been attended to, in the rearing of hogs. A few are reared by the small tenants and cottagers, near undivided commons, where they are allowed to wander about with their cattle and horses, during the summer and autumn, either feeding on the stunted grass, or turning up the soil in search of roots, &c. Others put a ring of stout wire in their snouts, to prevent their turning up the soil, and then pasture them along with their milch cows, until the beginning of winter, when they feed on grains about the barn doors; or, the ring being taken out of their snouts, they grub roots out of the arable land, and pick up any potatoes left in the soil. In short, very little care or expense is bestowed on them, until the beginning of February, when they are confined to the house, and fed on the refuse of potatoes, cabbage, and latterly oats, and a feed of boiled bear

bear occasionally. During the last fortnight's feeding, their drink is mixed with oatmeal seeds, and during the months of March and April, they are slaughtered, either for family use, or for sale in the weekly markets of Thurso and Wick. The average weight of a hog thus fed, is from 80lb. to 100lb. Dutch, the four quarters, which are sold at from *3d.* to *5d.* per pound, and the lard is sold at *5d.* per pound.

4. *Sties.*—The only sties used for them are small huts, made of turf, erected at the end of the cottage, or the tenant's stable or byre, with a door or hole large enough to admit the animal to pass out and in.

5. *Distempers.*—The only distemper to which this breed of swine is liable, is the leprosy, which is occasioned by starvation, improper or *warm* food, or carelessness in not attending to keep the animal in an airy clean place. This distemper may easily be prevented by care, by having clean airy sties, and occasionally giving them sulphur in their food.

A sow commonly brings from six to nine young ones at a litter. After these are a month old, either the whole, or a few of them are sold, at from *5s.* to *7s. 6d.* each; and in the course of from nine to twelve months, the purchaser will make from *30s.* to *40s.* by the sale of the pig, if properly fed. That is a clear proof, that the rearing and feeding of hogs, is a profitable concern for the small tenant or cottager; but in this remote corner, the great bar to the progress of this branch of rural economy, is the want of markets.

Experience has now shewn, that under a proper system, potatoes, yellow turnips, ruta-baga, and artificial

ficial grasses, can be raised here as well, and equally productive, as in any other county of Scotland. Let the land proprietors therefore import a larger breed of swine, to be distributed among their tenants and cottagers at prime cost, expenses included. Let it be a condition, when leases are granted, that the farmers shall annually plant an additional quantity of potatoes, for feeding swine; let yellow turnip seed be given them for the first year, to be sown, and the crop used in feeding a hog or more, as they can accomplish it; and let these farmers also sow some red clover for summer food to the pig; and lastly, let a market be established in each of the two towns of Thurso and Wick, where the small farmer will find a dealer to purchase his pork when ready. If such a plan as this were fairly begun in this county, the cottager would, in a few years, be enabled to pay from 20*s.* to 30*s.* per acre for his lot of arable land, in place of 10*s.*, now, in many cases, paid with much difficulty; and he would have treble the means he now enjoys, for the support of himself and family.

The Irish cottager pays from 3*l.* to 4*l.* per acre for his potatoe garden; but from the refuse of his crop only, he annually rears a pig, which will do more than pay his rent. At present, the Caithness cottager throws the refuse of his potatoes, &c. to the dunghill, in place of rearing a pig with it.

SECT. VII.—RABBITS.

THERE are rabbits in the sandy links of Reay, of Duncansbay, Freswick, and Reise.

1. *Breed.*

1. *Breed.*—The breed is a mixture of the common brown-backed, or silver-haired.

2. *Food.*—Their food is principally the grass on these sandy links, on which they usually pasture, but during the summer and harvest, as these sandy links are not inclosed, they commit depredations on the corn fields in their vicinity. Any rent paid for these small warrens, is but trifling.

SECT. VIII.—POULTRY.

1. *Turkies.*—Until within these last 20 years, there were no turkies reared in Caithness; but now, flocks of them are to be met with at the farm-yards of almost all the landholders, and principal farmers throughout the county. The turkey is a very tender bird for the first three months, and during that time, it requires much care and attention in rearing, but after that period, they are as hardy as the common poultry. There is no regular market for them here; the few that are sold, fetch from 2*s.* 6*d.* to 3*s.* each.

2. *Geese.*—The county of Caithness, from time immemorial, was reckoned the best in Scotland for rearing geese, and where the greatest number of them were reared. This was partly owing to the arable land being divided into small lots or farms, having in general extensive commons of green pasturage, in their neighbourhood, where the young flocks of geese roamed at pleasure, without any trouble, except bringing them home at night during the summer months, to preserve them from foxes. Many of these farmers also, were bound to pay their landlords so many geese in kind, as

as a part of their rent, which induced them to persevere in rearing annually flocks of geese. The price of a goose, about 30 years ago, during the month of August, before the stubble was ready for them, was from 7*d.* to 9*d.* each. These kind of payments, having been, in general, converted into a money-rent, and some of the commons being divided, of course fewer geese are now reared than formerly. Their price, in common with almost every other article, has much increased. It is now about 2*s.* in August, and 2*s.* 6*d.* after they are stubble-fed, about the end of harvest. Their feathers, (uncleaned) are now sold at 24*s.* per stone of 24lb. each. There are no geese reared in the Highland District of the county, from the want of the green pasture necessary for them while young.

As an instance of the instinct or natural sagacity of geese, it is known to be a fact, that a flock of geese were sent in an open boat from Forse, in the parish of Latheron, in this county, to Mr. Gray of Skibo, on the south boundary of the county of Sutherland, a distance of about 30 miles of sea, through the Murray Frith, and that, in the course of a few days, the same flock landed again at Forse, after having swam their way back.

3. *Fowls.*—About twenty years ago, while it was the general custom to pay fowls and eggs in kind, every farmer and cottager's wife, reared annually flocks of common fowls, from which they paid the stipulated number to their master, and generally had a few for sale. In those days a fat fowl was bought for from 3*d.* to 4*d.*, a cock at 2*d* to 3*d.*, stout chickens at 1*d.* to 1½*d.* each, and eggs at 1*d.* per dozen: now, since these payments in kind have been partly con-

verted

verted, the country people are not so industrious in rearing fowls. Hens now sell at 1*s.*, cocks at 10*d.*, chickens at 4*d.* to 6*d.* each, and eggs at 3*d.* per dozen.

4. *Ducks.*—These are not so generally reared as common fowls, but where a water-pond is near the farm-house, the farmer's wife commonly rears a few ducks; very few of them are brought to market; such as are sold, fetch about 6*d.* each. I have known several attempts made to rear ducks from the eggs of wild ducks, but whenever the young ducklings were able to walk, they either run away, or concealed themselves in holes or crevices, so as not to be found.

SECT. IX.—PIGEONS.

Advantages and Disadvantages.—The advantage of a well stocked pigeon-house is no doubt of great convenience to a family, because, where they are well attended to, a supply can be had from them during ten months in the year.—The only disadvantage attending them is, the depredations they commit on the corn in spring and harvest. This is seldom so great in the immediate vicinity of the pigeon-house, as at the distance of a mile or two, and, in this county they are not so numerous as to be considered of any moment. If they pick some of the seed in spring, they also destroy grubs in ploughed land, and the seeds of weeds.

Pigeon-Houses.—There are six pigeon-houses in this county, all built with stone and mortar; one in a conical form, of about seven feet diameter within, and 18 feet high

high, the inside of the wall being subdivided into holes for hatching. The others are built square, and roofed in, according to the common form. Where the pigeons are regularly fed, and otherwise attended to, the house is well stocked, with a numerous flock: but in general they are neglected, and in some cases, rats get into the pigeon-house, and destroy the young: starlings also, often destroy their eggs.

As there are no pigeons reared for the market in this county, I could obtain no account of their comparative expense and profit.

Pigeon dung is the very best manure for raising onions; and a ley of their dung, is allowed to be the best remedy for scouring coolers, to prevent blinking the worts in breweries.

SECT. X.—BEES.

The management of bees is not well understood in this county, and the climate is too cold for that industrious insect. Yet during a warm dry season, wild bees are general, and numerous in this county. They build their nests or hives in old walls, dykes, or in dry mossy knolls in moors, where heather bloom is abundant. Bee-hives have been tried in several gardens in this county, but have not been attended with success. In the year 1798, Sir John Sinclair, being determined to give a fair trial to the bee husbandry on his Langwell estate, he ordered 21 hives, with a stock of bees, from the southern counties, and employed a person who was recommended to him, to superintend them, through that winter, &c. They were brought to the garden of Langwell, situated in a warm valley, sheltered from the north and west by the Morven mountains. This superintendant was supplied with a stock of honey, to feed the bees when necessary, through the winter and spring. The result however was, that all the bees died during the winter and spring, it is said, in consequence of the superintendant or manager, having used the honey for his own purposes, and neglected the bees.

Regarding the superior sorts of Live Stock, some additional information will be found, in Appendix, F.

CHAP. XV.

RURAL ECONOMY.

SECT. I.—LABOUR.

SERVANTS.—1. *Price in Winter.* When farm-servants are engaged half yearly, the winter half year commences on the 28th November, and terminates the 20th June. For that term, a good farm-servant, fit to hold the plough, thrash corn, kiln-dry, and mill it, &c. receives about 3*l.* 10*s.* of wages, and 3½ bolls of cost, at 8½ stone, or 136 stone per boll; and lads, not fit to manage the plough, 40*s.* to 50*s.*, and three bolls of cost.

A woman-servant, fit to work at cart, &c., gets from 20*s.* to 24*s.* of wages, and two bolls of cost. Both the men and women get land and dung, to plant from one to four pecks of potatoes, in case they have agreed to remain during the ensuing summer half year. In cases where a male servant is married, he stipulates to have a milch cow maintained, and his wages are about 3*l.* Any married servant, capable of acting as a superintendant or *grieve*, has commonly 8*l.* in money, and seven bolls of cost, with maintenance for his cow summer and winter. Few labourers are hired by the day, through the winter months. In spring, they receive from 1s. to 1*s.* 6*d.* per day, according to the work in which they are employed. A woman hired by the day, receives from 8*d.* to 10*d.* during the spring months.

2. *Sum-*

2. *Summer.*—The male servants receive the same cost and wages in summer as in winter, with the addition of a chopin, (two pints), of skimmed milk per day, to ploughmen, till the middle of October. Women have the same cost and wages, as during the winter half-year. Herds from 15*s.* to 20*s.* of wages, and two bolls of cost, which is commonly given half oat and half bear-meal. Day-labourers employed to cut peats or hay, receive from 1*s.* 8*d.* to 2*s.* per day, and one meal, and for any other work by the day, about 1*s.* 6*d.* Women hired by the day, to assist at peats or hay, from 9*d.* to 10*d.* and one meal, and for weeding turnips, 8*d.* per day.

For raising marl, or such hard work, men get 2*s.* 6*d.* and women 1*s.* per day.

3. *Harvest.*—Men engaged for the harvest, receive from 30*s.* to 35*s.* of wages, and three firlots, or 102lb. in meal, *i. e.* such as can build corn-ricks, &c. The women engaged for the harvest, about 20*s.* of wages, and half a boll of meal for cost, from the commencement of shearing, until the corn and potatoes are ingathered.

A man hired by the day for harvest, gets 1*s.* 6*d.* and a woman 1*s.* per day.

4. *Year's Earnings.*—An unmarried farm-servant, fit for the plough, &c. earns in the year, from 6*l.* to 7*l.* in cash, three bolls and a half of oat-meal, and as much bear-meal; milk equal to 10*s.* 6*d.*, say 126 English quarts, at 1/4*d.*, and about two bolls of potatoes; the whole may be estimated at 14 guineas, reckoning the oatmeal at 20*s.* per boll. In cases where the keep

of a cow is added, the total year's earnings may be estimated at from 18*l.* to 20*l.* per annum.

Women employed by the year, as farm-servants, earn from 5*l.* to 6*l.* 10*s.* reckoning oatmeal at 20*s.*, and potatoes at 8*s.* per boll.

5. *Rise of Labour in given Periods.*—About the year 1770, the wages of farm-servants, such as were fit to hold the plough, and thatch the house, &c. (as was then the common expression), did not exceed from 6*l.* to 8*l.* Scotch, that is from 10*s.* to 13*s.* 4*d.* sterling in the half year. Women, and boys for herding cattle, from 3*s.* 6*d.* to 5*s.* sterling in the half year. They commonly received their victuals in the family, and if they got cost, the quantities were three bolls, half oat, half bear-meal to the men, and from one and a half to two bolls to the women half yearly, which is about one-fifth of the wages they now receive. In those days, a ploughman could purchase a suit of clothes, and a pair of shoes or brogues, at 10*s.* sterling; now he will pay 9*s.* for a pair of shoes, and even 25*s.* for a pair of boots to follow the plough.

In those days, labourers by the day, were seldom employed. Those who were hired to cut peats or bog hay, received from 8*d.* to 1*s.* per day, and a meal. Women from 4*d.* to 6*d.* per day; about half of what they now receive.

6. *Hours of Work.*—During spring and summer, ploughmen go out with the ploughs at six, and return at 10 A. M.; they again yoke at two, and return at six P. M The same hours are observed with carts.

Farm-servants, at any other work, consider from six in the morning, to six at night, as their regular working hours;

hours; taking an hour to breakfast, and an hour to dinner, from the beginning of March to the end of September, and during the winter months, as long as there is daylight. The same rule is observed by labourers hired for the day.

The above is the working hours observed on the best regulated large farms; but servants employed by the smaller tenants, get their victuals in the family, their master commonly works along with them, and of course no regular hours are attended to, but they work during almost all the daylight throughout the year, with the exception of meal hours, and occasional rest or relaxation.

7. *Piece-work.*—Labourers are employed by piece-work in making ditches, building dykes, trenching ground, quarrying stone, &c. as has been already noticed. Whenever work can be done by the piece, labourers should not be employed by the day, as they are apt to trifle away their time, and require to be well watched.

8. *Cottagers attached to Farms.*—Before the division of commons, almost every farmer had a cottager or two on the outskirts of his farm, bounding on the common. The cottager paid a limited number of days' labour in spring and harvest, to the farmer, and a trifle of money rent; he had a house and cabbage garden, and in many cases a cow and a few sheep, which pastured on the common; and he collected food for the cow through the winter, partly for work, and partly otherwise. Some of these cottagers paid a day in the week to the farmer, by the name of *cottar-work.* But where commons are divided, these cottagers disappear, from the want of means to feed a cow.

Upon a few farms, cottages are built for farm-servants who are married and have families. These resemble the *hinds*, as they are denominated in East Lothian, Berwickshire, and other counties in the south of Scotland.

As farms are enlarged, and the new system of husbandry becomes more general, this description of servants will become more advantageous, as they are more likely to remain in the farmer's employ, not being so flighty as young lads; and as their family grow up, their children may be usefully employed at weeding turnips, &c. &c. The greatest obstruction to this system is, (where coal is not the fuel), providing a sufficient quantity of peat for them through the season, because that is not so easy for the farmer, as furnishing a given quantity of coal, where it can be had at an easy rate.

9. *Expense proportioned to the extent of Land.*—The expense of cottages is already stated in the Third Chapter, as to Buildings.

SECT. II.—PRICE OF PROVISIONS.

The price of every article of provision has been increasing progressively, during this eventful war. About the year 1787, the price of beef in the Thurso and Wick markets, was from 1½*d.* to 2*d.* per pound, and now in 1810, from 4*d.* to 6*d.* per pound; mutton is now seldom below 6*d.* per pound, and some as high as 7*d.*; pork, in the season, about 4*d.* to 5*d.*; common fowls about 1*s.* each; geese and turkies as already stated. In the Thurso market, there is still a good supply of excellent fish, at moderate prices; for instance,

good

good haddocks, at 1*d.* each, or 1*s.* per dozen; cod of two feet long, at 6*d.*; ling, holibut, and turbot occasionally, in the same proportion.

For these several years past, oatmeal has been at from 20*s.* to 30*s.* per boll of 136lb., and in 1807, it was as high as 40*s.* per boll, and bear in the same proportion; potatoes at from 8*s.* to 10*s.* per boll of 384lb.; butter at from 10*d.* to 1*s.* per pound; common cheese at from 3*d.* to 4*d.* per pound. The farmer's ancient beverage, when he went to market formerly, was a bottle of good ale at 1*d.*, now ale of inferior quality, sells at 3*d.* per bottle, or 6*d.* per Scotch pint.

SECT. III.—FUEL.

THE fuel generally used in this county is peat or turf, cut in the peat-bogs or mosses, which abound in almost every part of it.

Coal is annually imported from Sunderland and the Frith of Forth, to the two ports of Thurso and Wick, which is used in the parlours and bed-rooms of the better class of the inhabitants; but peat is commonly used in the kitchens. About 20 years ago, peat was sold in the two towns at about 3*d.* per cart, which contained about a cubic yard; now it is sold at from 9*d.* to 1*s.* per cubic yard, according to its quality. English coal is imported to Thurso and Wick, at from 21*s.* to 30*s.* per ton, and Scotch coal at from 18*s.* to 21*s.* per ton of 20 cwt.

Circumstances of Management of Fuel, meriting Notice.—In a district where peat-bogs are abundant and extensive, and not far distant from any habitation, very

very economical rules for its management are not to be expected. They have two modes of cutting peats, horizontal, and perpendicular; *i.e.* when the peat-moss is not more than from one to two feet deep, the peat is cut perpendicularly, by a spade, called a *turskill*. This instrument is about nine inches long, with a heel at right angles to the right side, two inches and a half broad, with a perpendicular socket, (being the continuance of the heel), to embrace the wooden handle, about four feet and a half long; and in it is fixed a *foot-step* of wood, a few inches above the termination of the socket of the spade. The peat-cutter, holding the handle with both hands, with one push of the right foot, drives the spade into the moss, so as to cut out a peat, or turf, 12 inches long, and two inches thick: the breadth of the heel regulates the thickness of the peat. A woman stands on the bottom of the bank, whose business it is to seize the peat, as soon as the cutter gives it a jerk, to separate it from the bottom, and she throws it on the right side of the bank, where people are employed to spread them to dry. The mode of cutting peat horizontally, is the mode practised in many districts, and is too well known to require being particularly described.

English coal is much more economical than Scotch coal, as it cakes, and is, of course, more durable. I have seen one-fourth of coal-culm, and three-fourths of clay, beat up like mortar, with a little water, and then made into balls of about four inches in diameter: a few of these, when dry, put into the grate, with a few peats, make a good and an economical fire.

CHAP. XVI.

POLITICAL ECONOMY:

CIRCUMSTANCES DEPENDENT ON LEGISLATIVE AUTHORITY.

SECT. I.—ROADS.

BETWEEN the years 1776 and 1785, several lines of road were lined out, and formed, by annually calling out the inhabitants, to perform their six days statute labour on the King's highways. This was principally accomplished by the influence and directions of Sir John Sinclair, who assembled above 1200 men in one day, to make a line of road through Bencheilt, (a mountain in the parish of Latheron), which opened the communication from Dunbeath, direct through the interior of the county, to the town of Thurso, on the north coast; and, on another day, the same zealous friend to improvement, collected a considerable number of hands, and carts, to make a road through the Causeway-Myre, a deep bog, three miles long, in the parish of Halkirk, two miles to the south of the *Spittle-hill.* In this bog, some vestiges are still visible of a road, made by the order of Cromwell, during his protectorship, which gave it the name of the *Causeway-Myre.* These lines of road were formed in a convex manner, about 18 feet broad, but not *metled;** of course they could not be durable, consisting

* Metling a road, means covering it with broken stones, or gravel.

merely

merely of turf, or other soft materials, and requiring annual repairs.

About 20 years ago, Sir John Sinclair, as Representative of the County in Parliament, obtained an Act for commuting the statute labour of this county, and the commutation has been annually collected, at the rate of 30*s.* sterling for every 100*l.* Scotch of valued rent, as established an. 1702. It produces in all about 550*l.* per annum; which sum is annually expended on the repair of the roads, under the direction of the Commissioners of Supply. Several pieces of road have since been repaired and mettled, but the sum is too small to render that general benefit that was expected from it, and the people pay it with reluctance, especially in those parts of the county, where none of it has hitherto been expended on the roads. Some indeed contend, that if, during the period this commutation has been levied, the statute labour had been annually performed in kind, greater advantage would, before this time, have been derived from it.

The Proprietors of the county, however, have now embraced the benefit held out by a late Act of Parliament, granting an aid to the Northern Counties of Scotland, of one-half the estimated expense necessary to make the great lines of road, more especially from the Ord to Wick, and from Wick to Thurso. For that purpose, the Heritors have assessed themselves to the amount of five guineas per annum, for every 100*l.* Scotch of valued rent. The line of road from the Ord to Wick, commenced in the year 1811, and will be completed in the course of this year, (1812). The road from Wick to Thurso, is also in a fair train. As the great lines of road will be partly made at the public expense, the commutation for the old statute labour will soon be applied,

applied, in making and mettling the bye-roads, which will be the first effectual step towards the improvement of the county; as it will enable the industrious farmer, to carry his produce to market, and carry home extraneous manure, in the winter season; a measure at present impracticable, owing to deep and broken roads.

1. *Turnpikes.*—None are as yet established in this county; but by the County Road Act, tolls may be levied.

2. *Materials.*—There is either a flaggy rock, or free-stone, and in some cases whin-stone, to be had along all the intended lines of road in the county, with the exception of those places where deep bogs intervene; and there, knolls of a hardy dry gravel are to be had, for making or mettling the road.

3. *Expense.*—The expense of forming a road, 24 feet broad, and mettling it 12 feet broad in its centre, from 9 to 12 inches thick, may be computed at about 2*s.* 6*d.* per yard, or 210*l.* per Scotch mile of 80 Scotch chains long. In some cases, however, it is considerably higher.

4. *Farm-Roads.*—General Sinclair justly observes, that the proper direction and construction of farm-roads, merits much consideration, as they ought to be made subservient to the purposes of draining, and disencumbering the fields of stones, as well as of giving convenience for working up their several divisions. On his own estate of Lybster, he found it necessary to form almost every road, on stones placed in ditches three feet deep, and of considerable width, covered with the

coarsest

coarsest part of the clay taken out of them. Except on a few farms, such roads are seldom attended to. The expense must depend upon the breadth of the road, and the depth of mettling.

5. *Concave.*—None.

6. *Convex.*—All the roads formed in the county are convex, as best suited to carry off the water, but if well mettled, very little convexity is necessary, excepting where cart-wheels are conically made; in that case, a considerable convexity in the shape of the road, tends to lessen their friction.

7. *Application of Water.*—Not artificially applied to scour the roads.

SECT. II.—FERRIES.

There are two ferries from Caithness to Orkney; one at Scarscary, on Mr. Traill's estate, and the other at Huna, on the property of the Earl of Caithness.

At Scarscary, besides four fishing-boats, there is one large boat, for carrying horses, cattle, &c., and one small boat for passengers.

About fourteen years ago, the number of *stags*, or young horses, exported to Orkney, was about 320; and about 80 old horses, at an average, came from Orkney each year. But at present, there come from 250 to 300 horses from Orkney to Caithness.

At the above period, the freight of a horse, or *stag*, was only 1*s*. 4*d*.; at present it is from 3*s*. to 4*s*., according to circumstances.

The

The freight of the small boat, to Scapa, Stromness, or any part of the main-land of Orkney, 12 or 14 years ago, was 10*s*. 6*d*. It is now 21*s*. To any island near to Caithness, it is still 10*s*. 6*d*.

The proprietor asks no port-charges, but the ferry-man pays 16*l*. Scotch per annum, as ferry-rent.

At Huna, Captain Robertson of Warse informs me, that only one ferry-boat is kept for the passage between Caithness and Orkney. The fare is 9*s*. each time it crosses the ferry, which is twice a-week with the mail. For maintaining this boat, the postmaster is allowed only 40*l*. a year, by the Post-Office, which he says scarcely pays the expense. The 9*s*. fare goes to pay the hands. He says, that when the mail went but once a-week, the allowance was 25*l*. a-year; so that he has but 15*l*. more for performing double the work. The above fare of 9*s*. is for four hands. When more hands are requisite, the fare is 10*s*. 6*d*. If cattle were carried, the fare would be 21*s*., or somewhat less, if there are but few, according to agreement, and circumstances. If the full fare is made up, a single passenger may go for one shilling. It is seldom, that cattle go from Caithness to Orkney; but many are brought over from the latter, by a boat of larger dimensions, provided on that side of the ferry. The rates are not known, or fixed, depending on the agreement that can be made with the boat-owner, and according to the urgency for a speedy passage.

SECT. III.—IRON RAILWAYS, CANALS.

This county is not yet arrived at that progressive state of improvement, to require, or afford, iron rail-ways;

ways; and there are no canals in it. Indeed, as three-fourths of the county are bounded by the sea, canals are less necessary than good roads.

SECT. IV.—FAIRS.

There are about 20 annual fairs held in this county, a list of which will be found in the Addenda, No. XI.

SECT. V.—MARKETS.

There are weekly markets, held in the towns of Thurso and Wick, upon Fridays, where cattle, beef, mutton, pork, fish, &c. &c. are sold. The population, however, being but small, the sales at these markets are trifling, and merely a local accommodation.

SECT. VI.—WEIGHTS AND MEASURES.

By the statutes of King David II., who began to reign during the year 1330, the weights and measures of the county of Caithness, were the standards of Scotland. The law is thus recorded, in his Regiam Majestatem, chap. 14: "It is statute be King David, that "ane comon and equal weight, quhilk is called the "*weicht of Caithness*, (pondus Cathaniæ), in buying "and selling, sall be keeped and vsed be all men with-"in this realm of Scotland.

2d, "The law of God commands, thou sal not have "in thy bagg twa manner of weichts, ane mair and "ane

"ane less, neither sall thou have in thine house diverse "measures, ane great and ane other small, bot thou "sall have ane richt and just weicht."—Deut. cap. 25, 13th and 14th verses.

3d, "Gif ony man, agains the commands of God's "law, use any unequal weicht, he sall pay to the "King's Justice *aught kye* for his fault and transgres-"sion."

The circumstance, that the weight of Caithness should be the general standard, is not at all to be wondered at, for the town of Thurso, in Caithness, was formerly the great mart for trade, between Scotland and Norway, Sweden, Denmark, and the powers of the Baltic, and in consequence thereof, the weights established in that town, might, with great propriety, become the standards of the kingdom.

1. *Land.*—Land is measured in this county by the Scotch chain of 100 links, equal to 24 Scotch ells, or nearly 25 English yards long, which is about one-fifth larger than the English land-measure—1 acre=4 rood =160 falls=5760 square ells. In some cases, however, the English chain is used.

2. *Corn.*—The tenantry throughout the county use a vessel, by them called a *half firlot*, containing two pecks, and they give eight fills of it, for a boll of bear or oats. In measuring corn with it, the vessel is heaped, but in measuring meal, the roller is used to take off all above the stave. The regular corn-measure of the county, is either by firlots or by half bolls. The firlot should contain one bushel and a half and three quarts, Winchester measure, and of course, the half-boll measure contains double that quantity, so that the boll of

four firlots is just six bushels and twelve quarts, Winchester measure. Bear, oats, or malt, are measured by this standard. There is very little wheat, pease, or beans raised within the county, but the boll of these articles is understood to be only two-thirds of the bear boll, or four bushels and eight quarts.

Oatmeal is sold by the boll of 136lbs. Dutch, or eight stone and a half, and bear-meal at nine stone, or 144lb. The Dutch pound, is 17 ounces and a half Avoirdupoise.

3. *Liquids.*—All liquids, the produce of the county, are measured by the Scotch pint. The measure is made of Cornwall block-tin, thus:

One inch within its margin, or rim, there is a pin of the same metal; when it is filled to that pin, it holds 16, but to the top it holds 18 gills. In measuring spirits, it is filled to the pin, and ale is filled to the top: so that the pint of spirits is 16 gills, and the pint of ale 18. Twenty Scotch pints is reckoned one anker; $2\frac{1}{2}$ Scotch pints are nearly equal to an English gallon. Foreign spirits, and wine, are measured by the English gallon, and its subdivisions.

4. *Wood*—Is measured in the log, by the solid or cubic foot, or 1728 cubic inches; in deals, by the square foot of 144 square inches.

5. *Wool*—Is sold by the stone of 24lb. Dutch, and when English wool is retailed in the shops, it is sold by the English pound of 16 ounces.

SECT.

SECT. VII.—PRICE OF PRODUCTS COMPARED WITH EXPENSES.

For these last ten years, the price of every article for farming purposes, has been increasing annually. Servants' wages, as has been already stated, have also increased, and are still likely to increase, owing to the prolonged war in which we are necessarily engaged. Notwithstanding these disadvantages, the rent of land is equally on the increase. The farmer has hitherto been able to meet these increasing demands and expenses, from the great prices given for corn and cattle, for the last six years. Corn has sold at from 20*s*. to 30*s*. per boll, and the price of cattle has increased in the same period of time, from about 3*l*. to 4*l*. 10*s*. and even 6*l*. per head. This must have been occasioned by our successful commerce and manufactures, having diffused wealth through the nation, so that even this remote corner of the island feels its effect. Others again attribute it to the superabundant paper currency, and consequent depreciation of money. The prohibition of distilling from grain, has injured the Caithness farmer in particular, because he must annually lay down a proportion of his land in bear, (or bigg), to keep his land in heart, as a repetition of oat crops would prove injurious to the soil, and yet for the produce of his bear there is now, (an. 1810) no market. The general observation among the country people is, that if the price of victual keep above 20*s*. per boll, and the present price of black cattle continue, the farmer will make a shift to go on; but if either or both fall below the above prices, three-fourths of the tenantry of

this

this county will go to wreck, unless the price of labour, labouring utensils, and the rent of land fall in proportion.

In the course of my inquiries, I could not find that any accurate account was kept of the incidental expenses attending a farm, in order to proportion it to the produce of the farm. Few farmers are inclined to take that trouble, or to give such comparative information, should they have it in their power, because they will naturally suspect, that such inquiries proceeded from political views, connected with an increase of taxes, or from local motives, in order to raise their rents.

SECT. VIII.—MANUFACTURES.

It may not be unworthy the reader's attention, to have a short account laid before him, of the trades, or manufactures, which formerly existed in this remote district.

About forty years ago, exclusive of the shoe-makers who resided in the Towns of Thurso and Wick, there were one, two, or more itinerant shoe-makers in every parish, who went to the farmers' houses, and made shoes, or rather *brogues*, for the whole family, including the farm-servants, at the rate of twopence per pair; the shoe-maker and his apprentice being fed in the family during the time they were so employed. The farmer found the leather, hemp, and rosin. The leather being generally tanned by himself, cost him very little, and upon the whole, all the family were furnished with shoes at from 1*s*. to 1*s*. 6*d*. per pair. At that time the town shoe-makers sold, what was called dressed, or curried leather shoes, at from 2*s*. to 3*s*. per

3*s*. per pair. Now (1809) there are few or none of these itinerant shoe-makers.

There are no woods or shrubberies in the county to furnish bark for the farmer; taxes are high, and tax-gatherers more vigilant. The country people, both tenants and servants, purchase their shoes, (no doubt of a better quality than brogues, but not more durable), at from 7*s*. 6*d*. to 10*s*. per pair, for men's shoes, and 5*s*. 6*d*. to 6*s*. 6*d*. for women's shoes. Farm-servants pay from 20*s*. to 25*s*. for a pair of boots to follow the plough, whereas, in 1760, they wore *rillins* in the spring season. These were made of an oval piece of raw, or untanned horse or cow-leather, drawn together round the foot, by *thongs* of the same materials, through holes made in the margin of the skin, or piece of hide, and being thus faced on the upper part of the foot, with the hair towards the foot, they were warm and flexible, and they kept the mould of the ploughed land from annoying the feet. A pair of these might be valued at fourpence, and would last five or six weeks. The other parts of the servant's dress, were then simple, and cheap, as will afterwards be shewn.

About 40 years ago, weavers were settled through the country, for weaving the simple fabricks prepared by the farmers' wives and servants, for their own, and their husband's and children's apparel. Every farmer, and even cottager, had a small flock of sheep, of the native breed; these annually supplied a fleece of good wool, which the *gudewife* and her family carded and spun into yarn, either for blankets, for scourens, (coarse flannel), or *black greys*, (a kind of broad-cloth), or for Highland tartan, for the wear of the *gudeman*, herself and family, and perhaps some of it for sale, to the servants, in part of their wages, or to others. The weaver generally charged from 2*d.* to 4*d.* per yard for weaving it, and a peck of oat-meal was given as a bounty, for warping the web, and preparing it for the loom.

When the web was returned from the weaver, the *gudewife* got it washed in warm water, and if it was necessary to *full* it, that operation was thus performed: The house-door was taken off the hinges, laid on the floor, the web laid on it hot out of the water, then three or four women sat down round it, on a little straw, at equal distances, and all being ready, bare-legged, by the signal of a song, (similar to the *ràn-de-vashe* in Switzerland), each applied her soles to the web, and they continued pelling and tumbling it on the door with their feet, until the web was considered sufficiently fulled; then it was stretched out to dry, and was ready for the family tailor, or for sale, as the case might be.

If the tailor was wanted, he was sent for, and maintained in the family, until the clothes was made, and for his trouble, he received, annually, a quantity of victual, bear, or oat-meal, as might have previously been agreed upon. If the cloth was for the market, blankets sold at 10*d.* per yard, scourens at 8*d.* to 9*d.*, cloth at 1*s.*, and tartan, if the dyes were good, at 1*s.* to 1*s.* 4*d.* per yard. The *gudewife* was generally competent to dye the woollen yarn, either of a *blue*, *red*, *green*, *yellow*, or *black* colour, as might be required. That simplicity of life and industry are now gone, and instead of these native fabricks, nothing will do but broad-cloth from Leeds, and blankets and flannels from the southern markets.

In those days, coopers and tinkers were employed to make household vessels, and spoons; now these in most

most cases are superseded by crockery ware, and metal spoons.

These facts, exhibiting the manners of foreign times, are curious. Thence may be traced the progress of human improvement, and how agriculture and commerce, diverge out of the simplicity of the pastoral life, carrying luxury in their train. It may be proper to add, that in those days, linen was little used by the labouring class of society, and hence rheumatism was unknown. In modern times, every farm-servant wears linen, and as the heat of youth declines, rheumatism commences.

In regard to modern industry, it is to be observed, that the county of Caithness is well calculated for various manufactures; 1. As it possesses a number of fresh-water lakes, from which water-falls could easily be commanded, at a short distance from sea-ports, bounding on the North Sea and the German Ocean; 2. Because provisions are in abundance, and cheaper than in the more southern counties; and 3. The soil is, in general, capable of great improvement, and many hands could be usefully employed in the county, who hitherto, either emigrate to America, or go to Lanarkshire, to work at the manufactories in that flourishing district. The want of capital alone, has been the cause, why manufactures have not yet been tried on a large scale, proportioned to these advantages.

About the year 1789, Sir John Sinclair recommended a plan for erecting a tannery, and bleachfield, in the vicinity of Thurso, to which he subscribed to a considerable amount. Both these branches were accordingly set on foot. The tannery was, in the course of a few years, found to be a profitable concern, but the bleachfield, the reverse; partly owing to the want of a sufficient supply of pure water for the last stage of the bleaching process. From the most patriotic motives, Sir John Sinclair gave up his shares in the tannery, to the other partners, and took the whole shares of the bleach-field to himself. The tannery still continues a profitable undertaking: the bleachfield unproductive.

In the year 1804, a woollen manufacturer from Aberdeen, having come to this county, to find an eligible situation for himself, in order to encourage him, and to establish that species of manufacture in the county, Sir John Sinclair gave this manufacturer, the lease of a farm, near the village of Halkirk, upon very moderate terms, and he advanced about 600*l.*, to erect buildings and machinery for the woollen business on that farm, where there is a constant supply of water from the river. A house and machinery were erected, but owing (as I am informed) to a want of capital in the undertaker, the plan has not as yet made the progress that was expected.

A brewery was likewise erected, some years ago, on a large scale, in the town of Thurso. That business is still carried on, but the population is too scanty to afford sufficient demand for a regular business in the brewery line, in addition to a number of victuallers, *brousters*, or small brewers; who still carry on that business, and, from a greater facility to smuggle, can undersell the regular brewer.

At the village of Castletown, on the estate of James Traill, Esq., a ropery was commenced, and is still carried on, on a small scale; and were it not for the present state of our commerce with the Baltic, it would have been a profitable concern to the undertakers.

In the towns of Thurso and Wick, and in that village,

village, mechanics are settled, for making farming utensils, as carts, ploughs, harrows, thrashing-machines, &c. &c. to supply the farmers throughout the county.

In winter 1810, about 250 women and young girls were employed in the town of Thurso, plaiting straw for ladies bonnets. A few of them make up bonnets; but the greater part of the straw-plait is sent to London, from whence the prepared straw is imported. The straw-plaiters already earn at this employment, from 3*s*. to 5*s*. per week, which is very convenient for young women, whose parents reside in the town.

On the whole, these are the only species of manufacture hitherto attempted in the county under review. They do not employ many hands, and the extent, and the profit derived from them, are too trifling to have any particular effect on the price of provisions, or an increase of rent.

SECT. IX.—COMMERCE, AND ITS EFFECTS ON AGRICULTURE.

The same cause which retards the progress of manufactures, limits the extent of commerce in this county, namely, want of capital.

About 30 years ago, when we were at peace with Sweden and Denmark, and Caithness victual sold at from 8*s*. to 13*s*. 4*d*. per boll of bear, or oat-meal, several cargoes of victual were annually exported to Norway, and in return, fir-timber and iron were imported, at an easy rate At that time, Norway fir was retailed in this county at 8*d*. to 10*d*. per solid foot, and iron at

1*d*. to

1*d*. to 1½*d*. per pound. Foreign timber is now no less than from 3*s*. 6*d*. to 4*s*. per foot, and Swedish iron 4*d*. to 5*d*. per pound. At a more remote period, malt was exported from the port of Thurso, to Norway, and timber, iron, hemp, and flax, imported in return; and there are even some traditional accounts, that a few vessels from the port of Thurso traded to the West-Indies and to the Baltic.

The port of Thurso is well calculated for foreign commerce, as it has a good and safe roadstead, or harbour for ships, of any burden, at Scrabster Roads, and the access to the dry harbour in the river, is capable of great improvement. As soon as a vessel gets under way from this port, the German Ocean, or Atlantic, is open to her, and the *Pentland Frith* is no longer a terror to seafaring men.

From the year 1780 to about 1800, the merchants of Leith, Montrose, and Aberdeen, sent several cargoes of dressed flax annually, to agents employed by them, among the Caithness shopkeepers. These agents gave out the flax to be spun, by the young women, through the county; for which they received, about 10*d*. per spindle, or 2½*d*. per hank of 1200 threads. These agents had 1*s*. per spindle from their employers; the difference, being ½*d*. per hank, was their commission for risque and trouble. This flax was commonly spun to 2 or 2½ hank of yarn from the pound of flax, and the yarn so spun was returned to the merchants of Leith, &c. and there made into coloured thread for the foreign markets. Napoleon's decrees against commerce put an end to that branch of commerce. In so far as employing an additional number of hands, who occasionally were occupied in agricultural concerns, and the influx of the sums necessary to pay the spinners, it

was

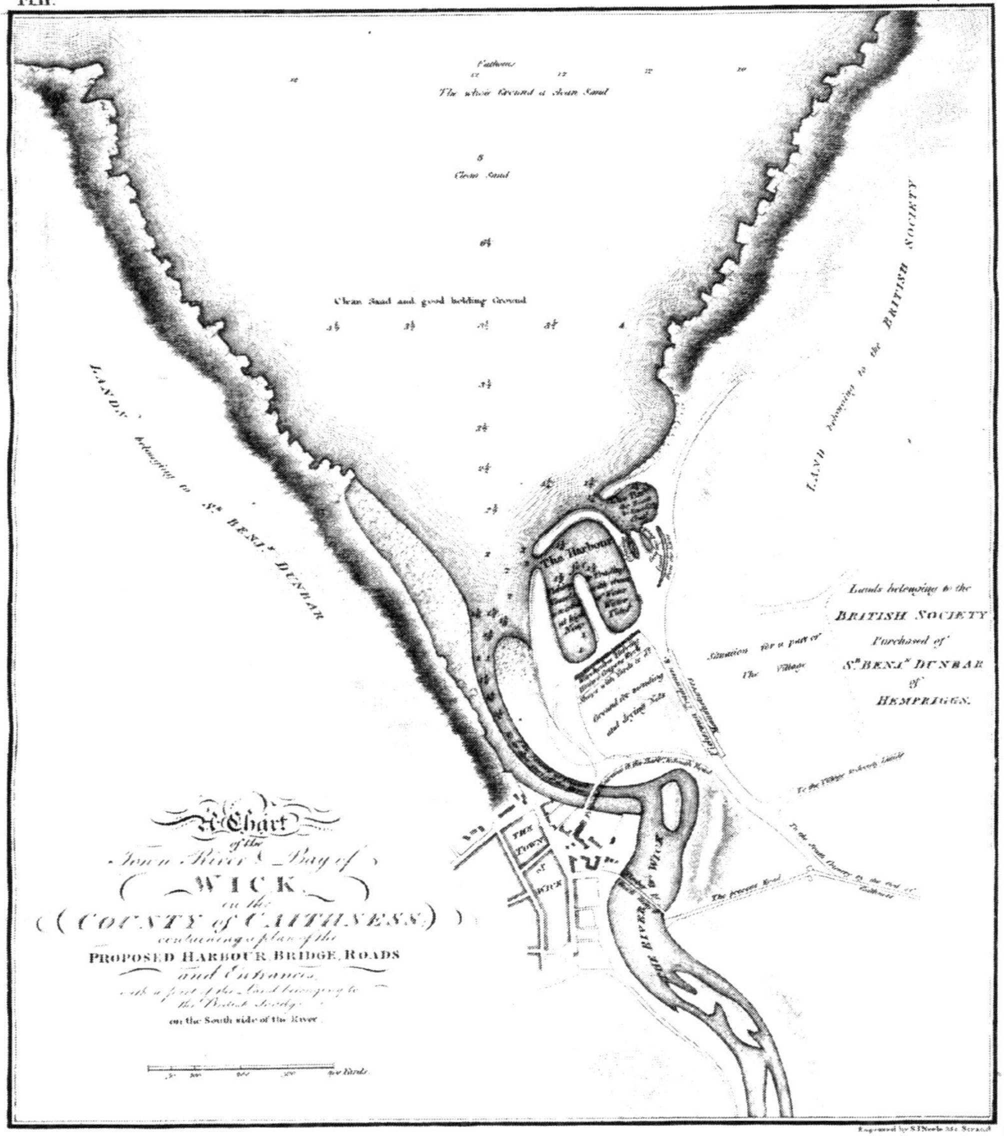

Fathoms
The whole Ground a clean Sand
Clean Sand
Clean Sand and good holding Ground
LANDS belonging to S.r BENJ.n DUNBAR
LAND belonging to the BRITISH SOCIETY
The Harbour
Ground for Spreading and drying Nets
Situation for a part of The Village
Lands belonging to the
BRITISH SOCIETY
Purchased of
S.r BENJ.n DUNBAR
of
HEMPRIGGS.
THE TOWN of WICK
THE RIVER of WICK
The present Road
A Chart of the Town River & Bay of WICK in the COUNTY of CAITHNESS containing a plan of the PROPOSED HARBOUR, BRIDGE, ROADS and Entrances, with a part of the Land belonging to the British Society on the South side of the River
Yards
Engraved by S.J.Neele 352 Strand

was beneficial to the county, and of course to its agriculture.

The principal branch of commerce which now exists in this county, is the herring fishery along the coast of the parishes of Wick and Latheron, where, from 30,000 to 60,000 barrels of fish, have been annually cured, and exported to the London, Leith, and Irish markets.

This fishery is likely to be greatly increased, by the erection of a Harbour at Wick, at the Settlement of the British Fishery Society; of which an Engraving is annexed. (See *Plate* II.)

The cod fishery has been for many years carried on, in the several havens or harbours of this county, but now it is the general opinion, that the London smacks, having fished regularly on the north coast of this county for about twenty years, have so injured the cod fishery, that not one-fourth of the number can be caught now on that coast, that were to be met with about twenty years ago*.

Great shoals of herring have frequently been seen on the north-coast of Caithness, in the Pentland Frith, &c. from the beginning of June to the 15th October, 1810; and preparations were made in the port of Thurso to give the herring fishery a fair trial with about 40 boats, in summer 1811; but the success did not answer the expectations that were formed of it. If it did succeed, it would greatly enhance the agricultural interests of the county, as the influx of men and money would fur-

* The increase of fish is said to be in the following proportion: a cod produces 3,686,700 eggs or spawn; a ling, 19,248,625; a flounder, of two ounces, contains 133,407; one of 24 ounces, 1,357,403; herrings weighing from 4 ounces to 5¾ ounces, from 21,285 to 36,960; lobsters, from 14 to 36 ounces, contain 21,699; mackarel, 20 ounces, 454,961; soal, of 14 ounces, contain 100,362 eggs.

nish

nish a market for the produce of the soil. The deep-sea fishery, however, is more likely to succeed in the early part of the season, because the water is too clear, or rather the nights too light, in June and July, so that the fish will see, and avoid the shallow nets used in the boat fishery; whereas decked vessels could go to deep water, and use deep nets, as the Dutch have been in the habit of doing, when their commerce was unrestrained. Scrabster Roads, near Thurso, is a safe road-stead, of easy access at all times of the tide, to such vessels as may be employed in the deep-sea fishery.

A considerable quantity of kelp is made from sea-weed (*Alga marina, et zostera marina)* along the Caithness coast, and sent coastways to Leith, Newcastle, &c., for the use of the glass-houses, soap-makers, &c.

There are a few sloops, of from 40 to 70 tons burden, which sail from the harbours of Thurso and Wick, to Leith, and occasionally to Sunderland, Newcastle, and London; they export fish, kelp, and oats, but more frequently convey mechanics, and labourers, as passengers, who go from Caithness in quest of work, to the southern counties; and by these vessels there is imported broad-cloth from Leeds, to supply the want of the cloth formerly manufactured in every family, from the wool of their little flocks; and cotton cloth and linens from Glasgow; tea, sugar, snuff, tobacco, and other articles from the London and Leith markets, and hardware goods from Sheffield, and Birmingham, &c., all which are retailed by the shop-keepers of the county; (See an Abstract of Exports and Imports, in the Addenda, No. VII). The commerce carried on in these vessels, (the herrings excepted), is of little benefit to the agriculture of this county, because the purchase of these imported commodities, drains away all the money that is

annually

annually realised from the produce of the soil, either in grain, or cattle, or from the industry of the inhabitants.

SECT. X.—THE POOR.

1. *Their Rates.*—None.

2. *Annual Receipts and Expenditure.*—See Addenda, No. I. and II., for the collections, fines, funds, &c.

3. *Work-Houses.*—None.

4. *Houses of Industry.*—None.

5. *Box Clubs—Advantages and Disadvantages.* Societies, or Clubs, have been formed in the towns of Thurso and Wick, and the village of Castletown, consisting of a number of mechanics, shopkeepers, and farmers, through the county, who have established bye-laws for the good government of their funds, &c. At present, there are in Thurso and its vicinity, 1. The Trades Society, consisting of 85 members. It commenced in 1785; the contribution is 1*s.* from each subscriber, per quarter; they pay 3*s.* per week to sick members, widows, &c. There are now eight widows, and three superannuated members, dependent on the society. Their present capital is 156*l.* sterling.—2. The Society of United Craftsmen; it commenced in 1796; contribute 1*s.* each per quarter; pay less or more to sick members, widows, &c. They have had many losses from mismanagement; have 130 members. Their present capital 250*l.* sterling. —3. The Fishers' Society: it commenced in 1793. In general,

general, the members are old men; they have had many burdens on their funds; they now pay to nine widows; their number 75 members. Capital 138*l.* sterling.—4. The Farmer and Craftsmen's Society, commenced in 1809; their number 156 members; capital already 75*l* —5. The Friendly Society, which commenced in October 1809; 43 members have subscribed; none are admitted above 35 years of age, and their quarterly contribution is 1*s.* 6*d.* each. Each member must contribute for seven years before he is entitled to receive any benefit from the fund: their capital as yet but small.—6. There is a society at Wick called the Friendly Society; they have contributed for many years, have a box, and keep a store for retailing oatmeal, to such of the brethren as require it; a plan which is attended with many advantages to those concerned.—7. There was a society formed at Castletown in 1798, entitled the United Farmers and Craftsman's Society of Castletown, consisting now (1809), of 164 members, and their capital is 340*l.* sterling. Their bye-laws consist of ten articles, and as they seem to be formed upon sound and good principles, they will be found in the Addenda, No. 13.

All these clubs or societies are found, from experience, to be very beneficial to such of the members, as from sickness, age, or infirmity, require such aid, and also to the widows and orphans of deceased members. Their laws seem formed upon similar principles; but those of the Castletown Club, I consider to be the most complete.

SECT.

SECT. XI.—POPULATION.

1. *General Facts regarding Population.*—A late publication makes the number of inhabitants on this globe to be 896 millions; of these 226 millions are Christians, 10 millions of Jews, 210 millions of Mahometans, and 450 millions of Pagans. Of those who profess the Christian religion, there are 50 millions of Protestants, 30 millions of the Greek and Armenian churches, and 90 millions of Catholics. The aggregate population being estimated at 896,000,000 souls, if we reckon with the ancients, that a generation lasts but 30 years, in that space of time, 896,000,000 of human beings will be born, and die; consequently 81,760 must be dropping to eternity every day; 3407 every hour, or about 36 every minute.

The following is given as an estimate of the population of Europe, viz.

Russia in Europe, ...	25,000,000
Denmark, ...	2,800,000
Sweden, ...	2,500,000
Poland, ...	9,000,000
Germany, ...	22,000,000
Hungary, ...	8,000,000
Great Britain, ...	11,000,000
Holland, ...	3,000,000
Turkey in Europe, ...	9,000,000
Italy, ...	13,000,000
Switzerland, ...	2,000,000
France, ...	28,000,000
Spain, ...	8,000,000
Portugal, ...	2,000,000
	145,000,000

Contrast

Contrast with this, the population of China, which, by Lord Macartney's suite, was estimated at 150,000,000 souls.

2. *Population of Caithness.*—In regard to the population of the district under review, every exertion has been made to procure accurate information, which will be found in the Addenda, (No. I. II. and III).

3. *Is the County over or under peopled?*—No county can be considered as being over peopled, where all the hands willing to work, will find employment, which is the case in this county. No doubt, owing to a limited commerce, and the want of manufactures that will employ many hands, a number of mechanics and labourers, go annually to the southern counties of Scotland, where mechanics are sure of constant work, and where the price of labour is still higher than in Caithness. As a proof, however, that the county is under peopled, it may be observed, that there is more corn produced, than is necessary to support the population, and if there were more capital to encourage manufactures and commerce, so as to form populous villages and large towns, to consume the produce of the soil, that alone would increase and improve the agriculture of the county, so that the soil would soon be able to maintain double the present population.

4. *Healthiness of the District.*—The county of Caithness is, and has been allowed to be, one of the healthiest in Scotland. About 60 years ago, when every farmer and cottager had his small flock of sheep, and wool was in abundance, the labouring people in general wore *scoorins*, (flannel of their own manufacture,)

ture), instead of linen, and in those days rheumatism was little known among them; but since the introduction of linen, as a part of their daily clothing, *consumptions*, *colds*, and *rheumatisms*, in the decline of life, are much more prevalent, than formerly was the case, among the labouring classes of the community.

5. *Food, and Mode of Living.*—The most numerous portion of the population of this district, namely, the small tenants, cottagers, and farm-servants, consume very little animal food, at any season of the year. Their mode of living is generally as follows:—For breakfast, about nine A. M., pottage, made of oat or barley-meal, with, or without some milk, or a piece of butter, as they may have it at command or not. For dinner, at three P. M., cakes made of oat or bear-meal, with some milk, or occasionally some boiled cabbage, but frequently bread alone, with a draught of cold water. For supper, oat or barley cakes, and *brochan*, (water-gruel made with oat-meal), with a little milk or butter to season it; and while the potatoe crop lasts, which is about six months in the year, an occasional meal of potatoes, boiled, the skin taken off, and then either mashed with a little milk or butter, or eaten whole, with or without milk. Some of the small tenants rear a pig, or hog, to be killed in March, and salted. A piece of it, with barley, makes *broth* for the family occasionally during the spring. Again, in the winter season, some of that class purchase a leg of beef, of about 60lb., which is salted, and used at times, to relish a pot of cabbage, or potatoes, during the winter.

In the summer season, (as has already been stated), the ploughmen are allowed an English quart of skimmed milk daily, which serves them with their oaten cakes. The female servants receive no other allowance for food, but two bolls of meal half-yearly, unless the farmer has some whey to spare; in that case, part of it is given to them gratis. These farm-servants dispose of a part of their meal, and some of them purchase butter or cheese for themselves. Thus the most numerous, useful, and industrious class of society, live in a simple and homely style, but are healthy, and contented. Their only extravagance is, endeavouring to have a piece of fine dress for church on Sunday; and should they go to a fair, or market, they like to taste an extra allowance of whisky, in order to be merry with their friends or sweethearts. They are now much more regular and moderate in these indulgences, than in former times, when their drinking at fairs, commonly terminated in cudgelling and bloody quarrels, which now a-days very rarely happen.

The mechanics in general, use more animal food than those engaged in agriculture; in other respects, they live on much the same kind of food as already stated, with the addition of tea to breakfast.

When beef was sold at 1½*d.* per pound, in the Thurso market, the Thurso fishermen made it a rule, to purchase a carcass of beef, for every person in the family, through the season; but in these times, one-fifth of that quantity must suffice.

The mode of living, among the superior classes of the population of this county, is similar to that usual in the Southern Counties of Scotland, except that they frequently use cakes of oat or barley-meal, well manufactured, in place of wheaten bread, as but little wheat has hitherto been produced in the county; and from habit, they like oat-cakes equally well. At the same

time,

time, there are two bakers in Thurso, and one at Wick, who import flour, and they have a tolerable trade, serving the wealthier families in the town, and occasionally those in the country.

CHAP. XVII.

OBSTACLES TO IMPROVEMENT.

SECT. I.—RELATIVE TO CAPITAL.

THE want of capital is much felt in this remote corner, the disadvantages attending which, are much increased by its distance from markets, for disposing of the produce of the soil; by the want of roads, to carry extraneous manure, &c. &c.; by the difficulty of procuring a supply of horses for the plough; and by the increased price of labour, and of agricultural implements of every description. All these circumstances combined, discourage people of capital from engaging in agriculture, in this district, where the culture of wheat, that great source of farming profit, has not hitherto succeeded.

Prices—Expenses. The fluctuation of the price of victual, (bear, oats, and oat-meal), or rather the want of a market for these articles, in the county, sometimes at any price, often compels the farmer to become the exporter of the produce of his farm to the southern markets. The want of home consumption for fat cattle, is likewise a great discouragement to any improved system, and the sale of lean cattle in the summer season, greatly depends on the chance of drovers coming to the county to purchase them. All these circumstances, and the want of some banking establishment, embarrass the

farmer,

farmer, and often disable him from regularly paying the demands upon him for rent, servants' wages, merchants' and mechanics' accounts, &c. &c. even though he may be possessed of produce equal to meet the whole, had there been a ready market within the county, as is the case in the more southern counties of the kingdom.

Want of power to Inclose.—The laws of Scotland, it is well known, are favourable to division and inclosure, otherwise the people of that country must have been starved long ago.

SECT. II. III.—TITHES, POOR'S-RATES.

NEITHER exist in this county.

SECT. IV.—WANT OF DISSEMINATED KNOWLEDGE.

IN May 1811, there was a circulating library established in the town of Thurso; whence publications on agriculture will soon be disseminated. Some copies of a most useful work, (the Farmer's Magazine), published quarterly at Edinburgh, are purchased by the country gentlemen and farmers; and as the people in general, are well educated, intelligent, and sagacious, agricultural knowledge would make rapid progress among them, were other obstacles removed.

SECT. V.—ENEMIES.

1. *Red, or Wire-Worm.*—This worm abounds in all fertile arable soil, but its depredations on agricultural produce are not much felt by the farmers of this county, as wheat is so little cultivated. Moles are said to pursue, and to feed upon this worm, and in this respect are useful.

2. *Slugs and Grubs.*—The grey slug, and the grub, are numerous in the Caithness soil, and destructive to the potatoes, and to the oat and bear crops, when they begin to vegetate, and appear above ground. There are many instances, of fields of several acres, sown with potatoe-oats, being stripped quite bare by the grub, during the cold N. W. winds, in the month of May, and their depredations continue until warm weather, and occasional showers, put a stop to their progress. Some people affirm, that the warm weather in June, brings the grub to the butterfly state; others maintain, that the grub, as well as the grey slug, remain in the same state during the whole season. The grey slug creeps up to the ears of the corn, in wet weather, during harvest, and feeds upon the grain.

3. *Rats and Mice.*—I have not heard of rats being troublesome in our corn-fields. Mice nestle among the corn in the summer season, and resort to the corn-yard in the end of harvest, as well as to barns, stables, &c. where they are destructive to grain.

Rats are not so numerous; but where they get possession, they do much mischief. They chiefly infest corn-mills and old granaries.

4. *Spar-*

4. *Sparrows.*—Such farms as have hedge-rows, or dry stone walls, or inclosures, are tormented with flocks of sparrows, who destroy much corn in the field, during the harvest.

5. *Other Vermin.*—In regard to other vermin injurious to the produce of the ground, the fly may be mentioned, so destructive to the young turnips; also moles, so troublesome in the field and garden, in May and June, turning up the soil, and throwing the young plants out of the ground.

There are but few plantations, of course but little shelter for rooks. There is one flock of them in the county, whose chief residence is in the garden of Brawll, where there is a plantation of tall trees. Their nests are sometimes destroyed, and in seed time and harvest, they are chased away from the corn fields.

6. *Means of its Prevention.*—It is well known, that the grub and the grey slug, keep under the surface of the soil in the day time, and that, with dewy nights, they crawl on the surface, and prey on the young plants of corn, principally potatoe oats, red oats, and bear. Some experiments have been made in this county, to prevent this mischief, by sowing the rough awns of bear, on the surface of the land, after it is sown and harrowed. And as far as these awns were sown, the grub does no damage to the crop; whereas, in any part of the same field, where no awns were sown, the crop has been greatly injured. This clearly shews, that the rough awns of bear, will prevent the movement or progress, and the consequent depredation, of that destructive vermin. Rolling the land with a

heavy roller in the night time, will destroy both the grub and slug.

Among various experiments with rolling, I will insert one, as transmitted to me by a gentleman in this county, in a letter, dated 16th August, 1808. "Last summer, the grub did much damage in a clover ley field of mine, sown with potatoe oats, and for three or four days, the mischief was spreading fast. I resolved therefore to apply a heavy cast-iron roller, weighing about 13cwt. about an hour before day-light, and, after a night intervening, to roll with it a second time. It perfectly stopped the progress of the grub, and even the part attacked, now bears a heavy crop, but not so forward as the rest. My servant who performed the rolling operation, said, that the first morning, the whole surface was covered with grubs; but that he observed very few of them the second morning."

"Having this year had a large summer fallow, it called my attention to the effect of the roller; and, from the application of my roller, (28 inches diameter) I am satisfied, that the stone and wooden rollers in use among us, are of little or no advantage. The weight of the stone roller is too great for its diameter. When applied to rough land, it is too heavy to work, and hops from clod to clod without effect. The want of weight in the wooden roller renders it of little effect."

A roller of small diameter, owing to its velocity, even with the slowest pace of a horse, cannot be made use of, without injury to the young plants of corns; whereas, the metal roller, of 28 inches diameter, would effectually crush the grub, and by its slow movement, would do no injury to the young plant,

but

but would rather be a benefit upon light-land, by pressing the soil about its roots. The only bar to the general use of these metal rollers, is the price, (20*l*.), which ordinary farmers cannot afford; but the awns of bear may be applied by the cottager, as well as the rich farmer.

To destroy rats; "slice cork into small pieces, then "fry them with some butter or other grease, and lay "them in places frequented by rats." They will eat the cork thus prepared, and, upon their drinking water, the cork will swell and kill them.

Good hunting cats, and spring-traps, are the most effectual means of destroying mice.

Sparrows may be destroyed by bear, steeped in a solution of arsenic, and the grain then strewed near walls or hedges in the month of June.

Moles are sometimes exterminated in this county, by means of spring traps, laid in their tracts under ground.

The corn and potatoe crops have frequently been injured by hoar frosts and mildews, more especially on the Highland straths of this county, during the months of July and August. The mildew fog rises from rivers, stagnant ponds, and lakes, or flow mosses, with calm evenings and a clear sky, and in the course of the night, it spreads over the adjacent flat land, accompanied by a hoar frost, which is dissipated by the rays of the morning sun. Their deleterious effects are first known on the potatoe haulms, which, by nine A.M. droop down, as if parboiled, and in the course of a few days wither, and become quite black; the potatoe crop makes but little or no progress afterwards. Corn exposed to this noxious vapour, if then partly full, will be much injured by the mildew; there having been many instances of oats so injured, as not to produce

produce one boll of meal from eight bolls of oats, and that of bad quality. Partly owing to draining, and partly to sowing the crop earlier than formerly, and the introduction of red oats, these frosts and mildews are not of late years so prevalent, or so prejudicial to the crops, as they were about 20 years ago.

In those days, it was remarked, that if a heavy shower of rain succeeded the hoar frost and mildew, before the beams of the morning sun struck the crop, no injury ensued. Farmers in the Highlands have made experiments, by running a long rope, made of heather, pulled by a person at each end, along the top of the corn, by the *dawn of day*, after a frosty night, to shake off the frosty dew, and they uniformly found, as far as this operation was performed, before the sun beams had reached the field, that the crop was much less injured, than where that plan had not been followed.

CHAP.

CHAP. XVIII.

MISCELLANEOUS ARTICLES.

SECT. I.—AGRICULTURAL SOCIETIES.

ABOUT the year 1794, several of the landholders, and some of the principal farmers in this county, formed an Agricultural Society, contributed a fund, by subscription, and made bye-laws, &c. &c. they met quarterly, for a year or two, but owing to many of the members being called off on the service of their King and Country, in Fencible Corps, &c. their meetings were discontinued, and the fund hitherto remains unappropriated to any agricultural purpose.

1. *Where wanting.*—It would tend to promote the interests of the plough, if the resident proprietors, and principal farmers in the county, formed themselves into two Societies, for the improvement of agriculture. Those of the parishes of Reay, Thurso, Halkirk, Olrig, and Dunnet, to meet occasionally at Thurso, and those of the other five parishes, at Wick. A fund should be raised, for the purpose of giving premiums to the best ploughmen, the best bulls and stallions, &c. &c. This would be a stimulus to farm-servants to become expert in their profession, and the live stock would soon be improved in their most essential properties.

CONCLU-

CONCLUSION.

MEANS OF IMPROVEMENT:

AND THE MEASURES CALCULATED FOR THAT PURPOSE.

THE first steps necessary to promote the improvement of this district, namely, the conversion of personal services, and the granting of leases upon liberal terms to industrious tenants, have been already carried into effect by Sir John Sinclair, the President of the Board of Agriculture, upon his extensive estates in this county, and that laudable plan has likewise been adopted by several of the other Landed Proprietors within the county. In many cases, the arable land has been *planked*; or converted into distinct farms, in place of the old system of tenants occupying it in run rigg, or *rigg and rennal*, as it was provincially termed. The prospect of good roads being soon made, is the next step to the effectual improvement of the soil. Improved species of oats, such as red, potatoe, and dun oats, have already been introduced, and prove beneficial to the farmer. But the rent of land, the rate of labour, also the prices of farm stock, and of utensils, have become so high, within these last ten years, that the produce of the soil, in bear and oats, will not, in common seasons, reimburse the farmer, as the market for his produce is distant and precarious, especially for bear, since the high duty on malt, and even the prohibition of distillation, prevents almost any sale of that species of grain, though it must form a part of the farmer's

rotation,

rotation, if he wishes to keep his land in any condition *.

For fat cattle, there is little demand, in any town or village within 100 miles of the county; and the sale of lean cattle, depends upon the annual demand from drovers, who come in the summer months, and call *trysts*, in various parts of the county, when the people assemble, and bring with them any cattle they may have for sale.

There is no bank, or even branch of one, at present, within 70 miles of the county, where the farmer could occasionally be accommodated, so as to meet any unexpected demand upon him, without being obliged to dispose of his victual, or cattle, at an under value; as now is too often the case.

In

* While the tax on malt made from bear or bigg, was levied in a fair proportion, compared to its intrinsic value, to that imposed on malt made from English barley, the farmer in the North of Scotland, found a market for all the bear he could raise on his farm; but owing to a misrepresentation of facts to our Legislators, the old proportion of malt tax is now altered, to the prejudice of the Scotch farmer, and consequently, there is no regular market for his produce of bear or bigg. From various experiments made, a pound averdupoise of English barley, contains about 10,000 grains, &c., and a pound of Caithness bear or bigg, contains about 19,000 grains at an average; from this it may be naturally inferred, that the English barley loses much less of its farina or saccharine quality, in the process of malting, than the *lean long* grains of bear or bigg do; that the same expense and labour are required to make a bushel of malt, from bear, as from barley, and therefore, that a bushel of malt, made from bear or bigg, should not pay above *one half* the tax imposed on a like quantity of English barley.

In order to promote the improvement of agriculture in the North of Scotland, it is absolutely necessary to encourage the growth of bear or bigg; because artificial grasses cannot be raised to advantage, but with this crop; when clover and rye-grass are sown with oats, its large leafy stalks prevent the free admission of sun and air to the tender plants of these grasses, and of course checks their progress, and, with a wet harvest,

In order to remedy these evils, and promote the improvement of the county, as far as climate and local circumstances will permit, the following measures are respectfully submitted to the consideration of the Board of Agriculture.

1. Let the Landed Proprietors of the county form themselves into one, or two Societies; establish a fund, for the purpose of giving premiums for the culture of winter wheat, in every part of the county, (the Highland districts excepted); circulating at the same time printed rules, for pickling the seed, and preparing the soil for it, and where the land is wet, recommending that it should be thrown up in drills, as if prepared for turnip, the seed to be sown broad-cast, in the month of August, or early in September, and lightly harrowed; the drills, as far as circumstances will admit of it, to have their side towards the north-west, the quarter from whence our most severe storms prevail. The drill husbandry would, in a great degree, carry off the superabundant moisture, and diminish the injurious effects, on the young plants of wheat, of a cold and variable climate.

Another mode of sowing wheat has been successfully invented by that intelligent agriculturist, the Sheriff Depute of this county, James Traill, Esq. The land is summer-fallowed in the usual manner, with the direction of the ridges as far as possible east and west;

harvest, it entirely destroys the young grass, whereas it never fails with a crop of bear; of course the North Country Farmer, must sow bear in the course of his rotation, or not attempt the improvement of his soil by green crops and artificial grasses. The bear crop is less liable to fail with a bad season, than the oat crop, as was experienced in 1782, and in 1800, when bear-meal was the chief support of the people in the North of Scotland, who could not purchase flour. Therefore its growth ought not to be discouraged by a heavy tax.

manured

manured in August with rotten compost, and ploughed in, in broad planks; then harrowed; and early in September the seed is sown, (after being pickled), by a double moulded drill plough, having two tin boxes containing the seed, upon an axle attached to two wheels of about two feet diameter. This machine is fixed to the muzzle of the plough. The tin boxes will hold about half a peck of wheat each, and have holes in them, the same as boxes for sowing beans. There is a broad strap of leather round each of the boxes, to cover the holes, and to prevent the seed from falling out. The plough, thus prepared for sowing, is brought to the north-east angle of the field, (supposing the field to run east and west), and previous to entering the soil, the left hand mould-board is put close to the beam, the other being extended by a swivel. The ploughman then proceeds in making a light furrow along the north-west side of the field, to the other end of it; having again turned the plough, and previous to entering it in the soil, he lays close the right mould-board, and extends the left one, and then shifts the leather strap off the holes of the left-hand box, and thus proceeds, with a light furrow, towards the east; the seed dropping from the left-hand box, in the south face of the first furrow, and the plough laying the furrow now turning, upon it. Having reached the east end of the field, he puts the strap on the holes of the left-hand box; and, after turning the plough to the land again, he lays close the left mould-board, and extends the right one; at the same time shifting the leather strap off the right-hand seed-box, and then proceeds; the seed now falling from the right hand seed-box, on the south-face of the last furrow, and is covered by this one.

He

He thus proceeds until the whole field is sown, and it is not afterwards harrowed. A strong vegetation appears in a short time; every drill of the wheat appearing in the hollows betwixt each furrow, and is thus sheltered from the severity of the storms, through the winter and spring. During these last two years that Mr. Traill has made this experiment, the returns have been abundant, and of good quality—from 40 to 48 bushels per Scotch acre. The quantity of seed sown is three firlots per Scotch acre; less was first sown, but it has been found, that by sowing thick, they have a heavier crop than otherwise.

To promote the culture of wheat, a flour mill ought to be erected in a central position, that the farmer might have a market within the county for his produce of wheat; because, were he to send it to the southern markets, prejudice would so operate against its quality, that it would not sell at more than two-thirds of the common market price. By thus encouraging the farmers in general, to make a fair trial of winter wheat, it is more than probable, that its culture might succeed in this county, to a greater extent than any partial experiments, hitherto made, may at present warrant.

Trials have been made with spring wheat, on land after turnips, and without being pickled, and in every case where it was sown before, or about the first of April, the crop was ripe about the beginning of October, but the returns were not abundant. It should be pickled and sown on land properly prepared, about the end of April, or beginning of May, and there is little doubt of its success; provided one-third more seed is sown, than of winter wheat; for it does not tiller.

2. The

2. The difficulty experienced by the farmer, in obtaining a supply of farm-horses from the south of Scotland, has already been noticed. To remedy this, let the Societies proposed to be erected, apply a part of their funds, to purchase and maintain in the county, a stallion of an approved breed, (for instance the Clydesdale), so as to enable the farmers to rear horses for themselves, more habituated to the climate, and of course more likely to answer.

3. The breed of black cattle in this county, are considered to be inferior to the generality of those in Scotland. It is now, however, proved, that the Skye breed will thrive, even in the Lowland part of Caithness, because in November 1806, the President of the Board of Agriculture, ordered 20 cows in calf, and a bull, from the Isle of Skye, to be brought to his own farm at Thurso East. In the course of that season, he gave 10 of these cows, and the bull, at prime cost, to a gentleman who had just taken a farm of 200 acres on his estate, within four miles of the sea coast of Thurso; the other 10 cows were given, on similar terms, to a farmer on his estate in the Highland part of this county. The experience of four years has now shewn, that the 10 cows, and their young stock, on the Lowland farm, retain their primitive shape, and pile of hair, as well as if they had remained in their native soil, on the hills of Skye. It is therefore the interest of the landholders and farmers of this county, to take the most effectual means for improving their cattle, by converting them into the real Highland breeds of Skye, or Argyle, as it is now ascertained, that they may obtain at least one-half more price for them, at the same age, than for their present mixed stock.

4. In every part of the county, where the arable

land is occupied by small tenants and cottagers, the culture of potatoes, and the rearing of hogs, is more practicable, than where land is occupied in large farms. In the county under review, therefore, if a proper breed of swine were imported, and sold to that class of people, at prime cost and charges, and if the culture of potatoes and clover, to feed these animals, were enforced, contracts might then be entered into, with some curers of pork in England, or some person employed to salt the pork at Thurso and Wick. The country people should then be taught, to make bacon in their warm, smoky houses; and that branch of rural economy, might thus be carried on, to considerable advantage, in the county of Caithness.

5. Under the old system, besides money-rent, and personal services, it was also customary, to pay a part of the rent in kind; namely, in victual, fowls, geese, and in some cases, hogs, or swine. The conversion of all these articles into money-rent, especially fowls, geese, and swine, has destroyed that industrious habit among the tenants, and cottagers' *wives*, of rearing poultry. While they were bound to provide a certain number annually for the Proprietors, they reared flocks of geese and poultry, at little or no expense, and of course had always a supply for any demand of that article, the price of which, added to their own comfort and convenience. They now rear very few; and their time is not employed in any other industrious pursuit. In a remote district, like this county, it is the opinion of many, that the mode most equitable to both landlord and tenant, is to have the rent payable, one-half in money, and the other in victual, so that the high or low price of produce, may be felt equally by landlord and tenant: it is also contended, that the small tenant, and

and cottager, should pay geese and poultry in kind, as a spur to industry.

6. The Landed Proprietors ought to establish a county bank, for the accommodation of every class of the community, as it is well known, that a well-regulated paper-currency, tends more to the improvement of the agriculture and commerce of the country, than any other measure that can be devised. Indeed, all plans of improvement, go on in a very languid manner, where that accommodation is wanting.

7. The knowledge of preparing peat-moss compost, on the Meadowbank system, either with dung or sea-weed, ought to be generally diffused, and even enforced, where necessary, as an excellent practice. The land should also be cleared from perennial weeds; the remains of the *run-rigg* mode of occupation, should be abolished; ploughing-matches should be established in every parish, and premiums given to the best ploughmen.

8. Establishing regular annual *trysts*, or fairs, for the sale of black cattle, that drovers of capital may be induced to attend them from the Southern Counties, as well as contriving some mode of selling the grain produced in the county, until manufactures are established, and population so increased in towns and villages, as to consume the produce of the county within itself, would have a most advantageous effect. Thirlage also, to particular mills, already partly given up, should be wholly abolished. The landlord should enforce and encourage the tenant to use extraneous manure, by draining the various lakes, and peat-bogs, where marl is to be met with throughout the county; by importing lime from Sunderland, to the ports of Thurso and Wick, and by disposing of it to the farmer,

 at

at prime cost and charges; he should also assist in procuring for him a change of the best seeds, of the sorts of grain best suited to the climate of the county; he should enforce the culture of green crops; and direct the tenant to raise rye-grass and turnip seeds on his own farm annually, so as to be less dependent on the seed-merchant, who often imports unsound seeds, and of inferior, or mixed qualities; and he should direct the farmer to have his turnip land in three divisions; one-third of white turnip, one-third of red-topped, and the remaining third of yellow turnip, or *ruta-baga*, by which he may command a supply of this excellent esculent, from the 1st of November to the 1st of May, and even later.

These measures, accompanied by the granting of leases, on equitable terms in regard to rent and duration, as well as proper clauses, in regard to a judicious rotation of crops, during the last three, or even five years of the lease, would effectually promote the improvement of this remote district, notwithstanding that nearly one-half of its extent, is under the fetters of a strict entail; a circumstance which, however much it may tend to perpetuate families, is very inimical, in an agricultural point of view, to the improvement of a country.

JOHN HENDERSON.

ADDENDA.

No. I.

Statistical Table of the County of Caithness, taken from the Statistical Account of Scotland.

1.	2.	3.	4.	5.	6.	7.	8.	9.	10.	11.	12.	13.	14.	15.
Parishes.	Volume of the Statistical Account.	Page.	Population in 1755.	Population in 1790 and 1798.	Increase.	Decrease.	Valued Rent, Scotch Money.	Real Land Rent, Sterling.	Ministers' Stipends, the Grain converted at 10s. per Boll.	Number of Scholars.	Schoolmasters' Emoluments.	Number of Poor.	Capital of Poor's Funds.	Annual Income of the Poor.
							£ s. d.	£ s. d.	£		£ s. d.		£	£ s. d.
1. Bower,	VII.	521	1287	1592	305	—	2761 16 0	1500 0 0	72	—	8 0 0	35	—	4 10 0
2. Cannisbay,	VIII.	142	1481	1950	469	—	3855 3 6	1300 0 0	105	—	18 0 0	—	—	12 0 0
3. Dunnet,	XI.	243	1235	1399	164	—	2309 12 6	950 0 0	90	90	6 13 4	—	400	22 0 0
4. Halkirk,	XIX.	1	3075	3180	105	—	3314 7 8	2200 0 0	80	—	6 0 0	—	—	5 0 0
5. Latheron,	XVII.	19	3675	4006	331	—	3940 14 5	1900 0 0	110	—	10 0 0	75	—	3 10 0
6. Olrig,	XII.	156	875	1001	126	—	—	900 0 0	70	—	9 0 0	—	—	8 0 0
7. Reay,	VII.	570	2262	2298	36	—	—	—	68	50	12 0 0	50	—	5 10 0
8. Thurso, town and parish.	XX.	493	2963	3146	183	—	5776 13 10	1714 5 6	110	242	—	—	50	25 0 0
9. Wick, ditto ditto,	X.	1	3938	5000	1062	—	—	—	124	—	—	150	—	12 0 0
10. Wattin,	XI.	279	1424	1230	—	194	1039 4 10	—	95	—	9 0 0	—	100	10 0 0
—	—	—	22,215	24,802	2781	194	—	—	—	—	—	310	550	107 10 0

Column 4, population in 1755, is	22,215		
Column 5, ditto in 1790-8,	24,802		
Increase,	2587		
Column 6, increase on the whole,	2781		
Column 7, decrease on ditto,	194		
	2587		
Column 8, valued rent, Scots,	£37,251	3	3
Or sterling,	3104	5	3¼
Column 9, real land rent, according to Sir John Sinclair,	13,929	0	0
Add salmon-fishing,	380	0	0
Houses in Wick and Thurso,	1200	0	0
	£15,509	0	0
Column 10, Ministers' stipend, including glebes,	£930	0	0
Average to each Minister,	93	0	0

Column 11, scholars in three parishes, 382; the population 6843; total scholars in the county thence computed at 1380; but several omitted, as Society Schoolmasters.

Column 12, Schoolmasters' salary, &c., perhaps 12*l.* each.

Column 13, poor in four parishes 310; population in these four parishes 12,896; total poor in the county thence computed to be 600.

Column 14, capital of poor's funds 550*l.* in three parishes; not stated what, in the other parishes.

Column 15, income of the poor 107*l.* 10*s.*; average 7*s.* 2*d.* each pauper.

Inhabitants in town of Thurso,	1612
Ditto in town of Wick,	1000
	2612

State of Property.

Five proprietors, from 7743*l.* 1*s.* to 2686*l.* 2*s.* 8*d.* of valued rent,	£21,153	14	7
Two ditto, from 2000*l.* to 1000*l.*	3092	16	6
Ten ditto, from 1000*l.* to 400*l.*	6902	7	4
Nine ditto, from 400*l.* to 200*l.*	2893	7	11
Eight ditto under 200*l.*	575	3	7
Bishop of Caithness,	1800	6	8
Town of Wick,	166	13	4
Town of Thurso,	666	13	4
Total,	£37,251	3	3

The following statement of the division of property, is taken from Sir John Sinclair's Survey of the Northern Counties:

	Sterling.		
Five proprietors, from 3240*l.* to 1000*l.*	£7740	0	0
Seven ditto, from 600*l.* to 400*l.*	3450	0	0
Twelve ditto, from 300*l.* to 100*l.*	2440	0	0
Six ditto, from 100*l.* to 50*l.*	450	0	0
Four ditto, under 50*l.*	29	0	0
Church lands,	900	0	0
	£15,009	0	0

Extent.

Sir John Sinclair's General View of the Northern Counties, makes the extent of Caithness 690 square miles; English acres 441,000; or Scotch acres 351,210; of which,

Arable,	18,000 acres.
Pasture,	36,000 ditto.
Moor or moss,	297,210 ditto.
	351,210 ditto.

Stock.

	Horses.	Cattle.	Sheep.
Halkirk parish,	1650	4963	2890
Thurso ditto,	534	937	688
	2184	5900	3578
In the other 8 parishes suppose 4 times as much, or	8736	23,600	14,312
	10,920	29,500	17,890

6000 horses, at 3*l.*	£18,000	0	0
15,000 cattle, at 2*l.* 10*s.*	37,500	0	0
9000 sheep, at 5*s.*	2250	0	0
Hogs, &c.	1000	0	0
	£58,750	0	0

Pasture.

10,920 horses, at 20*s.*	£10,920	0	0
29,500 cattle, at 20*s.*	29,500	0	0
17,890 sheep, at 2*s.*	1789	0	0
	£42,209	0	0

Statistical Table of the County of Caithness, taken from the Answers received from the Clergy of the sundry Parishes, in 1809-10.

1.	2.	3.	4.	5.	6.	7.	8.		9.	10.	11.	12.	13.	14.	15.	16.
Parishes.	Population in 1790-8, per Sir John Sinclair.	Population in 1810.	Increase.	Decrease.	Valued Rent. Scots.	Real Land Rent.	Ministers' Stipends, in Money, &c.	Ministers' Stipends, in Victual, ½ Bear.	Number of Scholars.	Schoolmasters' Salary, &c.	Number of Poor.	Capital of Poor's Fund.	Fines and sundry Collections.	Income of the Poor.	Money for Communion Elements.	Number of Society Schools.
					£ s. d.		£ s. d.	Bolls.		£ s. d.		£ s. d.	£ s. d.	£ s. d.	£ s. d.	
1. Bower,	1592	1485	—	107	2761 16 10	[Increased since the last calculation, but the particulars are not accurately known.]	50 0 0	128	200	24 0 0	50	100 0 0	6 0 0	11 0 0	8 6 8	—
2. Cannisbay,	1950	1806	—	144	3855 3 6		50 0 0	96	169	30 0 0	55	311 0 0	9 0 0	24 11 0	8 6 8	2
3. Dunnet,	1399	1440	41	—	2309 12 6		—	175	167	37 16 10	56	726 5 4	15 0 0	51 4 10	8 6 8	1
4. Halkirk,	3180	2532	—	648	3313 15 3		55 0 0	128	120	22 0 0	85	100 0 0	11 0 0	13 0 0	*8 6 8	2
5. Latheron,	4006	4206	200	—	4036 16 2		55 11 0	128	140	8 10 0	75	100 0 0	6 0 0	11 0 0	8 6 8	1
6. Olrig,	1001	1201	200	—	2396 5 4		—	175	120	30 0 0	34	100 0 0	7 0 0	12 0 0	5 0 0	1
7. Reay, (Caithness part of it),	1541	1292	—	249	2379 9 10		44 8 10	144	80	24 14 0	60	167 0 0	5 3 0	15 10 0	5 0 0	—
8. Thurso, parish and town,	3146	3470	324	—	5831 6 10		—	240	361	25 16 6	140	100 0 0	40 0 0	51 0 0	8 6 8	2
9. Wick ditto ditto,	3986	5080	1094	—	6536 13 2		50 0 0	160	320	32 0 0	120	250 0 0	30 0 0	42 10 0	8 6 8	3
10. Wattin parish,	1230	1257	27	—	1762 15 0		75 0 0	96	110	24 0 0	50	320 0 0	6 0 0	22 0 0	8 6 8	—
	23,031	23,769	1886	1148	35,633 2 1 †1583 0 8		379 19 10	1470	1787	238 17 0	725	2274 5 4	135 3 0	251 15 10	76 13 4	12

N. B. A part of the parish of Reay is within the boundaries of the county of Sutherland, and that part contains 825 inhabitants, exclusive of the number here.

There are twelve Society Schools in the county, viz. eight taught by men; salary from 10*l*. to 15*l*.;—and four by females; salary from 5*l*. to 3*l*. per annum, paid by the Society for Propagating Christian Knowledge.

* And 3*l*. to the session-clerk and beadle.

† By the returns from the Clergy, the valued rent is short 1583*l*. 8*d*. It should be 37,216*l*. 2*s*. 9*d*. The difference is the feu and tiend duties, payable to the Bishop, Crown, and to Sir John Sinclair, out of certain lands holding of them.

Statistical Table of the County of Caithness, taken from the Returns made to Government in July 1811, *in terms of Act* 51 *Geo. III. Cap.* 6, *by Parishes, viz.*

Answers to	Question First.		Second.	Third.	Fourth.			Fifth. Including Persons of every Age.		
Names of Parishes.	Inhabited Houses.	Occupied by how many Families.	Houses now building.	Other Houses uninhabited.	Families chiefly employed in Agriculture.	Families chiefly employed in Trade and Manufactures.	All other Families not included in the preceding two Columns.	Males.	Females.	Total of Persons.
1. Bower parish,	273	296	—	9	220	73	3	664	814	1478
2. Cannisbay,	578	399	1	5	313	43	43	857	1079	1936
3. Dunnet,	311	328	1	6	171	50	107	638	760	1398
4. Halkirk,	412	471	2	2	408	42	21	1132	1400	2532
5. Latheron,	722	722	—	18	629	85	8	1743	2183	3926
6. Olrig,	167	185	2	3	140	37	8	513	529	1042
7. Reay, (Caithness part of it),	301	301	1	3	296	3	2	625	831	1456
8. Thurso, town and parish,	572	748	2	18	306	216	226	1538	1924	3462
9. Wattin parish,	220	220	—	18	160	53	7	504	605	1109
10. Wick, town and parish,	945	1044	36	57	627	236	181	2394	2686	5080
Summary,	4301	4714	45	139	3270	838	606	10,608	12,811	23,419
Increase since the Returns made to Government in 1801,								425	315	810

The population of Caithness, per returns to Government in 1800, was as follows, viz.

	Total.
Bower parish,	1572
Cannisbay,	1989
Dunnet,	1366
Halkirk,	2545
Latheron,	3612
Olrig,	1127
Reay,	1541
Thurso,	3648
Wattin,	1246
Wick,	3986
	22,609

The town of Thurso contains 302 inhabited houses, 442 families; 844 males, 1108 females.

males	844
females	1108
	1952

Inhabited Houses:

Inhabited Houses		Families	
Burgh of Wick,	170		232
Suburbs:			
Louisburgh,	76		398
Pulteney town,	27		41
Bank-head,	22		26
Total,	295	Total,	697

890 males, 859 females.

Wick and Suburbs, 1749; of whom there are in the royal burgh, 489 males. 505 females.

994

Observations on the preceding Statistical Tables, principally on Table, No. II.

Columns 1, 2, and 3, in Table, No. I. contain the names of the parishes, and the volume and page of the Statistical Account of Scotland, in which a description of each parish is found, and the same applies to the names of parishes in Table, No. II.; to which these observations more particularly refer.

Columns 1, 2, 3, and 4, of Table, No. II. contain the population of the county of Caithness, in 1790-8; and in 1810, per the returns from the Clergy, shewing an increase of 738, on the whole.

The decrease in the parish of Reay, is owing to the establishment of sheep-farms, and enlarging the size of some arable farms, and increasing the rent, which induced several families, to settle at the manufacturing towns, in the southern counties of Scotland. The decrease in the parish of Cannisbay, is principally owing to a number of young men having gone into the navy, and engaged in the herring, and other fisheries, in various parts of the country. The decrease in the parish of Halkirk is, in some degree, owing to enlarging the extent of farms. The increase in the parishes of Wick and Latheron, is principally to be ascribed to the herring fishery on the coast of these parishes; and in particular at Wick, in consequence of the new harbour and fishing village, erecting there. In the parish of Olrig, the increase is owing to the number of houses erected in the village of Castletown, feued by the proprietor, James Traill, Esq.; and also to the progress made in the improvement of waste land in that parish. The increase in Thurso parish, is partly owing to the

increase

increase of houses in the New Town of Thurso, and to the improvement of waste lands in its neighbourhood, but also to the number of families, who, having failed in small farms, take up their residence in that town; where some of them become day-labourers, and others get upon the poor's roll.

The number of inhabitants in the country part of Caithness, and in small villages, is 20,068. The number in the burgh of Wick and its suburbs, 1749; and in the town of Thurso, 1952; total in the two towns, 3701; grand total of the towns and country, 23,769.

Column 5, contains the valued rent of the county of Caithness, as returned by the Clergy, which is less than the real valuation, as entered in the records of the county, namely, 37,256*l.* 2*s.* 9*d.* Scotch, or 3104*l.* 10*s.* 2¾*d.* sterling.

Column 6. The real rent of the county, cannot be accurately ascertained. The gross rent exceeds, it is supposed, 25,000*l.*; but the deductions are numerous, and heavy on the proprietors.

Column 7. The total income of the established Clergy of the county, converting the oatmeal at 20*s.* and the bear at 20*s.* per boll, being payable by equal portions at the fiar prices of the county, is as follows:

	£	s.	d.
Money stipends, per returns, amount to....	379	19	10
1470 bolls (half oatmeal, half bear), at 20*s.*	1470	0	0
The 10 glebes, (exclusive of the free manses), say, ...	100	6	10
For communion elements, ten parishes, as per column 14 of No. II. amount, ...	76	13	4
Total, ...	£2027	0	0

Which

Which divided among 10 Ministers, gives 202*l.* 14*s.* of average income to each. The stipend of the whole of the parish of Reay is included, because the stipend of the part of it which belongs to Sutherland, was not included in the calculation for that county.

Column 8, contains the number of scholars by the returns from the Clergy; total in the county, 1787, being to the inhabitants, in the proportion of one to 13⅓; but it is to be observed, that there are several private schools in some parishes, which, in some cases, have escaped the notice of the Minister, so that the number may be fairly computed according to the above proportion.

Column 9, contains the Schoolmasters' salaries, which is not so satisfactory as could be wished, because in some cases it is only the salary of the *Parochial* Schoolmaster, that is inserted, without computing his other income from school-fees, as Session-Clerk, &c. There are about 10 Society Schoolmasters in the county, who are allowed a salary of from 5*l.* to 15*l.* per ann. from the Society for Propagating Christian Knowledge; and these are permitted to take school-fees, from such as can afford to pay it, say from 1*s.* to 1*s.* 6*d.* per quarter. Some of these schools are kept by females, recommended for the benefit of teaching girls; and all the Society Schools, are annually visited and examined by the Ministers of the parish, who report to the Society the progress of the scholars, and the conduct of the Schoolmaster or Schoolmistress. Total income of the 10 Parochial Schoolmasters per this column, is 258*l.* 17*s.* sterling, which divided among 10, gives the average of 25*l.* 17*s.* 8¼*d.* to each Schoolmaster*.

Column

* The following more correct information, has been lately obtained, regarding

Column 10. The number of poor extends to 725, which is in the proportion of one to $32\frac{2}{3}$, to the total inhabitants of the county.

Column 11, contains the capital of the poor's funds, which amounts to 2274*l.* 5*s.* 4*d.*

The annual collections and fines, column 12, amount to 135*l.* 3*s.*

---

regarding the salaries and other emoluments, of the 10 Parochial Schoolmasters in 1811.

Parishes.	Annual Salary.						Remarks.
	In Victual.			In Sterling Money.			
	B.	F.	P.	£.	*s.*	*d.*	*Sterling.*
Bower, ...	—	—	—	22	4	$5\frac{1}{3}$	& $\frac{1}{4}$ acr. of garden, or 1*l.* 10*s.*
Cannisbay, ...	16	—	—	8	17	9	Ditto.
Dunnet, ...	—	—	—	22	4	$5\frac{1}{3}$	Ditto.
Halkirk, ...	—	—	—	22	4	$5\frac{1}{3}$	Ditto.
Latheron, ...	—	—	—	5	11	$1\frac{1}{3}$	Ditto.
Reay, ...	—	—	—	22	4	$5\frac{1}{3}$	Ditto.
Thurso, ...	—	—	—	22	4	$5\frac{1}{3}$	Ditto.
Olrig, ...	18	—	—	11	2	$2\frac{2}{3}$	Ditto.
Wick, ...	32	—	—	—	—	—	Ditto.
Wattin, ...	—	—	—	22	4	$5\frac{1}{3}$	Ditto.
Total, ...	66	—	—	158	17	9	

Total amount of money salary, per ann. is	158	17	9
Victual ditto, 66 bolls, or	66	0	0
Add a garden each, or 1*l.* 10*s.* say, ...	15	0	0
And Session-clerk fees, as Presenter, 40*s.* each, or, ...	20	0	0
Total is, ...	£259	17	9

Equal to nearly 26*l.* for each of the ten Schoolmasters per ann. exclusive of school-fees, which for reading English, is from 1*s.* to 1*s.* 6*d.* per quarter; for reading and writing, 2*s.*; for reading, writing, and arithmetic, 2*s.* 6*d.*; and for Latin, 3*s.* 6*d.* per quarter. Suppose the average number of scholars per ann. to be 25 at each school, and the average fees, 2*s.* per quarter, or 8*s.* per ann. that would average the school-fees at 10*l.* per ann. to each of the 10 Parochial Schoolmasters, and of course the average total income is above 36*l.* sterling per ann.

The

The total income of the poor, per column 13, amounts to 251*l.* 15*s.* 10*d.*; being about 6*s.* 11*d.* to each pauper.

But besides the above allowances, from interest of funds, fines, and Sunday collections, there is much given by private charity; the paupers stroll about from parish to parish, during the warm season of the year, when they collect meal, and other provisions, from the charitable disposition of private families, of almost every class of society; and when any poor person, or family, is afflicted by sickness, or otherwise, so as to confine them to their dwelling-houses, they are supported by the humanity of well-disposed families in their neighbourhood, who often do not wait to be solicited, to perform such acts of benevolence and Christian charity towards the distressed and destitute. It is already stated, that there is no poor's-rates in this county. There is from 2*l.* to 3*l.* allowed to the Session-Clerk, (the parochial schoolmaster), annually, out of the poor's funds.

State of Property.—More than one-half the valued rent of the county, namely, 18,777*l.* 13*s.* 3*d.* Scotch, is divided among nine Proprietors, of the name of Sinclair; one of whom is a Peer. There are two Proprietors of the name of Henderson; and two of the name of Horne; the remaining 20 Proprietors are all of different surnames. The names of the Landed Proprietors are as follow:

Roll of the Land-Proprietors' Names, in the County of Caithness, in 1811.

Right Honourable Sir James Sinclair, of Mey, Bart. now Earl of Caithness.

Right

Right Honourable Sir John Sinclair, of Ulbster, Bart. a Privy Councillor.

Sir Benj. Dunbar, of Hempriggs, Bart.

Sir J. G. Sinclair, of Murkle, Bart.

Sir Robert Anstruther, of Wattin, Bart.

William Sinclair, of Freswick, Esq.

James Traill, of Castlehill, Esq., Sheriff Depute of the County.

Mrs. Wemyss, of Stanstill.

James Sinclair, of Forss, Esq.

William Innes, of Sandside, Esq.

J. C. Sutherland, of Forss, Esq.

John Sinclair, of Barrack, Esq.

P. M. Threipland, of Toftingall, Esq.

John Horne, of Stircock, Esq.

—— Balfour, of Calder, Esq.

Colonel Benjamin Williamson, of Matlefield.

John Gordon, of Swiney, Esq.

James Smith, of Olrig, Esq.

Captain Sinclair Worth, of Duren.

David Brodie, of Hopeville, Esq.

Mrs. Sinclair, of Brabster.

Alexander Henderson, of Stempster, Esq.

James Horne, of Scouthell, Esq., W. S.

Alexander Osborn, of Latheron, Esq.

Thomas Fraser, of Banniskirk, Esq.

Patrick Sinclair, of Lybster, Esq. Lieutenant-General.

Miss Macleod, of Lynigar.

Alexander Sinclair, of Achingale.

Alexander Henderson, of Westerdale.

Alexander Cogle, of Campster.

Mr. Harry Craig, for a croft near Wick.

B. Water's heirs, ditto.

Bridgend's heirs, ditto.

And the Crown for the Bishop-lands in the county.

There is a great variety of surnames among the people of this county, no less than about 130; but the prevailing surnames are,—1. Sinclair;—2. Sutherland;—3. Campbell;—4. Swanson;—5. Henderson;—6. Murray;—and 7. Manson.

No. IV.

Extent of the County.

In Templeman's Survey of the Globe, he makes the County of Caithness 690 square miles, which is evidently more than its real extent. The medium of the various calculations I have made, to ascertain its extent, makes the county 616 square miles; and, adding one square mile for the Island of Stroma, 617¼ square miles, or 316,042 Scotch acres. The different sorts of land in the county, including that island, should stand as follow:

	Scotch Acres.
1. Arable land, of every description, infield, and outfield	40,000
2. Meadow, or haughs, near rivers, burns, &c.	2,000
3. Green pasture, common down, and partly moory clay	62,000
4. Under brushwood, and small plantations	850
5. Sand, in Dunnet Bay, &c. &c.	3,000
6. Mountains, or high moory hills, in the parishes of Latheron, Cannisbay, Halkirk, and Reay	71,200
7. Deep mosses, or flat moors, (502 less than the first account, for Stroma Isle)	130,261
8. Fresh-water lakes, 7680: rivers and burns, 743 acres	6,731
Total	316,042

The

The above is the most accurate computation that can be made, of the extent, and agricultural state of this district, which has hitherto been but partially measured.

No. V.

Produce of the County.

Live Stock.—The Ministers of five parishes, have sent the following returns of the live stock, within their respective bounds :

	Horses, young and old.	Black Cattle, young & old.	Sheep.	Swine.	Goats.
1. Cannisbay parish,	480	1518	1062	356	—
2. Latheron ditto, ..	730	2560	7500	90	40
3. Olrig ditto, ...	310	620	—	100	—
4. Thurso ditto, ...	504	1217	342	112	5
5. Wattin ditto, ...	558	1858	594	164	—
Total, ...	2632	7773	9498	822	45

The valued rent of these five parishes being 17,249*l.* Scotch, nearly one-half of the valuation of the county, deducting the towns: from local knowledge, therefore, and other sources of information, I compute the other five parishes at 2600 horses, 7060 cattle, 3250 sheep, 410 swine, and 20 goats; thus estimating the stock of the county at

5,234 horses, at 7*l.* 10*s.* (the average price per the parishes returned)		£39,240	0	0
14,833 cattle, at 4*l.* 4*s.*	ditto	62,298	12	0
12,748 sheep, at 12*s.*	ditto	7,648	16	0
1,232 swine, at 14*s.*	ditto	862	8	0
65 goats, at 6*s.*	ditto	19	10	0
	Total	£110,069	6	0

Sold

Sold out of the County annually.—For some years past, persons have come from Ireland, and have annually purchased, and drove out of this county, several hundreds of small horses, or ponies, to that kingdom; but, as considerable numbers of small horses are annually imported from Orkney, it may balance those sold out of it.

The number of black cattle, sold to drovers, is computed from 1200 to 1600, average 1400, which at 4*l.* 4*s.* each, is	£5880
700 sheep, from Langwell and Sandside, at 1*l.*	700
700 stone of wool, ditto at 1*l.* 10*s.*	1050
Total	£7630

There are numbers of cattle, sheep, and swine, slaughtered in the season, and consumed in the county; neither the amount, nor the value of which, can be ascertained, with any degree of accuracy.

Agricultural Produce.—It is generally supposed, that about four bolls and a half of bear, and four bolls of oats, per Scotch acre, may be considered as a fair average produce of the county *; and on that data, the following Table has been drawn up, from the best information that could be procured.

* Some contend, that a boll may be added to that average of oats, and half a boll to the bear; but it is better, in such calculations, to be within, than without the mark.

Crops.	Scotch Acres.	Bolls per Acre.	Average Price per Boll.	Produce per Acre. £	s.	d.	Total Produce Sterling. £	s.	d.
			s.	£	s.	d.	£	s.	d.
Oats, either potatoe, red, dun, black, or grey,	30,000	4 bolls	12	2	8	0	73,000	0	0
Bear or bigg,	6000	$4\frac{1}{2}$ do.	20	4	10	0	27,000	0	0
Wheat,	10	7 do.	30	10	10	0	105	0	0
Potatoes,	500	20 do.	8	8	0	0	4000	0	0
Turnips,	350	$12\frac{1}{2}$ ton	8	5	0	0	1750	0	0
Pease,	20	4 bolls	20	4	0	0	80	0	0
Flax, when seed can be obtained,	20	—	—	10	0	0	200	0	0
Outfield land in natural pasture,	2000	(See pasture)	(See pasture)	—			—		
Sown grass, clover and rye-grass,	800	180 stone	8d.	6	0	0	480	0	0
Fallow,	300	—	—	—			—		
	40,000								
Natural meadow, haugh or bog hay,	2000	60 do.	6d.	1	10	0	3000	0	0
							112,935	0	0
Pasture for 5232 horses for the summer months, at 12s.				£3139	4	0			
Ditto for 14,833 cattle ditto, at 10s., including town and hill pasture,				7416	10	0			
Ditto for 12,748 sheep, Cheviot and natives, at 2s.				1276	16	0			
Ditto for 1232 swine, at 3s				184	16	0			
Ditto for 65 goats, at 2s.				6	10	0			
							12,023	16	0
Total,							124,958	16	0

According to the foregoing calculation,

Acres.				Bolls.
The 30,000	produce	120,000	bolls of oats, averaged at $\frac{2}{3}$ meal, is	80,000
The 6000	produce	27,000	ditto of bear, averaged at $\frac{5}{4}$ ditto, is	33,750
The 10	produce	70	do. of wheat, averaged at do. do. is	105
The 20	produce	80	do. of pease, averaged at do. do. is	80
36,030		147,150	bolls of grain, or in meal, ...	113,935

And the 500 acres of potatoes, produce about 10,000 bolls, of 24 stone weight. The whole would be nearly equal to five bolls of meal, and about half a boll of potatoes, for each inhabitant of the county, young and old. Perhaps one-fifth more than what is necessary, to maintain the population through the year, along with animal food, milk, and other vegetables. But since the introduction of large horses on the principal farms, they require considerable quantities of oats; and it is remarked, that there is not now so much grain exported from this county, as was the case about 20 years ago; about which period, from 20,000 to 30,000 bolls were annually sold out of it.

There is little or no wood sold from the natural shrubbery, which is fast decaying, and the small plantations, are principally for ornament, and not for profit or sale.

Manufactures, Fisheries, Minerals.—It has already been stated, that there are no manufactures of any moment in this county. While the trade with the Continent was unrestrained, the spinning of flax, for coloured thread, was generally carried on here. It appears, by the Custom-House books, that, in 1793, 41,040 spindles of linen yarn were shipped. The price of spinning, at 1*s.* per spindle, is 2052*l.* sterling. The

war

war has destroyed this branch of industry, from the want of flax.

The Thurso tannery, may produce about 2100*l.* per annum, partly tanned, and partly curried leather: the duties paid by it to the revenue, are about 109*l.* per annum, and the price at which the leather is sold, about 22 times the duties, which, at an average is 1½*d.* per pound, say .... £ 2100

The Thurso bleachfield may produce, from bleached linen	300
The kelp, manufactured along our shores, about 140 tons, may annually produce	1400
The fisheries may be computed as follows:	
Herring fishery, from 1st of July to 30th September, annually about 40,000 barrels, or say that the industry of man brings 20*s.* for each barrel out of the sea	40,000
The cod fishery, much less than in former times, say	550
About 40,000 lobsters, sold to the London smacks, at 3*d.*	500
Salmon fishery, about 1200 kits, of 36lb. at 40*s.*	2400
Total	£47,550

About 15 years ago, the river Thurso alone, produced 2500 kits of salmon, in one season, which, at 30*s.*, is 3750*l.* But that river has been lately mismanaged, by fishing in the close season of the year, and keeping the cruives shut all the year round. It will require a jubilee to recover its former amount.

Exclusive of the above, there are about 20 fishing smacks, from Gravesend, which fish regularly for cod and ling, on the north coast of Caithness, and they have

have, in a great degree, destroyed the cod fishery on our shores.

There are about 160 fishing boats in the several creeks and harbours on the coast of Caithness, whose crews may be averaged at five persons each boat. They occasionally fish for haddock, cod, ling, skate, turbot, and cuddings, &c. &c. in the season. Those in, or near to the towns of Thurso and Wick, dispose of their fish daily, haddocks at 1*d*. each, and other fish in proportion; others along the coast, dispose of their fish to the country people, *i.e.* barter them for meal, butter, cheese, and such other commodities as the one party have to give, and the other require for the subsistence of their families. Their produce I do not reckon, as it is consumed in the county.

For the last two years, a straw-plait manufacture has been carried on in the town of Thurso; the prepared straw is procured from London, and the plait returned to that market. The number at present (1811), employed in this manufacture is 260 women and girls. Their average earnings now may be computed at 3*s*. each per week, equal per annum to 2028*l*. In the course of another year, it is supposed that they will become so expert at the business, that they will average at least 5*s*. each per week, or 3380*l*. per annum. This branch of industry has the additional benefit, that it is performed by young girls, who are not capable of performing any labour that would require great exertion, and who would otherwise live in idleness at the expense of their parents.

There is also some salted beef, and butter, sent from this county to the Leith market annually; likewise tallow, goose-feathers, quills, calf-skins, and other skins, raw, exported; total about 1330*l*.

There is no productive mineral in this county. A vein of lead-ore, of good quality, was discovered at Skinnet, five miles from the sea-port of Thurso; but no fair trial to work it has hitherto been made. There is lime-stone, and marl, in various parts of the county, as already stated, but not wrought for sale.

Recapitulation of the Produce of Manufactures; Commerce and Fisheries; and Miscellaneous Articles.

	£
1. The Thurso tannery, gross produce, about	2,400
2. The ditto bleachfield, ditto	300
3. Kelp, manufactured from sea-weed, about	1,400
4. The herring fishery, but a considerable part of the fish is caught by strangers, who come to the county, during the fishing season, and cure the fish at Wick, &c.	40,000
5. Cod fishing, only about	550
6. Lobsters	500
7. Salmon fishery, in the rivers, about	2,400
8. The boat fishery for haddock, &c. sold to the town and country people, suppose about	1,500
9. The straw-plait manufactory, at Thurso	2,028
10. Grain, viz. bear, oats, and oatmeal, exported, about	10,000
11. Salted beef, butter, tallow, calf-skins, &c. feathers, &c.	1,330
Total	£62,408

No. VI.

No. VI.

General View of the State of the County of Caithness.

Extent in square miles		617
in English acres, statute measure		395,053
in Scotch acres		316,042
in arable land	40,000	
in meadow	2,000	
in green pasture, &c.	62,000	
in brushwood, and small plantations	850	
in barren sand, at Dunnet bay, &c.	3,000	
in mountains, or high moory hills	71,200	
in deep peat mosses, and flat moors	130,261	
in fresh-water lakes, rivers, &c.	6,731	
		316,042

Horses	5232
Cattle	14,833
Sheep	12,748
Swine	1,232
Goats	65

	£	s.	d.
Value of live stock	£110,069	6	0
Value of agricultural produce	114,958	16	0
Value of manufacturing, commercial, fishery, and mineral produce	62,408	0	0

Number of Proprietors, including the Crown for the Bishop-lands	34

Valued rent, Scotch	£37,256	2	9
Ditto, sterling	3,104	10	$2\frac{2}{3}$

Number of inhabitants, (in 1755, 22,215), in 1798	23,031
Ditto, in 1810, per Table No. II.	23,769
Increase, (in 55 years, from 1755, about 1554), in 12 years, from 1798	738
Number of fighting men, from 18 to 45 years, per militia lists	2,809
Ditto, from 16 to 60 years of age	4,072
Inhabiting towns*, viz. Thurso 1952, in Wick and suburbs 1749	3701
Inhabiting the country part, and small villages	20,068
Number of inhabitants to each square mile	$38\frac{1}{2}$
English acres to each inhabitant, nearly	$16\frac{2}{3}$

	£	*s.*	*d.*
Ministers' stipends 379*l.* 19*s.* 10*d.*, and 1470 bolls, say at 20*s.*, is, with glebes and communion elements	2027	0	0
Average to each Minister, nearly	202	14	0

* The town of Thurso contains 1952 inhabitants, of whom there are
  - 18 shopkeepers, or merchants
  - 20 inn-keepers and alehouses
  - 5 shops for retailing whisky
  - 51 house-carpenters and wheel-wrights
  - 12 blacksmiths
  - 2 tin-smiths
  - 22 coopers
  - 80 tailors
  - 32 masons
  - 55 shoemakers
  - 52 weavers
  - 2 watchmakers, and
  - 1 boat-carpenter.

Scholars

Scholars 1787			
	£	s.	d.
Parochial Schoolmasters' salaries, and common emoluments	258	17	0
Average to each Schoolmaster, formerly about	25	17	8¼
Average to ditto, at this time, (1811)	36	0	0

Poor 725			
	£	s	d.
Capital stock of poor's funds	2274	5	4
Annual income of the poor	251	15	10
Average to each	0	6	11

No. VII.

Abstract of Imports and Exports into and from the Port of Thurso, County of Caithness, in the Years 1793 and 1803, per the Custom-House Books.

N. B. Strathnaver is included within this Port of Thurso.

Commodities.	Anno 1793. Imports. Quantity.	Anno 1793. Imports. Denomination.	Anno 1793. Exports. Quantity.	Anno 1793. Exports. Denomination.	Anno 1803. Imports. Quantity.	Anno 1803. Imports. Denomination.	Anno 1803. Exports. Quantity.	Anno 1803. Exports. Denomination.
Snuff	5283lb.	—	—	—	8150lb.	—	—	—
Tobacco	2207lb.	Stalks	—	—	1144lb.	Roll & St.	—	—
	157lb.	Roll						
Whisky	75lb.	Galls.	—	—	89 galls.	—	—	—
Wine	122lb.	French	—	—	7 galls.	French	—	—
	897lb.	Not Fr.	—	—	914 galls.	Not Fr.	—	—
Rum	152lb.	—	—	—	503 galls.	—	—	—
Gin	—	—	—	—	134 galls.	—	—	—
Brandy	—	—	—	—	23 galls.	—	—	—
Salt	20,896 bush.	English	443 bush.	English	59,143 bush.	English	2216 bush.	English
	14,377 bush.	Foreign	1775 bush.	Foreign	500 bush.	Foreign	—	—
	204 bush.	Scotch	335 bush.	Scotch	438 bush.	Scotch	—	—
Coals	43 chald.	English	—	—	806 chald.	English	—	—
	241 tons	Scotch	—	—	585 tons	Scotch	—	—
Cinders	—	—	—	—	26 chald.	English	—	—
Tea	1856lb.	Black	—	—	9972lb.	Black	84lb.	Black
	8lb.	Green	—	—	94lb.	Green	—	—
Sugar	40cwt. 3qrs. 8lb.	Brown	—	—	227cwt. 1qr. 2lb.	Brown	—	—
	169cwt. 2qrs. 5lb.	Refined	—	—	514cwt.	Refined	—	—
Coffee	36lb.	—	—	—	40lb.	—	—	—
Dry cod	—	—	5 tons 2cwt. 9lb.	—	—	—	9 tons 7cwt.	—

Wet cod	—	—	224 barrels	—	—	—	229 barrels	—
Salmon	—	—	448 barrels	—	—	—	38 barrels 400 kits	— —
Herrings	—	—	627 barrels 6840 barrels	Red White	— —	— —	3732 barrels 3854 ditto	Red White
Barley	3 tons 12cwt. 3qrs.	Hulled	—	—	6 tons 11cwt. 2qrs.	Hulled	—	—
Bear or bigg	1qr. 4 bush.	—	646 qrs.	—	—	—	3481qrs.	—
Pease	6qrs.	—	—	—	37qrs. 2 bush.	—	—	—
Oat-meal	31 tons 4cwt. 1qr. 4lb.	—	614 tons 9cwt. 1qr. 16lb.	—	60 tons	—	311 tons	—
Wheat-meal	34 tons 13cwt. 3qrs.	—	—	—	17 tons	—	—	—
Oats	66qrs. 3 bush.	—	6 qrs.	—	82qrs. 4 bush.	—	128qrs.	—
Wheat	—	—	—	—	15bush.	—	—	—
Biscuit	3 tons	—	—	—	6 tons 2cwt.	—	—	—
Butter	—	—	7 tons 13cwt. 2qrs. 24lb.	—	13cwt. 2qrs. 11lb.	—	2t. 9c. 2q. 26lb.	—
Cheese	2qrs.	—	8cwt. 22lb.	—	19cwt. 2qrs. 24lb.	—	—	—
Wool	196cwt. 5lb. 15lb.	Raw Combed	148cwt.	Raw	103cwt. 3qrs. 3lb.	Raw	477cwt. 17lb.	Raw
Hides	—	—	—	—	No. 710.	—	No. 16	—
Yarn	32 sp. 500qrs.	Cotton Linen	—	— —	1cwt. 2cwt.	Cotton Linen	— —	— —
Brimstone	2qrs.	—	—	—	—	—	—	—
Candles	224lb.	—	—	—	128lb.	—	—	—
Cotton wool	—	—	—	—	200lb.	—	—	—
Copperas	2cwt. 3qrs. 2lb.	—	—	—	5cwt 2qrs. 14lb.	—	—	—
Corks	144 gross	—	—	—	588 gross	—	—	—
Cordage	2 tons 6cwt.	—	—	—	5 tons 1cwt.	—	—	—
Dye stuffs	16 casks	—	—	—	166 bags, &c. 2 tons	—	—	—
Cork	—	—	—	—	2cwt.	—	—	—

Commodities.	Anno 1793. Imports. Quantity.	Denomination	Exports. Quantity.	Denomination.	Anno 1803. Imports. Quantity.	Denomination.	Exports. Quantity.	Denomination.
Earthenware	49 crates	—	—	—	114 crates	—	—	—
Bricks	No. 28,000	—	—	—	No. 30,012	—	—	—
Tiles	No. 14,500	—	—	—	No. 9742	—	—	—
Flax	3 tons 19cwt.	Undress'd	—	—	7cwt.	—	—	—
	45 tons 11cwt.	Dressed			28 tons 11cwt.			
Beef	—	—	363 barrels	—	5 barrels	—	254 barrels	—
Copper	4cwt.	Wrought	—	—	—	—	—	—
Furniture & apparel	15 loads	—	5 loads	—	26 loads	—	13 loads	—
Glass	5 cases	—	—	—	53 crates, &c.	—	—	—
Liquorice	3cwt. 1qr. 4lb.	—	—	—	1cwt. 3qrs.	—	—	—
Currants	2cwt. 1qr.	—	—	—	3cwt. 2qrs. 4lb.	—	—	—
Figs	1cwt. 2qrs.	—	—	—	2cwt. 1qr. 3lb.	—	—	—
Plums	23lb.	—	—	—	—	—	—	—
Confections	—	—	—	—	6cwt. 3qrs. 8lb.	—	—	—
Prunes	1cwt.	—	—	—	—	—	—	—
Raisins	5cwt. 1qr. 22lb.	—	—	—	6cwt.	—	—	—
Candy	1cwt. 27lb.	—	—	—	3cwt. 15lb.	—	—	—
Haberdashery	241 bales & boxes	—	167 bales and boxes	—	111 bales, &c.	—	15 bales, &c.	—
Hardware	24 casks and boxes	—	82 casks and boxes	—	228 casks	—	14 boxes	—
Hats	3 boxes	—	—	—	54 boxes	—	—	—
Hemp	2 tons 5cwt. 1qr. 26lb	—	—	—	5 tons 1cwt. 1qr.	Dress'd	—	—
					2 tons 10cwt.	Undress'd		

Honey	20lb.	—	—	—	1qr. 3lb.	—	—	—
Hops	15cwt. 8lb.	—	—	—	—	—	—	—
Hoops	No. 122,500	Wood	—	—	No. 238,600	Wood	—	—
					No. 40,500	Iron	—	—
Cart-wheels	76 pair	—	—	—	95 pair	—	—	—
Harrows	—	—	—	—	58 pair	—	—	—
Fanners	1 pair	—	—	—	6 pair	—	—	—
Riddles and scythes	8 doz.	—	—	—	6 doz.	—	—	—
Spades	6 doz.	—	—	—	8 doz.	—	—	—
Indigo	1cwt.	—	—	—	20lb.	—	—	—
Iron	6 tons 13cwt. 2qrs. 7lb.	Wrought	5 tons 9cwt. 2qrs. 24lb.	—	26 tons 14cwt.	Wrought	—	—
	18 tons 17cwt.	Unwro't			24 tons 3cwt.	Unwro't	—	—
Lead	10cwt.	Bird-shot	—	—	3 tons 3cwt.	Bird-shot	—	—
Leather	2tons 12cwt. 3qrs. 22lb.	Tanned	3 tons 10cwt. 1qr. 13lb.	Tanned	13 tons	Tanned	2 tons 12cwt.	Tanned
Molasses	3 tons 14cwt. 2qrs.	—	—	—	5 tons 6cwt. 3qrs.	—	—	—
Logwood	6cwt.	—	—	—	1cwt.	—	—	—
Linen cloth	3400 yards	—	3400 yards	—	—	—	1570 yds. for	bleaching
Ditto yarn	41,040 spindles	—	41,040 spindles	—	—	—	—	—
Linen and woollen drapery	60 bales & boxes	—	3 bales	—	458 bales	—	—	—
Lintseed	72 bush.	—	—	—	92 bush.	—	—	—
Lemons & oranges	—	—	—	—	8 boxes	—	—	—
Fishing lines	—	—	—	—	No. 101	—	—	—
Madder	2cwt.	—	—	—	3cwt.	—	—	—
Nails	1cwt.	—	—	—	10cwt.	—	—	—
Green oil	18 gallons	—	—	—	42 gallons	—	—	—
Lintseed ditto	33 gallons	—	—	—	84 gallons	—	—	—
Whale ditto	20 gallons	—	—	—	—	—	96 gallons	—
Oilmen's ware	2 casks	—	—	—	8 casks	—	—	—

Commodities.	Anno 1793. Imports. Quantity.	Denomination.	Exports. Quantity.	Denomination.	Anno 1803. Imports. Quantity.	Denomination.	Exports. Quantity.	Denomination.
Onions	16 bush.	–	–	–	20 bush.	–	–	–
Herring barrels	–	–	No. 307	–	No. 3389	–	No. 1127	–
Ditto hogsheads	–	–	No. 17	–	No. 20	–	No. 22	–
Salmon barrels	–	–	–	–	No. 20	–	–	–
Ditto kits	–	–	–	–	No. 1200	–	–	–
Brown paper	27 bundles	–	–	–	24 bundles	–	–	–
Ordinary ditto	14 reams	–	–	–	11 reams	–	–	–
Pepper	1qr. 6lb.	–	–	–	2qrs.	–	–	–
Gunpowder	1cwt.	–	–	–	2cwt. 3qrs.	–	–	–
Rice	2cwt. 1qr.	–	–	–	6cwt. 2qrs.	–	–	–
Rosin	1cwt. 2qrs.	–	–	–	3cwt. 3qrs.	–	–	–
Soap	14cwt. 2qrs. 12lb.	Soft	–	–	2t. 1[illegible] 3q. 20lb.	Soft	–	–
	3 tons 10cwt. 2q. 22lb.	Hard	–	–	9t. 3c. 1qr. 16lb.	Hard	–	–
Starch	2cwt. 3qrs. 12lb.	–	–	–	4cwt. 3qrs. 2lb.	–	–	–
Bed feathers	–	–	7cwt. 2qrs. 20lb.	–	–	–	17cwt. 1q. 1lb.	–
Kelp, including kelp from Lord Reay's country	–	–	561 tons	–	–	–	123 tons	–
Tallow	–	–	2 tons 8cwt. 1qr. 20lb.	–	–	–	19cwt. 2q. 8lb.	–
Alum	16cwt.	–	–	–	11cwt 2qrs.	–	–	–
Battons	2 hun.	Foreign	–	–	2 hun.	British	–	–
Deals	61 hun. 3 qrs. 26 odds	British	–	–	67 hun.	Ditto	–	–
Deal ends	–	–	–	–	11 hun.	Ditto	–	–

Spars	17 hun. 14 odd	British	–	–	12 hun 1qr. 6 odd	British	–	–
Rails	15 hun. 1qr. 24 odd	Ditto	–	–	62hun. 2qr. 24odd	Ditto	–	–
Plough-beams	3qrs. 18 odd	Ditto	–	–	3 qr.	Ditto	–	–
Hazle cuts	24 hun.	Ditto	–	–	4 hun. 3 qr.	Ditto	–	–
Handspikes	–	–	–	–	3 hun.	Ditto	–	–
Harrow-bills	–	–	–	–	3 hun.	Ditto	–	–
Fir timber	339 load 4 ft.	Foreign	–	–	{ 116 hun. { 2417 pieces	Foreign –	–	–
Oak timber	–	–	–	–	31 load	–	–	–
Ditto plank	–	–	–	–	7 load	–	–	–
Lath wood	8 fa. 3 qrs.	Foreign	–	–	{ 11,325 feet { 16 bundles	–	–	–
Mahogany	–	–	–	–	80 feet	–	–	–
Porter	92 hogsh.	–	–	–	390 hogsh.	–	–	–
Potatoes	211 hogsh.	–	–	–	108 bush.	–	–	–
Clover-seeds	10cwt. 2qrs. 2lb.	–	–	–	12cwt.	–	–	–
Rye-grass	186 bush.	–	–	–	370 bush.	–	40 hogsh.	–
Bird-seeds	2 bush.	–	–	–	3 bush.	–	–	–
Garden-seeds	4 bags	–	–	–	2 bags	–	–	–
Slates	No. 32,600	–	–	–	No. 47,600	–	No. 39,280	–
Stones	–	–	–	–	–	–	12 tons	–
Staves {	504 hun. 20 odd	Barrel	–	–	928h. 2q. 24 odd	Barrel	–	–
	45 hun. 3 qrs. 10 odd	Hogsh.	–	–	8hun. 1qr. 30 odd	Hogsh.	–	–
	10 hun. 2 qrs. 20 odd	Pipe	–	–	21h. 1 qr. 30 odd	Pipe	–	–
Tar	61 barrels	–	–	–	187 barrels	–	–	–
Twine	3qrs.	–	–	–	11cwt.	–	–	–
Vinegar	566 galls.	–	–	–	5700 galls.	–	–	–
Vitriol	4cwt.	–	–	–	6cwt.	–	–	–
Hare-skins	–	–	–	–	–	–	12 doz.	–

Commodities.	Anno 1793. Imports. Quantity.	Anno 1793. Imports. Denomination.	Anno 1793. Exports. Quantity.	Anno 1793. Exports. Denomination.	Anno 1803. Imports. Quantity.	Anno 1803. Imports. Denomination.	Anno 1803. Exports. Quantity.	Anno 1803. Exports. Denomination.
Calf skins	–	–	22 doz.	–	–	–	61½ doz.	–
Deer ditto	–	–	–	–	–	–	3 doz.	–
Rabbit ditto	–	–	2 doz.	–	–	–	3 doz.	–
Goat ditto	–	–	–	–	–	–	6 doz.	–
Otter ditto	–	–	4 doz.	–	–	–	3 doz.	–
Apples	16 bush.	–	–	–	11 bush.	–	–	–
Ashes	1 ton 11cwt.	Pearl	–	–	7cwt. 2qrs.	Pearl	–	–
	3cwt.	Pot	–	–	2 tons 11cwt. 1qr.	Pot	–	–
Bark	40 tons	Oak	–	–	2 tons 12cwt.	Oak	–	–
Black beer	–	–	–	–	100 galls.	–	–	–
Bottles	–	–	–	–	152 gross	–	–	–
Wool-cards	–	–	–	–	23 doz.	–	–	–
Beer	–	–	–	–	–	–	243½ galls.	–
Nolt-hair	–	–	–	–	1 ton 3cwt.	–	–	–
Provisions	–	–	–	–	–	–	24 boxes	–
Quills	–	–	–	–	–	–	No. 24,000	–
Malt	–	–	–	–	30qrs.	–	–	–
Ton- { Inwards	5454	–	–	–	7122	–	–	–
nage { Outwards	5891	–	–	–	6211	–	–	–

No. VIII.

A Statistical Table of Five Parishes of the County of Caithness, in 1810.

Particulars.	Dunnet Parish.		Cannisbay Parish.		Wattin Parish.		Bower Parish.		Olrig Parish.	
	Houses.		Houses.		Houses.		Houses.		Houses.	
Houses inhabited	290	—	397	—	220	—	275	—	171	—
By how many families	304	—	397	—	220	—	275	—	180	—
Uninhabited houses	15	—	4	—	4	—	10	—	16	—
	Males.	Females.	Males.	Females.	Males.	Females.	Males.	Females.	Males.	Females.
Persons married	223	223	298	298	284	284	229	229	148	148
Children	353	385	440	396	254	269	306	338	221	182
Children at school	86	81	95	74	73	54	96	32	80	71
Persons married having no children*	24	24	7	7	13	13	28	28	12	12
Wives whose husbands are absent	—	8	—	1	—	2	—	4	—	4
Women employed in domestic affairs	—	376	—	404	—	61	—	29	—	61
Persons chiefly employed in agriculture	188	59	366	53	321	415	360	334	241	279
Employed in trade or handicraft	54	2	37	14	37	8	49	33	61	—
Not comprised in the three preceding classes	47	11	461	472	115	112	3	2	240	224
Not natives of the parish	84	104	27	33	177	266	91	96	148	101
Not natives of the county	8	15	19	11	9	29	8	7	16	5
Sickly for three months or more	9	3	4	5	1	1	4	3	6	3
Disabled from work by sickness	8	6	14	13	7	18	3	16	6	8
Servants	49	75	43	49	86	184	88	114	89	120
Bachelors having houses	26	—	16	—	22	—	11	—	7	—
Persons residing in families, but not constituent members	2	4	4	7	14	20	4	1	4	1
Indigent, on the poor's roll	9	50	11	44	5	54	15	35	14	20
Unmarried females having houses	—	26	—	27	—	21	—	21	—	3
Widowers	29	—	12	—	8	—	19	—	16	—
Widows	—	75	—	54	—	53	—	72	—	34
Persons of from one to 21 years of age	375	399	465	467	301	306	348	371	304	303
——— from 21 to 45	118	160	201	259	136	216	167	211	162	240
——— from 45 to 60	108	128	146	157	71	90	77	123	53	67
——— from 60 to 80	58	81	47	57	46	53	54	63	21	41
——— from 80 to 100	7	6	3	2	2	8	2	8	5	8
——— above 100	—	—	1	1	—	—	—	—	—	—
Total males	666	—	863	—	560	—	643	—	544	—
Total females	774	—	943	—	697	—	776	—	659	—
Total population	1440	—	1806	—	1257	—	1419	—	1203	—
Left the county within these three months	—	—	—	—	8	8	—	—	—	—

Among other interesting particulars, it appears from the above Table, that the number of females at, or below 21 years of age, is 33 less than the number above that age; and that the number of males, in the five parishes at, and below 21 years, is 233 more than the number above that age; and upon the whole, that the number of both sexes above 21 years, is 200 less than the number at, and below 21 years of age.

It is to be regretted, that similar returns could not be procured from the other five parishes, so as to render this Table complete.

* There are 84 couple married in the five parishes, who have produced no children. There are 84 widowers, and 288 widows!

No. IX.

State of the Population of the Parish of Thurso, Anno 1801.

	Women whose Husbands are absent.	Unmarried Females having Houses.	Bachelors having Houses.	Widowers.	Widows.	Persons Married.	Houses. Inhabited.	Houses. By how many Families.	Uninhabited Houses.	Children*. M.	Children*. F.	Servants. M.	Servants. F.	Persons residing in Families, but not constituent Members of the Family. M.	Persons residing in Families, but not constituent Members of the Family. F.	Females employed in Domestic Affairs.	Persons chiefly employed in Agriculture. M.	Persons chiefly employed in Agriculture. F.	Persons chiefly employed in Trade. M.	Persons chiefly employed in Trade. F.	Persons not comprised in any of the preceding Classes. M.	Persons not comprised in any of the preceding Classes. F.	Males.	Females.	Total Number of Persons.
Town District	26	23	41	18	82	275	360	469	51	363	408	51	150	83	164	678	—	—	464	16	365	435	831	1127	1958
Country District	2	14	23	15	40	253	342	350	33	326	360	77	121	73	113	—	486	556	52	11	229	336	767	903	1670
Town and Country	28	37	64	33	122	528	702	819	84	689	768	128	271	156	277	678	486	556	516	27	594	771	1598	2030	3628

* Children at school in 1801, 215.

No. X.

A Comparative View of the Expense of Husbandry, &c. &c. in the County of Caithness, at different Periods, as below stated.

	Anno	Oatmeal Cost to Farm-Servants per Annum.	Price per Boll.	Total Price of the Oatmeal.	Bear-meal Cost per Ann.	Price per Boll.	Total Price of Bear-meal.	Price of Bear and Oatmeal to Servants.	Pairs of Shoes.	Price per Pair.	Money Wages per Annum.	Total of Cost and Wages per Annum.	Wages in Harvest, without Cost.	Wages in Harvest, with Cost.	Value of the Daily Apparel of a Farm-Servant.	Dress Apparel of a Farm-Servant.	Wages for Day-Labour, with Victuals.	Wages per Day, without Victuals.
		B. F.	£ s. d.	£ s. d.	B. F.	£ s. d.	£ s. d.	£ s. d.		s. d.	£ s. d.	£ s. d.	s. d.	s. d.	£ s. d.	£ s. d.	s. d.	s. d.
Male servants,	1750	3 0	0 8 0	1 4 0	3 0	0 6 0	0 18 0	2 2 0	2	1 8	1 0 0	3 5 4	9 0	5 0	0 9 1	0 16 9	0 4	0 6
	1790	3 0	0 12 0	1 16 0	3 0	0 10 0	1 10 0	3 6 0	2	5 6	3 0 0	6 17 0	27 0	15 0	0 18 4	2 8 5	0 8	0 10
	1798	3 0	0 14 0	2 2 0	3 0	0 13 0	1 19 0	4 1 0	2	7 0	5 0 0	9 8 0	40 0	26 0	2 6 9	3 4 0	0 10	1 0
	1810	3 2	1 5 0	4 7 6	3 2	1 0 0	3 10 0	7 17 6	2	10 0	6 10 0	15 7 6	52 0	32 0	2 5 0	3 10 0	1 0	1 6
Female servants,	1750	1 2	0 8 0	0 12 0	1 2	0 7 0	0 10 6	1 2 6	2	0 10	0 6 8	1 10 10	6 0	2 6	0 12 0	1 6 9	0 3	0 4
	1790	1 2	0 12 0	0 18 0	1 2	0 10 0	0 15 0	1 13 0	2	3 6	1 0 0	3 0 0	18 0	10 0	1 5 0	1 13 6	0 4	0 6
	1798	1 2	0 14 0	1 1 0	1 2	0 11 0	0 16 6	1 17 6	2	4 6	1 12 0	3 18 6	23 0	15 0	1 14 2	6 6 4	0 4	0 8
	1810	2 0	1 5 0	2 10 0	2 0	1 0 0	2 0 0	4 10 0	—	—	2 8 0	6 18 0	32 0	20 0	2 0 0	4 5 0	0 6	0 10

N. B. The cause of the reduction of price in apparel in 1810, is owing to the low price of manufactured cotton cloth; and in the year 1750 there was nothing used but home manufacture, when wool was abundant, and at low prices.

During the Years	1750.	1790.	1798.	1810.
	£ s. d.	£ s. d	£ s. d.	£ s. d.
A cow with calf, cost	0 15 0	3 10 0	5 5 0	7 0 0
A ditto without ditto	0 12 0	2 8 0	4 0 0	5 10 0
A horse or garron, for the plough	1 10 0	3 7 0	7 0 0	12 0 0
A three-year old wedder, in season	0 2 6	0 7 6	0 12 0	1 5 0
A lamb	0 0 6	0 2 6	0 4 0	0 10 0
A sow or hog	0 2 6	0 10 6	0 15 0	1 10 0

During the Years	1750.	1790.	1798.	1810.
	s. d.	s. d.	s. d.	£ s. d.
A goose, in September	0 6¼	1 2	1 8	0 2 6
A hen	0 2	0 4	0 6	0 1 0
18 eggs in 1750, for a dozen, now 12	0 1	0 1¼	0 2	0 0 3
A stone of butter, (24 lb.)	5 0	15 0	18 0	1 2 0
A stone of cheese, ditto	2 6	4 0	6 0	0 8 0
1lb. of beef or mutton, by the quarter	0 1½	0 2½	0 4½	0 0 6

N. B. The above Comparative Tables refer chiefly to the expenditure of the general class of Farmers or Occupiers of land. Persons farming on a more extensive scale, have a much greater expenditure, in maintaining their servants, purchasing farming utensils, &c. &c.

No. XI.

Fairs annually held in the County of Caithness.

Date.	In what Parish	Name.	Where held.	Commodities sold at each.
February 3	Cannisbay	Candlemass	Freswick	Woollen and other stuffs, the produce of the county.
March 15	Olrig	Olrig	Olrig	Cattle, &c.
29	Bower	Camster	Camster	Ditto.
May 15	Ditto	Rood fair	Lairal	Woollen stuff, &c.
June 21	Olrig	June fair	Lysag	Cattle, &c.
July 4	Thurso	Petersmass	Thurso	Horses, woollen stuff, &c.
27	Halkirk	James fair	Spittlehill	Horses, cattle, lambs, &c. &c.
August 1	Wick	Hill fair	Hill of Wick	Cattle, &c. &c.
8	Reay	Trust fair	Reay	Ditto ditto
	Latheron	Lammass	Bridgend	Ditto.
29	Dunnet	Marymass	Dunnet	Cattle, horses from Orkney, &c. &c.
Septemb. 2	Thurso	Ditto	Thurso	Ditto ditto, and merchant goods.
29	Wattin	Rood fair	Backlass	Ditto ditto.
October 26	Ditto	Wester fair	Wester	Ditto.
November 1	Latheron	Little market	Bridgend	Cattle, and creels, &c. rom the brushwood.
7	Bower	Lukesmass	Reaster	Cattle.
21	Ditto	Stanstill fair	Stantill	Ditto.
26	Ditto	Bower fair	Bower	Ditto.
27	Olrig	Trothemass	Olrig	Ditto.
Decemb. 27	Wattin	Magnusmass	Wattin	Ditto.

A weekly market held at Thurso every Friday, and at Wick every Tuesday, throughout the year.

No. XII.

Return of the Number of Marriages, and Births, in the Seven following Parishes of the County of Caithness.

[There is no Register of Burials kept, and no Return from the other three Parishes.]

Anno.	Bower Parish. Marriages.	Bower Parish. No. of Births. Males.	Bower Parish. No. of Births. Females.	Cannisbay. Marriages.	Cannisbay. No. of Births. Males.	Cannisbay. No. of Births. Females.	Halkirk. Marriages.	Halkirk. No. of Births. Males.	Halkirk. No. of Births. Females.	Latheron. Marriages.	Latheron. No. of Births. Males.	Latheron. No. of Births. Females.
1786	12	29	14	7	19	27	22	42	[illegible]	22	[illegible]	40
1787	9	24	13	14	31	32	15	41	36	19	59	40
1788	20	20	9	7	20	34	12	31	35	28	5[illegible]	55
1789	9	9	7	14	28	29	17	37	29	21	62	51
1790	18	16	17	15	41	18	19	32	45	20	56	74
Total	68	97	60	57	139	140	85	183	179	110	24[illegible]	258
1806	16	26	15	14	23	18	9	48	3[illegible]	4	66	47
1807	10	17	17	15	23	10	12	48	35	12	51	55
1808	9	22	16	6	21	17	19	39	40	18	48	41
1809	9	22	22	10	18	11	9	38	5[illegible]	20	50	59
1810	5	17	20	9	19	21	10	31	27	24	43	53
Total	49	101	88	54	103	77	59	204	188	78	258	255

Anno.	Olrig Parish.			Thurso.			Wattin.		
1786	4	15	14	25	63	48	8	24	22
1787	5	19	11	29	39	46	8	21	10
1788	3	11	7	20	52	45	11	15	18
1789	4	10	13	28	29	44	13	14	20
1790	3	13	17	26	66	61	8	20	25
Total	19	68	62	128	249	244	43	94	95
1806	3	25	19	17	59	52	6	22	11
1807	9	22	13	26	39	48	5	23	12
1808	3	13	9	25	55	44	5	15	15
1809	10	10	18	12	38	37	6	10	12
1810	5	15	16	22	44	36	6	10	14
Total	30	85	75	102	235	216	28	80	64

Mrs. Cowper, midwife, in the town of Thurso, has, from 1790 to April 1811, attended the birth of 787 boys, and 729 girls; total 1516; being 58 boys more than of girls.

Grand total in the ten years, from 1786 to 1810—Of Marriages 915; males born 2138; females born 2003; more than females by 135; producing 4½ children to each marriage.

No. XIII.

Regulations of the Society of United Farmers and Craftsmen, of Castletown, in the County of Caithness.

At Castletown, the 14th February, 1798, and the 38th year of the Reign His Majesty King George the Third, whom God long preserve.

"We, the Farmers and Craftsmen, in and about Castletown, having met, it was proposed and unanimously agreed to, that it is expedient, and necessary, for us to form ourselves into a Society, and to raise a fund, for the aid and assistance of such members, their widows, and offspring, whom it may please God to reduce to indigence and want. We, therefore, resolve to unite ourselves into a Society, which shall be known, and called, by the name of the United Farmers and Craftsmen of Castletown, for the ends and purposes aforesaid; and further, we bind and oblige ourselves to abide by the following Rules and Regulations, and such others as may hereafter be judged proper to adopt.

Article I. *Admission of Members.*—1. That no person is to be admitted into the Society, but he who is a Protestant by profession, and of a good moral character, sound in mind and body, and, to all appearance, able to provide for himself and his family. 2. That at the commencement of the Society, persons be admitted at the age of 60, but after the Society amounts to 100 Members, no person shall be admitted above the age of 40 years. 3. That no person shall be admitted into the Society as a Member, until he is recommended at least by two Members of the Society, with whom he has

has been acquainted for a sufficient time before; and until he is personally present, unless for reasons satisfactory to the Society.—4. That sons of Members, of the foresaid description, be admitted after the expiration of six years from the commencement of the father; upon paying half entry money, provided their age does not exceed 30 years.—5. If a Member has no son, his son-in-law shall have the same privilege.—6. That notwithstanding the said regulations, no person shall be admitted, without the voice of a majority of the Members of the Society.

II. *Times of Meeting.*—1. That the Society shall meet on the second Wednesday of February, May, August, and November, annually, during the existence of the Society.—2. That the Society shall meet at twelve noon, on the February meeting, which shall be deemed the annual meeting, for the election of office-bearers and other business, and at noon on the other quarterly meeting days.

III. *Election, and Duty of the Office Bearers.*—1. That a Member shall be chosen annually by a majority of votes to bear the office of *Preses*; who shall maintain good order, take the sense of the meeting, and sanction their resolutions by his subscription, and also choose a Depute to officiate in his absence.—2. That a Member shall be chosen annually, to bear the office of Treasurer, who shall pay the sums allowed weekly to each sick, superannuated, or otherwise indisposed Member, and account for the same next quarterly meeting thereafter.—3. That four Members shall be chosen annually, as Stewards, to bear office quarterly in rotation, and the Steward for the quarter shall visit each

each sick or otherwise indisposed Member within a mile and a half of Castletown.—4. That four Members shall be taken from the roll quarterly, to bear office as Managers, who, together with the other office bearers, shall be a Committee to determine in all causes that may occur between the quarterly meetings, not provided for in the Articles; but their determination shall be no longer binding than the first quarterly meeting, unless sanctioned by the Society.—5. That a Member shall be chosen annually to the office of Clerk, who is to attend all the meetings of the Society and Committees.

IV. *Collections.*—1. That during the first year of this Society, each person admitted shall pay as entry money five shillings sterling, but after that period it shall be in the power of the Society, to raise the entry money from time to time, as shall be thought proper. 2. That each Member shall pay 1*s.* quarterly, as quarter-pennies.—3. That in case the fund of the Society, by sick Members' annuities, or otherwise, should be brought to the sum of ninety pounds sterling, each Member shall pay in proportionally over and above the ordinary quarter-pennies, until the fund shall exceed that sum, as much as the Society shall deem needful. —4. That at the death of a Member, or Members, within the space of six years from the commencement of this Society, each Member shall pay in his respective share, of what sum may be given out for the interment of the foresaid Member or Members.—5. That any Member residing in England or Ireland, shall be allowed two years and a half to remit his quarterly payments without any fine.—6. That any Member leaving Great Britain and Ireland, will be allowed six years to remit his quarterly payments, without a fine.—7. That Members residing

residing in Scotland, and not in Caithness, will be allowed 18 months to remit their quarterly payments, without any fine. Members in Caithness, at ten miles distance, to be allowed one year to remit their quarterly payments without fine.

V. *Fund.*—1. That all or part of this fund shall be laid out, if required, in purchasing any commodity, that may be for the joint interest of the Members, or given out on lawful interest, until the next annual meeting.—2. That no more than 20*l.* sterling shall be given out to any one Member at one time.—3. That no Member shall receive any sum upon interest until he finds two cautioners, and all of them satisfactory to the Society.

VI. *Box.*—1. There shall be a box with three locks, and three keys, different from one another, to hold the money, books, bills, or other papers belonging to the Society.—2. That two keys shall be kept by two of the Stewards, each quarterly, and the other by the manager for the quarter; the box to be deposited in the Treasurer's House.

VII. *Benefit.*—1. That any Member who is rendered unfit to provide for himself and family, by sickness, accident, or otherwise, shall receive three shillings sterling per week, for the space of six weeks, and if he is not likely to recover, shall receive two shillings sterling for other six weeks, if so long sick.—2. That any Member continuing sick for more than three months, and in all human probability not likely to recover; or, having failed through old age, or infirmity, shall be put upon the superannuated list, and receive fifteen

shillings

shillings sterling quarterly or, their proportions paid weekly as the Society shall see cause.—3. That every widow of this Society shall receive *two-thirds* of the superannuated Member's allowance, and that paid quarterly.—4. That if a Member die before his widow is entitled to the annuity, she shall continue the quarterly payments, until she is entitled to the annuity, and then she shall receive as formerly stated.—5. That orphan children of deceased Members shall receive 10*s*. sterling yearly, less or more, as the Society shall deem fit, until they arrive at ten years of age.—6. That a Member's widow marrying, her annuity shall be immediately withdrawn, and if there be any children of the first marriage, who shall appear to be in indigent circumstances, they shall receive the orphan's annuity.—7. That on the death of a Member, 1*l*. 15*s*. shall be paid from the fund of the Society, and on the death of a Member's widow, 1*l*. sterling for defraying funeral charges.—8. That Members not residing within one mile and a half of Castletown, shall attest their claims on this Society, by two satisfactory Members, or in failure of that, by the Minister and one of the Elders of the parish they reside in.

VIII. *No Benefits*.—1. That no money shall be paid out, from the fund, until the capital amount to 120*l*. sterling.—2. That no Member shall receive any benefit until his name shall have been six years on the roll.—3. That any Member in arrears to this Society, shall not receive any benefit until the same is regularly paid up.—4. That any Member who shall bring disease on himself, by any unlawful means, shall not receive any benefit while thus indisposed.—5. That any Member who shall waste or destroy any part of the

Society's funds by pretended sickness, or otherwise, shall be expelled the Society.—6. That if any Member fail to pay in his quarterly payments for three quarters successively, and not appearing or sending, the fourth quarter day, before the books are shut, his name shall be struck off the roll, unless two-thirds of the Society shall declare in his favour.—7. That any Member who shall curse, swear, or take the *Divine Name* in vain, while in this Society, shall be reproved by the Preses, and provided he continues in such practices, he shall be expelled the Society.—8. That if any Member come into the meeting intoxicated with liquor, so as to occasion any quarrel, or be troublesome in the meeting, he shall be reproved by the Preses and fined, and if he continues in such practice, he shall be expelled the Society.—9. If any Member be found guilty and convicted of any enormous crime, in any of His Majesty's Courts of Justice, he shall upon such conviction, be immediately expelled the Society, and if he should happen to leave a widow or children, whose necessity may call for assistance, they shall be referred to the generosity of the Society.

IX. *Fines*—1. That if a Preses refuses to bear office after he is duly elected, he shall pay a fine of two shillings sterling, a Treasurer one shilling and sixpence, a Steward ninepence, of fine.—2. That if the Preses, and all those holding office, are not present, within half an hour of the time appointed for the meeting, he or they so absent, shall pay a fine of sixpence each.—3. That if a Member residing within 10 miles of Castletown, is absent from the yearly meeting of the Society, he or they shall pay a fine of sixpence each.—4. That if a Member fail to pay, or send his quarterly payment,

payment, he shall pay a fine of twopence for the first quarter, threepence for the second, and fourpence for the third quarter.—5. That if a steward for the quarter fail to visit the sick, or otherwise indisposed Member, residing within the limited distance, weekly, within 48 hours after notice is sent to him, he shall pay a fine of sixpence for each offence.—6. That on the death of a Member or Member's wife, or widow, any Member failing to attend his, or her funeral, when duly warned, and residing within two miles of the deceased, shall pay a fine of sixpence.—7. No Member shall be allowed to speak in the meeting, but upon the business thereof, after the books are opened, until they are shut, under the penalty of a fine of sixpence for each offence, nor direct his discourse to any of the Brethren, while they are engaged in the business of the meeting, but to the Preses. Neither shall more than one person speak at one time, so that one may not interrupt the other, or occasion confusion, such offence to be determined by the meeting, and the offenders liable to what penalty they may inflict.—8. That any Member may deliver his opinion respecting the business of the meeting, at the time under consideration, and that, with freedom and impartiality, and speak or be silent, as the Preses shall direct.—9. That if any Member be found, a backbiter, talebearer, or busy body; and shall privately inform against any of his brethren of the Society, concerning any matter that shall happen in a meeting, which shall be prejudicial to them, or any individual among them, or, which might occasion any quarrel; and in particular, any Member who shall inform against another voting in opposition to a Member who is absent, such informer or informers shall forfeit a penalty of 2*s*. 6*d*. for the first offence, 3*s*. for the second, and if he continue such practices, shall be expelled the Society.—10. That if any Member refusing to pay a fine on conviction, his money shall not be received, nor he any longer accounted a Member, unless a majority of the Society declare in his favour.

X.—*Of the Society in general.*—1. The Society being composed of Members of two professions, viz. Farmers, and Craftsmen, therefore, to prevent all disputes, or grumbling, that might hereafter arise, in disposing of the money of this Society to Members, it is hereby resolved upon, that it shall be proportioned between the two professions, and laid out accordingly, if required, and if not required, that it shall be laid out as formerly specified.—2. That it shall be in the power of the Society, to make or add new Articles, and alter, or amend, those already made, as they may see necessary; but such new articles or amendments, shall not be in force until passed into a law, in a yearly full meeting of the Society.—3. That no less than two-thirds of this Society, can be a majority, sufficient either to make, alter, or amend, any of the Articles already made, or to dispose of any of the funds of the Society: but in choosing office-bearers, or any small matter, a majority of *one* shall be sufficient.—4. It is hereby expressly declared and agreed upon, that the said fund shall always remain at Castletown, and that at least four Members, managers of the fund, reside in, or within one mile of the village. That the box shall not be broken up, nor the money shared or divided, so long as five Members shall remain, and hold it a Society. If any Member in, or out of the place, mention the breaking of the Society, he shall upon full proof and conviction thereof, be excluded the Society.

—5. If

—5. If any doubt shall arise, with respect to the meaning of these Articles, the sentiment and judgment of a majority of the Society shall determine the point.

(Signed) GEORGE BRUCE, Preses.
DAVID BAIN, Clerk."

Then follows the certificate of the Clerk of the Peace, that the said Articles were read in presence of, and approved by the Justices of the Shire of *Caithness*, at their General Quarter Sessions.

No. XIV.

Copy of Papers regarding the Herring Fisheries on the Coast of Caithness, and the Means of Improving the same.

AT a Meeting of the Magistrates of Thurso, held there, on Tuesday the 15th day of August, eighteen hundred and nine years, for the purpose of considering the practicability of establishing the Deep-Sea Herring Fishery, on the Northern Coast of Caithness;

GEORGE PATERSON, Esq. the eldest Magistrate, and Baillie of the Town, being in the Chair;

There was laid before the meeting, the evidence of Mr. Donald Miller, master of the sloop Alexander, of Thurso, also the evidence of William Swanson, fisher in Thurso, and of several other fishermen belonging to that town, from which it is evident,

1. That great shoals of herrings appear upon the Northern Coast of Caithness, and Strathnaver, (extending from Dunnet-Head to Cape-Wrath), as early as the

months of May and June, and that such an early fishing is less likely to be interrupted by bad weather, and that the fish caught, can be brought to a better market, than if the fishing were to take place at a later period of the year.

2. That though, from the clearness of the nights in the summer season, the herrings could not be got with the small nets employed at present on the Coast of Caithness, which are only about twenty-two feet deep, (unless the weather happened to be dusky) yet that with deep nets, such as are used by the Dutch, which are 35 feet deep (as their experience on the Coast of Shetland has clearly ascertained), they might be caught even at that season of the year, in such quantities as to be a very great national object.

3. That a Fishery in the Deep-Seas, is more to be depended on, than in Lochs, or Arms of the Sea; where, though the herrings may occasionally resort in great quantities; yet, at other times, they frequently abandon such stations for years.

4. That for the Deep-Sea Herring Fishery, no place can be better situated than Thurso, and its neighbourhood; and that Scrabster Roads, in the Bay of Thurso, would be the best station for decked vessels to rendezvous for that fishery, instead of Brassa Sound, in the Shetland Islands, which is situated at so great a distance from the Northern Coast of Caithness.

And, 5. That it would be of the greatest possible advantage to those who are engaged in the Northern Fisheries in general, to have an opportunity of employing their hands and vessels, on the Coast of Thurso, in the months of May, June, and a part of July, and on the Coast of Wick, during the remainder of July, and the months of August and September.

It

It was therefore Resolved—1. To send certified copies of the evidence already obtained, to the Honourable the Fishery Board at Edinburgh; to the Right Hon. George Rose; to Mr. Rickman, Secretary to the Commissioners for Highland Roads and Harbours; and to Mr. Salton, Secretary to the British Fishing Society, accompanied with specimens of Herrings caught near Thurso, and cured in the Dutch style, requesting at the same time to know, if any additional information was necessary, to enable them to judge of the importance of the proposed fishery, and of the propriety of countenancing, and supporting the measures recommended for its establishment.

2.—That it would be highly material, if some Dutch Fishermen were settled at Thurso, for the purpose of instructing the Fishermen on the Northern Coast of Caithness, in the Dutch mode of catching and curing Herrings; and also in their mode of carrying on the cod and other herring fisheries; and that the Fishery Board be requested to send a supply of such fishermen, if it should be in their power.

3. That it would be of the greatest importance, with a view of establishing the proposed Herring Fishery, that a Harbour was constructed at Thurso, being the best situation on the Northern Coast, for a general *depôt;* where salt, and cask, and all the other materials necessary for the fishery, might always be kept in readiness; and where the fishing vessels might be sheltered during the winter season, when they are unemployed in the fishery.

4. That from the peculiar importance of this fishery, which might be carried on to a very great extent, the establishment thereof, is an object well entitled to the assistance and support of every friend to the fisheries,

to the improvement, and to the prosperity of the country; and in order that such support might be obtained, it would be highly expedient, to erect a Company, with an adequate capital, for carrying on the same on a great scale, under parliamentary sanction.

5. That such an establishment would not only prove highly advantageous, in a public point of view, but there is evey reason to believe, would also yield a handsome profit to those who engaged in it. That the success of the Dutch Herring Fishery, was principally owing to the following circumstances: 1. That it was carried on earlier in the season, than was usual with other herring fisheries (beginning on the 24th of June); that they had nets of great depth, the lower parts of which could not be seen by the fish, even in the clearest nights; that they trusted to the deep-sea fishing, which has always been found less precarious than the fishing carried on in lochs, and that they carried it on with a great number of vessels, by means of which, they were enabled to find out the shoals of herrings even in the open sea; and

6. That, as it is proposed that the fishery on the Northern Coast of Caithness, shall be carried on upon the same principles, it can hardly fail to be equally profitable, and indeed will probably prove more so, possessing as it will do, superior advantages, for it would be nearer the Ports of out-fit, it can commence in the month of May, instead of June, and the fish caught in consequence thereof, be brought earlier to market, and will fetch a better price.

Evidence of William Swanson, Fisher in Thurso, corroborated by the Declaration of about 30 other Fishermen of that Town.

William Swanson, fisher in Thurso, aged 52 years, declared, That, about the year 1790, he was employed in the bounty fishing, for several years, on board of vessels belonging to different ports;—That they generally fished in the lochs in the West Highlands;—That about the same time, he also tried the herring fishery, in a small boat, in the Pentland Frith, principally between Dunnet Head and Strathy Head; and that though the herring was numerous along that coast, the fishers could not be successful in small boats, but, that if they had decked vessels, that would have kept the sea, they would have been very successful.

That the herrings appeared off the coast, this season, in the month of May, and he had also seen them at the same time for many years past;—That owing to the clearness of the nights at that season of the year, it is difficult to catch them with small nets, unless the weather is dusky.

That great bodies of herrings are at the Offing, being about half a league from the different headlands; and that sometimes they are seen 18 miles off the coast, all the way from Dunnet-Head to Cape Wrath.

That they appear upon the northern coast of Caithness, about a fortnight, or a month, earlier than on the east, or Wick coast, and are much the same as to size and quality.

That he has seen the Dutch catch herring off the coast of Shetland, and other parts of the North Sea and German Ocean, in vessels called *busses;* that their nets

were

were of great length, and 480 meshes deep, which is three times the depth of nets used by Thurso fishers;—That the largest and best fish keep nearest the ground;—That the declarant has no doubt, even with the clear weather, that with nets used by the Dutch, the herring fishing would be off this coast early in the season, and the deep-sea herring fishing, with decked vessels and deep nets, according to the Dutch mode, would answer well from Dunnet-Head to Cape Wrath.

That it would be of great advantage to such a fishing, to have a Harbour at Thurso, where salt, and casks, and other materials for the fishing, might be stored up, in considerable quantities, and always at hand; and that the fisheries could be carried on, on this coast, with particular advantages, owing to Scrabster Roads, in Thurso Bay, being such an excellent place for shelter, in case of bad weather.

That if the herring fishery were to be carried on along this coast, it would be desirable to have harbours at Sandside-Head, and Portskerra, for the accommodation of boats and small vessels; but that the great harbour, and place for stores and materials, should be at Thurso;—that a fishing-smack has lately come from the westward, to Scrabster Roads, (the Friends, of Greenwich, William Nauct master), who said, that the herring appeared in such great shoals about three miles to the west of Cape Wrath, that, if he had proper nets, he could have filled his vessel in one day.

That there is a great variety of fish upon this coast, particularly in the summer and harvest.

That great numbers of smacks, for supplying London with cod, rendezvous here, and carry on the fishing on this coast;—That he has seen 25 smacks in Scrabster Roads at once, and 35 between Dunnet-Head and

and Cape Wrath;—That the cod and herring fishery might be prosecuted at the same time, and by the same vessels; and that the cod fishing might be carried on, when the season for the herring was over;—That the Thurso fishers, from 40 to 50 hands, are willing to be employed in the herring fishery, and that a number of fishermen, all along the north coast, would do the same, if they met with suitable encouragement.

(Signed) WILLIAM SWANSON.

The above having been read to the remainder of the Thurso fishers, was corroborated by them.

(Signed)

ALEXANDER SWANSON, JOHN FINLAYSON,
ANDREW NICOL, D. MACALASTER,
JOHN SIMPSON, DAVID LEED.

Observations on the Means of Improving the Fisheries, on the Coast of Caithness, by Mr. Alexander Fulton, of Greenwich.

IN the first place, it would require a Harbour to be built in Scrabster Roads, as vessels at all times would *take* a harbour there, when they could not enter into the Harbour of Thurso.

It would be proper also to enlarge the Harbour of Thurso, and to have a single pier-head on the west side of Murkle Bay also, which would be very requisite, as, in case of strong westerly winds, the boats would have a place of safety to run into, should they be driven to the eastward of Thurso Harbour. With all these advantages

vantages in their favour, the fishing in the bays of Thurso and Dunnet might be carried on, to the great advantage of all that neighbourhood. The open boats employed in the fishery, should be from 10 to 13 tons each; manned with from seven to nine men each.

The boats to be built on the plan of the Murray Frith boats, as they are best for fishing in the bays and harbours on the west coast of Caithness; but on the east coast of Caithness, larger vessels would answer much better, as it would enable them to use a much greater number of nets, and of course enable them to catch a much greater number of herrings. Those vessels should be from 40 to 50 tons burthen, built and decked like the Yorkshire cobles, and rigged with lug-sails; such boats and vessels should be built with wood of the growth of Scotland, which would come much cheaper than foreign wood. These vessels should be fitted with tanks in their holds, three feet square, made tight, instead of barrels, wherein herrings might be salted directly as they are caught, being first gib'd, which is done by drawing the guts out at the gullet with a small knife. By this means, the blood is drawn from the fish, and the fish will be cured much better. After being 24 hours in salt, the herrings should be taken out of the first pickle, and resalted; they would then want no more, till landed at Thurso, when they might be barrelled, for the home market, or for exportation. It would be very material to have such tanks, to save time and trouble, as they will not require any coopers on board of those vessels. Thurso also being so near the Shetland Islands, these vessels might be employed, in the early part of the summer, on the coast of Shetland, and might make several voyages in the season. They might also be employed in catching cod

and

and ling, for salt-fish, and when dried on the beach at Thurso, would always find a market.

The open boats might also be employed in catching herrings, in the lochs of the West Highlands; all this might be accomplished, were persons of skill and capital to embark in the trade.

In order to encourage the herring fishery, the best mode would be to give a bounty, according to tonnage, for vessels of not less than ten tons, or more than sixty, the bounties to be lessened in proportion to the increase of tonnage; a higher bounty to be given at the first outfit, a lower bounty the second year, and none the third. This would encourage a number of spirited adventurers to come forward, and would be the means of establishing a most advantageous fishery. It would also be proper, to take off the duty on the materials used in the fishing trade, as lines, twine, sail-cloth, &c. unless the bounty granted would indemnify the adventurer.

Copy of a Letter from the Right Hon. Sir John Sinclair, Bart. to the Secretary of the Fishery Board, dated Thurso Castle, 20th August, 1811.

SIR,

I herewith inclose some questions, put by me to Mr. George Miller, your fishery officer at this port, regarding the establishing Dutch fishermen there, together with his answers; and I have no hesitation in stating my full conviction, after maturely considering the subject, that Thurso is the best situation, perhaps in Europe, for carrying on the Deep-Sea Herring Fishery.

In

In addition to the reasons urged by Mr. Miller, it is proper to observe, that the herrings appear, in the neighbourhood of Thurso, in the end of May, or beginning of June, whereas they do not appear on the eastern coast of the county, until the end of July, or beginning of August. The only difficulty in carrying on the herring fishery at Thurso, is the clearness of the night in June and July. The Dutch found the same obstacle to the success of the herring fishery on the coast of Shetland, and they were obliged therefore, to use *very deep nets*, which the fish will not see, even in the clearest night. This renders it necessary to have deeper nets than boats can well manage. By adopting the Dutch plan, in the neighbourhood of Thurso, there is no doubt, that the earliest, and best fishery in Europe, can be established there.

There are only two places that can stand in competition with Thurso. The first is Peterhead, but there are no herrings in that neighbourhood, and the attention of the people there, is distracted by a variety of other objects; the other place is Wick, and the adjoining village of Pultney Town; but there, they are accustomed to carry on so successfully a fishing by boats, that it would not be easy to induce them to alter their system; whereas Thurso has every advantage for such an experiment, and no particular object, at present, to distract its attention from following up the pursuit. I hope, therefore, that the Fishery-Board will resolve to try an experiment at Thurso, with at least a part of the Dutch fishermen, proposed to be settled in Scotland, and scarcely a doubt can be entertained of their meeting with perfect success.

I remain, Sir, &c.

(Signed) JOHN SINCLAIR.

Queries

Queries by the Right Honourable Sir John Sinclair, Bart., and Answers by Mr. George Miller, Officer to the Fishery-Board at Thurso, regarding the Advantages of establishing Dutch Fishermen at Thurso.

Query 1.—Is not Thurso a favourable situation for fitting out herring-busses, and for the settlement of Dutch fishermen, &c.; and what are the grounds upon which you form that opinion?

Answer.—Thurso, without any doubt, is a most, if not the most eligible situation, for fitting out herring-busses, either for the deep-sea fishery, or open-sea fishing; also, as a place of settlement for Dutch fishermen, for the following obvious reasons:

1st, It has a very good natural dry harbour, capable of admitting vessels of 150 tons, and which, by building a pier, can be very highly improved, and made to receive vessels of from 200 to 300 tons.—2d, It has a most safe and commodious winter, as well as summer roadstead, (Scrabster Roads), within less than two miles from the dry harbour.—3d, Being situated at the northern extremity of Great Britain, it has ready access to the western, northern, and eastern seas, and is about mid-way between the summer herring fishery, near Shetland, and the winter herring fishery, in the West Highland Lochs, neither being distant above a day's sail, with a fair wind.—4th, It has at present, an infant herring fishery, which commences early in June. —5th, House-rent is low, and all the necessaries of life, (fuel perhaps excepted, which at the same time is not dearer than in other places where coal can be had by sea), cheap, and easy to be obtained.—6th, The inhabitants

habitants are in the knowledge and practice of manufacturing herring-nets, and curing herrings, as practised in Scotland.

Query 2.—Are there other fishings in the neighbourhood of Thurso, besides the herring, in which the Dutch fishermen might be employed?

Answer.—Besides the herring-fishery, (which hitherto has not been carried on, but on a small scale, at Thurso), there is good haddock, tolerable good ling, and the best cod fishing, between the North Foreland and Cape Wrath, which is well known to the Masters of the English cod fishing-smacks, who supply the London market from the immediate neighbourhood of Thurso.

For about 20 years past, the English smacks have been in the practice of fishing cod, within sight of the town of Thurso, from the beginning of September to the end of March: it is not uncommon to see, in good weather, from 20 to 30 smacks, fishing cod at the same time, near the town; and in bad weather, they take shelter in the roadstead of Scrabster Roads.

(Signed) Geo. Miller.

Thurso, 16*th Aug*. 1811.

On the best Modes of consuming Herrings.

When herrings are pickled in the Dutch manner, it is recommended to prepare them for use likewise in the Dutch mode, which is greatly to be preferred to any hitherto invented.

Herrings, when they come first in the season into Holland, are generally eaten with French beans. They are likewise eaten just before dinner, and at all times in the

the manner the English eat anchovies, or while taking wine, either at a dessert, or after dinner, for a relish as well as refreshment.

On taking the herring out of the keg, (which should always contain sufficient pickle), cut the belly open, to take out the melt or roe, and to take entirely away the mucus, or matter, generally lodged to the ribs and the backbone. Let the fish be clean washed with cold water, inside and out. Then pour on sufficient milk, just warm at the first to cover the herrings, so as to soak therein for half or three-quarters of an hour, according to the length of the time the herrings may have been in pickle; afterwards taken out, and wiped clean, to be laid on a dish for use. At this time, with a sharp knife, cut sufficient from head to tail, on the back, just to take off the fin, and only to divide the skin; when with a silver fork begin, at the neck or shoulder, to roll the skin on the fork, which will easily come off, and be stript from the shoulder to the tail, on the one side, and which likewise do in the same manner on the other.

After this, instead of cutting them straight across into pieces, cut them in a sloping direction, about a finger's breadth, beginning at the shoulder, and so continuing on to the tail.

In this manner they dress them amongst the respectable classes abroad, such herrings being deemed even a great luxury; and it is found, by the experience of ages, that herrings so cured and eaten, are not only highly healthful, but in some cases have prevented consumptions. Indeed the Dutch proverb is, "When the herrings come in, the Doctor goes out;" meaning his professional services are superseded by the general use of herrings.

No. XV.

Hints regarding the best Rotation of Crops, for the County of Caithness, and the other Northern Districts of Scotland. Communicated by Sir John Sinclair, Bart.

It seems absolutely necessary, to think of some new plan of cultivation, or rotation of crops, in the Northern Districts of Scotland. Bear, formerly the great source of profit, will no longer indemnify the farmer, or enable him to pay an adequate rent; wheat being of sure sale, is certainly a proper article to try; and if sown early, (on which the whole depends), not only good crops may be produced, but also grain of excellent quality. In order to ascertain how far wheat would answer, the following rotations are recommended, by an intelligent South Country Farmer, to the attention of those who may wish to try so important an experiment, either on light or strong land.

1. *On Light Land.*—It is more than probable, that a fallow is absolutely necessary to clean the land, and that five furrows would be necessary, the first rotation. Begin to plough early, at furthest in the end of May, or beginning of June. Lay on 30 cubical yards of good dung, per Scotch acre, and 30 bolls, or 120 bushels of Sunderland lime. The dung and lime to be laid on with the last furrow. Sow as early in September as possible; three bushels of seed will do, if sown early, if not, more is necessary: both red and white from Essex may be tried, or old seed from Scotland, but always of the very best quality. In April, harrow

the wheat, roll and sow grass-seeds, which will produce, the next year, a good crop, without injuring the wheat. The rotation then to be as follows.

Proposed rotation on light land: 1st year, fallow; 2d year, wheat; produce probably 10 bolls per acre; 3d year, hay; 4th year, pasture; 5th year, oats; 6th year, turnips; 7th year, bear; 8th year, hay; 9th year, wheat, on one furrow.

2. *On Strong Land.*—It is much more difficult to form a good system for raising wheat on strong land, than on light, at least in a northern climate, where beans are a hazardous crop. A fallow with five furrows is absolutely necessary. Begin to plough early in spring, and sow the wheat early in September; a greater quantity of manure is necessary for this kind of soil, namely, from 35 to 40 cubical yards, and 150 bushels of lime per Scotch acre. Grass-seeds with lime is hazardous in strong land; beans would be the best second crop, if not bear or barley. If bear is sown, take one furrow immediately after harvest, and two in the spring; with the bear sow grass-seeds; and after one year's hay, and one year's pasture, break up with oats, and continue the same rotation, beginning with a fallow.

Proposed rotation: 1st year, fallow; 2nd year, wheat; 3d year, beans, or bear, and grass-seeds; 4th year, hay; 5th year, pasture; 6th year, oats; then fallow, &c.

The above hints being submitted to the consideration of some intelligent farmers in Ross, and Cromarty, the following observations regarding them were transmitted to Sir John Sinclair.

 Communi-

Communications from Mr. Archibald Dudgeon, of Arbol, in Ross-shire, addressed to Donald M'Leod, Esq. of Geanies.

Arbol, 18*th May*, 1807.

SIR,

I beg leave to submit to you, the following observations, on the "Hints regarding the culture of wheat, in Caithness," which if you judge worthy of transmitting to Sir John Sinclair, they are at your service.

1. *Light Land.*—1st, The cultivation of wheat on light land, after fallow, is regarded as hazardous. To speak professionally, it frequently throws out in the spring, or in other words, a number of the plants die, which generally renders the crop a poor one. 2dly, Where land has got a full dose of lime, and wheat the first crop that is sown thereafter, (unless the season is uncommonly good) the lime militates seriously against the quality. The operation of lime upon the soil protracts the period of ripening, at first, and although the quantity of dung to be administered, would be very beneficial in counteracting this, still it appears to me advisable, to give potatoe oats the preference, the first round. Were the foregoing two objections obviated, the preparation in other respects is excellent. Provided it is meant that the ploughings for the fallow are to be preceded by a ploughing before winter, (which is necessary to make fallow work kindly the next summer), and that harrowing and gathering of quickens, is carefully attended to betwixt each ploughing.

Three bushels per acre of seed, is plenty on rich lands well prepared, but upon the average of soils, and preparations, four bushels will be more eligible. It is surely well judged to get the seed from England; and I have

I have heard it alleged, and I doubt not on good reason, that the northern counties should have their full supply of seed annually from the south. In place of what is laid down, I would substitute the following

Rotation for light lands.—First round: 1. Fallow; 2. Potatoe oats; 3. Grass; 4. Grass; 5. Grass; 6. Wheat. —Second round: 1. Turnips; 2. Potatoe oats; 3. Grass; 4. Grass; 5. Grass; 6. Wheat.

The preparation for wheat, after the three year old grass: "To be ploughed the latter end of August, or beginning of September, well harrowed, and allowed to lie for two or three weeks, then seed-furrow it across the first ploughing."

2. *Strong Land.*—Wheat, after a well-wrought fallow, on strong lands, is considered as a sure and valuable crop; while the remark, as to sowing seeds on such soil in the spring, (unless critically attended to), holds good; at the same time, the idea of beans should be abandoned. In Ross-shire, it is a difficult matter to raise them to perfection, and several of the best farmers in the county, have given them up. Beans require a much longer season to ripen, than our climate in the North, favours us with. On good dry bottomed land they will do; but on these, turnips will be found a more advantageous crop. Beans being excluded entirely from our husbandry, is not a serious loss. I would propose the following

Rotation for strong lands.—First round: 1. Fallow; 2. Potatoe oats; 3. Grass; 4. Grass; 5. Wheat. —Second round: 1. Fallow; 2. Wheat; 3. Grass; 4. Grass; 5. Wheat.

Potatoe oats succeeds the first fallowing, as the land is supposed to be newly limed. Grass-seeds should be sown with wheat as early in April, as the land will bear horses without poaching it, taking care not to allow it to become hard and dry, before the seeds are sown. It is having the business executed at that nice juncture, betwixt wet and dry, which insures success. Early sowing in Caithness, will assuredly be advantageous, as soon after the 20th September as possible. The quantity of dung, for both soils, appears to me greater than a farm can furnish at the beginning, and greater, at an after period, than is advisable to apply at one time. I consider from 20 to 25 cubic yards sufficient for an acre, if it is well rotted dung. On the other hand, the proportion of lime appears under par. In place of what is recommended, I should suppose, from 160 to 180 bushels of lime shells, on the light lands, and 200 to 240 on strong land, *i. e.* about 70 bolls of slack lime for light land, and 91 bolls for strong land, seem to me necessary.

General Remarks.—While the reduced value of bear and barley, imperiously requires that these grains be expelled from the list of rent paying crops, in order to meet the increased expense of husbandry; and further, that the value of lands, be made to keep pace with the progressive advance on lands in the south; while these call for a new system, still, extensive practice should be cautiously gone into, (by those paying rents), till experience justifies their projects. Wheat is unquestionably the most profitable grain we grow, and the soil of Caithness, in general, has every appearance of being suited for its culture. Although the rotations I have submitted, strike me as good, I have not the presumption to say they are the best for that county. The gentlemen and farmers thereof, must be better

better judges than a stranger; and when they are about to introduce the cultivation of a description of grain, which promises to add much to the opulence of their county, they will, no doubt, by well-conducted experiments, ascertain the true *rules* on which they should act.

I remain, Sir,
With due respect,
Your most obedient Servant,
(Signed) ARCHIBALD DUDGEON.

To Donald M'Leod, Esq. of Geanies.

Extract of a Letter from George Middleton, Esq. Cromarty, regarding the best Rotation of Crops in Caithness, dated Cromarty, 24th May, 1807. Addressed to Sir John Sinclair, Bart.

I know so little of the soil or climate of Caithness, that I cannot well judge of the proper rotation of crops there. But I think your climate moist, and your soil mostly incumbent on a wet bottom. I would not advise, therefore, your sowing much wheat, till after three or four years experience, as it may not ripen well. In some seasons, even here, it will not come to perfection, where the situation is exposed. I have one farm, three miles west from this, rather high, where I find it not prudent to risk much wheat, though the soil is very rich. I think you will find the potatoe, or Polish oats, more certain pay, after fallow, excepting in very good soils, and favoured situations, for inferior wheats are very unsaleable.

I think fallowing absolutely necessary in all wet bottoms, whether the soil be strong or light. Turnips may likewise be considered as a fallow. As there are many farms, where no dung can be had but from its own produce, there will not be nigh enough to cover a sufficient breadth of fallow, at the rate of thirty cubic yards per acre, along with lime. A less quantity of dung, therefore, must often be tried. There is no rule to be invariably followed, regarding the number of ploughings for a fallow, as much depends on the climate and soil; but you should plough and harrow in the driest weather, until the land is perfectly clean. The ridges should be made round, and from 15 to 18 feet broad, and gathered up at least twice, by the middle of September. If wheat is to be tried, it should be sown immediately; for on early sowing all depends. Take care to keep off all the surface-water at the ends of your field, by clearing it to the level with spades, where necessary. Where you intend oats for your fallow, gather it up in the autumn, in the same manner as for wheat, and sow on that furrow in spring, without further ploughing; harrowing well, or scarifying the surface before sowing. Oats are found to grow well by following this plan. You may sow grass-seeds with the oats, or on the wheat crop, in the middle of May, and harrow it. Sowing oats on a winter furrow, is a Northumberland practice, and I never knew it fail where the land is clean.

Where it is intended to sow oats, if the fallow has not been got perfectly clean, plough again in spring before you sow. If you try Polish oats, sow thick, and at least five firlots to the Scotch acre. The following rotations are submitted to your consideration.

First Rotation.—On soils of a middling quality, where no dung can be got but the produce of the farm, first year, fallow; second year, wheat, or oats; third year, hay,

hay, or pasture; fourth year, pasture; fifth year, pasture; sixth year, oats; seventh year, turnips or fallow; eighth year, oats; ninth year, pasture; tenth year, wheat or oats.

Second Rotation.—On the best soils, where more dung can be got than is produced on the farm, first year, fallow; second year, wheat; third year, barley, and grass-seeds; fourth year, hay, or pasture; fifth year, wheat or oats, with a light dunging.

I would by no means advise beans, for they will not ripen here, except on favoured spots and in good seasons.

The probable return of wheat, may be stated at, from seven to eight bolls; of potatoe oats eight quarters; of Polish oats, on your best land, after fallow, you may expect ten quarters per Scotch acre.

I have found, after many years trial, that oats is a safer crop than bear or barley after turnips, and it will probably be more so, in your climate*: and oats are always of ready sale in the London market. The seed you sow of Polish, or potatoe oats, should always be changed as often as they become mixed with black oats.

I am,

(Signed) GEORGE MIDDLETON.

---

* Oats binds the soil more than bear, and therefore grass-seeds do better with the latter; but on soils of only middling quality, and scanty manure, oats is more productive than bear, and ought to be preferred. The Polish species is too late for the Caithness climate.

No. XVI.

No. XVI.

Queries regarding Cottage Gardens, and Cow-keeping, on a small scale, in the vicinity of Peterhead and Aberdeen.

Query 1. What is reckoned the best quantity of ground for a tradesman, who does not keep a cow, but cultivates a small garden?—*Answer*. One acre of ground is reckoned sufficient, for the purpose of raising potatoes, and other vegetables.

Q. 2. What is the rent he generally pays per acre?—*A*. The rent per acre is four pounds, near the town.

Q. 3. What advantage does he derive from his garden?—*A*. The advantage he derives from it chiefly is, that of supplying his family with vegetables, particularly, *potatoes, turnips, coleworts*, &c., and the labour, to a tradesman or mechanic, occupied in a sedentary employment, is conducive to health. Besides potatoes, turnips, &c. he sometimes sows a small quantity of grain (bear or bigg) with grass-seeds: the grass crop he lets.

Q. 4. What is the best quantity of land for a person keeping a cow?—*A*. Three Scotch acres.

Q. 5. What is the best rotation of crops to follow?—*A*. The best rotation is thus: 1. Potatoes after grass on light land, or oats after grass on strong land; 2. Potatoes after oats; 3. Bear after potatoes, sown down with grass-seeds: the grass may lie three years.

Q. 6. What rent is paid for such land near the town of Peterhead, and at a distance from it?—*A*. The rent per acre near the town, is 4*l*.; and about a mile distant, 2*l*. 10*s*.

Q. 7.

Q. 7. What is the expense of culture?—*A.* The expense of the culture of one acre, sown down with bear, and grass-seeds, and the profit of the bear crop, &c. will appear from the following

Statement.

Charge.	£	s.	d.	*Discharge.*	£	s.	d.
Expense of one acre, sown with bear and grass-seeds, is,							
1. Manure, ...	3	0	0	Produce of the bear crop, seven bolls at 20*s.* per boll,	10	10	0
2. Seed, bear, and labour, ...	2	10	0	The first year's hay crop on the ground,	10	0	0
3. Grass-seeds, ...	1	5	0	Second year's do. do.	8	10	0
4. Rent for three years, at 4*l.* ..	12	0	0				
5. The profit of one acre for the three crops, 3*l.* 8*s.* 4*d.* per ann.	10	5	0				
	£29	0	0		£29	0	0

N. B. Land in the immediate vicinity of the town of Thurso, is let at from four guineas to 5*l.* to tradesmen or mechanics: the crops they raise are chiefly potatoes, turnips, bear, and artificial grasses, broke up after two years with oats; and at one mile and a half from the town, they would not give 20*s.* per acre of rent, from the difficulty of carrying manure to it, and the distance being inconvenient to themselves to labour it.

No. XVII.

Note from a Correspondent, on the Size of Ridges, when Waste Lands are brought into a state of Cultivation.

Many circumstances tend to convince me, that in bringing waste lands into a state of cultivation, it is most material to make the ridges wide and high.

New

New land, more especially where the bottom is *till* or flat rock, is very apt to be wet and spongy, retaining a great superfluity of water, which prevents any manure, whether lime, dung, or marl, from operating on it successfully. But this great obstacle to the improvement of waste lands, would be obviated by making the ridges wide, and raising them high. By this means also, the land might be dunged, ploughed, and barrowed, and afterwards pastured on, at times when it would otherwise be impracticable.

I have seen very good corn raised on new land in *lazy-beds*, when it could not be obtained in any other way usually practised. This was entirely owing to the height of the ridges, and the consequent dryness of the land, so that the manure acted upon it. *To cottagers bringing in new lands, the plan is to be particularly recommended*, not only for their potatoes, but for their other crops; but as it is impracticable to cultivate large tracts with the spade, the best plan to pursue *with the plough*, is to widen the ridges to 18 or even 30 feet, raising them in proportion by repeated gatherings, without splitting the ridge; by means of which the land would be kept dry. Some ground, in this way, would be lost by the furrow; but as soon as the land was brought into a thorough good order, and of as fine and firm a consistency as the old land, the plan of small level ridges might be adopted.

It is not improbable, however, that in many parts of Caithness, where the land is flat, on a *tilly* bottom, the plan of wide and high ridges, would be preferable to any other, as a likely mean to obviate the disadvantage of a wet climate.

The Author has 30 acres of waste land now under the

the operation of the plough, in the county of Caithness, and owing to its *tilly* bottom, it is a complete puddle in wet weather, notwithstanding several hundred yards of covered drains, having been made in every hollow of it. He is now going to make it into ridges of 20 feet wide, and to raise them as much as the depth of the soil will admit, before he can apply manure with any probability of success; as no manure will ferment the soil while it is wet and poachy.

No. XVIII.

Copy of an Advertisement, regarding a Lead Mine discovered in the Hill of Skinnet, the Property of Sir John Sinclair, Bart.

" *Valuable Lead Mine to be Let.*—The hill of Skinnet, in the county of Caithness, North Britain, has long been remarkable for very promising indications of some valuable mines. Considerable quantities of mundick or pyrites, were found in it, also *terra ponderosa,* and some small specimens of lead itself; but it was in the month of September last, that a vein of lead ore, about 12 inches in width, was discovered; and the ore it produced, upon being assayed, at a very skilful refinery, yielded at the rate of 68$\frac{1}{7}$ per cent. of lead; the produce of silver in the ore that has been yet discovered, has been inconsiderable.

" This vein produces what is called " *bouse ore.*" It is most advantageously situated, being easily drained, and lying within four miles of the town and harbour of Thurso, with which a communication may easily be opened. A regular vein having been fallen upon, it

would

would not be difficult or expensive to trace it, until the great body of lead, which the hill probably contains, is discovered. There are also several appearances of other mines in that neighbourhood, both on the same, and other estates, which might be wrought at the same time.

"It is proposed to let this mine to a respectable Company, for payment of a certain portion of the produce, the Company being obliged to work the mine, so as to give it a fair trial.

"Proposals for that purpose may be addressed to the proprietor, Sir John Sinclair, Bart. M. P. Charlotte-square, Edinburgh, who will furnish any additional information that may be necessary.

"*Edinburgh, 20th November*, 1804."

Several specimens of the ore mentioned in the above advertisement, having been circulated, it may be proper to state the result of the experiments which have been made in various places, for ascertaining the value thereof.

1. H. Davy, Esq. Professor of Chemistry in the Royal Institution at London, writes in the following manner, regarding the quality of the ore,—"I have completed the analysis of the lead ore from your estate. It gives, by a common assay, sixty-one in the hundred parts, of lead. Accurate analysis, however, proves, that it consists of seventy-one of lead, and twenty-nine of sulphur. I congratulate you on being possessed of so valuable a substance; it is one of the richest species of potters' lead, and the price of lead is now excessively high."

2. Mr. Jameson, Professor in Natural History in the University of Edinburgh, gives the following account of

of the analysis.—"The lead ore I find to contain in the hundred parts,

Lead, ... 69

Sulphur, ... 14

A small portion of earthy matter, and a minute portion of silver. The exact proportion of silver, I have not ascertained, the analysis being still unfinished."

3. The following are the results of the assays at Blaydon refinery in Northumberland.

"Bouse ore from Caithness, Scotland. Assay for lead. —Taken eight averdupoise ounces of the ore, and calcined it on an open fire, in an iron ladle; it burned with a blue sulphuric flame, and suffocating smell, supposed to be uncombined sulphur. Loss by calcination, 4drs. or $\frac{1}{32}$ per cent.

	oz.		per cent.	
The remainder mixed with 4oz. of carbonate of potash, and fused in a crucible, produce of lead, ...	$2\frac{1}{2}$	=	35	25
The scoria or slag, collected and mixed with half its weight of iron filings, and melted, produce of lead, second operation, ...	3	=	37	5
Whole produce of lead, ...	$5\frac{1}{2}$	=	68	75

"Assay for silver—Taken 2oz. of each of the above parcels of lead: weight of the two beads of silver, $\frac{1}{128}$ grains—15dwts. 7grs. 5 per cent."

Since the original vein was discovered, some labourers, in digging a ditch, 200 yards from the spot where it was at first met with, found again the same kind of ore, so that there is every reason to suppose, that the quantity in that neighbourhood is very considerable.

In

In a letter from Mr. John Simons, of London, to George Sinclair, of Ulbster, Esq. dated Edinburgh, 13 April, 1749, he stated, that he had found some pieces of lead ore, in the Hill of Skinnet; and added, that he and a company from London would take a lease of it, in case the property of that part of the said Hill, (then a common), was adjusted with the other proprietor concerned.

It may not be improper to add, that the direction of the seams in the rock where the lead ore was found in the Hill of Skinnet, is about S. W. and N. E.; that the beds, or strata of the rock is nearly horizontal, the seams vertical, with ochry faces, and in some cases, white sparry seams; that the rock is of a flag nature, the strata thickening, after digging down about six feet.

No. XIX.

On the Improvement of Waste Lands.

It is, as already stated, computed that there are about 62,000 acres of inferior green pasture, partly moory, within this county; of this extent it may be fairly stated, that there are 20,000 acres, of so little an elevation above the level of the sea, that it may be improved, and cultivated, so as to produce at least 8*s*. per acre, of increased yearly rent, or 8000*l*. per annum.

Of the immense tracts of peat-moss in the county, it may be computed that there are 1200 acres of low lying, rotten, or dead moss, capable of being improved by paring, burning, and gravelling with calcareous clay, &c. so as to produce good crops of oats, turnips, and hay,

hay, may be valued at 6*s*. per acre of increased rent, or 360*l*. per annum.

Of the 40,000 acres of arable land computed in the county, it may without exaggeration be stated, that there are 15,000 acres of the description of land called, *out-field* or *afterwall*, which yield only a scanty crop of grey oats, once in three or four years; and are then allowed to gather a sward of native sorrel, knot-grass, or marigold, for pasture; present value, say 4*s*. per acre; and as this land is commonly on a dry bottom, by applying *lime*, or *marl*, and its consequent judicious mode of management to this land, it may, in the course of a few years, be improved, so as to produce an increased rent of 10*s*. per acre, or 7500*l*. per annum.

Therefore 20,000 acres of inferior pasture or common, would produce an increased rent of 8*s*. per acre,

or	£8000
The 15,000 acres of outfield land, 10*s*. per acre, or	7500
The 1200 acres of peat-moss, 6*s*. per acre, or	360
Total increased rent, at about 8*s*. 9*d*. per acre, is	£15,860

The increased produce of the above land, at the rate of 26*s*. 4½*d*. per acre = 3 rents, amounts to 47,580*l*. In the view of additional population, it is well known, that a female farm servant, has for her support, annually, four bolls of meal, and 48*s*. of money wages. Upon this data, I will suppose that 8*l*. per annum is sufficient for every human being, men, women and children, consequently 47,580*l*. will furnish sustenance for 5947 additional inhabitants. And the addition to the national capital, at 25 years' purchase, would be 396,500*l*. But should the culture of wheat be generally tried, and prove successful, the increased rent, in that event, from the remaining 25,000 acres of the better kind of arable land, *i. e.* such as now produces bear or bigg, may fairly be calculated at 15,860*l.*; so that the whole increased rent that the county may be made to produce, may be 31,720*l.*; the increased produce, would then be three rents, or 95,160*l.*; the addition to the national capital, at 25 years' purchase, 793,000*l.*; and the increase of population, at 8*l.* each, 11,895 souls.

All this theoretical calculation is practicable, were there capital to execute it. The tax upon horses employed in agriculture in this county, where they cannot be wrought for more than seven months in the year, is the same as paid in other parts of the kingdom, enjoying a better climate, and where they can be employed for eleven months in the year.

The tax upon the rent payable by the farmer, is also a bar to improvement, because in many, if not in most cases, it is a tax upon ideal profit only. And many other taxes are levied in this remote county at the same rate, as are paid in other parts of the United Kingdom, enjoying many advantages, not within the reach of the inhabitants of this county. It is, therefore, a subject not unworthy the attention of Government, to consider whether it would not be a wise policy to tax the remote parts of the kingdom, in a manner suited to their limited resources, circumstances and situation, or, to give premiums for the encouragement of the agriculture of such districts, adequate to the inequality of the taxes payable by them, which would in time realise in whole, or in part, the political result, hinted at in the above calculations.

No. XX.

No. XX.

Extracts from the Regiam Majestatem—Statutes of King Robert II. page 57.

" *The Assize of Weichts and Measures, Cap.* 22.

1. " King David's common elne contains threty-seven measured inches, with the inches of three men, ane meikle, ane middel, and ane lytel, and sal stand conform to the middel inch, or conform to three grains of bear without the tailes."

2. " The stane to weigh wool and other things, should have fiveteen punds; an stane of walx, aught. Twelve London punds makes a stane."

3. " The pound sould weigh twentie-five shillings, and this was in the time of the assize aforesaid, and the pound contains fiveteen unces."

4. " In the time of umquhill King Robert Bruice, the great Conquestor, first of that name, the pound of silver contained twenty-six shilling, four pennies, in respect of the minoration of the pennie, or money of that King frae the money of King David aforesaid."

5. " The ounce contained, in the time of King David aforesaid, twentie pennies. In the time of the said King Robert the First, it contained twentie-ane pennies; bot now in our days, that is, of King Robert the Third, in the zeare of grace 1393, the ounce of his money contains thritty-two pennies."

6. " The stirlin, in the time of King David, did weigh thrity-twa grains of gude & round quheat; bot now it is otherwise, be reason of the minoration of money."

7. " The

7. "The boll sould contain an sextarius; that is, twelve gallons, and sal be in the deepness nine inches, with the thickness of the tree, and in the roundness above it sal contain three score and twelve inches in the midst of the ourtree, and in the inferior roundness it sould contain three score and eleven inches."

8. "The gallon sould contain twelve pounds of water, that is, of sea water four pounds, of rynand water four pounds, and of standane water four pounds."

9. "The inche, in all measures, sould be measured at the root of the nail, and sould be in length conform to three grains of gude bear without the tailes."

XXI.

On Scarcities in Caithness.

In Malthus's Treatise on Population, he states, that Scotland suffered severely from scarcity and disease, during the years 1680, 1688, 1740, 1756, 1766, 1778, 1782, and 1783, particularly in 1680, so many families perished from these causes, insomuch, that for six miles of a well-inhabited district, there was not a smoke remaining, in the parish of Duthill, in Morayshire. I was therefore induced, to inquire into the state of the Session Records of the parish of Thurso, in this county, as to the number of marriages and baptisms, during those years of general scarcity in Scotland. By that record, it does not appear that the county of Caithness had experienced much want during the scarcity of those times. The record was not then, perhaps, very regularly kept, but I was favoured with the following copy of it as it stands, from that intelligent gentleman, the Rev. Mr. Munro,

Munro, Parochial Schoolmaster of Thurso, to whom I feel much obliged for various pieces of Statistical information.

Table of Marriages and Baptisms in the Parish of Thurso, from 1672 to 1784.

Years.	Marriages.	Baptisms.	Years.	Marriages.	Baptisms.
1672	16	95	1741	16	45
1673	—	109	1742	25	—
1679	—	60	1744	—	77
*1680	—	66	*1756	—	69
1681	—	91	1757	—	67
1684	21	86	*1766	—	90
*1688	29	102	1767	—	88
1689	32	—	*1778	—	101
1703	—	76	1779	—	97
1708	33	—	*1782	24	119
1728	29	41	*1783	27	88
1738	40	81	1784	15	84
*1740	17	87			

Remarks.—During this period, there are several years omitted altogether, and the number of marriages in various other years. Those alluded to by Mr. Malthus, as years of scarcity, are marked thus (*), and there does not appear, that there was any serious diminution in the progress of the population of this parish, during those years; from which it may safely be inferred, that the scarcity was not very severe in any part of the county of Caithness, because the inhabitants of the town of Thurso, would be the first to feel its effects. This was owing to their bear crop being productive, and indeed the growth of that grain ought at all times to be promoted, as a guard against scarcity and want. This can only be done, by diminishing the present high tax on malt made from bear, or bigg, to at least one-half of the tax charged on malt made from English barley.

No. XXII.

An Account of the Commencement of Manufactures at Thurso, and in its Neighbourhood.

The first attempt to establish any manufacture at Thurso, or its neighbourhood, was in the year 1788, when a subscription was set on foot for that purpose, of which the following is a copy, together with the names of the original Subscribers, and the sums they respectively subscribed.

We, the Subscribers to this paper, taking into our consideration, the great advantages that would result from the establishment of Manufactures at the towns of Thurso and Wick, do hereby agree, as soon as a proper plan can be formed for that purpose, to pay into the hands of Sir William Forbes, James Hunter and Co. bankers, in Edinburgh, the sums of money annexed to our respective subscriptions, according as the same may be called for, by such Directors as may be appointed for managing the same; under this special provision, that the Manufactures to be established, are approved of by a majority of the Subscribers, and that no person is to be bound for more than he actually subscribes for; and that each Subscriber shall subscribe the sum of 25*l.* sterling, at least, which is to be a share in the said stock, and shall have a vote in the election of Managers or Directors of such Establishment, together with an additional vote for every additional two shares he subscribes.

List of Subscribers to the Manufacturing Scheme in Caithness.

No.		Shares.	£	s.	d
1	Sir John Sinclair, Bart., of Ulbster	12	300	0	0
2	Mr. William Innes	2	50	0	0
3	Mr. Patrick Swaney	2	50	0	0
4	Mr. Donald M'Leod	1	25	0	0
5	James Horne, Esq. W. S. Edinburgh	1	25	0	0
6	Mr. Donald Robeson, Writer, Thurso	1	25	0	0
7	Mr. James Nicolson, Surgeon, Thurso	1	25	0	0
8	Mr. Ben. Calder, Oldfield	1	25	0	0
9	Mr. William Henderson	1	25	0	0
10	Mr. Daniel Miller	1	25	0	0
11	Mr. John Miller, jun.	1	25	0	0
12	Mr. George Miller	2	50	0	0
13	William Sinclair, Esq. of Lochend	2	50	0	0
14	Mr. William Wilson	1	25	0	0
15	Mr. Hugh Mackay, Glengolly	1	25	0	0
16	Mr. Alexander Manson	1	25	0	0
17	James Traill, Esq. of Hobbister	4	100	0	0
18	Ben. Williamson, Esq.	3	75	0	0
19	Mr. George Sinclair, of Geise	1	25	0	0
20	James Sinclair, of Harpsdale, Esq.	1	25	0	0
21	Sir James Sinclair, Bart. of Mey	1	25	0	0
22	George Mackay, Esq. of Bighouse	1	25	0	0
23	Captain Patrick Campbell, of Barcaldine	1	25	0	0
24	Mr. William Manson	1	25	0	0
25	Alexander Sinclair, Esq. of Forss	1	25	0	0
26	Sir John Sinclair, Bart. of Murkle	2	50	0	0
27	Mrs. Mackay, of Scotstoun	1	25	0	0
	Shares	48	£1200	0	0

The progress that was made in the undertaking, will appear from the following paper, addressed to the Board of Trustees for the encouragement of Manufactures in Scotland:

 " *Caithness*

"*Caithness Manufactures.*

"The attention of the Board of Trustees for the Encouragement of Manufactures and Improvements in Scotland, is most earnestly requested to the following observations, on the advantages which may be expected from their exciting and encouraging a spirit of industry in the county of Caithness.

"It is only within these two years past, that any attempt has been made, in that part of the kingdom, to establish manufactures. If properly encouraged, it cannot fail to be attended with the most beneficial consequences, from the many natural advantages which it possesses. Two-thirds of the county are surrounded by the sea, which, though unfortunately rather deficient in harbours, yet abounds with fish of various kinds, for the sustenance of the people. The country is in general well inhabited, and it has two towns, Wick and Thurso, admirably situated for trade. It produces considerable quantities of grain, insomuch that it exports at present from 10,000 to 20,000 bolls per annum. There is also abundance of peat for fuel, and every appearance of coal; and the people are far from being deficient in industry, when they meet with encouragement.

"The plans which have been under consideration, within these two years past, are as follow:—First, to establish a *tannery*, which is already going on, and to which it is hoped that the Board will give some assistance. The great and increasing demand for leather, and the number of *small hides and skins*, in the county and its neighbourhood, (which proportionably are the most valuable), were strong inducements for engaging in that plan as early as possible.

"Next, a *bleachfield* was begun, on as large a scale

as

as seemed calculated for the commencement of such an undertaking; and the Subscribers to that attempt flatter themselves, that, considering their remote and northern situation, and the many disadvantages under which all new attempts must necessarily labour, they will receive as much encouragement as the Board has hitherto bestowed in any case of a similar nature.

"The soil and climate of Caithness seem to be admirably calculated for raising Flax, and for carrying on all the different operations of the *linen manufacture*. By distributing flax-seed, erecting lint-mills, and other encouragements, there is every reason to believe, that the linen manufacture may be carried on there to a very great extent.

"It is also proposed, to erect a manufacture of *coarse woollens*, for the consumption of the country people, as soon as a proper person, with some capital of his own, can be discovered for managing such an undertaking, who will be able to carry it on at his own risk, and for his own behoof, with the assistance which he will receive from the Subscribers.

"On the whole, the attention of the Trustees is the more earnestly requested to these plans, since the industry of that corner of the kingdom, is at present at that particular crisis, when proper encouragement will bring forward the most rapid improvements, such as will do credit to the patronage of the Board, and must prove of general benefit to the kingdom: whereas, if such a spirit is now neglected and depressed, it is impossible to say when it will again revive with equal energy.

"N.B. Persons wishing to engage in any manufacture in Caithness, or desirous of taking a share in the concern,

concern, may apply to Mr. Horne, Writer to the Signet, Edinburgh; or to Mr. William Henderson, merchant, in Thurso. There are also many eligible Farms to let in Caithness; and every encouragement will be given to those who incline to settle in that county, in the farming line.

" *Edinburgh, Nov. 30, 1789.*"

No. XXIII.

On the Establishment of the Flax Husbandry, and the Linen Manufacture in Caithness. By Mr. Paton.

The aptitude of Caithness for the growth of flax, and the linen manufacture, may appear from what follows.

It is admitted, that the climate in Caithness is rather inferior to that of the southern counties of Scotland, and the seasons fit for agricultural labour, rather shorter; but it is evident, that vegetation is more rapid, and that the soil is equally good, appears from the weighty crops of hay, turnip, bear, and oats, it produces*; and when properly attended to, yields as good flax as any in Scotland: and although rain is more frequent in Caithness, than in some of the more southern counties, yet it is much more moderate, and this is greatly in favour of the growth of flax, which requires a good deal of moisture; hence Holland is so famous for flax. But to give an evident proof of the

* I have had common bear on my little farm, that weighed 18½ stone per boll. I had potatoe oats last year, of such superior quality, that they were mentioned in the newspapers, and Mr. Traill's factor offered me 3*s.* per boll above the highest current price for seed: they weighed about 15 stone per boll.

aptitude

aptitude of Caithness for the growth of flax, one acre of land under that crop, which I had under my charge, gave 50 stone of scutched lint from the mill, 16 lb. to the stone, and it heckled to 9 lb. per stone, which, to the best of my recollection, spun to five hesps from the pound. This crop would have sold in other districts, accustomed to the flax husbandry, at 50*l*. sterling. I also raised two acres of flax, and although the land was considered only in an ordinary state for that crop, yet I had 70 stone of good flax, that spun three hesps from the pound, and heckled to 10 lb. from the stone.

I have known greater produce than any of the above, though not in such large parcels, yet these smaller parcels, are no despicable proof of what the soil and climate is capable of. Besides, it is well known, that flax requires more labour than any other crop, the weeding, pulling, rippling, or thrashing out the seed, watering, spreading, lifting from the grass, making it up for the mill, &c.; all this being done by women, whose wages are much lower than in the more southern counties, occasions a very considerable saving, and it is greatly owing to cheapness of labour in the different branches of the linen manufacture, and the raising partly of their own flax, that the Irish rival us so much at market. Farther, the interim between the hay and corn harvest, is the proper season for pulling, watering, and preparing the flax for the mill, and as women have little to do at this season of the year, they may not only be easily obtained, but may be had at reduced wages. Again, Caithness abounds with marl, and although any water free from iron ore, when prepared in proper pits, will water lint, yet marl water gives it a superior gloss, and the pits retain the

water

water more closely. Thus it appears, that Caithness is peculiarly adapted for the flax husbandry, from the nature of its soil and climate, the low price of labour, the abundance of labourers, the superior quality of the water and watering ponds, and the plenty of ground fit for drying the flax: on the whole, wherever good bear and oats can be raised, so can good crops o flax, and that Caithness is a good corn country, is evident, from the quantities of grain it produces, more especially within these few years, since improvements have been carried on so rapidly.

As Caithness is peculiarly adapted to the growth of flax, so it is for the linen manufacture at large. It is well known, that the Irish undersell us at market, owing to the low price of labour, and their growing their own flax, both of which might be the case in Caithness, where there is cheap and good land for growing flax, plenty of hands to manufacture it, and labour moderate. In proof of this, the spindle of yarn, that is spun in Caithness for 1*s.*, cost 1*s.* 4*d.* further south, and the yarn is as well spun here as there. Caithness is likewise a healthy country, with plenty of fuel, and a regular supply of provisions, as beef, mutton, pork, meal, fish, &c. at reasonable and cheap rates; indeed there is not a more plentiful and cheaper market in Scotland than in Thurso. There also may be had, different excellent falls of water for machinery, either for linen, cotton, or bleaching. There is already a bleachfield on a large scale in the country, where linens are finished in the highest style, after the Scotch and Irish methods. There are also several lint mills, on the most approved plans, and if the flax husbandry were encouraged more, they may all be soon required. It is no mean proof of the fitness of Caithness for the growth of

flax,

flax, and of the desire that the people have for raising it, that there is this year at the bleachfield, above 600 pieces of linen of considerable length, all made from flax of the growth of Caithness.

No. XXIV.

Hints regarding the Means of promoting the Improvement of the County of Caithness, in North Britain. By Sir John Sinclair, Bart.

The most likely means of promoting the improvement of this remote district, are as follows:

1. The erection of a large town, to be a market for the Agricultural productions of the county, and the centre of its commerce, and manufactures, whence various establishments, of a similar nature, on a smaller scale, might spread over all the neighbourhood, as is the case in regard to Manchester, Glasgow, &c. There can be no doubt, that Thurso, from the many natural advantages it possesses, is the situation, the best adapted for that purpose; nor indeed can any place be better calculated for a large manufacturing and commercial city, or a kind of Metropolis to the neighbourhood.

2. The formation of a harbour for carrying on the fisheries and foreign commerce on a great scale, which may be constructed at Thurso with peculiar advantage, and,

3. Completing the roads of communication, and the bridges of the county.

For effecting these important purposes, it is proposed to erect, by Act of Parliament, a Joint Stock Company, with

with a capital of 50,000*l*., a sum adequate to the objects in view, and which might be laid out in a manner, that would not only yield the usual legal interest, but even a profit to the subscribers.

1. To complete the New Town of Thurso, would require a capital of 30,000*l*. The houses, to yield profit, ought not to be on a large or expensive scale. We shall suppose, that thirty houses are built at the rate of 300*l*. each, hence 9000*l*.; and 105 houses, at 200*l*. each, or at the expense of 21,000*l*., which would amount in all to 30,000*l*. Houses of the first sort, would let at 20*l*. a year, and of the second, at 12*l*. 10*s*. yielding, on the whole, per annum, the following income:

30 houses at 20*l*. rent each, ...	£600
105 houses at 12*l*. 10*s*. each, ...	1312
	£1912

Hence there would arise an annual profit of 412*l*. per annum, in addition to the legal interest, of five per cent.

2. The Harbour proposed to be erected at Thurso, would require 6000*l*., in addition to what public aid can be procured, and the interest of that sum, would be amply furnished, by a moderate tonnage tax on the shipping, even on the present trade, which, if a Harbour were constructed, would be increasing every year, and would soon become a very pofitable concern.

3. The roads and bridges in the county, including the bridge of Wick, would require 14,000*l*. to complete them, in addition to public aid. The road and bridge money paid by the county, is perfectly sufficient to defray the interest of that sum, and tolls, if necessary, might be erected, in aid thereof.

It must evidently appear, from the preceding observations,

servations, that nothing is wanted, *but capital*, to effect the great improvements above-mentioned, there being sufficient funds to defray more than the legal interest. We shall next proceed therefore to state, how that capital may be raised.

It is well known, that various important improvements have been carried on in other places, by the erection of joint stock companies, particularly in the case of canals, where the profit of the undertaking was not so certain as in the present instance. Why should not the same plan succeed here?

The inducements to subscribe, even to those who have no local attachments, are sufficiently tempting. The security for the payment of the interest, is unquestionable, the chance of profit is great, and as it is proposed, that the company shall be erected by parliamentary authority, there is no risk of additional demands, beyond the sum subscribed, or farther responsibility.

The plan the most likely to be generally acceptable, for raising the capital required, would probably be as follows:

Let the sum be raised by 2000 shares, at 25*l.* each, the money to be paid by instalments, in five years, with an interest at the rate of five per cent. to those who advance the money at once.

It is supposed that one fifth part of the sum, say 10,000*l.* will be subscribed in the county of Caithness itself, and in other parts of Scotland; but as by far the greater part of it must be raised in England, the directors must be chosen, and ought to hold their meetings, in London, as in the case of the British Fishing Society. There ought, however, to be a Committee of Proprietors in Caithness, to controul the expenditure there, and to conduct the proposed improvements, subject

ject to the superintending authority of the Directors in London.

These general hints will explain the outlines of the proposed measure, by engaging in which, persons possessed of capital, will have an opportunity of laying it out with profit, and also, it is hoped, *with peculiar satisfaction.*

What indeed can be more gratifying to a feeling and intelligent mind, than to promote the improvement of a district, naturally possessed of many advantages, but which hitherto, in consequence of its remote situation, has been unfortunately neglected, and which requires nothing, but the assistance of some opulent, and public spirited individuals, to rise to consequence, and to wealth; and here it may be proper to observe, that the expenditure of the same sum, which would scarcely be felt in some situations, would operate here as a charm, establishing, in a valuable part of the kingdom, *more directly*, industry, and commerce, and *circuitously*, even agricultural skill and enterprise, with all their attending advantages.

Thurso, 16th August, 1799.

N. B. There is every reason to hope, that as soon as peace is restored, and that money abounds, at a low rate of interest, some plan of the nature above sketched out, may be carried into effect.

No. XXV.

No. XXV.

Memorandum regarding a Rendezvous for Merchant Ships in the North Seas.

A Rendezvous for merchant ships sailing to the Baltic, has hitherto been in some harbour in the Orkney Islands; but there is every reason to believe, that Scrabster Roads, on the west coast of Caithness, is much better calculated for that purpose. It is large enough to hold from 200 to 300 sail at a time, is well sheltered from all quarters, no tide-way, good holding ground, from eight to ten fathom water, and sufficient room to work out with any wind that blows. In consequence of its possessing these advantages, it is, during the most tempestuous seasons of the year, the principal resort of the fishing smacks who supply the London market with cod; and it is well known, that the masters of those smacks, are the best pilots, from Gravesend, to Cape Wrath in Strathnaver.

Scrabster Roads has another advantage; that it is near the thriving town of Thurso, which is surrounded by a plentiful country, whence a fleet may be supplied with any articles for which it may have occasion.

On these grounds, it is earnestly requested, that the Lords Commissioners of His Majesty's Admiralty, would have the goodness to direct an inquiry to be made into the advantages attending Scrabster Roads, as a proper place of rendezvous in the North Seas, and would fix upon that harbour, if, upon inquiry, it should prove so well calculated for the purpose, as is above represented.

No. XXVI.

Hints regarding the Harbour of Thurso.

It is a great advantage to any *tide Harbour*, like that of Thurso, to have such an excellent roadstead as Scrabster, in its immediate neighbourhood, where vessels may remain at anchor in safety, until they can get into the harbour itself; but that circumstance, instead of being an objection, is an argument in favour of having a Harbour at Thurso, because it removes the only possible objection to it, as being a *tide Harbour*.

The idea of erecting a new village or town at Scrabster, is quite impossible, both from the elevated nature of the ground about it, and the want of that most essential article, *water*. It would require, indeed, many years, and many thousand pounds, to erect such a town as Thurso, in any part of that neighbourhood, were a situation to be met with, liable to no objections.

There is, perhaps, no town in the north, better situated than Thurso, for the Cod and Herring Fisheries, for the whale fishery, or for a trade with the West Indies, and the Baltic. The greater part of the cod that supplies the London market, is caught in that neighbourhood. The herrings appear on that coast a month earlier, than on that of Wick. It is situated in the centre of a fertile, and an improving district, and it wants nothing but a harbour, to make it a place of great commercial importance. Being situated on a river, is a point of infinite consequence to a large town, nor is it of less importance, that if a proper harbour is made, it would be *land-locked*, and consequently would be a place of perfect safety, at all seasons

sons of the year. The building of boats, and other vessels, might also be carried on with great advantage in a place so situated.

There is no place in Scotland, indeed, where the formation of a Harbour would do more good, or where public aid would be more usefully expended.

No. XXVII.

Resolutions of the Freeholders of Caithness, regarding the Exertions made by Sir John Sinclair, Bart. for Promoting the Prosperity of the County.

At the Borough of Wick, and within the Council House, and Common Court Place thereof, the 26th Day of May, 1807; betwixt the Hours of Twelve and Two in the Afternoon;

At a Court of Freeholders of the County of Caithness, met for the pupose of electing their Representative to Parliament, Sir Benjamin Dunbar of Hempriggs, Bart. Preses; It was moved by Mr. Sinclair of Freswick, that the Thanks of the Freeholders of this County, be given to Sir John Sinclair of Ulbster, Bart. Member, now elected for the fourth time, for this County, without opposition, for his uninterrupted attention to promote the improvements of Agriculture, and Rural Affairs, as well as of the useful Arts and Sciences of the Nation at large; but particularly, for his constant attention to the general interests of this his native County; for the introduction of Agriculture, and the Arts, and the promotion of Commerce, Manufactures, and Fisheries, particularly for his active and successful exertions, in laying the foundation for extending Fishings and Com-

 merce,

merce, by procuring Harbours at Wick and Thurso, and thereby encouraging the cultivation of Lands, by opening a Market for its produce, and increasing the Population of the County, usefully employed: Which Motion was seconded by Mr. Sinclair of Barrack, and unanimously adopted by the Meeting.

(Signed) BENJAMIN DUNBAR, Preses.

Extracted from the Minutes, by
JOHN ROSE, Sheriff Clerk.

No. XXVIII.

Hints submitted to the Consideration of the Select Committee, to whom the Survey and Report of the Coasts and Central Highlands of Scotland, made by the Command of the Commissioners of His Majesty's Treasury, has been referred; including some Observations on the Advantages of Domestic Colonization.

[This is the Paper, on which was founded the Improvements which have since been carried on in the Northern Districts of Scotland.]

INTRODUCTION.—The subject that has been referred to the Committee, is unquestionably one of the most important that could possibly be submitted to the consideration of any respectable or intelligent body of men. About two hundred years have now elapsed*, since the British Government has almost exclusively directed its

* As far back as the reign of James I. there was a public lottery, the profit of which was appropriated to the expenses attending the establishment of our Colonies in North America.

attention

attention to the cultivation of its foreign possessions, leaving the improvement of its territory at home to the exertions of individuals. The adoption of such a plan might be justified, if every acre in the United Kingdoms were cultivated to the best advantage, and if, after all, we could neither find food for our people, nor employment for the capital we were possessed of; but surely, until that is the case, we should not be rash in wasting abroad, what can be employed at home to much more advantage.

It is unnecessary, at this time, to dwell on the fatal consequences which this country has experienced from Foreign Colonization, *carried to the extent it was*. It appears that our American Colonies alone cost us above 40 millions, in addition to all the expenses of the various wars connected with those establishments, which amounted to above 200 millions more. What happy effects might not have been expected, had only a small proportion of those sums been dedicated to domestic improvement!

Lord Bacon, whose works throw as much light on politics, as on philosophy, in a work entitled, "Certain Considerations touching the Plantation in Ireland," or the new settlements begun in that country, written in the reign of James I., thus states his opinion regarding the means of promoting domestic colonization:

"For the third, I will never despair but that the Parliament of England, if it may perceive that this action is not a flash, but a solid and settled pursuit, will give aid to a work, so religious, so politic, and so profitable. And the distribution of charge, (if it be observed), falleth naturally into three kinds of charge; and every of those charges respectively ought to have its proper fountain and issue; for as there proceedeth from your Majesty's royal bounty and munificence, the gift of the land, and the other materials, together with the endowment of liberties; and as the charge which is private, as building of houses, stocking of grounds, victual, and the like, is to rest upon the particular undertakers; so, whatever is public, as building of churches, walling of towns, town-houses, bridges, and causeways, or highways, and the like, ought not so properly to lie upon particular persons, but to come from the public estate of this kingdom, *to which this work is like to return so great an addition of glory, strength, and commodity**."

The principles which Lord Bacon thus established, were actually carried into effect by the celebrated Frederick of Prussia, who, fortunately for his kingdom, having no distant possessions to attend to, was led to dedicate his active mind to domestic improvements, promoting the cultivation of wastes, the introduction of new settlers from foreign countries, (instead of permitting emigrations from his own), the building of cottages, the draining of marshes, the forming of canals, the division of commons, (for the encouragement of which premiums were given), and other objects of a similar nature. The sum he annually laid out for those purposes, (a particular detail of which will be found in Count Hertzberg's Works), was very considerable, for the narrow resources of his kingdom, amounting to no less a sum than 300,000*l.* sterling per annum; but instead of being impoverished by such liberal grants, he thereby increased his revenue so much, as to leave behind him a treasure in specie, to the amount of about twelve millions sterling. What might not then be

* See his Works in folio, vol. iv. p. 406.

effected

effected in this country, were similar measures to be pursued?

As the year 1803 will, it is to be hoped, be a distinguished æra in the annals of this country, *for the commencement of Domestic Colonization*, it is extremely desirable, to have such a plan formed, as may do credit to the new system, and may refute, by the evidence of facts, any objections that can be urged against it.

The northern part of Scotland, to which the Report referred to the Committee principally relates, possesses within itself various resources, which may render it one of the most valuable possessions belonging to the British Crown.

Though, (except along the coast), it is in general unfit for agricultural operations, yet it produces a superior breed of cattle, and, it has lately been ascertained, might maintain a fine-woolled breed of sheep. The hills also are full of mines and minerals of the most valuable sorts, and the sea coasts abound with fish of the greatest variety and value.

The number of inhabitants in the Northern Highlands, may be calculated at above two hundred thousand souls; and as far back as the time of Harrington, Scotland in general, was justly considered as an invaluable nursery for the armies of Great Britain*. But as in those mountainous districts, more especially since inoculation has been introduced, population increases as fast as in North America, unless new means of occupy-

* "Scotland being a martial country, will make a larger provision of a good auxiliary militia; and in regard to auxiliaries, Scotland will be a greater revenue to you than if you had the Indies."—Harrington's Oceana and other works, folio edit. p. 187 and 458.

ing the people, are from time to time pointed out, perpetual emigrations must be the necessary consequence.

For the purpose of furnishing such employment, the Report referred to the Committee, very properly suggests, 1. Roads; 2. Bridges; 3. Harbours; 4. Naval Stations; and 5. Canals. Some observations on each of these, shall be submitted to the reader's consideration.

1. *Roads.*—The most important means of improvement certainly is, roads of communication, as that is the foundation on which the whole system must depend. That there ought to be a road from one extremity of the island to the other, with branches diverging from the main road, where necessary, is essential in various points of view, as, 1. for the purpose of communication with the seat of government; 2. for the marching of troops; 3. for the easier conveyance by post, of commercial intelligence; and 4. that the cattle and sheep reared in those remote districts, may be conveyed with the greater ease and safety to the more fertile counties, where they are prepared for consumption. The roads alluded to in Mr. Telford's Report, are so essential for those purposes, that this part of the Plan does not require any particular explanation. It is to be observed, that the districts through which those roads are to be conducted, though unable to make any great exertion, yet would most readily contribute what they could, to promote so important an object, and that the expense might be greatly diminished by employing the army, the militia, and the volunteers, in carrying on such works.

2. *Bridges.*—It is well known, that no roads can be complete

complete without bridges, and that they are particularly necessary in a country, where even the smallest streams are apt to be unexpectedly swelled into torrents, and soon become dangerous to the traveller. No bridges can be more essential than those mentioned by Mr. Telford; and the sum which it is proposed the public shall contribute for their erection, is not likely to be objected to.

3. *Harbours.*—If the safety of commerce, or the improvement of the fisheries, are objects worth attending to in those remote districts, it is evident that they cannot be obtained without the advantage of harbours. An impartial and intelligent traveller, (the late Mr. Pennant), who visited those remote districts many years ago, states, in the following words, the result of his inquiries into that subject: "At a little distance, (he observes), from Sinclair Castle, near Staxigo Creek, is a small herring fishery, the only one on the coast: *cod and other fish abound there;* but the want of ports on this stormy coast is an obstacle to the establishment of the fisheries on this side of the country*." It is singular, that it should be reserved to these times, to act upon the facts he had collected. The advantages to be derived from the harbours recommended in Mr. Telford's two Reports, can hardly be questioned, both with a view to the fisheries, and to the general commerce of the country. In regard to the proposed harbour at Wick, in particular, *it is in fact a national object;* for it would furnish shelter, not only to the coasting trade, but to the foreign commerce of the kingdom. Within these few years past, about 30 vessels have

* Third edition, vol. i. p. 182. The Tour was taken ann. 1769.

been

been wrecked upon that coast, the greater part of whom, and their valuable cargoes, would probably have been saved, had there been a harbour there.

4. *Naval Stations.*—The acquisitions that France has made, of the coasts and harbours of Flanders and Holland, renders it absolutely necessary to have some Naval Stations on the Eastern Coast of Scotland, for the protection of that part of His Majesty's dominions, and the Baltic and other trades passing to the north. Aberdeen and Cromarty, might certainly be made serviceable for that purpose: but for any establishment on a great scale, the peninsula at Peterhead, described in Mr. Telford's first Report, is by far the most valuable; and indeed there is hardly such a situation, for a Naval Arsenal, in almost any part of Europe.

5. *Canals.*—For many years past, the idea of cutting a canal from Fort William to Inverness, has been recommended to the public attention, and is at last submitted to the consideration of Parliament. As that subject is so fully explained in the Report, it seems unnecessary to dwell more upon it in these cursory observations.

Such are the means of improvement recommended in these Reports. Let us next consider, 1. The expense which the plan will occasion. 2. The advantages that may be derived from it; and 3. What would be the best mode of carrying it into effect.

1. *The Expense.*—The expense of carrying on each of these important improvements, shall be separately touched upon.

1. It is proposed in the Report, that a sum not exceeding

exceeding 96,000*l.* shall be granted by the public, for certain roads and bridges in the northern parts of Scotland, and that a similar sum shall be paid by the land-owners of those districts where they are to be made. The general principle of this proposal certainly cannot be objected to: but it is submitted, whether the proportions to be expected from the land-owners, ought not to vary, according to situation and circumstances. It cannot be supposed, that districts hitherto inaccessible, can afford as much as those which have already been enriched by commerce and intercourse; and if this is admitted, any difference of contribution that may arise in consequence thereof, might be defrayed out of the fund arising from the balance of the Forfeited Estates, which was, originally, especially appropriated for the improvement of that part of the kingdom *.

2. The expense of harbours for the improvement of the fisheries, is stated at 6000*l.*; but that sum is certainly inadequate for so important an object. It is a fortunate circumstance, that the property of a tract of country, where an admirable harbour may be formed, peculiarly adapted as a central point for carrying on the Deep-Sea Herring Fishery, has lately been acquired by that public spirited Society, constituted for the special purpose of improving the British Fisheries. The Society is certainly well disposed to make every possible effort which its moderate capital will admit of, to promote so useful an undertaking; but it is to be considered, that it has a new settlement entirely to create; that the Harbour of Wick, is not only of importance to that neighbourhood, but may afford shelter and protection to a

* The proper proportion seems to be as follows: to the south of Inverness the land-owners should advance one-half, and to the north thereof, one-third of the sum granted.

number

number of vessels employed both in the coasting trade and in foreign commerce; and in fact, that it lays a foundation for establishing the Deep-Sea Herring Fishery, from which this country would derive more profit, and naval strength, than from almost any new undertaking to which its attention can be directed.

3. The expense of the proposed Naval Stations, amounting only to 60,000*l.*, 27,500*l.* of which it is proposed shall be raised by private subscription, does not seem to require any further explanation, than what is contained in the Report.

4. The Caledonian Canal is undoubtedly a great national object, and I have no doubt, if peace had continued for some years, that numbers of persons would have readily taken a concern in it, as a fair mercantile speculation. At present, it can only be executed by the Public, and when completed, the Nation would not only be indemnified for the expense, by the advantages of which it would be productive; but if it answered the objects in view, of shortening, and rendering safer and more commodious, the communication between the Eastern and the Western Coasts of the Island, it possibly would yield a surplus to the Exchequer.

5. Regarding the road from Carlisle to Port Patrick, it is only necessary to observe, that every thing that can possibly facilitate the intercourse between Great Britain and Ireland, cannot fail to have the warmest approbation of those, who are real friends to the prosperity and happiness of the united kingdoms.

On the whole, if the Public were, in the course of seven years, to be at the whole expense that is above suggested, amounting in all to 501,450*l.* what is it, compared to the advantages which may be expected from

that

that expenditure? Is it possible to suppose, that the nation, either directly or indirectly, would not be benefited, even in a financial point of view, to a much greater extent than the interest of the sum expended, namely, 25,000*l.* per annum? But when it is considered, that at so moderate an expense, the commerce of the country will be facilitated; that in the course of a few years, some millions of property may probably be saved from being either wrecked and lost, or captured by the enemy; that many thousands of industrious or useful inhabitants will be prevented from abandoning their native country; and that the foundation of improvement will be laid in many extensive and valuable districts; who can possibly refuse, giving every possible aid to measures, of a nature so peculiarly beneficial and important?

2. *Advantages which the Country may obtain, were the proposed Measures carried into effect.*—There is nothing from which this country would probably be enabled to draw more substantial benefit, than to be enabled to make a fair comparison between foreign and domestic colonization, in regard to all the leading points of political importance, as population, agriculture, commerce, manufactures, revenue, naval strength, and military power.

1. *Population.*—As to population, there can be no comparison between the two systems. The people you have at home, you have always at your own command, and they must furnish you either with men and money, or with both; whereas the inhabitants of a distant colony, may have a jealousy of the mother-country, or may wish to become independent, or may join your most inveterate enemies, or may be conquered by them. The

The population of a domestic colony, therefore, produces strength; that of a remote one engenders weakness, and becomes the source of debility.

2. *Agriculture.*—It is evident also, that such encouragements as those above suggested, may greatly promote the Agriculture of a country, and may contribute to render it independent of foreign nations for grain. Though the northern parts of Scotland, are in general far from fertile, yet the new modes of improving wastes, which have been lately introduced there, (in particular the fen husbandry, and the burning of a clayey surface), are likely soon to alter the whole face of the country, and may possibly in time enable it to furnish those inferior qualities of grain, as oats and rye, which we have hitherto been obliged to import, in such quantities, and at such an expense, from foreign nations. Without, however, roads of communication, to carry on and to promote the internal improvement of those districts, and harbours to import lime, and to export the produce that has been raised, agricultural improvements, to any great extent, cannot be expected.

3. *Commerce.*—Nothing is more desirable for a maritime power, than to extend the navigation and commerce of every part of its dominions. Were the measures above alluded to, to be carried on, there can be no doubt, that not only the coasting trade would be improved, but that a very advantageous commerce might be carried on with the Baltic, and the West Indies, by which the number of our seamen, and the produce of our customs, would be considerably augmented.

4. *Manufactures.*—For the purpose of employing those who may not find the means of occupation in agriculture, commerce, or the fisheries, it would be desirable to have some of the coarser manufactures esta-

blished

blished in the North, more especially those which we are at present obliged to import from foreign countries, as Osnaburghs, Silesias, and the like. And if the improvements which are in contemplation were carried on, and succeed to the extent that may be expected, there can be no doubt, that these districts would furnish a new and advantageous market for the manufactures of England; and rival in that respect, those foreign colonies, in the principal benefit that can be derived from them.

APPENDIX.

No. I.

ACCOUNTS

OF THE

IMPROVEMENTS CARRIED ON IN THE COUNTY OF CAITHNESS,

FOR THREE YEARS, ENDING ANNO 1803.

An Account of Various Measures, calculated for the Improvement of the County of Caithness, carrying on in the course of the Year 1801.

1. Mr. Headrick, and Mr. Bushby the Mineralogical Surveyor, have been sent North, by the Barons of Exchequer in Scotland, to bore for coal at Scrabster, in the neighbourhood of Thurso, on lands belonging to the Crown, where there is a great probability, that a very valuable mine of coal will be discovered.

2. Mr. Telford, a respectable and intelligent engineer, has received orders from the Treasury, to survey the harbours on the coast of Caithness; in particular, those of Wick, Thurso, and Dunbeath; and to estimate the expense of making the same. Some public assistance may be expected for carrying on these impor-

tant undertakings; in the promotion of which, the Directors of the British Fishing Society, and Mr. Vansittart, Secretary to the Treasury, have much interested themselves.

3. For the purpose of improving the Fisheries on the coast of Caithness, Government has sent north, free from expense, some Dutch fishermen, to be employed in the herring fishing at Wick.

4. Mr. Charles Abercrombie, so celebrated for his skill in lining out roads, has received orders from Lieutenant-General Vyse, authorised for that purpose by Lord Pelham, Secretary of State for the Home Department, to line out the roads, about the Ord, and hills of Berriedale, and along the borders of Caithness and Sutherland, so as finally to settle the direction, throughout a tract of country, which is reckoned the most difficult to make of any in Scotland.

5. Application is made to Government for authority to lay out a sum of money, this year, in making the roads of the county, to be repaid out of the balance of the Forfeited Estates in Scotland; with a view, not only of carrying on so essential an improvement, but also of furnishing a number of industrious labourers with the means of subsistence.

6. A person from Perth, well acquainted with the Linen Trade, has examined, in the course of this year, the advantage which Caithness possesses for carrying on that manufacture; and has placed them in so striking a point of view, that no doubt is now entertained of its being soon established on a large scale, in the county. Some flax is already raised, and great quantities of yarn spun, wove, and bleached, to as great perfection, as in any part of Scotland

7. When the harbour of Dunbeath is made, it is proposed

proposed to carry on a regular intercourse with the opposite coast of Moray and Banff, for the purpose of importing lime from Portsoy, &c. and for exporting cattle, too large for sending round by the heads of the Friths, or in too good condition to be driven to any great distance, through a rugged country.

8. A number of Farmers from the Lothians, and other southern counties, have been examining the farms in Caithness, where it is supposed that several of them will settle. They have every inducement to do so, as the crops in Caithness were abundant for the last two years, when they failed in so many other districts.

9. Robert German, from the county of Cambridge, has come to Caithness, with the peculiar sort of ploughs, adapted for trying the fen husbandry, as practised in Lincolnshire, Cambridgeshire, &c. This is the most profitable of all farming; producing, at a small expense, great crops of grain, grass, rape, tares, turnips, &c. by paring and burning mossy lands, not worth, in their present state, a shilling per acre. There is every reason to hope, that this important improvement will answer, equal to the most sanguine expectations of those by whom it has been introduced.

10. Mr. Stephens, junior, proposes being in Caithness in October, to examine to what extent watering of land, and draining, can be carried on in the county, that such essential improvements may be pursued, with proper spirit, in the course of next season.

11. The resolutions adopted by the Gentlemen of the County, last year, for establishing winter herding, preventing the casting of feal and divot, and including other branches of police, have already had so beneficial an effect, that it is resolved to enforce them as much as possible. Indeed, all the intelligent Farmers

in the county, are so sensible of the advantages resulting from them, that it is hoped no compulsory measures are necessary, to insure their observance.

12. Mr. Scott, a respectable builder from Edinburgh, is employed in erecting houses in the New Town of Thurso. He has discovered a very valuable freestone quarry in the neighbourhood, which will be of the utmost service in promoting the building of that town; and it may become an article of export to London, and other places, being of an uncommon good quality. The town of Thurso now contains about 2000 inhabitants; and has increased about 400 within the last ten years.

13. The trees which have been planted in the hilly parts of the county, promising to answer, it is proposed to carry on plantations there on an extensive scale, and to establish nurserymen, by whom the Gentlemen of Caithness may be supplied with young trees, accustomed to the soil and climate, and consequently more likely to thrive than any that can be imported.

14. Some promising veins of *Copper*, and of *Lead Ore*, and specimens of the most beautiful *Marble*, having been discovered in different parts of Caithness, Mr. Hutchinson, of Alstonmoor, in Cumberland, came north to examine them; and is so much pleased with their appearance, that he intends, in conjunction with his friends, to establish a company for working such as are likely to be the most productive and valuable.

15. The introduction of the *Cheviot Breed of Sheep* has succeeded so completely, that it is proposed to increase them considerably. The flock of one proprietor already amounts to between 3000 and 4000, and he proposes augmenting the number to 10,000, which will probably be the largest flock, of so valuable a sort, in the

the island. Materials will thus be furnished for the establishment of a woollen manufacture, which has been long much wished for.

16. Though *Sheep* must be the staple article in the hilly districts, yet *Cattle* ought to be principally attended to in the plain country, until there is a market for considerable numbers of fat sheep. The cattle of Caithness are much improving in quality, particularly those which have been crossed with the Galloway breed. In order to accommodate the drovers, who may wish to purchase them, and that the cattle may be brought to their proper value, it is proposed to hold stated fairs, in the beginning of the months of June, August, and September, which several considerable dealers have already engaged to attend.

17. A regular and frequent communication with other places, is essential to the improvement of any district. To obtain that advantage for Caithness, it is necessary that a Daily Post should be established to the two principal towns; and it is to be hoped, that an intended application to the Postmaster General for that purpose, will be successful. It is farther proposed, to have packets, or vessels that will sail at fixed periods from Leith, to the towns of Wick and Thurso; and also to carry on an intercourse with the metropolis, by means of the fishing smacks which supply the London markets with cod and other fish, and which rendezvous, for several months in the year, at Scrabster road, near Thurso.

18. Instead of applying, either to Courts of Law, or to Parliament, for authority to *divide the Commons*, it is not unusual, at present, to refer the same to the decision of one or more Gentlemen of the county, who are not interested in the division; and so much are the

proprietors, in general, disposed to promote such measures, that a favourite toast here is likely soon to be realized—" May a *Common*, be an *uncommon*, spectacle in Caithness."

19. The late scarcities have pointed out the necessity of improving the agriculture, and extending the cultivation of the kingdom. In regard to the latter point, there is every reason to hope, that the county of Caithness will not be deficient. A great extent of *waste lands* have been improved, this year, in various parts of the district; and the crops promise amply to repay the expense, more especially on mossy lands. The spirit of enclosing and cultivating wastes is now so prevalent, that one Gentleman has pledged himself, that he and his tenants shall improve 500 acres in the course of next year; and a subscription paper is proposed, to ascertain the quantity which the different Proprietors of the county will undertake to improve, in the course of next season.

20. As *Education* is the basis of all permanent improvement, it is intended, immediately, to erect an Academy at Thurso, where all the principal branches of education will be taught by proper masters. A boarding-school for girls, has already been established there, and is conducted much to the satisfaction of the town and neighbourhood; and as Thurso will soon rival, in regard to the important article of education, any town of its extent in Scotland: That, joined to the cheapness of provisions, and other conveniences, must be a great inducement to persons of moderate income to settle there.

It will appear, from the preceding enumeration, what a variety of important improvements are now carrying

rying on in Caithness, which the late favourable seasons, and the high price of the articles which the country produces, have greatly tended to promote. In the course of last spring and summer, from 400 to 500 labourers came in from the neighbouring counties in quest of work; and hitherto they have all found occupation in building, enclosing, ditching, trenching, road-making, and other substantial improvements. Indeed, such has been the happy situation of Caithness, during seasons which have unfortunately borne so hard on other places, that no person, either living in it, or who chose to come into it from any of the neighbouring districts, have felt the want, either of food or employment.

An Account of various Measures, calculated for the Improvement of the County of Caithness, carrying on in the course of the Year 1802.

The account which was published about twelve months ago, of the improvements carrying on in the county of Caithness, anno 1801, having met with a very favourable reception, I am thence induced to continue the same plan for the current year 1802. The utility of such statements can hardly be questioned. They serve not only as memorandums to the inhabitants of the district to which they relate, inciting them to persevere in the plans therein suggested, but they also furnish a number of useful hints to other places; and they have a strong tendency to excite a general spirit of cultivation and improvement throughout the whole country. On these grounds, I hope that the publishing of such annual reports, instead of being confined to this remote county, will spread over the kingdom in general.

 1. The

1. The trial for *Coal* at Scrabster, unfortunately has not hitherto answered; but there is still reason to hope, that deeper bores may be successful. In the interim, several Gentlemen in the county have employed a skilful Surveyor to search for other minerals on their respective estates; and he has already discovered considerable quantities of marl and limestone; also clays, valuable for making bricks and tiles, and for potteries; some manganese, and lead ores, have also been found. The particulars of the whole will be laid before the public, as soon as the survey is finished.

2. An act for making a *Harbour at Thurso*, having passed in the course of the last session, that important undertaking is to be set about, as soon as a proper Contractor for executing the same can be got. It is intended to make the harbour as complete as possible, so as to admit vessels of from 300 to 500 tons, at least in spring tides; also to have a graving-dock; a regulating-weir, and a slip for ship-building. The whole expense will probably exceed 10,000*l.*; but it is desirable to lay a foundation for that extensive commerce to which Thurso, from its situation and other advantages, seems to be so justly entitled. About 20 houses have been already built in the New Town of Thurso, and about 20 more will probably be erected next year, in addition to a number of houses recently built in the Old Town; so that accommodation will soon be found for those who may be inclined to settle in this thriving place, and to carry on commercial, and other branches of industry. Such is the spirit of improvement in that neighbourhood at present, that some enclosed land near Thurso has let as high as 5*l.* per acre.

3. The *Herring Fishery* on the coast of Caithness was rather more successful this year than the last, above

above 10,000 barrels having been caught. Had the proposed harbour at Wick been erected, which we trust will be the case next year, the fishery would of course have been carried on to a much greater extent. Some casks, of different sizes, were cured in the Dutch style, and, it is believed, were of equal good quality: but it is impossible to carry on that branch of the fishery with much success, until harbours are made upon the coast, to accommodate, and, in cases of necessity, to shelter, the persons who may engage in the deep-sea fishery.

4. The celebrated pass of the *Ord of Caithness*, of which Mr. Pennant, in one of his northern tours, has given so terrific, but so just a description, has long been remarkable for the steepness of the ascent, and the danger of the road across it. In consequence of directions sent by Lord Pelham to Lieutenant-General Vyse, it was surveyed this summer by that excellent engineer Mr. Charles Abercrombie, who has discovered a mode of conducting the road without the smallest difficulty or danger; and the ascent, instead of being so uncommonly steep, will not exceed one foot in thirty, in any part of it. There is every reason to hope that something effectual will be done for the roads and bridges of the North, in the course of the ensuing Session of Parliament.

5. The *Establishment of Various New Branches of Manufacture* are in contemplation, several proposals having been given in for that purpose; in particular—for a woollen manufacture—for the spinning and weaving of hemp—for the making of bricks and tiles—for the manufacture of soap and candles, &c. &c. Ship-building has already begun at Ham, and a ropery at Castlehill. The branches formerly established in this county have succeeded so well, that a gentleman in the south of Scotland, who had taken a share in them, to the amount of

25*l.*,

25*l.*, and who probably never expected to hear of it again, was lately agreeably surprised to be informed, that he might receive 65*l.* for his share in the concern.

6. Some Farmers from the southern parts of Scotland, have already taken farms in Caithness, and more are expected. There is every reason to believe, that when the prejudices against a northern soil and climate are removed, numbers will be glad to settle in a district where they will enjoy many advantages, amply compensating for any inconveniences, to which they may be subjected. An excellent system of improvement is now adopted; that of letting the old stock land, and a part of the adjoining commons, to substantial farmers, on improving leases; and then to divide the remainder of the commons among the smaller tenants, whom it is necessary for that purpose to remove. By these judicious measures, the population of the country is preserved, whilst its improvement will be rapidly accelerated.

7. The *Cultivation of Wastes* is going on with spirit, and with as much success as could be expected, in a season so little calculated for improvement. One Proprietor has ploughed between 500 and 600 acres of waste land; the whole of which, and even more, would have been under crop this year, had the weather been favourable. The plan of dividing commons, also, by a submission to the gentlemen in the neighbourhood, is found to answer. An extensive and valuable tract, amounting to about 2500 acres, has been divided this year, at a very moderate expense; and another, exceeding 4500 acres, is now in the same train. An opportunity is thus afforded of providing for the smaller tenants, who must be removed, where farms are enlarged; and also of settling any disbanded soldiers and others, who may be inclined to cultivate wastes at home, instead of flying to the wilds of America.

8. The

8. The most extensive experiment tried, in cultivating waste land this year, and successfully carried through, was as follows: On the 7th of April last, five men from Westmoreland, accustomed to paring and burning, began to pare, with the breast-plough, a tract of common containing about 80 Scotch acres. A sufficient number of hands were, at the same time, employed in surrounding the whole with a ditch, and subdividing it by cross-drains, into four enclosures. In such a season, when hardly a peat could be got sufficiently dry for use, it was impossible to expect, that the land, thus pared, could be burnt in proper time for cropping. However, by great exertions, in the short space of about five months, the whole 80 acres were pared, burnt, enclosed, subdivided, ploughed, and partly sown with rape, turnips, &c. The ground thus brought into cultivation, was set up to auction, to see what it would fetch; and was let, on a lease for 21 years, for 20*s.* per acre; with an increase of 5*s.* per acre, at the end of the first ten years. The expense of this improvement may be thus estimated:

	£	*s.*	*d.*
1. Paring and burning per English acre, ...	1	17	0
2. Spreading the ashes, ...	0	3	0
3. Ploughing for seed, ...	0	10	0
4. Harrowing for ditto, ...	0	3	0
5. Enclosing and sub-dividing into fields of 22½ English acres each, with a ditch and a sod wall, ...	0	15	0
Total per English acre, ...	3	8	0
6. One-fifth additional, to ascertain the expense per Scotch acre, ...		13	6
Total per Scotch acre, ...	£4	1	6

In

In a favourable season, the first crop would have paid all the expense, both of the cultivation and enclosure; but if it did not, there is surely sufficient inducement to improvement, if, at an expense of about 4*l.*, you can have an income of 20*s.* per acre. By the above plan, the landlord runs little risk; he merely carries on the great outlines, leaving the minuter details to be managed by an active and attentive husbandman, who is much more likely to do justice to the progress of the improvement, than any proprietor, were he even constantly resident upon the spot.

9. The last spring and summer were so hostile to every attempt, the success of which depended on the operation of fire, that it retarded much the progress of *Fen Husbandry* in Caithness. Notwithstanding every disadvantage, however, between 200 and 300 acres have been pared with the fen plough, and about 50 acres burnt, and laid down with rape, chicory, grass seeds, &c. After the ashes from the first paring and burning have been spread, it has been found a most useful practice, to use Cook's cultivator, so as to bring the land into good tilth; and this plan is particularly necessary if new land is cultivated on the fen system. Where this instrument was used, which was to the extent of about 20 acres, the rape and grass seeds are particularly promising.

10. Many tracts of waste land have a stetile crust on the surface, generally of a peaty nature, and, consequently, easily burnt, while the soil below is commonly clay, and capable of being rendered fertile. Some lime the surface of such soils; others bury the crust by trench ploughing—both of them tedious and expensive operations. But the true mode is, to extirpate the principle of sterility, by the following process: during winter, plough the land three or four inches deep, so as to reach the

clay; cross-plough it in spring; and, as soon as the clods are dry, burn the whole surface in large heaps, spread the ashes, and sow oats, bear, turnips, rape, or grass seeds, according to the season during which the burning can be accomplished. About 12 acres were treated in this way, and at once brought, from being coarse, rugged, and barren, into a capital state of tillage and fertility. The expense did not exceed 50*s*. per acre.

11. There is no soil naturally more unproductive, nor more difficult to render fertile, then a cold and coarse clay. The usual mode of improving that soil, is, by a strong dose of lime, which, including the expense of carriage, cannot be calculated at less than from 5*l*. to 10*l*. per acre. From some experiments tried in the central counties of England, there was reason to believe, that burning the whole surface of such a soil, was a cheaper and better mode of improvement. As this was a most material point to ascertain, it was intended to make a trial on a large scale; but, owing to the uncommon wetness of the season, only five acres could be completed. The expense was as follows —

	£	*s.*	*d.*
6 tons of coal and culm, at 16*s*. per ton	4	16	0
Carriage of ditto from the shore to the field ..	0	10	0
40 cart load of peats, at 1*s*. each	2	0	0
Additional expense of carriage, 13 of these cart loads being brought from a considerable distance	1	0	0
126 labourers (including women and boys) for gathering and burning the sods, at 1*s*. on an average	6	6	0
Spreading the ashes, at 6s. per acre	1	10	0
Total	£16	3	0

or

or about 3*l.* 14*s.* 6*d.* per Scotch acre. Every thing is here stated at the highest rate; yet there is hardly any mode (unless in the immediate vicinity of dung or lime) where that kind of soil could be made equally productive, at double, or even triple the expense. It is proper to remark, that the best mode of burning the clay, is in sod kilns, similar to those in which they burn limestone in several districts.

12. A number of other Agricultural Experiments have been tried, in the course of this year. They are too numerous to be detailed in a paper of this description; but, the result of some of the most important of them, it may be proper briefly to mention. 1. It appears that winter wheat is a much hardier grain than winter rye. 2. Winter tares cannot be depended on in the northern part of the island; but they may be sown early in Spring with much advantage, and answer better than what are called Spring tares, being much hardier. They should be sown, however, immediately after the land is ploughed. 3. There is reason to believe that carrots will answer on fen or mossy land, if a sufficient quantity of ashes is spread on the ground where they are sown; and it is probable that lime, and other manures, may raise that valuable crop on peaty soil. 4. It is desirable to cultivate oats having only one pickle, instead of two or three. The grain is plumper, ripens earlier, and is much less liable to shake: the sample, also, is more equal, and, consequently, must fetch a better price at market. 5. An acre of moss land, after being pared and burnt, was sown, on the 30th of May, with grass-seeds alone, (red clover, rye-grass, with a small mixture of other grasses), and on the 30th of September it was fit to mow. The plan of laying down land, even in good heart, to grass, without a crop of grain, cannot

not be too strongly recommended; but it would seem to be a system peculiarly well adapted for new lands. 6. It would appear, that the northern parts of Scotland produce peat, the ashes of which is equal in quality to the Berkshire, when burnt by the same process. 7. Chicory is likely to prove a valuable addition to British herbage.

13. Some extensive improvements have been recently made in this county by *draining*, in particular at the loch of Duren, where a great tract of valuable land, and an inexhaustible quantity of the richest marl, have been secured by two spirited proprietors, at a very moderate expense. Similar useful undertakings have also been carried on at the dam of Achingils, and the moss of Wydell.

14. A variety of other means of improvement are in contemplation. *Regular trysts*, for the sale of cattle, are to be established. Inns, where still wanting, are to be built, partly on the principles of a tontine, and partly on the plan, that the freeholders, and other proprietors of the county, shall each subscribe a certain sum annually, towards paying the rent of an attentive innkeeper, till it appears that the profits of his business will enable him to go on without that assistance. An application is made to the Post-Office to have a daily post established, instead of the present mode of only three times a week. Some villages are planned out for carrying on the fisheries, and different branches of manufacture. An application has been made to Government, requesting that circuit courts may be held, at least once a year, to the north of Inverness, which, in various respects, would promote the improvement of the more northern counties; and a petition will be presented, as soon as the new Parliament assembles, complaining of the degrading situation in which the county is placed, sending, only alternately with Bute, a Member

to

to the Imperial Parliament, and, consequently, being every seven years totally unrepresented.

CONCLUSION.

Such are the measures now carrying on in this Northern District. If persevered in, and successfully carried through, there can be little doubt that the county of Caithness, however remote, and at present almost inaccessible, will soon reach a very high degree of prosperity and of improvement.

October, 1802.

An Account of various Measures, calculated for the Improvement of the County of Caithness, carried on in the course of the Year 1803.

Introduction.—The measures which were in contemplation, for promoting the prosperity of this remote district, have been considerably checked by the renewal of hostilities with France, which so unexpectedly took place at the commencement of this year. A state of war must, in general, be unfavourable to all sorts of improvements. The difficulty in obtaining capital to carry them on with spirit; the scarcity of hands, owing to the demands of the Army and Navy; and, in remote situations, the trouble attending the procuring seeds and other articles by sea, from distant parts of the country, and skilful labourers, where they are necessary for the introduction of any new system, are all hostile to active and great exertions. But if that was the case on former occasions, it is still more so at present, when we are threatened with all the horrors of of conquest, by the most powerful state that has arisen in modern times; and when people in general, seem more inclined to consider what are the best means of preserving what they have got, than of acquiring more. It were much to be regretted, however, if such a spirit were to become general. If that should be the case, this country would soon become unable to persevere in so arduous a contest. The best foundation of its strength, is the cultivation and produce of its own soil, and if, in addition to the other calamities of war, we were to be under the necessity of depending on foreign nations for any large proportion of our subsistence, at a time when our commerce must necessarily be considerably diminished, our wealth would quickly disappear, and our distresses would accumulate to a height which might produce the most disastrous consequences. This is a subject which, it is to be hoped, will soon attract the attention of parliament; and that some system will be adopted for the purpose of furnishing the landed and the farming interests, with the means of carrying on the cultivation and improvement of the country, if possible with greater energy than ever, as the best mode of enabling us to prosecute the present war, with additional spirit and success.

In addition to the calamities of war, the last season also, was, on the whole, highly unfavourable to agricultural improvements. The spring and the beginning of summer were cold and ungenial; and though the months of July and August were dry, and consequently well calculated for the operation of burning, yet from the want of rain at that critical period of the season, the crop of this year has but little straw, and though the quality of the grain is wholesome, yet it is hardly equal in quantity to the average produce of Caithness. This is the more to be lamented, as the preceding crop turned out a worse one than any remembered in that county for some years.

1. *Improvements of Wastes.*—This most important object was carried on to a considerable extent, during the year 1803; preparations having been made for that purpose, previous to the war breaking out. The dryness of the summer was favourable to burning, a species of improvement of important consideration. On the whole, in the course of the last season, probably *above a thousand acres* might be put in a progressive state of cultivation, of which about 430 were in the hands of one proprietor.

The best system of improving commons, that have a good depth of soil, with a rough surface, and that is capable of being burnt, is now pretty well ascertained, in so far as regards this Northern District. The land should be ploughed in the winter months, cross-ploughed in spring (that the clods may not be crumbled to pieces by the winter frosts), and burnt in summer; the ashes then spread, and ploughed in; and early next year, after being well harrowed, should be sown with oats and grass-seeds. In a better climate, the burning may take place earlier, and oats or bear may be sown the first year; and where sheep are abundant, a crop of turnips may be taken, but, on the whole, the plan above mentioned, is the best that has hitherto been attempted in this district; though slow, yet, being done gradually, requires few cattle and servants, and is sure of success. There is no other mode by which many thousand acres of waste land in this county could possibly be brought in, with nearly the same advantage. To give such land a sufficient dose of lime, would require from 5*l.* to 10*l.* per acre, according to the distance of conveyance; whereas, by this system, the expense does not exceed from 2*l.* to 3*l.* per acre; and the first crop of oats

alone

alone will pay the whole expense of the improvement, including the enclosure.

2. *Paring and Burning.*—Several skilful hands were brought from Westmoreland this year, in order to carry on the system of paring with the breast-plough, and then burning the turf thus obtained. In all, about 100 acres were treated according to this plan. From the thinness of the turfs, several acres of land thus prepared, might have been burnt, and laid down with oats in the course even of this year; but unfortunately the men were detained at Leith for about three weeks, waiting for a conveyance by sea to Caithness, and consequently were too late in coming. Little do those who live in the southern part of the kingdom know the disadvantages under which their northern brethren endeavour to rival them in improvement. About 50 of these acres were pared and burnt, with a view of providing for some small farmers, whom it was necessary to remove, in order to complete the cultivation and enclosure of an extensive tract of country in the neighbourhood. These farmers are continued in their old possessions till Whitsunday next, when they remove to their new farms. The 50 acres is to be cropped by the proprietor, which will entitle them to the benefit of the straw; and some acres are also to be laid down with grass-seeds for them. They are also to have about 50 acres of valuable pasture, adjoining to their arable land. Their lease is for 15 years. The rent is sufficiently moderate, namely, 3*s*. per acre for the first five years, 6*s*. for the second five, and 9*s*. for the third five, and half as much for the pasture land. But though the rent is low, yet that is compensated by the satisfaction of establishing a new colony of farmers, on a barren waste, on a system that is likely to encourage their exertions,

 and

and which, at any rate, will necessarily promote the improvement of that part of the country.

3. *Fen Husbandry*—It was of the greatest importance to try the fen system of husbandry, near the sheep farms established in this county, with a view of raising winter provision for that valuable stock. Unfortunately, however, there was no flat or low-lying mossy ground in that neighbourhood. It was necessary, therefore, to plough the sides of hills considerably elevated, and above the level of the sea. The seasons of late having been peculiarly unfavourable for this important species of improvement, its progress has been greatly retarded; but, on the whole, the prospect of success is at present flattering. About 60 acres has been laid down with rape, turnip, and grass-seeds, and the appearances of these crops are promising. A hardy species of grass, peculiarly adapted for mossy land, has been brought from the fens of Cambridgeshire, and it is proposed to try a long small white oat, from the neighbourhood of Whittlesea-Mere, in Huntingdonshire; which, from its hardiness and earliness, will, it is believed, succeed. Next season will certainly decide to what extent this system ought to be prosecuted in a hilly district. In a flat country, abounding with deep bogs, or mosses, there can be no doubt of its being infinitely preferable to every other.

4. *Commons.*—An extensive common having been divided not far from the town of Thurso, a considerable part of which, though rather elevated in point of situation, yet was capable of cultivation; one of the proprietors, whose share amounted to above 2000 English acres, was anxious to try what could be effected for the improvement of so valuable a tract. The whole was, in the first place,

place, divided in 50 lots, varying, in extent, from 12 to 20 acres, and upwards, according to circumstances, and the divisions marked by the plough, which was itself a troublesome business. Three modes of improvement were then adopted. 1. Some lots the proprietor himself undertook to improve, by paring and burning, in the manner already described, in order to provide settlements for some small tenants, to be removed in the neighbourhood. 2. Some lots were let to new improvers, who became bound to cultivate them at their own risk and expense; and, 3. A number of other lots were annexed to the neighbouring farms, under the obligation of improvement. Where this plan is practicable, it is certainly an excellent mode of improving commons, as a farmer has many advantages, which it is unnecessary here to point out, for bringing in, at a cheap rate, the waste lands in his vicinity. One spirited improver (Mr. George Miller, of Whitefield, near Thurso) deserves to be particularly commemorated upon this occasion. Observing the success of the new modes of improving waste lands, which had been introduced into the county, he offered a rent of 40*l.* per annum, for about 200 Scotch acres, in that part of the common which happened to be in his neighbourhood. The lease is rather long, namely, for 31 years; but it was desirable to encourage an active and judicious improver, who began ploughing his new farm almost before the ink was dry upon his lease; and though the land was intrinsically valuable, yet this was the first instance, in that part of the kingdom, of drawing such a rent from a tract of land that formerly had yielded nothing.

5. *Sheep Farming.*—It was generally believed that Caithness was but ill adapted for a sheep stock; and when not only sheep were introduced into the Highland

parts of the county, but also so superior a breed as the Cheviot, it was foretold, both in the southern, and in the northern parts of Scotland, that the plan could never answer, and that it would necessarily be attended with considerable loss. The attempt, however, has been most successfully carried on for several years; and, with a view of ascertaining the practical effects of the experiment, the grazings that were put under sheep, were advertised to be let The commencement of a war is certainly an unfavourable time for letting land, more especially at such a distance from the metropolis; but the success of the sheep system, in those parts, was so uncontrovertibly established, that some of these grazings, which ten years ago had only paid 87*l.* 16*s.* a year, were let at 600*l.* per annum; and, in the opinion of intelligent men, were worth 100*l.* more. It was thought adviseable, however, to give peculiar encouragement to the first farmer (Mr. James Anderson), who resolved to carry on a new system, on so extensive a scale, in so remote a district; more especially, as he was likely to do ample justice to the plan. A higher rent will be obtained for the other grazings still to be let in the same neighbourhood; and, on the whole, there is reason to believe that no agricultural improvement has hitherto been made, with more profitable results; a tract of country having been thus raised from a rent under 200*l.*, to above 1200*l.* per annum.

It is earnestly requested, that Highland Proprietors, more especially those with moderate incomes, will make themselves masters of a plan, which experience has thus sanctioned; and by which, at a moderate expense, they will not only render themselves and their families opulent, but will likewise greatly promote the industry, and increase the wealth of their country.

6. *Cattle.*—The introduction of the best breeds of cattle into a district, according to the various purposes for which they are destined, is a most important mean of improvement, which cannot be too anxiously attended to. Several experiments, with that view, have been tried in Caithness, in the course of this season: among the rest, Col. Williamson has introduced the Argyll breed, which there is every reason to hope will answer. Mr. Paterson has brought some oxen from Aberdeenshire for ploughing, and some cows from Buchan have been sent north, of a sort, considering their size, famous for the quantity of milk they produce*. It is proposed to compare this breed, with the Ayrshire cows, so celebrated for the Dairy, some of which have been brought by Mr. Dunlop to the neighbouring district of Strathnaver.

* The Buchan cows are not so well known as they deserve to be. The best sort are polled, generally of a dark or brown colour. They commonly weigh, when fattened, from 17 to 18 stone, (16 pound Dutch weight to the stone). They are of so thriving a quality, that they are generally fat at the end of the autumn, without much attention having been paid to their food, and though fleshy, they continue to milk well. Though their size is small, they will give from 6 to 8, and even as high as 14 Scotch pints of milk per day, (equal to as many English quarts). They are fed principally with oat straw in winter, which is found greatly preferable to bear or barley straw. Sometimes they also get what they call *plotted hay*, or hay with boiling water thrown on it. Some sea-ware is also given them, which is very conducive to milking well; but above all, they have a practice in the neighbourhood of Peterhead, of giving them green kail in April, which is sown in the spring preceding, transplanted in June or July, stands the winter season better than turnip, and vegetates very strong in April. By adopting this plan, the dreadful interval for the farmer, between the winter and summer feed, might in a great measure be filled up. In general, from 10 to 12 Scotch pints, or English quarts, of their milk, give a pound of butter. They have made near Peterhead butter-milk cheese, but it answers better when the butter-milk is mixed with other milk.

7. *Improvements by small Tenants.*—It is certainly desirable, to preserve, as much as is consistent with the improvement of a district, its old inhabitants, who are attached to it by many ties, and who might not for some time feel themselves equally comfortable in other situations. It is difficult, however, to adhere to this principle, where the tenants are poor in circumstances, have little skill in Agriculture, and have not even cattle or intruments of husbandry calculated for carrying on any proper system of cultivation. A plan, however, has been fallen upon, which tends in some measure to obviate these objections. Some small tenants have been prevailed upon to enter into an agreement with a considerable farmer in their neighbourhood, by which he engages to plough for them, the waste land attached to their farms, at the rate of fifteen shillings per Scotch acre, the price not to be exacted until a twelvemonth after the work is executed, when they will be enabled to pay the expenses from the crops they raise. The plan has been so much approved of, that the small tenants in one district, have had about 60 acres of waste land ploughed for them on this system, in the course of this season. Their own miserable cattle and instruments of husbandry, could never have broken up such a soil, but when once it is properly ploughed, they are able to manage it tolerably well by their own exertions; and in process of time, they will probably become more opulent, and abler to do justice to their farms.

8. *Towns and Villages.*—The increase of towns and villages, is one of the surest signs of the prosperity of a country; and in this important particular, the county of Caithness is not deficient. Several houses have been built this season in the new town of Thurso. The village of Castleton,

Castleton, erected by Mr. Trail, goes on prosperously; and it is impossible to pass through that thriving place, without feeling much satisfaction at the industry that seems to prevail there, and the contented looks, and comfortable circumstances, of the inhabitants. A new village, called Brodie's-Town, from the name of its spirited founder, is rising on the eastern coast of the county, in a situation admirably calculated for the herring-fishing. Some progress is making in the erection of a village at Halkirk; and it is expected next year, that the British Fishing Society will make some exertions towards establishing a fishing settlement on the feu it has obtained from Sir Benjamin Dunbar, in the neighbourhood of Wick.

9. *Roads and Harbours.*—The attention that has lately been paid to the improvement of the northern parts of Scotland, must do infinite credit to the Legislature of this country, if the measures they have chalked out are prosecuted with proper zeal and energy. A foundation has thus been laid for a new system, not of foreign, but of domestic colonization, which will be found infinitely preferable to the cultivation of distant settlements. By the acts which were passed, certain sums were granted for carrying on the Caledonian Canal, and for making roads, and building bridges, in the northern counties, under the direction of Commissioners appointed to oversee the expenditure of the money, but they were enacted too late in the season, to expect that much could be done in carrying on such great undertakings, in the course of the present year. In consequence, however, of the correspondence that has been established between the Commissioners and the Gentlemen of Caithness, there is reason to hope, that considerable progress will be made, in the course of the ensuing

ensuing season. It cannot be doubted, if this district were made accessible, and proper roads of communication carried through it, that it would soon rival more southern districts in various descriptions of improvement.

It is proper here to add, that a thousand pounds have been granted, from the public funds of Scotland, for erecting a harbour at Wick; and there is every reason to hope, that that important undertaking will be carried on with proper spirit in the course of next year. As Wick is the true centre of the deep-sea herring fishery, the erection of a harbour there, is perhaps one of the most important objects to which the public attention could be directed, or in which the public money could be employed.

10. *Miscellaneous Articles.*—1. The establishment of a woollen manufacture, at the new village of Halkirk, has taken place this year. The machinery has been already erected, and from the prices which Mr. Walker, the manufacturer, has demanded, the Farmers in the neighbourhood are satisfied, that they cannot manufacture their wool so cheap, by their own servants, as by him; whilst, at the same time, it is done by his machinery in a manner greatly superior.

2. This year also, a post-chaise and a pair of horses have been set up by Mr. Ryrie, innkeeper at Thurso, which is likely to answer. It is singular, though there had been some attempts to keep post-chaises at Inverness, yet that they were all given up in the year 1773. Mr. Ettles set one up in 1775; which was then the only one so far north. There are now seven kept in Inverness alone, one or two at Tain, and one at Kessock. It is proposed to have, next year, a diligence on the Highland road from Perth to Inverness, and it is to be hoped that, in due time, the plan will be

extended

extended to Caithness. The advantages of having such modes of conveyance, from one end of the kingdom to the other, are inestimable.

3. Mr. John Reid, of Heathfield, near Thurso, laid down a small field of bear, which he could not get sown till the 24th of June last: it was cut down on the 24th October, and produced upwards of ten returns of good merchantable grain. It would probably have produced two or three seeds more, had it been sown earlier; but this experiment tends to prove, that in very unfavourable seasons, a crop of bear may be laid down much later than is commonly imagined, and with the prospect of a handsome return.

4. A limework is intended to be carried on, on the estate of Major Innes of Sandside, which it is hoped will be a source of great improvement to all that neighbourhood.

Conclusion.—Some prejudices, it is said, are entertained against the publication of such accounts of local improvements, as if they originated from other motives than a sincere and ardent wish to promote the prosperity and interests of the country. But how could it otherwise be known by the public, what is doing in so remote a district as Caithness, which is so seldom visited by strangers? and can it be questioned, whether these hints may not in various respects contribute to the benefit of other counties? Is it of no consequence, that the success of the Cheviot breed of sheep, beyond the possibility of doubt, should be spread over all the Highland districts, and the way pointed out, by which the rent and value of that extensive tract of country, may in many cases be increased six-fold? Is it nothing to have facts authentically published, regarding the various modes of improving waste

waste lands, by some of which, the expense of the improvement is repaid by the first crop that the ground produces? And is no benefit to be derived, from a knowledge of the success attending the introduction of new breeds of cattle, new sorts of grain, new kinds of grass, &c.? Above all, can it be doubted, that the country at large is interested, when new towns and villages are erected, and new manufactures and other improvements successfully carried on? Instead therefore of objecting to the publication of such accounts, as unnecessary, which is all that can be urged, for it is impossible that any detriment can arise from them, it would be much better for public-spirited individuals, to promote, as much as possible, the adoption of such a plan in all the various districts in the kingdom; in order that experiments happily adopted in one county, may prove the source of similar improvements in other places.

Edinburgh, 25th Nov. 1803.

Appendix to the above Statement.

Among the numerous commons in the county of Caithness, the most extensive and valuable is known under various names, as the Hill of Forse, of Scrabster, &c. and in all, it is supposed that this tract contains about 8000 acres, mostly green ground, and capable of cultivation. The necessary steps have been taken, for having this common divided by arbitration; and a plan has been formed, connected therewith, which cannot fail to give satisfaction to every friend to the improvement. It is founded on certain resolutions adopted by the magistrates, and other inhabitants of the town of Thurso, of which the following is a copy:

At

At a meeting of the Magistrates and Feuers of the town of Thurso, assembled to take into consideration the propriety of applying to parliament for a division of those commons called the Hills of Forse, Scrabster, Aust, Geise, Ormly, Thurso, Pennyland, Holburnhead, and Brims, and all the mosses, muirs, and other waste lands connected therewith, the following Resolutions were adopted:

I. That it appears to this meeting, in many respects, extremely material, that such extensive commons, containing, it is supposed, about 8000 acres of land, by far the greater part of which is capable of improvement, should be brought into cultivation as speedily as possible.

II. That it is peculiarly desirable to bring forward such a plan at the present time, as the division of so extensive a tract may furnish the means of occupation and subsistence to numbers of persons in the northern districts of the Highlands, who may otherwise be reduced to the most poignant distress, in consequence of their plans of emigration having been checked by legislative provisions, and no means of subsistence having been pointed out to them.

III. That in the course of the division, a portion of these commons will belong to the Crown, as proprietor of the lands of Scrabster: there is reason to hope, from the great attention paid by His Majesty's Government to the situation of the Highlanders, that these allotments of waste lands, may be appropriated by the Crown for so beneficial a purpose as that of forming new settlements for natives of the Highlands; and it being also probable, that Government may be desirous of making such settlements on a large and liberal scale, that it would be adviseable to dispose the allotment of the waste lands that may belong to the town of Thurso (exclusive of the mosses) to the Crown, at any fair price that may be fixed upon

upon by the Commissioners appointed by the Act; and that the price received for the same, shall be employed in paving the streets, improving the harbour, and carrying on other public works, the most likely to be advantageous to the town and neighbourhood.

IV. That were this plan carried into execution, three objects of great public importance would at once be accomplished; it would have a tendency to promote the improvement of a town, situated in the remotest part of the kingdom; it would be the means of speedily bringing into cultivation an extensive tract of valuable land, now lying totally useless; and the hope of such a settlement would cheer the heart of many as brave and worthy subjects as any in His Majesty's dominions, whose prospects at this time are truly deplorable.

V. That a copy of these Resolutions, together with the sketch of a plan for making a Royal Colony at Scrabster, be transmitted to His Majesty's Ministers, to the Commissioners appointed by Act of Parliament for carrying on the roads and bridges throughout the Highlands, to the Barons of His Majesty's Exchequer, to the Officers of the Crown in Scotland, and to the Highland Society.

Sketch of a Plan for establishing a Royal Colony at Scrabster, in the County of Caithness, on a Tract of Common, which will be allotted to the Crown, together with some Waste Lands to be purchased in its Neighbourhood.

Let us suppose that 3000 acres in all are employed in making the intended settlement, of which one half belongs to the Crown, and the other half must be purchased.

It is proposed, on part of the land, near the burn, or water

water of Scrabster, to erect a village for labouring people, and to divide the remainder into small farms.

The village to consist of a hundred houses, each house to have, at an average, 3 acres of land attached to it, which would enable each settler to keep a cow, (of the breed of that country), summer and winter. It is supposed that this quantity of land, namely, 3 acres, might be cultivated by means of that excellent instrument the *Cascroum*, (a kind of foot plough), which the Highlanders can manage with great dexterity, and which is too little known.

As the place is entirely a new settlement, and the settlers, with their families, must in general come from a considerable distance, they will require at least 10*l.* for each family, to assist them in building a house, enclosing their land, &c. but they would be able to pay at the rate of 10*s.* per annum, after the first seven years, by which the public would be amply indemnified for all the expense which they occasioned; and, in process of time, that rent might be increased.

As to the small farms, it is proposed, that they should consist of 10 acres each, one acre for the house and garden, and the other nine to be divided into three portions for a rotation of grain, grass, and green crops. These small farmers would be possessed of some property of their own, though at the same time, might require, perhaps 20*l.* each, to assist them in buying seed, working cattle, &c. but they would also be able to pay at the rate of 10*s.* per acre after the first seven years, and their rent might afterwards be increased.

It is supposed, that to the amount of 2500 acres might be divided in this way into 250 farms; this, with 100 settlers in the village, would make 350 families; which, at six to a family, for their children are very numerous,

(more

(more especially since inoculation has been introduced) would make in all 2100 souls.

The expense attending the proposed colony, would be as follows:

	£
1. Value of 1500 acres, to be purchased at 4*l.* per acre, (the remaining 1500 being the property of the Crown)	6000
2. Expense of surveying, allotting and dividing the same	500
3. Allowance to 100 village settlers, 10*l.* each	1000
4. Allowance to 250 small farmers, 20*l.* each	5000
	£12,500

At the end of seven years, the settlement would produce, at the rate of 10*s.* per acre, 1500*l.* per annum, with the prospect of a considerable increase.

It is proper to add, that the settlement is situated not far from the sea, in a bay, well calculated for carrying on the cod and other fisheries, in which the people would partly employ themselves: so that this colony would prove a valuable nursery for seamen, besides being in other respects so useful.

Let this plan be compared with any scheme of foreign colonization, and it will not be difficult to decide which is entitled to a preference.

Minutes

No. II.

An Account of the Improvements carried on by Sir John Sinclair, Bart. Founder, and first President, of the Board of Agriculture, on his Estates in Scotland.

The reader of this Report, will probably be desirous of knowing some particulars, regarding the nature and extent of the improvements carried on by that individual, who originally pointed out to the British Parliament, the advantages to be derived from the establishment of a Board of Agriculture, and by whose exertions, every obstacle to the formation of that Institution, was successfully surmounted. With the view of gratifying any wish of that sort, the following account is drawn up.

It is the more necessary that such information should be communicated to the public, because, from the remoteness of the situation where these improvements have been carried on, (at the northern extremity of the Island), there are few who have it in their power to examine them in person, and without ocular inspection, and indeed some previous knowledge of the ancient state of the district, it is hardly possible to believe, that a person engaged in such a variety of other occupations, of a literary, a political, and even a military nature, and who, from the situation he held, as President of the Board of Agriculture, was under the necessity of residing so much in, or near the metropolis, could have found leisure, successfully to carry on, under many disadvantages to be afterwards explained, any extensive plan of improvement, in so remote a part of the kingdom, 700 miles distant from the capital.

In a paper which Sir John Sinclair drew up some years ago

ago, detailing the commencement of his improvements, he has remarked, "that it is a peculiar disadvantage at-"tending the cultivation and improvement of a remote "and neglected district of a country, that every thing "is to be done, and that a great variety of new and im-"portant objects must be attended to, at one and the same "time. Those who live in a part of the Island, that has "already made considerable progress, can hardly form "an idea, of the difficulties which must be surmounted, "when towns and villages must be erected, as centres of "communication and business; when roads and harbours "must be made, for the sake of domestic and of foreign "intercourse; when manufactures must be established, "to provide employment for the surplus population which "an improved system of agriculture, and the enlarge-"ment of farms, necessarily occasion, and when new "breeds of animals, new instruments of husbandry, and "persons skilled in new modes of cultivation, must be "introduced from distant parts of the kingdom. If it is "possible, however, by the application of a great capital "and of great attention, successfully to carry on these "objects together, the one has a tendency to promote, "and to encourage the other; the spirit that is excited for "the improvement of one article, rouses a similar spirit "of energy in regard to another; and a new race of peo-"ple is, in a manner, formed, who, from a state of torpor, "ignorance, idleness, and its concomitant poverty, are "animated to inquiry, roused to exertion, and impelled "to obtain by their industry the acquisition of wealth*."

Situation, and Extent of the Estate.—The Estate, the im-

* See Sketch of the Improvements now carrying on, by Sir John Sinclair, Bart. printed ann. 1803.

provement

provement of which it is proposed briefly to describe, is situated in five parishes in the county of Caithness, namely, Thurso, Halkirk, Reay, Wick, and Latheron. The county is valued at 37,256*l.* Scotch, and the property in question is estimated at 7843*l.* or nearly one-fourth of the total amount. Caithness is supposed to contain above 395,000 English acres; as a considerable part of this property is in the Highland districts, and consequently of great extent, it is calculated that the estate must comprehend more than one-fourth of the whole surface of the county, or above 100,000 acres.

Original State of the Property.—Nothing could be more unpropitious to improvement, than the state of this estate when it originally came into the possession of the present Proprietor. With the exception of a few large farms, or what are called *mains*, (that is, lands annexed to mansion houses), it was in general occupied by a number of small farmers, to the amount of, from 800 to 900 in all, who held their possessions in what was called *rig and rennal*, or intermixed with each other; and beyond the outer fence of this motley farm, there were nothing but undivided commons, in which the neighbouring proprietors had a conjunct interest. The rent was paid partly in money, but principally, according to the old feudal system, in various articles in kind, as grain, lamb, poultry, eggs, &c.

In order to render the following account more distinct, it is proposed to arrange it under seven general heads; and to describe, 1. The improvements carried on in the immediate neighbourhood of the town of Thurso; 2. Those on the east side of the river Thurso; 3. Those on the west side, and in the Highland district; 4. Those carried on in the parish of Wick, and the lower part of the parish of Latheron; 5. Those on the estate of Langwell; 6. To give a general view of the improvements already accomplished; and, 7. Those still in contemplation.

I.

Improvements in the immediate Neighbourhood of the Town of Thurso.

Perhaps the principal circumstance, favourable to the improvement of the estate, was this, that at one of its extremities, it surrounded the sea-port town of Thurso, and though it was, at the period when those improvements were begun, almost destitute of manufactures, or of foreign commerce, (some trade to Norway alone excepted), yet still the existence of such a town was a circumstance from which considerable advantages were to be derived. No extensive improvements can be carried on without the vicinity of towns and villages; nor would it have been easy to have collected such a number of people, and to have erected the houses necessary for their accommodation as Thurso furnished, in the life of one man, unless at an expense which few private individuals could afford.

From the bridge across the river Thurso, near that town, there is to be seen a considerable tract of land, now completely enclosed, and rendered fertile, and a number of excellent farm-houses, in every direction, rendering the whole as fine a prospect as can any where be contemplated in so northern a district. Indeed no scene would be more complete, had it been possible to have surrounded the fields with trees and hedges; which, however, the climate, and the vicinity of the Northern Ocean, have unfortunately rendered impracticable.

It

It is proposed to begin our description of this part of the Estate, with the improvements carried on in the more immediate neighbourhood of this town.

Farm of Thurso-East.—The farm in the possession of the Proprietor, is the first which he is naturally desirous of improving. Some progress had been made in the cultivation and inclosure of some fields, when it came into Sir John Sinclair's possession, to the extent of perhaps fifty acres; but small farmers held possessions within 300 yards of the house, a public road transversed the principal fields, and an extensive common in its immediate neighbourhood remained undivided. The whole, however, is now completely changed. With the consent of the neighbouring gentlemen, the public road is altered so as to suit the inclosures made; every field is brought into a high state of fertility; the common is divided, improved, and let to industrious tenants; and the whole estate, as it may be called, for it contains about 500 Scotch, or 600 English acres, is now as improved a tract of country, as any in the north of Scotland.

Thurso Castle.—This ancient mansion house, which was originally built, it is said, in the year 1660, has been recently thoroughly repaired, and is a great ornament to the whole neighbourhood. At no great distance, Harold's Tower was erected, in memory of a battle fought with the Danes, where a Harold Earl of Caithness was slain: from its elevated situation, it has a most advantageous effect. The view from it, comprehending a great extent of improved country, the town, the river, and the celebrated Bay of Thurso, the rocky promontories of Holburn-head and Dunnet, and the Orkney Islands at a distance, is truly picturesque.

Farm of Mount Pleasant.—The farm next to Thurso-East, is called Mount Pleasant, from the beauty of its situation. It contains sixty acres of most fertile arable land, inclosed and improved by the proprietor, and about sixty acres more which had been inclosed many years ago; on this farm there is an excellent house and offices. Such are the effects of inclosure and improvement, that the lower part of this farm, formerly rented at only 14*s.* per acre, is worth at present about 4*l.* to a farmer, and some part of it is now let at even 5*l.* per acre, as an accommodation to the inhabitants in the neighbourhood.

Farm of Spring Park, including Dixonfield.—Spring Park, possessed by Mr. Mathers, contains above thirty-three acres of inclosed arable land, with an excellent house upon it; and the same industrious farmer has taken a new improvement, called Dixonfield, containing about eighty-four acres more, where a most extensive experiment was made, (which is described, in Appendix, p. 11), to bring a considerable tract of waste land at once into a state of cultivation, and which, to those who saw it, seemed like magic; above eighty English acres, of land perfectly waste, being, in three months, inclosed with ditches, improved by paring and burning, and covered with a crop.

Oldfield.—This farm, including Mount Vernon, an improved piece of common attached to it, contains about eighty-one acres. There is an excellent house upon it, beautifully situated, and every justice is done to its cultivation, by its present respectable occupier, Col. Williamson. It was for some time in Sir John Sinclair's possession, by whom the fields were rendered regular, the inclosures carried on, and the commons ploughed up, and a foundation laid for their complete improvement.

Manson-

Mansontown.—A field containing twenty-five acres, lay within sight of the town of Thurso, in a most miserable state. It was inclosed, ploughed, and reduced into order by the proprietor. It was then let to Dr. Manson, of Thurso, who has already erected a neat cottage upon it, and who will soon render it as fertile as any land in the neighbourhood.

Clay-Field—There is no soil naturally more unproductive than a cold wet-bottomed clay, unless it is invigorated by manure. With a tract containing about fifty-two Scotch acres, the plan of burning the surface was tried, as practised in Leicestershire. It was thus put into a state capable of being rendered highly fertile, with the aid of lime and dung, as is sufficiently evident, from the parts of it which have been under crop.

Mill, and Circular Cottage.—The want of a good mill, capable of grinding even in the dryest seasons, was much felt in the neighbourhood of Thurso. It was therefore resolved to erect one on the *haughs* of Stainland, though the expense was likely to be considerable. For the accommodation of the miller, a circular house or cottage was built, the roof gradually diminishing like the top of a bottle. It has a singular appearance, and would have answered completely, had the mason done justice to the construction; at present, it is apt to smoke. It cost about 50*l*., and from the strength of its shape and materials, it is likely to last for ages.

On the other side of the river, a number of objects, equally gratifying, present themselves to the eye.

Public Walk.—A Public Walk, intended for the accommodation of the inhabitants of Thurso, is a striking object from the bridge. It is advantageously situated along the banks of the river, ornamented with shrubs and trees, which it is hoped will thrive under the shelter of the buildings erected in the New Town, and there are few places of public resort, whence a finer stretch of fertile fields can be seen. The ground between the walk and the river, is cultivated as a garden.

Wilsonton.—At the head of the Public Walk, Mr. Wilson has erected a good-looking house and offices, on a spot beautifully situated, which was granted to him in perpetuity, to encourage him to ornament the neighbourhood by its construction. No place could be better calculated for a neat and elegant villa, adjacent to a thriving town.

Juniper Hill.—Mr. William Henderson, a respectable merchant in Thurso, has built, a little higher up the river, another comfortable house, and has taken some land in the neighbourhood, which he is improving by every means in his power.

Heathfield.—The Offices erected on the farm of Heathfield, are also seen from the bridge, and the exertions made by Mr. Reid for the improvement of that place, do credit to his skill and industry.

Ormly.—The house possessed by Major Rose, on his farm of Ormly, is most favourably situated, and is surrounded by some of the finest fields any where to be met with, where the modern system of husbandry is carried on with great spirit and success.

Wester Ormly.—This improved farm was first brought into

into order by Mrs. Douglas, sister to Mr. Dawson of Frogden, who was justly accounted the best farmer in the southern counties of Scotland. On her quitting it, Mr. William Henderson, writer in Thurso, took it, and has carried on improvements there which do him infinite credit. There is also a comfortable house on this farm.

Ormly Boll-sowings.—A beautiful field near Thurso, was called the *Boll-sowings*, being let to the people of the town, in lots sufficient to sow a boll of barley. The old rent was only about 20*s*. per acre. It contained in all, about 50 acres. It is now inclosed, and brought into a complete state of cultivation. Some of the fields are let at four guineas per acre; and Mr. James Davidson has taken above eight acres, for which he pays at the rate of five guineas per acre; the highest rent paid in this neighbourhood.

Thurso Garden.—That the town of Thurso, and the shipping frequenting the harbour and bay, might be supplied with so essential an article as vegetables, seven acres were inclosed, to be occupied as a garden, and let at a moderate rent, that the gardener might have no plea for charging exorbitant prices.

Whoever impartially considers the variety and extent even of these improvements, would naturally consider them as sufficient to have occupied the exclusive attention of a long life. These, however, comprehend but a small proportion of the whole that has been accomplished.

II. *Im-*

II.

Improvements on the East Side of the River Thurso.

Stainland.—In carrying on the improvement of an extensive Estate, it is necessary, in the first place, to establish some large farms, with a view of inducing persons of a competent property, to direct their attention to agricultural pursuits, and to show a good example of improved husbandry to their neighbours. With that view, Sir John Sinclair took into his own hands the farm of Stainland, originally possessed by eight small tenants; and having brought it into a proper state of cultivation, and erected substantial offices, he let it to Mr. William Shireff, at a very moderate rent, to induce him to build a suitable dwelling house, (which he has done), and to complete the improvement of the farm, in which some progress has been made. It is necessary, however, in all such cases, to tie down the farmer to a regular progress in improvement, for instance, that of liming or marling a certain number of acres every year, otherwise it may not be carried on either so rapidly, or to that extent, that might be looked for.

Baintown.—It does not necessarily follow, that the enlargement of farms should occasion depopulation. The smaller farmers may be encouraged to settle in towns and villages, or small lots of land, (what might be called *cottage farms*), given to them. Several farms of that description, have been formed in the neighbourhood of Stainland, and a tract of about 30 acres, improved for that purpose, is now occupied by cottage farmers.

Geise

Geise Little.—This farm, containing above sixty acres, is advantageously situated on the banks of the river Thurso. A substantial house and offices have been erected there, but as it is better adapted for grass than grain, its present occupier, (Col. Williamson), has converted it into a sheep-farm, with a view of supplying the town of Thurso with mutton and lamb.

On the size of Farms.—However desirable it may be, to establish some large farms, with a view of inducing persons possessed of competent property, to become farmers, and to show a good example to the neighbourhood, yet a mixture of small farms, is not to be neglected in a thinly peopled country; and it was impossible to think of venturing to overturn the system adopted in an extensive tract of country, inhabited by several hundred souls, who are undoubtedly entitled, to have their interests and situation attended to by their landlord. Sir John Sinclair, therefore, resolved to divide considerable tracts, situated on both sides of the river Thurso, into farms of about 20*l.* rent per annum; but even this was on a greater scale of occupation than formerly, the farms having previously paid on an average, only at the rate of 5*l.* per annum: hence even that system was objected to, as tending to depopulate the country.

Plan for the Establishment of small Farms on a regular system.—In order that justice might be done to the new system, it was resolved to have regular plans drawn up of the different farms—to ascertain in what manner they could best be divided into distinct possessions—to have the houses placed in such situations as were the most central and advantageous—to have comfortable and substantial houses and offices built, and to have them thatched

with

with clay and straw, instead of *divots* or thin turf, (which makes a great havock of the surface, wastes a great deal of ground, is a very indifferent roof, and requires constant repairs)—to abolish services of every sort—to prohibit the carrying or selling of peat or turf to the town of Thurso, (which prevents those tenants, who follow that practice, from collecting manure for their farms)—to induce the tenants themselves to burn coal instead of peat, (which may be done to advantage, since the impolitic tax on coal has been abolished; they would thus be enabled to bend their whole attention to the improvement of their farms)—to abolish *thirlage*, or a restriction to particular mills—to provide better mills than at present, and to endeavour to make the miller a separate profession, that he might have the whole charge and trouble of bringing the corn to the mill, and of carrying it to market—to tie down the tenants to a regular rotation of crops, until the advantages of an improved system of husbandry were perfectly understood—to assist them in procuring proper seeds, particularly clover, rye-grass, and turnips—and to establish some mode of selling them marl at an easy rate, and of delivering lime at Thurso, at the lowest price at which it could be imported, so as to render the use of *feal* or turf perfectly unnecessary.

By these, and other measures, as the distribution of small premiums, to encourage their industry, &c. there was every reason to believe, that the farmers established on this new footing, would soon become as happy and respectable a set of small tenants, as any holding the same extent of ground, of equal rent and value, in any part of the kingdom.

It was also intended, to print and circulate hints among them, to the following effect, in order to inculcate the principles upon which an improved system of husbandry

can

can best be carried on, the only means by which the farmer can be placed in a comfortable situation.

Hints to Farmers.—It is certainly necessary to contrive the means of cultivating the ground, at as cheap a rate as possible, more especially as the wages of servants are becoming higher every day; ploughing, therefore, with a light plough, and with two horses, (still better if with two oxen) without a driver, is most earnestly recommended.

Every tenant ought to have the complete and exclusive possession of his own farm. Inclosing, therefore, and winter herding, are absolutely necessary.

No tenant ought to take a farm without a sufficient capital.—Prepare that capital before hand, and place no dependence upon credit.

No farmer ought to take more land than he can stock and manage, and indeed ought to have some ready money on hand, for bad times. Better to cultivate 50 acres well, than 100 in a slovenly manner.

No farmer should begin without a knowledge of his profession. It requires an apprenticeship of several years to learn the most common trade, and, as farming is a complicated business, a previous knowledge of that art is indispensably necessary.

Endeavour to raise good grain, for it will always sell, even in years of plenty; whereas it is only in dear and scarce seasons, that there is any demand for grain of an inferior quality.

Let your stock of cattle, horses, &c. be of the best sorts, and more remarkable for real utility than for beauty or fashion.

Endeavour to breed your own stock, and be assured that they will thrive better with you, than any you can purchase.

Go

Go seldom to market, and when you go, let it be to sell, rather than to buy.

Be not above your profession, and always consider it as the first that any man can follow.

Learn the smallest minutiæ of your trade. He will never be a good general, who does not know his exercise.

Consider your landlord as a friend, whose interest and yours, when well understood, are the same.

Keep your land always in good heart. It is both for your credit and your interest to do so, even at the close of your lease. Your next farm will be got on better terms, for every landlord will struggle to get you.

Be not afraid of trying experiments, but let them be on a small scale at first, and few at a time.

Show a good example of industry to your servants. You cannot expect that others will do for you, what you will not do for yourself.

Admit no guest into your house, who cannot live upon the productions of his own country.

Lay up one half of your profits, and live comfortably upon the other.*

---

* In order that some of these hints might be better remembered, a few of the most important were versified, to the following purport:

Let this be held the Farmer's Creed:
For stock seek out the choicest breed,
In peace and plenty let them feed;
Your fields sow with the best of seed,
Let them nor dung, nor dressing need;
Inclose and drain them with all speed,
Extirpate then each noxious weed;
AND YOU WILL SOON BE RICH INDEED.

The

The following is a list of the principal farms, on both sides of the river of Thurso, and the extent of each, where this system has been in a great measure established.

Names of Farms.	Arable Land.	Moor and Pasture.	Total.
	Acres.	Acres.	Acres.
Wydell	237	172	409
Todholes	70	75	145
Shalmistry	30	40	70
Achingils and Swarty	120	50	170
Sordell	123	102	225
Sibster	144	56	200
Quoycrook	24	16	40
Halkirk	67	15	82
Leurary	50	170	220
Harpsdale	270	350	620
	1135	1046	2181

The total consequently amounts to about 2181 Scotch, or 2617 English acres. The whole of this extensive tract is put in a train of improvement, and the most intelligent of these small farmers already acknowledge, that they have been greatly benefited, where they have rigorously attended to the plan laid down to them.

There are two distinct farms on the east side of the river, called Carsgo and Hoy, containing about 250 Scotch acres of arable land, and 130 acres in moor and pasture, on which some improvements have been made, but not to any considerable extent.

III.

Improvements on the West Side of the River Thurso.

Thurdistoft.—This small farm contains about sixty-three Scotch acres, including moor or pasture. The improvements on it are carried on with much spirit and success, by by Captain James Henderson, to whom a lease has been granted of considerable endurance, to encourage him to make the necessary exertions for bringing the whole farm into a state of proper cultivation.

The Bleachfield, and Farm attached to it.—A bleachfield was erected on the river Thurso, which has been let to Mr. Paton, with a small farm attached to it, containing about fourteen acres, including moor and pasture. The arable part of the farm is cultivated with much attention and industry, insomuch, that the produce is calculated to be at the rate of ten bolls of bear, and twelve bolls of oats, per Scotch acre.

Glengolly.—This farm contains about seventy-five acres, of which forty are arable. The soil of the arable part is excellent; but, owing to some cross water-runs, it is difficult to bring the fields into a regular shape.

Whitefield.—This farm contains about seventy acres, of which sixty-two are arable. The soil is unfortunately shallow, but every exertion is made by the spirited occupier of the farm, Mr. George Miller, to render it productive. He has built a substantial house and offices upon it, much to the advantage of the farm, and greatly to the ornament of the neighbourhood.

Geise.—This beautiful farm, containing about 135 Scotch acres, of which sixty-three are arable, is possessed by Mrs. Captain M'Lean, who is carrying on, with much spirit, several improvements on it. This farm has the advantage of an excellent garden, and of a bed of marl.

In the neighbourhood of the farm of Geise, Captain John Henderson has undertaken the improvement of two new

new farms, Henderland, containing ninety Scotch acres, and Janetstown, containing forty-four, which, under such skilful management, there can be no doubt will soon be brought into a state of productive cultivation.

How.—The farm of *How*, contains 101 Scotch acres, of which about twenty-five are arable. The whole farm will soon be brought into a productive state, by the exertions of so active an improver as Mr. George Miller, of Whitfield.

Upper How, or George Town.—This farm contains about 200 Scotch acres of a *common* recently divided, the improvement of which has been undertaken by Mr. George Miller, of Whitfield. It is the greatest attempt of the sort by any farmer in the northern parts of Scotland. Above 100 acres have been already brought into a state of cultivation, and there is no doubt that the whole will, in process of time, be improved, by so enterprising a farmer.

Buckies.—This farm contains about 107 acres of arable land, (including about thirty-four improved waste land); and about 179 acres of moor or pasture. Mr. John Davidson, the occupier, has erected upon this farm an excellent house and offices, and is carrying on its improvement, with much spirit and success.

Aimster.—This farm contains in all about 281 acres, of which about 108 are arable. An excellent house and offices have been erected by the occupier, Captain John Henderson, and the more fertile part of the farm, will soon be brought into as good order as any in Scotland.

Skinnet.—This beautifully situated farm is occupied by

Mr. Daniel Miller, whose industry and exertions equal those of any farmer in the kingdom. It contains about 805 acres, of which 167 are arable, and it is already rivalling, in its appearance, the best cultivated farms in the southern parts of the kingdom: what a change, from its miserable appearance, under the old system, of small farms, and intermixed occupations.

Nursery and Planting Ground.—At the bottom of the farm of Skinnet, four acres are laid out for a Nursery, and seventy-two acres for Plantations. If this plan answers, which is as yet in its infancy, it must be productive of great advantages to all that neighbourhood, as well as ornamental to the country.

Common in the Hill of Skinnet.—In the division of an extensive common, called the Hills of Skinnet and Leurary, about 1706 Scotch, or 2134 English acres, were allotted to Sir John Sinclair, a considerable proportion of which was capable of cultivation, and, fortunately, at the same time, the old arable lands adjoining were out of lease. The plan therefore, which it was thought fittest to adopt, in such circumstances, was this:—to let off the arable land, and part of the contiguous waste lands, in large farms, of from 200 to 300 acres; and in order to accommodate the small tenants, who had formerly occupied the farms thus enlarged, to divide the remainder of the common, into small farms or lots, and to let them on the following terms.

Plan of letting small Farms in the Hills of Skinnet and Leurary.

1. The farms in general, to consist of about twenty-five acres each, one acre for the house, garden, &c. and the

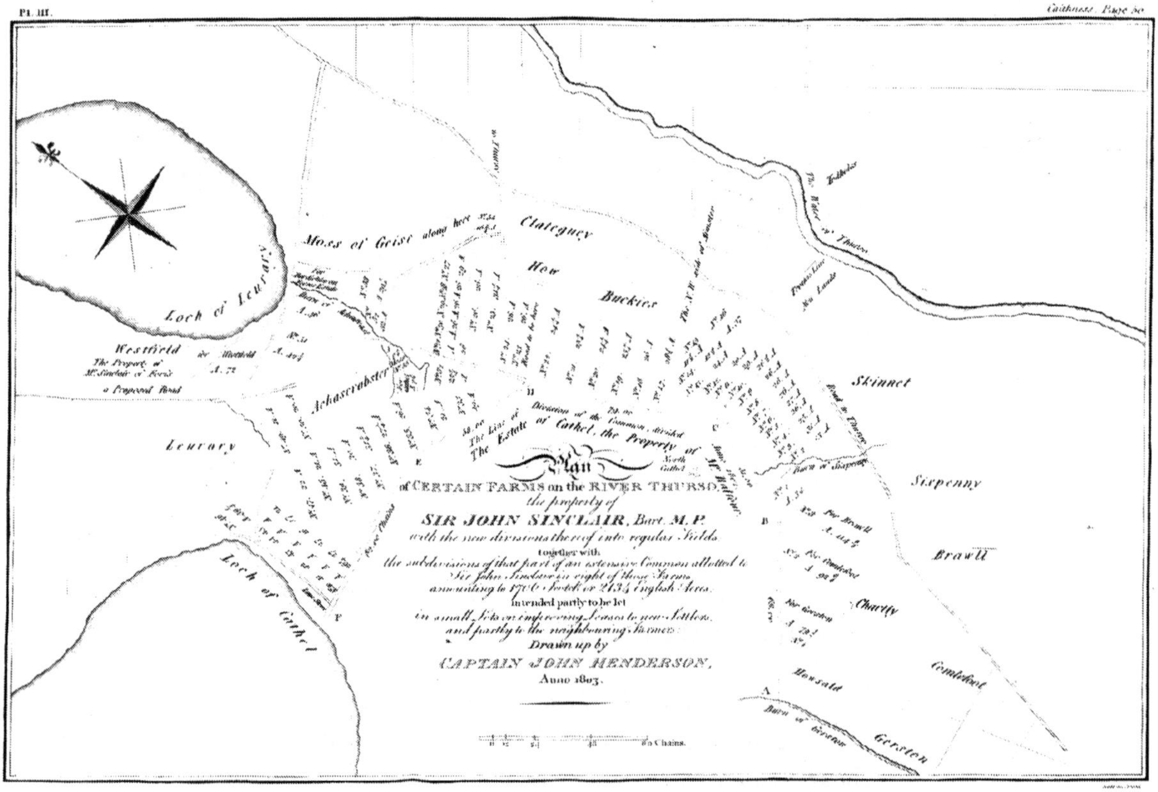
Plan
of CERTAIN FARMS on the RIVER THURSO,
the property of
SIR JOHN SINCLAIR, Bart. M.P.
with the new divisions thereof into regular Fields
together with
the subdivisions of that part of an extensive Common allotted to
Sir John Sinclair in right of those Farms
amounting to 1706 Scotch or 2134 English Acres
intended partly to be let
in small Lots on improving Leases to new Settlers
and partly to the neighbouring Farmers:
Drawn up by
CAPTAIN JOHN HENDERSON,
Anno 1803.
80 Chains.
Loch of Leurary
Westfield
The Property of
Mr. Sinclair of Forss
a Proposed Road
Moss of Geise along here
Clateguey
How
Buckies
Achascrabster
Leurary
The Line of Division of the Common, divided
The Estate of Cathel, the Property of
North Cathel
Skinnet
Sixpenny
Brawll
Charlty
Comlefoot
Housald
Gerston
Loch of Cathel
The Water of Thurso

the remaining twenty-four acres to be subdivided into fields of four acres each, calculated for a rotation of six years.

2. The lease to be for twenty-one years; the rent, for the first seven years, to be from one shilling to five shillings per acre, (according to its value), with a gradual increase, during the remainder of the lease.

3. Each tenant is to get a sum in money at his entry, to assist in building houses, &c. on finding security to lay out the same properly, and to leave houses of that value at the issue of the lease; to be allowed also a certain additional sum, according to the value of the house when he removes. The houses, gardens, &c. to be placed as directed by the Proprietor.

4. The farm to be divided into six fields of four acres each. Twelve acres to be cultivated in the first three years, and four acres every year afterwards, till the whole is brought in. After the first seven years, the tenant to be bound to have eight acres in corn, eight in pasture, four in green crops, and four in sown grass, either cut green, or made into hay; the rotation to be as follows: 1. Fallow or green crops; 2. Grain with grass-seeds; 3. Grass, either made into hay, or cut green; 4. Pasture; 5. Pasture; and 6. Oats; and so on till the end of the lease. In case of removal, the incoming tenant to be allowed to sow grass-seeds on the field, which, under the above rotation, ought to be laid down with grass.

5. The tenants to be allowed a sum in money at their entry, for inclosing, on their finding security for executing the same, according to a regular plan, with an additional sum at the issue of the lease, according to the value of the inclosures.

6. The tenants to keep no sheep without the express

leave of the Proprietor, as they are so destructive to hedging, planting, and similar improvements.

From the annexed Engraving, (*Plate* A), it appears, that there are above fifty new farms planned out upon this common, in addition to the waste land attached to the old arable fields. Every exertion was made to bring this extensive tract as quickly as possible into cultivation; and some progress was made in it, even the first year. The great difficulty was, to provide straw and hay for the new settlers, until they could raise those articles themselves, for the cattle and horses they required. To cultivate an extensive tract of waste land, without having some arable land in the neighbourhood, whence food can be procured for cattle, can hardly be attempted with much prospect of success, and it is the neglect of attending to this circumstance in the commencement, that has occasioned so many failures in the improvement of waste lands.

Brawll, &c.—There are several other farms on the west side of the river Thurso, called Brawll, Gerston, &c. which it may next be proper to mention. The gardens of Brawll, containing about seven acres, have long been celebrated as the greatest ornament of that neighbourhood; and the farm of Brawll is supposed to be peculiarly calculated for grazing. Captain George Swanson lives in a substantial house at Gerston, and is improving the arable part of his farm.

The lands of Leurary have been already mentioned. To those of Assary and of Brawlbin, lying in the parish of Reay, little has hitherto been done in the way of improvement.

The Strathmore.—This is an extensive Highland District, where there are a number of farms belonging to the

Estate

Estate on which some improvements have been made, in particular by Mr. Sinclair Gun, and Mr. John M'Donald, at Achascoriclet. On some of these farms, in particular Rumsdale, the Glut, and Dalganachy, the Cheviot sheep have been tried, and that plan would answer, if these lands were connected with other farms, to which the sheep might be driven in the winter season, and were principally kept for summer pasture.

IV.

Improvements in the Parish of Wick, and the lower part of the Parish of Latheron.

On the East Coast of Caithness, the improvements of this estate have likewise been carried on with considerable spirit and success, more especially on the lands of Keiss, Tannach, Thrumster, Ulbster, Easter Clyth, Wester-Clyth, and Roster.

Keiss.—This valuable estate contains about 2930 Scotch acres, divided as follows, viz.

	Scotch Acres. A.	R.	P.
1. Infield	343	3	27
2. Outfield	57	1	11
3. Meadow	22	0	30
4. Pasture	700	2	2
5. Moss, &c.	1806	1	13
Total	2930	1	3

There is an excellent house upon the estate, and it possesses many advantages, from its vicinity to the sea, though, for want of a harbour, the Herring Fishery cannot be carried on to the extent that might otherwise be practicable.

Tannach.—Some improvements have been carried on in this farm. A good farm house has been erected on it, and about 30 acres of waste land have been improved.

Thrumster, Ulbster, and East Clyth.—Captain Brodie, who occupies these farms, has carried on their improvement with great spirit and success. He has drawn up the following statement of the expense which his improvement have occasioned; an uncommon instance of exertion in so remote a part of the kingdom.

State of Improvements by David Brodie, Esq. of Hopeville, on the Lands of Thrumster, Ulbster, &c. the Property of the Right Hon. Sir John Sinclair, Bart.

				£	s.	d.
1. *Village of Brodie's Town, or Sarclet.*						
21 houses, built of stone and clay, with tile roofs, at 35*l.* each				735	0	0
Clearing the harbour, to receive a sufficient number of boats for the inhabitants, by blasting and removing rocks and large stones				135	0	0
Making a new winding road, for access to the harbour				80	0	0
				950	0	0
2. *Mains of Ulbster.*						
Draining the Moss of Scammal	£40	0	0			
One inclosure of stone dyke from waste ground, and making the same into arable land in good condition	70	0	0			
Road to the Moss of Ulbster	40	0	0			
				150	0	0
3. *Creek of Whalego.*						
Clearing the harbour, by blasting and removing large stones, and building a platform for boats, to secure them from being carried away	53	0	0			
Making stairs in the face of the rock, to lead down to the boats	8	0	0			
				61	0	0
Carry forward				£1161	0	0

Brought

4. *Creek of East Clyth.*

Brought forward		£1161 0 0
Blasting and removing rocks and stones, for making it accessible to boats		70 0 0

5. *Mains of Thrumster.*

New mill-house, 80 feet long, containing thrashing-mill, corn-mill, and barley-mill, with a brick-kiln, all slate-roofed, including machinery and loft	560 0 0	
Byre adjoining, 80 feet long, thatched roof	70 0 0	
Slate roofing, and fitting up an old barn for a stable, 80 feet long, including new wood for the roof	80 0 0	
A feeding-house and byres adjoining, 150 feet long, thatched, roofed partly from the old roof of the barn	150 0 0	
House at the road-side, of two stories, tile-roofed, thatched over	160 0 0	
Barn adjoining ditto	50 0 0	
New smiddy, and cart and plough-maker's shop	60 0 0	
New dwelling-house, with two wings and sunk cellars, the whole timber of best Memel log, as per valuation	1030 0 0	
New oval garden, forced by blasting and quarrying rocks around the Pictish tower, and carrying earth to cover rocks, formerly all rugged crag, and an eyesore on the farm	250 0 0	
Road from mill to house and stable, 400 yards, metled	40 0 0	
6076 yards of stone dyke, snap-topped	303 16 0	
5457 ditto ditch, with turf dyke and front	136 8 6	
9336 ditto open drains	153 12 0	
9050 ditto covered drains	226 5 0	
730 ditto of stone dyke and hedge	54 15 0	
Mill lead and dam dyke	35 0 0	
780 yards canal in the meadow	39 0 0	
Expense of cut from the Loch of Buckego	36 0 0	
		2724 16 6

6. *General Improvements.*

20 new houses thatched, for additional settlers on the lands, 40*s.* given each settler, to furnish timber, they building the walls	40 0 0	
40 acres of more arable land, made from waste ground, at 5*l.*	200 0 0	
		240 0 0
		£5095 16 6

Wester Clyth and Roster.—These farms are now occupied by Dr. James Henderson, with a number of sub-tenants, and several improvements are carried on in them, in particular, by dividing the land occupied by the sub-tenants into regular lots. There are, at present, about 400 Scotch acres cultivated, and above 1600 acres more are capable of improvement. Dr. Henderson's principal attention has hitherto been directed to the improvement of the Fisheries; and, already, he has increased the number of boats employed in the Herring Fishery, from one, to above 30 large boats, besides several small ones. These are principally manned by persons living on the estate, (some of them new settlers), and by their exertions, above 3000 barrels of herrings, have been caught in the space of one year.

V.

Improvements on the Estate of Langwell.

This is perhaps the most extensive plan of improvement that has hitherto been attempted by any private individual. The tract in question, contained above 27,000 English acres, of which about 500 acres were natural brushwood, about 250 acres were arable, and the remainder consisted of lands in a state of nature, partly hilly, and partly peat bog. Along the vallies, a number of small farmers had formerly cultivated a little arable land, but depended principally, both for the payment of their rents, and their subsistence, on rearing a small breed of black cattle, kept in the hills and muirs. Nothing could be more miserable than the whole state of the district. It yielded but a trifling rent to the Landlord, whilst at the same time the Tenants were unable, except in very favourable seasons, to procure the common necessaries of life. The scene has now greatly altered, and the following description of the improvements on that

Estate,

Estate, in a Letter dated the 21st April, 1803, from the Clergyman of the district at that time, the Rev. Mr. Mackintosh, must be read with peculiar interest.

"This day I had a pleasant walk through some of the "improvements of Langwell, where many and various "scenes occurred to my view, the novelty of which could "not fail to arrest the wandering eye, and to fill the "mind with interesting ideas, contrasting ancient rusticity "with modern refinement.

"All the banks at the Inver are either ploughed or "trenched. Such as are tilled since last year, are in "excellent condition; little labour and expense would "now make them produce crops corresponding to the "most sanguine expectations.

"The fen husbandry is carrying on with alacrity and "success: a great deal is already done, and all more "promising this year than the former.

"I extended my survey to the new colony at John-"ston, which is not the least flourishing part on this "estate; and in the course of a few years, it will become "one of the best places in the district.

"I returned by the new Park, which abounds with pre-"sages of future prosperity, and clearly demonstrates, "that perseverance is the great quality of a good hus-"bandman. The appearance of grass there, is far beyond "my expectation, and promises amply to reward the "pains bestowed upon it.

"The improvements at Achastle, are arduous, exten-"sive, and very flattering;—*arduous*, from the immense "rocks which it is often necessary to remove;—*extensive*, "as the old lands bear no proportion to the new, and "the new are extending daily;—and *flattering*, because "in a great measure under promising crops already; and "I am persuaded that in a few years, the lower parts of

"the

" the new grounds will prove far superior to the old
" arable land, though it was reckoned very fertile.

" As to the woods, both natural and planted, they are
" all in a flourishing state. The natural and artificial
" beauties of Langwell, are well known, and at this sea-
" son of the year are charming beyond description."

To improve rich and fertile districts, with a favourable soil and climate, and in the neighbourhood of good markets, is attended with little difficulty; but to bring hilly districts, in a remote part of the kingdom, to a state of profitable production, is a very different attempt. A variety of obstacles must, in that case, be surmounted, arising from soil, climate, distance from market, bad roads, and a number of other discouragements, which nothing but zeal and industry can possibly enable a Proprietor to overcome.

Of all the means of bringing a mountainous district to a profitable state, none is so peculiarly well calculated for that purpose, as the rearing a valuable breed of sheep: a small proportion alone of such a description of country, can be fit for grain; and, in regard to cattle, for every pound of beef that can be produced in a hilly district, three pounds of mutton can be obtained, and there is the wool into the bargain: besides, wool is an article easily transported, of essential use, for which there is in general a regular demand, and which is capable of great improvement. Sheep also, generally sell with less variation of price than cattle, and are easily driven to market. It was therefore resolved, to improve this extensive property, by converting it from cattle, into sheep-farms.

The great difficulty in carrying on the improvements of this Estate, arose from the circumstance of its being occupied by above eighty small tenants, who did not pay in all above 250*l.* per annum. Nothing could be more

absurd

absurd than to suffer such an extensive and valuable district, to be employed almost in nothing but in breeding an inconsiderable number of cattle, and feeding some red deer that wandered about the upper parts of the estate. Humanity, however, required, that above 500 individuals, who inhabited the estate, should not be driven from their ancient possessions, without having some other means of subsistence pointed out to them: hence it was necessary to proceed with caution, in extending the system of sheep farming, and to form some plan of provision for the people.

The following measure was at last adopted for that purpose,—that of giving them two Scotch acres of arable land, or at least fit to be rendered arable, with a house and garden, to each of those little farmers, under the name of "*Cottage Farms*," the Proprietor becoming bound, for the first year or two, to employ them for 100, 200, or 300 days in the year, as the cottager chose, paying for his labour so much grain, and so much money, in proportion to the number of days agreed upon. Thus the cottager, in a manner, received rent from the landlord, instead of paying any. No plan could succeed better, as a means of introducing industry into a district. It required, not only the labour of these cottagers, to carry on a variety of improvements, essential in an extensive tract of country, formerly almost in a state of nature, but it was necessary to employ a number of experienced labourers, from other places, to assist them, whose example was of much use.

It was soon found, that the plan was admirably suited to the temper and spirit of the Highlander, who was not fond of constant labour, but had no objection to work for a certain number of days, provided he had the remainder of his time free and uncontrouled. By adopting

this

this plan, every possible means were taken, neither to diminish the number, nor to crush the spirit, of a brave and hardy race of men, whose services in war might be so eminently useful; whilst at the same time, a habit of industry was introduced, far beyond the expectations of those who were best acquainted with that property in its former state, when hardly a single labourer could be procured in it. Measures were also taken, to furnish the women with employment: a number of spinning wheels were distributed among them, made by wheel-wrights who were set up for that purpose. The whole was certainly an operose and complicated system; but as it has answered beyond expectation, it is impossible not to recommend the adoption of a similar plan, to the attention of those, who may be desirous of improving a Highland Estate, without depopulating their country.

The advantages which have resulted from these improvements, in a pecuniary point of view, are very great, the Estate in question having, in the space of a few years, increased in value, from under 300*l.* to above 1600*l.* per annum, or more than five rents.

VI.

General View of the Improvements already accomplished.

The great object of all the measures above detailed, was, to lay a foundation for the future improvement of the estate, it being impossible to do more at once, considering its extent, and its disadvantages in regard to climate, markets, &c. The following statement will point out the amount, 1. Of the old arable land, where the farms have been inclosed, or regularly divided into distinct possessions; and, 2. Of new lands improved and brought into a state of cultivation.

1. *Arable*

1. *Arable Land, inclosed, or otherwise improved.*

	English Acres.
1. Arable land on the east side of the river Thurso,	2719
2. Ditto on the west side of the river,	1742
3. Ditto in the lands of Harpsdale, Leurary, Assary, Brawlbin, and the Strathmore,	1150
4. Ditto in the parish of Wick, and lower part of the parish of Latheron,	1450
5. Ditto on the estate of Langwell,	150
Total,	7221

2. *Waste Lands improved.*

	English Acres.
1. Waste lands on the east side of the river Thurso,	1582
2. Ditto on the west side,	1786
3. Ditto in the lands of Harpsdale, Leurary, Assary, Brawlbin, and the Strathmore,	150
4. Ditto in the parish of Wick, and lower part of the parish of Latheron,	210
5. Ditto on the estate of Langwell,	350
Total,	4078
Add the old arable land,	7221
Total land improved on Sir John Sinclair's estate, by himself, and by the encouragement given to his tenants,	11,299

The improvement of the soil, however, was not the sole object to be kept in view. A variety of other particulars, and more especially the following, merited attention.

1. *Farm*

1. *Farm Houses.*—The necessity of having good farm houses and offices, both for the accommodation of the farmer, and as an ornament to the country, need not be dwelt upon. There is hardly an estate in the northern parts of Scotland, where there are so many good houses and offices, as on the one in question; indeed, in some cases, they are rather better than the size or value of the farms would require.

2. *Roads.*—Without the accommodation of Roads, no district can be improved; and it is one of the principal disadvantages attending the county of Caithness, that its soil in general, consists either of clay or peat, and that the materials are rather of a softish quality, which renders it extremely expensive, both to make the roads, and to keep them in repair. The greatest exertion, perhaps ever made in Scotland, in road-making, was when about 1270 men were assembled by Sir John Sinclair in one day, to make a road along the side of a hill called The Bennichiel. Such are the difficulties, however, attending the making of roads in Caithness, that had it not been for the encouragement given by Government, it is not probable that much would have been effected, in that line of improvement, in our time. As without Inns also, roads would not be complete; for the benefit of travellers, one was erected on the estate of Langwell, called Berriedale Inn. Though the situation of the Inn itself is beautiful, yet as the country round is bleak and unhospitable, it increases the pleasure of the stranger, to find himself so comfortably accommodated.

3. *Plantations.*—It is a most unfortunate circumstance, for this part of the kingdom, that it is so extremely ill calculated for planting. The county of Caithness, being a promontory at the extremity of the Island, two-thirds of

it

it is surrounded by the sea, the spray from which, in addition to the violence of the winds, is extremely injurious to the growth of trees. The soil of a great part of the district also, lies on a flat rock, which prevents the roots of the trees from penetrating to a proper depth; hence, even when they do survive, they are extremely stinted in their growth. The establishment of a nursery at Skinnet has been already taken notice of. Some attempts at raising trees have been made on the farm of Thurso East. At Brawll, in the interior of the county, they have answered, where they were carefully attended to. That part of the county, however, that joins to Sutherland, on the Eastern Coast, is the best adapted for plantations. Instead of being a flat, it is of a hilly nature, and there is every reason to hope that trees will grow to considerable perfection, both along the banks of the rivers, and the sides of the hills. The number of trees planted on this part of the estate, in the years, 1806, 1807, and 1808, were as follows, viz.

Scotch firs	319,000
Larch	8,600
Ash	4000
Mountain Ash	2000
Elm	8000
Sycamore	5000
	345,600

Considerable plantations were also made, both before, and since the years above mentioned.

4. *Mines.*—It is generally admitted, that Mines constitute the natural wealth of a hilly district, and there is no reason to suppose, that the higher parts of Caithness are an exception to the general rule. A vein of lead, with a mixture

a mixture of mundick, was discovered near Skinnet, on the property of Sir John Sinclair, and miners from Derbyshire came North to work it; but after they had made some progress, they were unfortunately called away. So promising a vein, however, ought not to be lost sight of. Mines, it is supposed, are likewise to be found on the estate of Langwell.

5. *The Fisheries.*—There is, probably, no district in Europe, better calculated for carrying on the Fisheries, either in point of profit, variety, or extent, than Caithness. No less a number than 45 different sorts of fish are caught, either in the fresh waters belonging to the county, or in the seas by which it is surrounded. The greater part of the cod, brought to the London market, are caught at present at no great distance from the town of Thurso, and the fishing smacks employed to catch them, rendezvous at Scrabster Road, in its immediate neighbourhood. But no branch of the fishery is so important as that of herring, whether they are to be cured for domestic and European consumption, as the Dutch herrings are, or to be sent to our West India Colonies.

Aware of the importance of the Fisheries to the prosperity of Caithness, Sir John Sinclair made every exertion in his power, as early as circumstances would admit of it, to promote their success. In the year 1787, he prevailed on the Messrs. Fall, of Dunbar, to re-establish the Cod Fishery, which had been neglected for many years. He furnished capital to John Sutherland of Wester, and Mr. John Anderson of Wick, which enabled them to commence a Herring Fishery on the East Coast of the county, which has since become very productive, having yielded, in one year, above 60,000 barrels of herrings, and which may be carried on to almost any extent.

6. *Harbours.*—It is not to be questioned, that a commercial country cannot prosper without harbours: they are indispensable also for the success of the fisheries, and they are of great importance likewise in an agricultural point of view, for the importation of lime, and the exportation of the productions of the soil. There are few places where harbours are naturally so perfect, as not to require the improvements of art; and, where the assistance of art is necessary, it generally occasions a very considerable expense. As harbours were too costly operations to be carried through at the sole expense of a district, only commencing its career of improvement, every exertion was made by Sir John Sinclair, to procure public aid for accomplishing such important objects. With aid thus procured, one Harbour, that of Wick, or Pulteney Town, has been completed, at an expense of about 12,000*l.* greatly to the advantage of all that neighbourhood; and an Act has been obtained, for constructing a Harbour at Thurso, which, it is to be hoped, will be carried into effect at no great distance of time.

7. *Commerce.*—It is surely unnecessary to state, how essential Commerce is, for the prosperity and improvement of any country, were it only for the purpose of providing a market for the surplus productions of agriculture. Had the farmer only to supply his own family with food, his operations would soon become languid; but when he can dispose of any surplus, either to be consumed at home, or exported abroad, and in exchange can obtain the various articles for which he may have occasion, his industry necessarily increases, his energy and activity double, he accumulates wealth or capital, and is thus enabled, to extend his sphere of cultivation—to improve his stock—the grain and other articles he sows—the instruments of hus-

bandry he uses, &c. &c. Thus the intercourse and commerce that take place between the farmer, and those who follow other occupations, tend to their mutual comfort and prosperity. Hence it is a most unfortunate circumstance for any district, if it does not enjoy the advantages of domestic, and even of foreign commerce.

Hitherto the commerce of the county of Caithness has been extremely insignificant; it principally consisted in exporting,—not manufactured articles,—but the raw productions of the soil, as grain and cattle, together with some fish; and in importing timber, groceries, woollens, &c. It is now in contemplation, however, not only to carry on a trade with the Baltic, but also a direct commerce with the West Indies. Inquiries have been made for this purpose in several of the West India islands; and there is reason to hope, that an advantageous intercourse will be carried on, as soon as the harbours of the county, in particular that of Thurso, are completed.

8. *Manufactures.*—It is a great disadvantage to the county, that no extensive Manufacture has hitherto been established in Caithness, as it would have greatly tended to promote its agricultural interests. Some attempts, however, on a small scale, have been made, and not without success; particularly by the erection of a tannery at the town of Thurso; the Bleachfield, situated on the river Thurso, near Thurdistoft, has been already taken notice of; and a Woollen Manufacture has been established near the village of Halkirk. It is probable, however, on the whole, that some branch of the Linen Manufacture would stand the best chance of succeeding in Caithness; and with that view a lint-mill, and bleachfield, were erected. From the specimens of linen manufactured in Caithness, it evidently appeared, that there was nothing

in

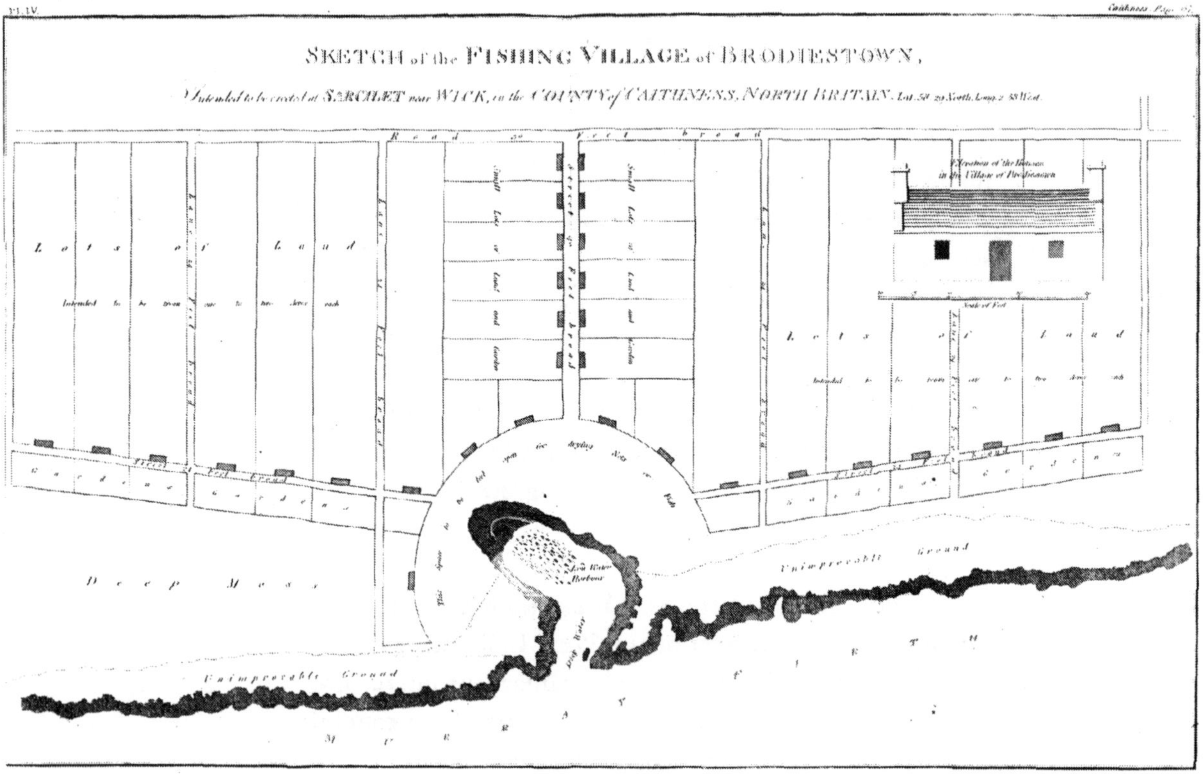
SKETCH of the FISHING VILLAGE of BRODIESTOWN,
Intended to be erected at SARCLET near WICK, in the COUNTY of CAITHNESS, NORTH BRITAIN. Lat. 58. 29 North, Long. 2. 58 West.
Road 30 Feet broad
Lots of Land
Intended to be from one to two Acres each
Small Lots of Land and Garden
Street 40 Feet broad
Elevation of the Houses in the Village of Brodiestown
Scale of Feet
Gardens
Space to be left open for drying Nets or Sails
Low Water Harbour
Deep Water
Deep Moss
Unimproveable Ground
MURRAY FIRTH

in the soil or climate of the county, to prevent flax from being raised, and linen manufactured and bleached there, equal to any in Scotland.

9. *Villages.*—The advantages of having villages scattered over a country, are too well known to require any particular elucidation. When properly situated, they often lay the foundation of large towns and cities, but even in their humbler state, they are of infinite service, by collecting a number of useful mechanics and tradesmen together, by furnishing hands, either to carry on such manufactures as are the most essential in every district, or to assist the adjoining farmers in their agricultural operations, and by acting as a common centre, where fairs and markets may be held, or little shops set up, or schools established, for the education of the children in the neighbourhood. It is extremely desirable therefore, that a number of villages should be founded on different parts of an extensive property. Two have already been set on foot on this estate, and have made some progress.

The first village is on the sea coast, at a place formerly known by the name of Sarclett, but now changed to *Brodie's-town**, in compliment to its public spirited founder, (David Brodie, Esq. of Hopeville,) who undertook to build, and to finish, in the most substantial manner, thirty-one houses, in three years, upon receiving twenty guineas for each house, for which he agreed to pay 5 per cent. for the first seven years, and 7½ per cent. during the remainder of his lease. (See *Plate* IV. for a Plan of the Village and Houses). Mr. Brodie undertook these, and the other improvements on the farms he occupies, (the expense of which has already been detailed), from an anxious wish,

* It is a proper rule to lay down, as a mode of promoting improvements, to call any new farm or village, after the name of the Founder.

that

that whilst such great things were going forward in the neighbourhood of Thurso, those parts of the Estate, situated on the Eastern Coast of the County, should not be neglected.—It is a peculiar advantage, therefore, attending the rousing of a spirit of improvement, that when once it fairly takes root, it runs with rapidity from one part of an extensive property to another. Successful exertions in one part; excite a corresponding zeal in another; and if the measures thus undertaken, are planned with judgment, carried on with skill, and persevered in for any length of time, a progress is made, beyond the most sanguine expectations of those who have engaged in such undertakings.

The establishment of inland villages ought also to be encouraged, for the reasons already detailed. To promote so useful a system, the village of Halkirk has been commenced. It is situated on the banks of the river Thurso, about six miles from the sea, and has the advantages of a church, a bridge over the river, and that several roads meet there. (For a Plan of the Village, see *Plate* V). A Woollen Manufacture has also been erected, in its immediate neighbourhood, it being the best situation for that branch of business in Caithness.

10. *New Town of Thurso.*—It must in general be admitted, that no district can reach any great degree of prosperity, without having a considerable Town erected in it; and that countries are usually powerful and prosperous, in proportion to the size of the cities which are found in them. Wherever a number of inhabitants are collected together, they furnish a market for the agricultural productions of the neighbourhood, which of course, increase with the demand. A large town also, necessarily implies, persons with sufficient capital to promote internal industry, and to carry on foreign commerce:—it

also

PLAN
of a Village to be erected at
HALKIRK.

REFERENCES

Represents the Houses on the Lots.
Land now Arable.
The boundary of the Glebe and of Milntown.
A Cairn.
The present School House.
Bridge Street and the main Street to be 60 Feet Broad.
The other Streets from 24 to 36 Feet Broad.

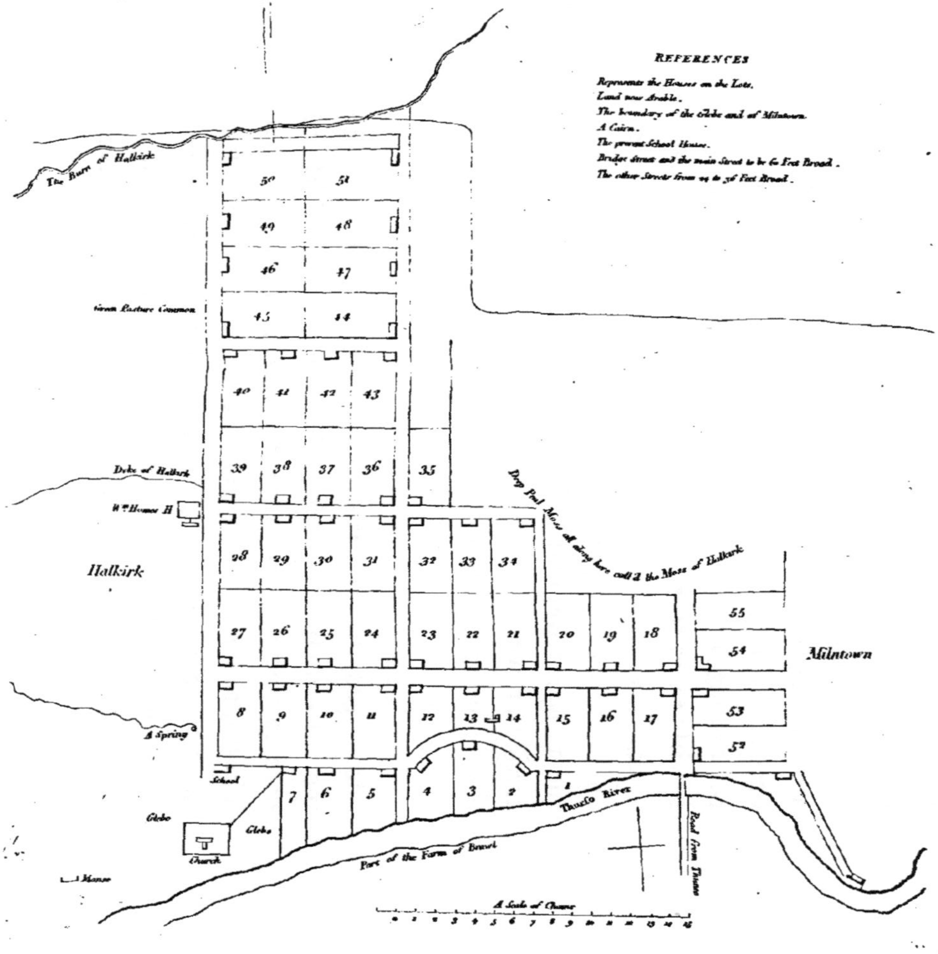

Plan of the NEW TOWN of THURSO in the County of CAITHNESS North Britain
now Building on the Property of SIR JOHN SINCLAIR of Ulbster, Bar.t

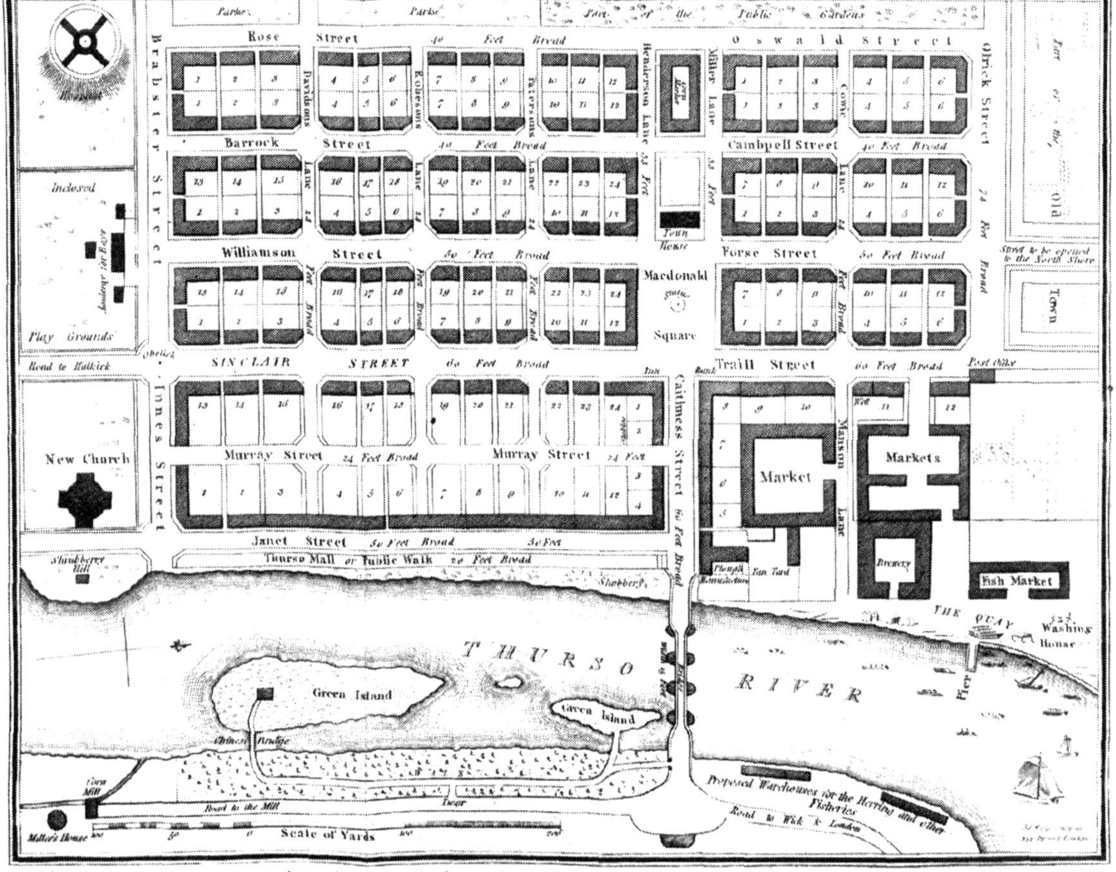

The New Town of Thurso is admirably situated on a gentle ascent with a southern exposure in a well cultivated & fertile country on the Banks of a River about to be made Navigable & near a Harbour capable of great improvement. No place can be better calculated for the Fisheries in general for foreign Commerce or domestic Manufacture. Possessed of such advantages the Proprietor resolved to build it according to the most regular plan that could be contrived and in a manner not only ornamental but also peculiarly well adapted for preserving the health & promoting the convenience of the Inhabitants. The Streets have every advantage that can be derived from a complete circulation of air & the public walks along the banks of the River will be remarkably pleasant & healthy. The different Markets being placed between the Old and the New Town will tend much to the accommodation of the Inhabitants. The Plan may be carried on to any extent either to the North or West that may be thought most advisable & it is also proposed to have another Town on a regular system built on the opposite side of the River as soon as an increase of Inhabitants will render it necessary.

also implies, establishments for the education of youth, churches for religious instruction, hospitals for the benefit of the sick, institutions for promoting various branches of art and science; and other marks of prosperity, civilization and improvement. On these grounds, the increase of old, or the establishment of new towns or cities, have justly been considered, as one of the most striking marks of the flourishing state of a nation.

Impressed with these ideas, Sir John Sinclair was happy to find, a town in his own neighbourhood, (Thurso), admirably situated for every species of improvement. There was an old town, which contained about 1600 inhabitants, but the houses were very irregularly built, and in many places crowded on each other. He was thence induced, to resolve on building a New Town, on different principles, and where regularity was strictly to be observed.

In forming a plan for that purpose, the reader will perceive from the annexed Engraving, (see *Plate* VI), how much the comfortable accommodation of the inhabitants has been attended to, and if that plan is carried into execution in the manner proposed, (which must require time to fully accomplish), there is every reason to believe, that in point of beauty and convenience, it will not be surpassed by any erection of the same extent, of which Europe can boast. The New Town of Thurso, according to the annexed Plan, will only contain about 300 houses, but when a town so advantageously situated, is once fairly set agoing, it is impossible to say, to what a height of prosperity it may ultimately be carried. Indeed no town can be better situated. It is built on the banks of a considerable river, where it enters a beautiful bay, at the entrance of the Pentland Frith, and opposite to the Orkney Islands. The soil on which it is placed is dry, and the new town proposed to be erected, is situated on a gentle slope facing the

the south. The harbour, in spring tides, will at present receive vessels of about 100 tons, and when the proposed improvements in it take place, ships of a much larger size may enter. The harbour, it is true, must always be a tide one, but fortunately it has, within two miles of it, that celebrated anchorage ground called Scrabster Roads, which is equal to any of its extent, for security and convenience. No town can be better situated for manufactures, or commerce, being within a few hours sail of the German and Atlantic Oceans. The town is likewise admirably situated for the Fisheries, that important source of northern wealth; and at present the fishing smacks, which supply the London market with cod, being driven from the Dogger-bank, rendezvous in its neighbourhood. Indeed such is the variety of fish in that part of the kingdom, that twenty-four different sorts have been put upon the same table, in the course of one day, without an extraordinary exertion. Thurso has also the advantage of excellent sands, where a bathing-machine may be erected. An Academy is now in contemplation, where all the principal branches of education will be taught by proper masters: a Boarding-school for girls has been established, which has been conducted much to the satisfaction of the town and neighbourhood; and as Thurso will thus rival, in the important article of education, any town of its extent in Scotland, that, joined to the cheapness of provision, and other conveniences, must be a great inducement to persons of moderate incomes, to settle there.

In forming the plan of a New Town, it was judged extremely necessary to have it laid out, not only in the best manner that experience could suggest, but also to have the various public buildings necessary to be erected, planned on the best principles, and the most approved construction. The private houses are all to be built according

to

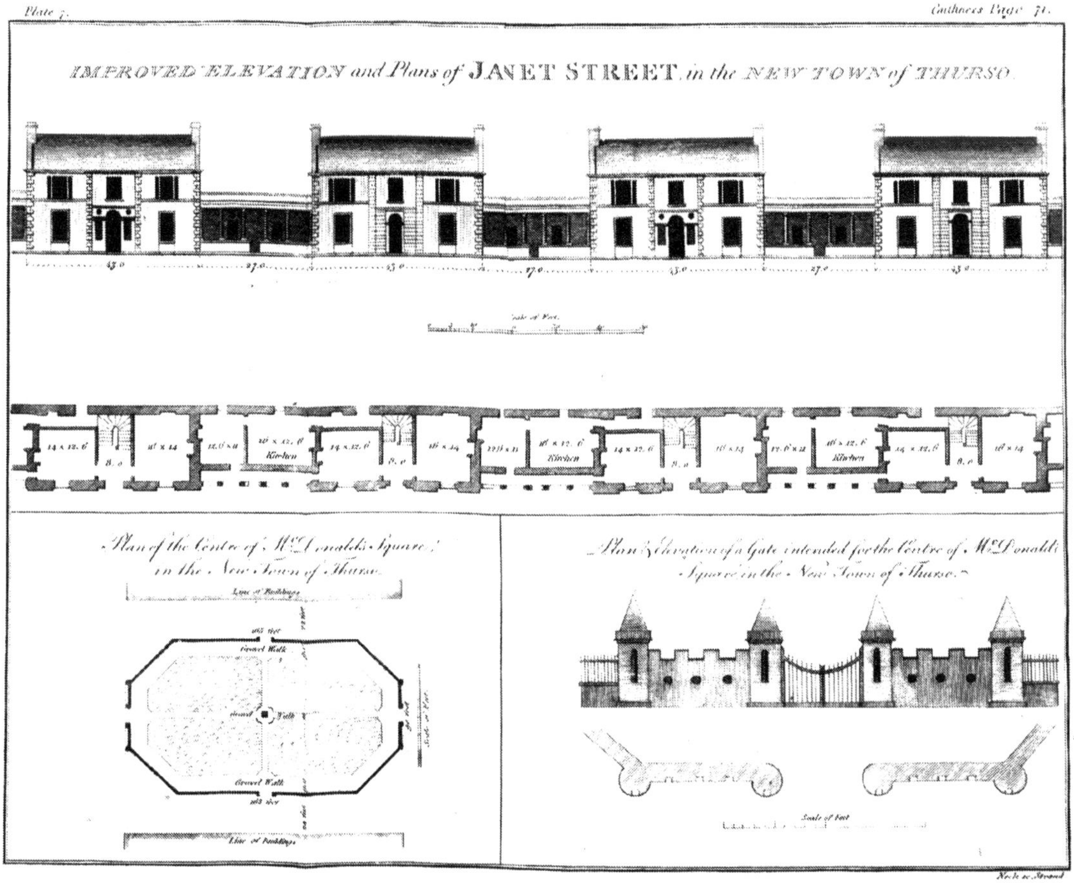

Neele sc. Strand

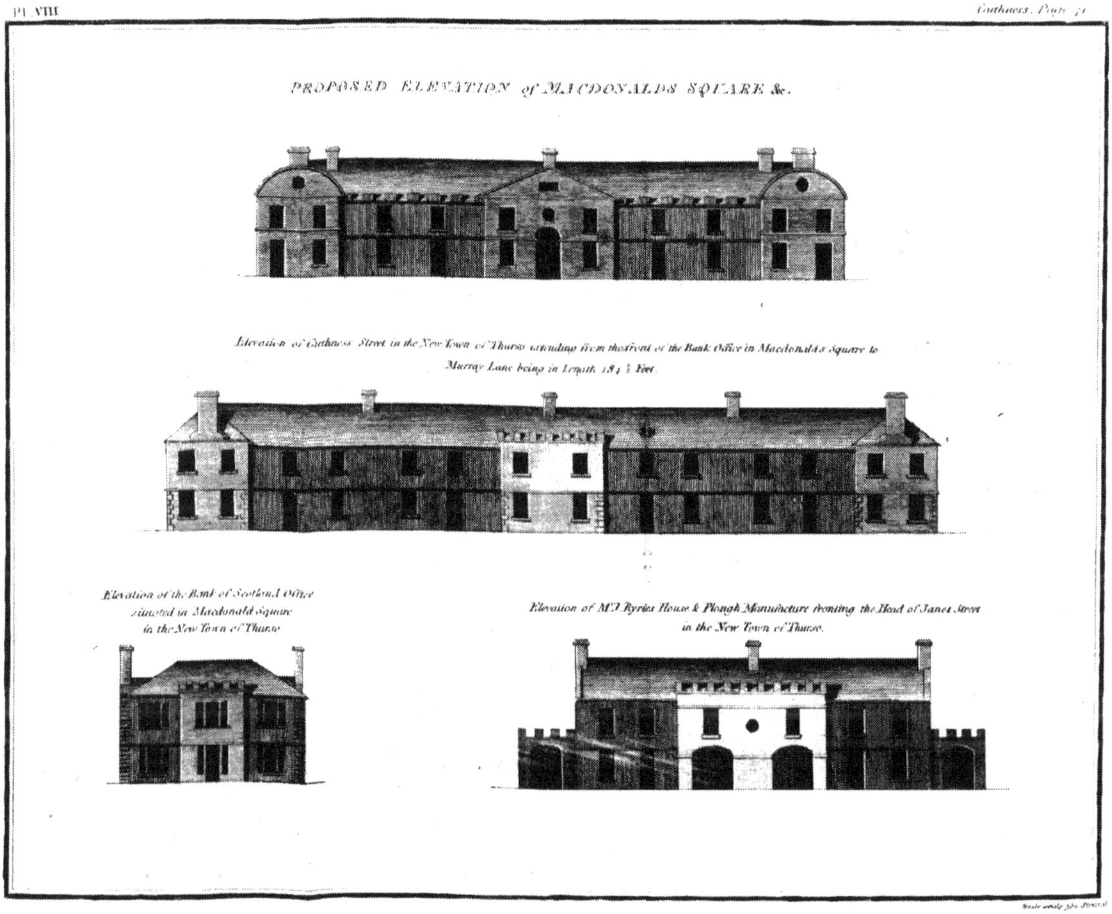
PROPOSED ELEVATION of MACDONALDS SQUARE &c.
Elevation of Caithness Street in the New Town of Thurso extending from the front of the Bank Office in Macdonald's Square to Murray Lane being in Length 184 ½ Feet.
Elevation of the Bank of Scotland Office situated in Macdonald Square in the New Town of Thurso
Elevation of Mr. J. Ryries House & Plough Manufacture fronting the Head of Janet Street in the New Town of Thurso.

to a specific plan, laid down for that purpose, and from which no individual, who takes the ground, is permitted to deviate. Several private houses have been already built in different parts of the town, so as to mark out the intended streets. As the Public Walk is already made, the bridge built, and as every spot fit for the plough, within sight of either, is inclosed and cultivated, the prospect from the public walk, or the bridge, is uncommonly beautiful.

To explain the nature of the Elevations which have been preferred, there are annexed, 1. An Engraving of Janet Street, which fronts the Public Walk, (see *Plate* VII.), where several houses have been already built, according to the form laid down; and, 2. The Plan of Macdonald Square, &c. (see *Plate* VII.), which has likewise commenced.

It was a most satisfactory circumstance, attending these exertions for the improvement of Thurso, and of its neighbourhood, that a Youth, at a very early age, was tempted to express his feelings on the subject, in Verses, of which the following is an exact copy, without any alteration whatever, which it may not be improper here to insert, as the first poetic effusions on the improvement of that town.

VERSES,

ADDRESSED TO SIR JOHN SINCLAIR,

On his Plan of Building the New Town of Thurso, and carrying on other Improvements there,

BY HIS AFFECTIONATE SON, GEORGE SINCLAIR;

WRITTEN IN THE THIRTEENTH YEAR OF HIS AGE.

" See where yon town in modest guise appears,
" Where wealthy Commerce flourishes, tho' late,
" Where yonder bridge its stony arches rears,
" (How different all from its first shapeless state!)

" See where the ploughman breaks the yielding soil,
" And the gay shepherd tunes his rural lay;
" Or, where the vessel, fraught with foreign spoil,
" Unloads its treasures at the crouded quay.

" On moors, once cloth'd with rank obtrusive weeds,
" The playful lambs frisk to the shepherd's strain,
" On fields—the corn, (no rock its growth impedes),
" Displays its ears bent down with ripen'd grain.

" Great was the man who first these wilds adorn'd,
" Who taught the rude and unproductive land
" To yield such plenteous gifts, and wisely scorn'd,
" To waste his time with unimproving hand.

" Alas! how fatal for the world his death;
" Who e'er can cease to mourn so kind a friend!
" The poor continue with their latest breath,
" To wail their bounteous benefactor's end."

Such are the praises which in future age,
Each rustic to thy memory will pay,
The converse such, in which he must engage
With strangers, when near Thurso's walls they stray.

Praiseworthy deeds! how happy must thou be,
To greet such blessings to thy honour pour'd!
All, in true colours drest, thy worth must see,
Since to these great attempts you've nobly soar'd.

While

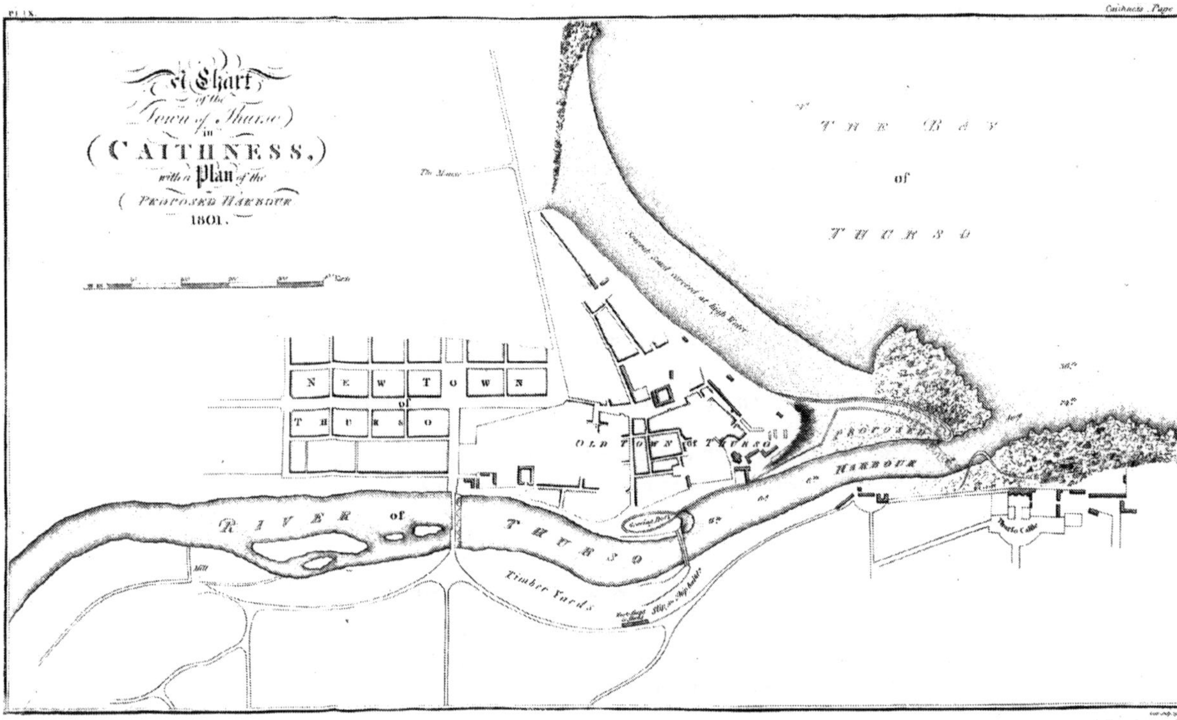
A Chart
of the
Town of Thurso
in
(CAITHNESS,)
with a Plan of the
(PROPOSED HARBOUR
1801.
The Manse
THE BAY
of
THURSO
NEW TOWN
of
THURSO
OLD TOWN of THURSO
PROPOSED
HARBOUR
RIVER of
THURSO
Timber Yards
Mill

While in such plans you glory, and engage,
  Let me the Muse's duteous aid implore,
Let me peruse attentive History's page,
  And in my mind true learning's treasure store.

Be it my care to cull the flowers that blow,
  In Homer's verse, or Maro's polish'd line,
Forbid it heaven, my time should idly flow
  Nor reap these harvests which the heart refine.

Harrow on the Hill, Nov. 1802.

VII.

Additional Improvements still in contemplation.

The Improvements above described, may be considered as in a manner accomplished; lands to the extent of above 11,000 English acres, have been all put in a train of improved cultivation;—a number of substantial Farm Houses and Offices have been built;—Roads carried on;—Bridges erected;—Plantations formed;—Miners employed in digging for Ore;—successful Fisheries set on foot;—a most useful Harbour constructed;—some branches of Manufacture established;—Villages commenced;—and the foundation of a New Town laid, which has already made considerable progress: much, however, of the Plan originally formed, remains to be effected, the execution of which, the difficulties of the times have hitherto retarded.

The first object which it would be desirable to accomplish, is, the Harbour of Thurso, a Plan of which is annexed (see *Plate* IX). An Act has been obtained for that purpose, and some public aid may be expected from the balances arising from the Forfeited Estates in Scotland; but it is hardly possible, at present, to raise a fund, fully adequate to that undertaking. Until that Harbour is made, the

the Plans in contemplation, for the extension of the Commerce of Thurso, cannot be attempted.

It is proposed to erect a number of Public Buildings at Thurso, (Engravings of which are annexed), as soon as the prosperity of the Town will admit of it: among these are, 1. a new Church (see *Plate* X.);—2. an Hospital, on a construction peculiarly well calculated for preventing the spreading of infectious disorders (see *Plate* XI.);—3. an Academy (see *Plate* XII.);—and, 4. a Public Wash-House and Laundry, (see *Plate* XIII).

These Plans were all prepared, after much inquiry regarding the best construction of such buildings; and are here given, as they may furnish hints, which may be useful in other places, where similar objects are in contemplation.

CONCLUSION.

SUCH is the general nature of the Improvements, as originally planned out, and which, to a considerable extent, have been executed, on this extensive property. Numerous are the disadvantages under which it was attempted. It was necessary to bring many thousand acres, from almost a state of nature, into a progressive state of improvement;—to arrange a plan for that purpose on judicious principles;—to provide adequate funds for accomplishing it;—to rouse, among the inhabitants of the district, the spirit necessary for so great an undertaking;—to procure, from other districts, the hands required for various branches of the proposed system of improvement*;—to make a total alteration in the situation, the

* This is done under many disadvantages, in a remote district. In 1802, Sir John Sinclair prevailed on a dozen of natives of Westmorland to

Pl. X.

PLAN of the *PROPOSED CHURCH* for the *NEW TOWN* of THURSO.

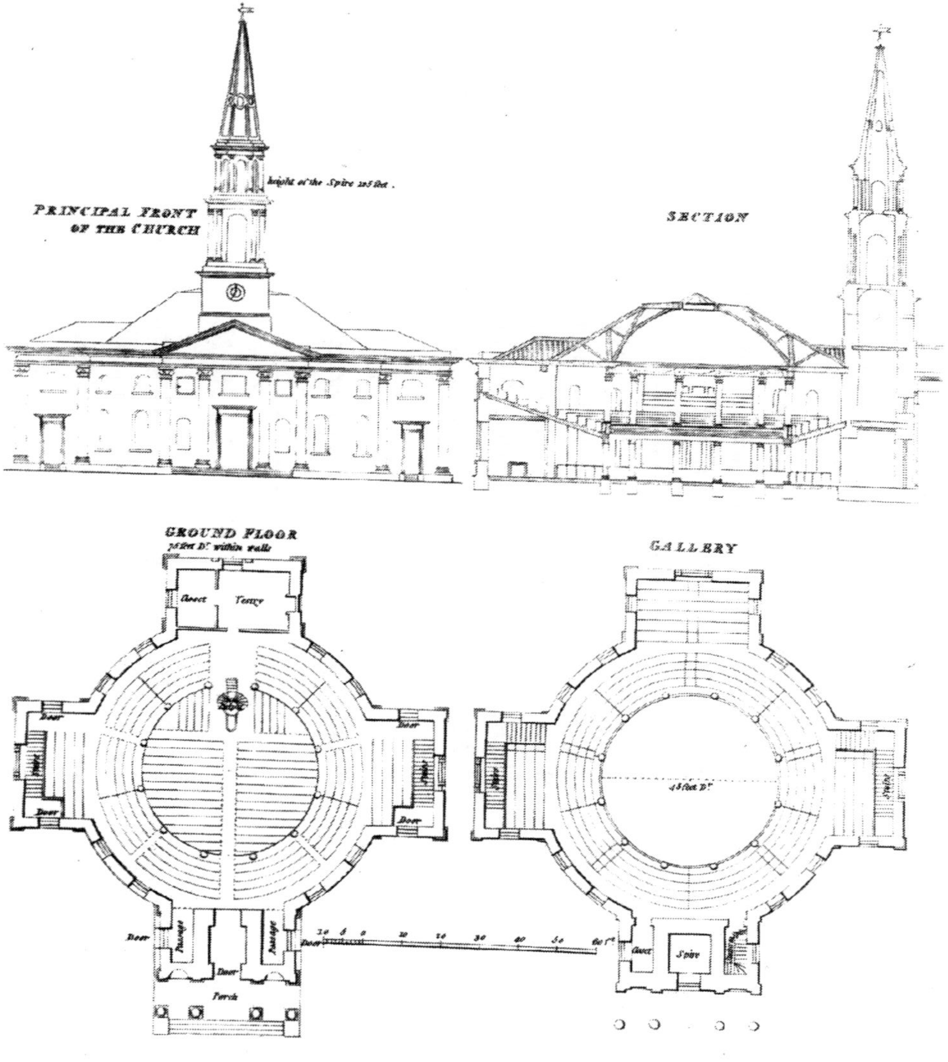

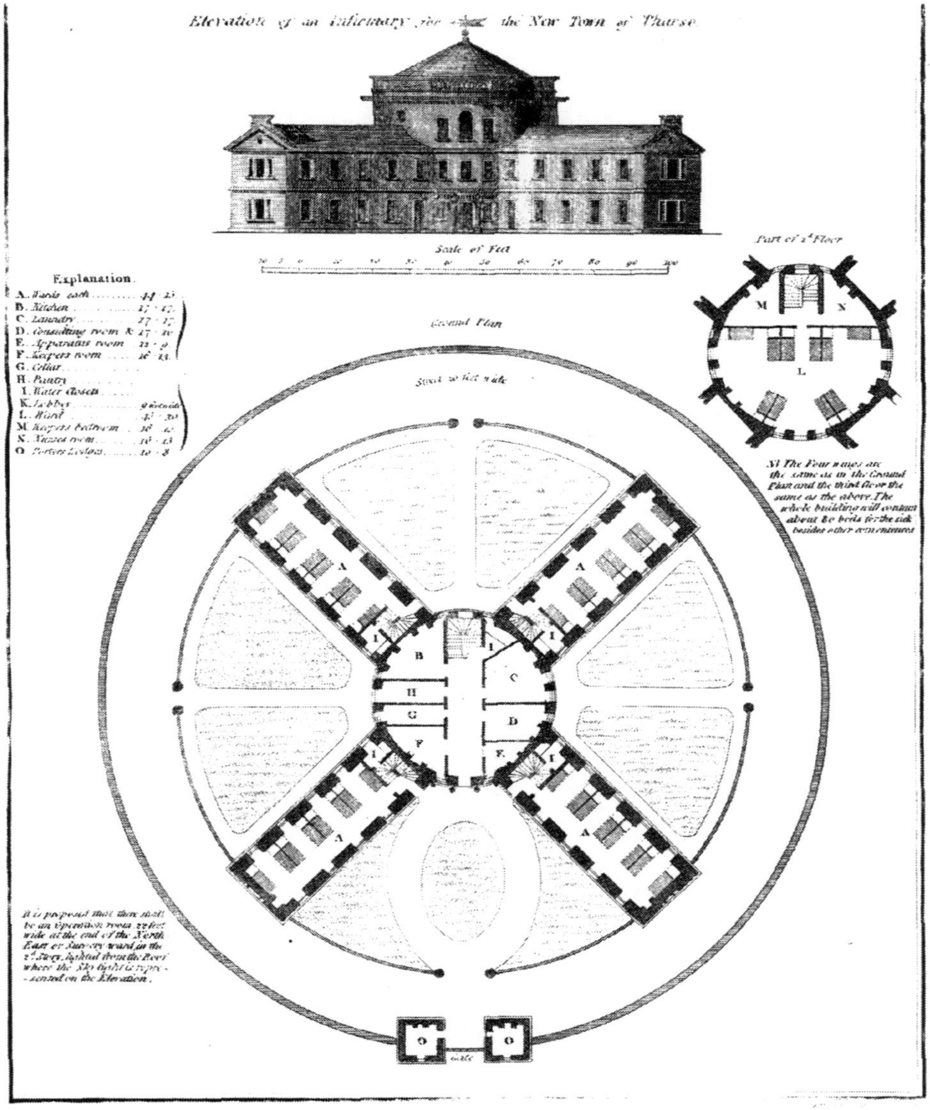
Elevation of an Infirmary for the New Town of Thurso
Scale of Feet
Part of 2d Floor
Ground Plan
Explanation.
A. Wards each ... 44 · 25
B. Kitchen
C. Laundry
D. Consulting room &
E. Apparatus room
F. Keepers room
G. Cellar
H. Pantry
I. Water Closets
L. Ward
M. Keepers bedroom
N. Nurses room
O. Porters Lodges
NB The Four wings are the same as in the Ground Plan and the third floor the same as the above. The whole building will contain about 80 beds for the sick besides other conveniences
It is proposed that there shall be an Operation room 22 feet wide at the end of the North East or Surgery ward in the 2d Story, lighted from the Roof where the Sky light is represented on the Elevation.

SKETCH of NORTH or ENTRANCE FRONT of AN ACADEMY for the NEW TOWN of THURSO.

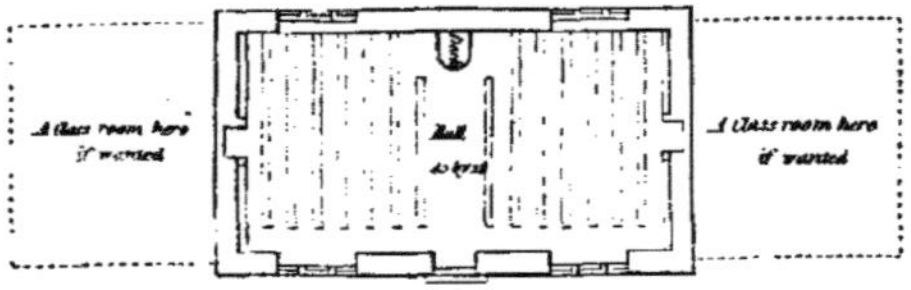

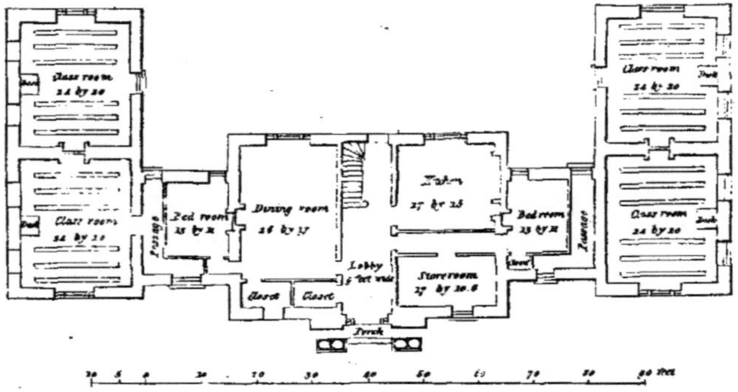

SECTION of WASHHOUSE.
and LAUNDRY.

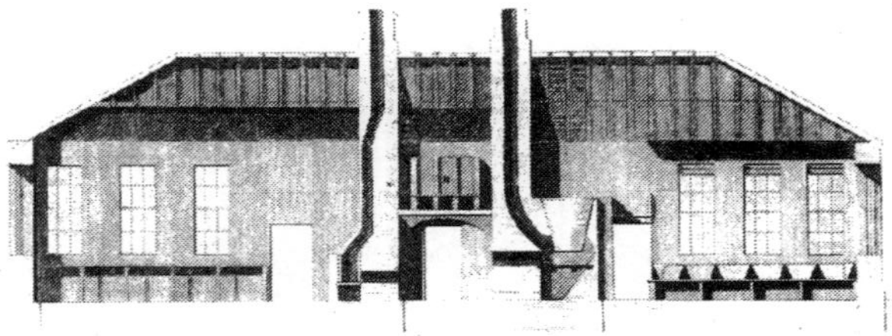

ENTRANCE FRONT.

GROUND PLAN.

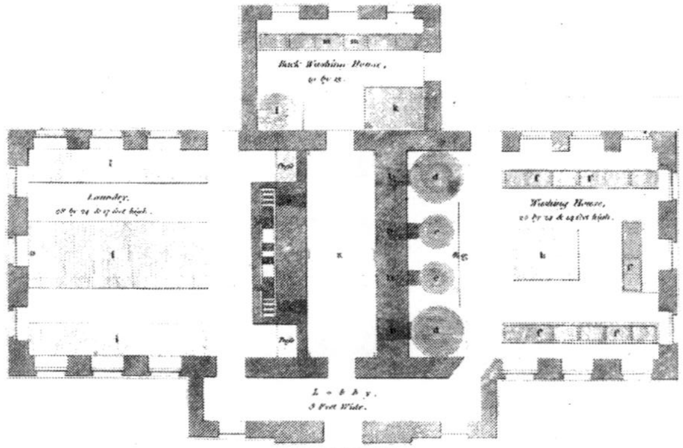

REFERENCES.

To a Plan of a Public Washing-House & Laundry for the New Town of Thurso,
Designed by Alex^r. M^c.Innes, 13th. July 1801.

a. The Coal Vault from whence the fires are supplied, 5 feet wide.
b. The fire places for the Boilers.
c. Ditto for the Stoves for heating Irons, drying Clothes &c.
d. Boilers for the Washing water.
e. Ditto for heating the Suds.
f. Washing Tubs each having Stopcocks for warm and cold water, and Suds if necessary, also a plug in the bottom for letting off the Suds into a Reservoir.
g. A Pump for raising the Suds from the Reservoir into the Boilers.
h. A Table to lay the Washed Clothes upon.
i. Tables to dress the Clothes upon.
k. A Cistern for collecting the Suds from the Boilers &c. by means of a pipe, for the use of the Poor people; this cistern has a pump at one corner for raising the Suds into a boiler by a Spout over the Roof of the Coal Vault.
l. A Boiler for the Suds for the use of the Poor people.
m. Tubs for Ditto.
n. A Reservoir for supplying the Boilers and Tubs with Cold Water.

NB. A Mangle may be placed at the end o of the Laundry, and pipes may be conveyed from the Stoves through the Laundry for Drying Clothes. Ropes may also be placed for hanging clothes on, to be raised or lowered at pleasure by means of Pullies.

the habits, and the prejudices of the former occupiers;—to surmount the obstacles arising from a want of roads and harbours;—to contend with a most unfavourable climate;—to make up for a deficiency of markets;—and to carry on such an undertaking, in the midst of a foreign war, which diminished the number of labourers, checked circulation, more especially in the distant parts of the kingdom, and added to burdens which had already been severely felt: all these unfavourable circumstances united, have rendered it impossible, in many cases, to do more, than to lay the foundation of Improvement. In fact, the measures above detailed, relate to such a variety of particulars, that they resemble more a system, calculated for the establishment of a new colony, or the improvement of a great province, than of a private estate. It was unfortunately impossible, properly to attend to the execution of such a plan, and at the same time to fulfil the duties incumbent on the President of the National Board of Agriculture. To assist that Board, however, in carrying on the general Improvement of the Country, was such an object, that every idea of private interest necessarily gave way, to promote so essential a public benefit.

London, 10th May, 1812.

---

to go to Caithness, to introduce the Paring and Burning system. They had got on board a ship, and had actually set sail from Leith, on the 20th of March, when most unfortunately, another vessel run foul of that ship, and damaged it so much, that it could not proceed in its voyage; some of them were discouraged from proceeding, and the others were detained several days at Leith and Edinburgh, which prevented their reaching Caithness as early in the season as they ought to have done.

No. III.

No. III.

The following intelligent letter, will explain the difficulties which the Proprietors and the Farmers of Caithness experience, in getting an adequate price for their produce.

Letter from Thomas Pinkerton Esq. to Sir John Sinclair, regarding the Sale of certain Caithness Productions.

SIR,

I am favoured with your Note of the 3d inst. inclosing copy of a letter to you from James Traill, Esq. respecting the purchase of beef, and other articles of provision in the county of Caithness; and shall be very happy if I can render you any service, in promoting the interest of that county, either by my advice, or in the sale of any of the articles therein mentioned.

With respect to the curing of beef, I have again and again attempted that business at Leith, where good large fat cattle can be purchased, and every other convenience found, for carrying on an extensive business of this kind; but I have always failed in the attempt, notwithstanding I have had contracts with Government for the beef which I cured at that place. The cattle, though many of them were of a good size, were mixed with some of a smaller breed, and whenever the small beef was discovered on inspection, it caused the whole cargo to be rejected, the loss on which was greater than all the profit gained by what was received into the government stores. I understand the cattle in the north of Scotland are of a very small breed, and are therefore very unfit for salting. No cattle

cattle are killed for the Navy, that weigh less than five cwt. each, the four quarters. Beef cut from small cattle, gets very hard after being six or twelve months in salt; the fat boils away, and a piece of eight pounds weight, when put into the pot, will not weigh half that weight after it is boiled, whereas a piece of beef cut from the carcass of a large fat ox, will eat nearly as well twelve months, or even two years, after being salted, as when first cured, and will shrink little in boiling. Besides the inferiority of the cattle, the salt laws are a prohibition to the curing of beef in Caithness. A cwt. of salt, with the duty, costs here about 40*s.*, whereas in Ireland it does not cost 10*s.* The duty is something less I believe in Scotland than here; but still it will cost 10*s.* per cwt. more for the salt necessary to cure one cwt of beef than it does in Ireland. The Irish have therefore the advantage of 10*s.* per cwt. on every cwt. of beef they cure. Very good beef can be purchased in Ireland for 3*d.* and 3½*d.* per pound; this low price, with the advantage of the salt-laws, quality of beef, local situation, long experience in the business, &c. &c. renders the plan of curing beef in Caithness, or in any part of Scotland or England, totally out of the question.

As to the articles of oats, and oat-meal, oats always command a ready sale here, and any quantity can be sold at the market price, which fluctuates from 24*s.* to 34*s.* per quarter of eight bushels, and a bushel of good oats should weigh about thirty eight pounds. Oat-meal is not much in use here, but for the Navy, for which the Victualling Board contract occasionally, for quantities of about 200 tons: their wants are very uncertain, and as they must not be disappointed, I am well convinced they will not trust to so distant a quarter as Caithness for supplies. If, however, these articles can be purchased considerably cheaper there than in the southern counties of Scotland, (when

(when difference of expense of freight, &c. is taken into consideration), I have no hesitation in saying, that any quantity the county can procure, will find a ready sale at this market; but every thing will depend upon the price and quality of the articles.

As to butter and cheese, I have never seen any Scotch cheese that would at all answer this market; it is sent in large quantities from England to Scotland, and has never, to my knowledge, been imported from Scotland to this country for sale. Large quantities of good Dutch cheese have been imported here for some years past, which sells from 3*d.* to 4½*d.* per pound. I have sent it frequently to Scotland, where it fetches 6*d.* per lb. which is a strong proof that cheese from Caithness will not answer at this market. Of butter I have a different opinion. I have frequently seen very good butter imported from Scotland, and there is no doubt but any quantity will sell here, if the quality is good, and the price reasonable; but every thing will depend upon these circumstances. The price of butter fluctuates much here: it got up a few months ago, from 80*s.* to 120*s.* per cwt.; it has fallen of late from 120*s.* to 90*s.* and I expect will be still lower. The rise was occasioned by the French Decree, for preventing all communication between this country and Holland, &c. which prevented for a while the importation of butter, cheese, &c. from Holland, and the fall in the price is occasioned by a relaxation of the said Decree: we have therefore now immense supplies of butter, cheese, and corn, from both Holland and France. The Victualling Board contract once a year for butter, and the Contractor is bound to supply all that is wanted for the year. I am not acquainted with the quality of the butter from Caithness, but have reason to think it is not fit for the Navy, which is of very little consequence, as any supply that

that

that county could procure, would be no object worth the attention either of the Government or Contractor, besides, as good a price, perhaps better, can be obtained in this market, than is paid either by Government or the Contractor.

If your friends will say at what prices they will engage to ship the articles of oats, oat-meal and butter, and what quantities can be procured, as also on what terms they can procure freight to London; and in the mean time will send forward a small quantity of each article, by way of a sample, I could soon decide how far it would answer to engage farther in the business.

Should you want any further information on this head, I will wait on you, at any time you may think proper to appoint.

I remain, &c.

Your most obedient Servant,

THOMAS PINKERTON.

No. 1, *Adelphi Terrace,*
7th July, 1807.

No. IV.

THE following is the valuable Letter from Mr. Traill, alluded to in the above communication.

Letter from James Traill, Esq. of Hobbister, to Sir John Sinclair, on the Sale of the Agricultural Productions of Caithness.

Castle-Hill, 25th May, 1807.

MY DEAR SIR,

IN reference to the subject of our conversation, when I had the pleasure of seeing you last Saturday, I beg leave

leave to state to you, that, (as it appears to me), there is no way in which you can so effectually promote the agricultural interests of this part of the kingdom, as by opening a ready market for its produce. This consists chiefly of grain, cattle, and the produce of the dairy.

Our grain consists principally of bear, or bigg, and oats. The latter I may venture to state as very little, if any thing, inferior in quality to the average produce of Scotland, and might be very advantageously employed as an article of supply for the fleet, if manufactured into meal. The former is a very inferior species, to even the best Scots bigg, and certainly much more inferior to English barley, though very absurdly placed on the same footing with it, in the legislative provisions for regulating the exportation and importation of corn. Wheat is a grain not altogether unknown, but never hitherto successfully cultivated, in this part of the kingdom; and, considering the disadvantages we labour under, in point of climate, it must be regarded as extremely doubtful, whether that species of grain, which is acknowledged to be the source of the opulence of the South Country Farmers, shall ever become a staple commodity of this county. If it does, it can only be effected by a change of system, tending to increase, to such a degree, the fertility of the soil, as may be sufficient to overcome every disadvantage of local situation. This object is only to be accomplished by the extensive introduction of sown grasses and green crops, for which our soil and climate are peculiarly adapted, and which would be cultivated with a degree of success equal to what has been experienced in any part of the kingdom, were it not for our distance from every market, and the utter impossibility of turning to account the produce of these crops. It is here, (as it appears to me), that the great obstacle to our advancement lies; and I am firmly

convinced,

convinced, that, could this obstacle be in any measure removed, you would soon have the satisfaction of seeing your native country, rival in its industry and opulence, many of those that are more highly favoured by nature.

The only mode that has occurred to me, of supplying this deficiency of internal market, is, by endeavouring to procure for us, some Government contract for oatmeal, beef, pork, butter, cheese, &c. for the supply of the Navy, to a certain limited extent;—or, what I should prefer, that some Victualling Agent should be appointed to purchase up those kinds of stores for Government use, at such prices as they are commonly supplied elsewhere; or perhaps both plans might be blended in this manner: A certain number of the gentlemen, or farmers of the county, might undertake to furnish such provisions, to a limited extent, by way of experiment, to be paid for at the same rates as they are furnished elsewhere by contract; and an Agent for Government, settled in the country, to judge of the quality of the articles brought forward, and to superintend the process of cutting up, salting, and curing. This person might receive his remuneration at the hands of the Contractors, though employed by Government, in order that the articles contracted for might come to the public use, without any additional charges.

I cannot perceive any objection to this plan, other than that it is out of the customary routine, and that it might be thought, if the commodities we had to offer, were fit for the use of the Navy, we might find the means of competition without all this precaution; but the difficulties we have to struggle with, from our remote situation, are unknown in the southern parts of the kingdom. If any public notice is given of such supplies being wanted, the contract is filled up almost before we can hear of it. If we feed stock with a view to it, unlike other situations, where the disappointed candidate finds some other vent, perhaps on terms not less advantageous than those he originally looked to, ours remain a dead stock, altogether unsaleable, and the whole expense incurred in feeding, is just so much money thrown away.

To these circumstances I may add, that there are so many little things in the detail of the management, that require the attention of a man practically acquainted with the business; and that fashion, or habit, in so many ways influence the result of an experiment of this kind, that we could hardly expect to succeed in a struggle, against the various interests and prejudices which might oppose themselves to us. Whereas, it does not occur to me, in what respect the public would be injured, by an attempt to bring into notice the remote parts of the empire, under a system of regulation such as I have suggested, which effectually provides against every imposition, from any inferiority in the quality of the commodities offered to their use, while it in no respect enhances the price.

I ever am,

With the greatest respect,

MY DEAR SIR,

Your faithful and obedient humble Servant,

JAMES TRAILL.

Sir John Sinclair, Bart. &c. &c.

No. V.

No. V.

Minutes and Observations drawn up in the course of a Mineralogical Survey of the County of Caithness, An. 1802. *By* JOHN BUSBY, *Mineralogical Surveyor, Edinburgh.*

1802. *August* 2.—Set off this morning for Westfield, the property of Mr. Sinclair of Forss. First finished a well at the house of Westfield. The strata in the well is much distorted and broke, by a dyke stretching through the well. To the north-west and south-east is a bituminated stone, which effervesces with acids, and rises in broad flags; the bitumen is volatilized by exposure to the air, and leaves the strata grey-coloured. The thick strata does not soon decompose, and answers admirably well for stone dykes. The proprietor has had long experience of its durability, in several parts of his estates near Oust. Bored, and found shell-marl, two feet thick. Near the same place, I found bog iron-ore.

3.—Examined the quarry near Westfield; found the dip one in five, dipping south-east.—Surveyed the lime-stone at Achahater; found the upper stratum to be three feet thick. By digging down, found a continuation of lime-stone, colour blue; gave directions how to open the quarry to advantage. This stone is near to the Loch of Calder.—Bored for shell-marl between Forss and Achloke.

4.—Bored for shell-marl in the Red Park, and found two feet thick of it. Surveyed the slate quarry of Achascrabster; the description of the nature of the slate, to be found under the head of Buckies, as they are all of one kind, only differing a little in perfection from each other. Bored nearthis place for shell-marl.

 5.—At

5.—At Forss, found an inferior limestone of a blue colour, dip south-east one in six. At Crosskirk found several stratums of the blue limestone, from 19 to 16 inches thick; dip north-west. Made several bores, to ascertain the soil. Bored for shell-marl at the same place.

The principal part of the shell-marl in the Loch of Westfield lies on the north-west side. By Mr. Sinclair of Forss's information, the greater part of the Loch is of a rocky bottom.

6.—Set out to survey the estate of Shebster, the property of the Rev. Mr. Nicholson. Bored for shell-marl in the mosses of Shebster.

7.—Bored for shell-marl in ditto. Examined the lime rock at the hill of Achabay; the rise and dip cannot be well known, as the rock is very rugged, uneven, and much detached. The lime appears of good quality. The thickness of the rock should be ascertained, to determine a proper mode of working the quarry, &c. Bored for shell-marl below Achearmanach: found it at Classoharn; presented a blue limestone of thin stratum; dip north-west, one in four; the full thickness is not yet ascertained. Bored for shell-marl; found it four feet thick.

9.—Began surveying the estate of Sandside, the property of William Innes, Esq. First guaw west from the house, found a fine lime-work, seemingly about ten feet thick; the stratum dips to the north, that is, to the sea. A little to the west of this there is another lime rock, four feet thick; the cropping out to the surface of the dip is north-west. Third guaw west of this, the red granite comes boldly down to the sea; it is interspersed with several veins of granite, and large veins of feldspar. On the east side of this ridge of granite, is the strata which is general on the coast near Sandside, to wit, a bluish calcareous freestone, of considerable thickness, thin stratums of indurated clay, and thin stratums of bluish

slates,

slates, &c. Examining the strata in contact with the granite rock, I found it rising to the granite, and even overlapping it; although at the distance of less than fifty yards, it is dipping to the granite; there is no mark of extraordinary convulsion on the strata; it is of a pretty sudden dip, one in three, and is very hard. Next to the granite, on the west side of it, is the dibrous of the granite, and other stones, covering in part more than fifty yards of coast, in a stratum uneven in thickness. The stratum covered dips to the granite, and is of the same nature as that on the east side. Those who dwell on theories, should mark this fact: it is not very often that we have the opportunity of seeing what is termed the primitive rock, and the secondary rock, in contact with each other in such a state. About two hundred yards west from the above, is a very good lime rock presented eight feet thick, dipping to the north-east. Some of this rock has enclosed some pieces of granite and other stones, such as above described; I find the stretch is near a mile. At this place there is a great extent, with little or no cover upon it. This day I finished the well at Sandside.

11.—Bored for shell-marl in Loneturadal. Bored for shell-marl in the moss of Clausgoel. Bored for shell-marl in Benjamin's Moss; found presented at the wooding moss at Clashelcas, a reddish freestone rock, dipping one in four. Found in John Ivick's burn, grey granite from the top to the bottom of it; found the hills of Binroy, Kenmore, and Bengow, consist of grey granite. Bored for shell-marl at the head of Bingbrach. Bored at the sides of the Loch of Clackningill for shell-marl; the channel is composed of decomposed granite, chiefly white quartz. Found at rear of the above, the black oxyde of manganese, of considerable purity, imbedded in decomposed red granite; it is an irregular vein. Bored for shell-marl in many places in the line of the same burn, nearer to the sea.

 12.—Examined

12.—Examined the fine lime-quarry presented at Erylaive; dip north-east. This strata is a similar dip with the surface of the ground, forming a trough, as the following figure

Bored for shell-marl in Borlum's meadows and Blourisker. Found at Fresgo a vein of lead, matrix limestone.

13.—Found at Burnfield a tolerable vein of lead, stretching north and south.

16.—Found presented a brown freestone rock, dip north-east at the mill of Shurary. Found at the sides of the Loch of Shurary, small wilkes, which indicate shell-marl in the Loch. Ascended the hill of Shurary: about half way up the hill presented a fine lime-rock, dipping to the hill; the hill consists of red freestone, limestone, &c. Bored for shell-marl at Ferweelk, Blurefat and Stanelcut. The lime-rock at Achabater, eastward from the above, seems to be the same stone, and of nearly the same quality; the colour is blue, and the stretch of the hill corresponds. Bored for shell-marl at Auchnechy and Brubster, the property of Sir Robert Sinclair: found two feet thick of shell marl, and a quagmire full of it.

17.—Travelled to Rumsdale; a little before I arrived at Loch Culm, the stratified rock is presented: this, without exception, is the wildest low-lying ground I ever travelled over. As far as I can see, the surface is pretty near a level, over many thousand acres of the strongest heath I ever beheld. From the above place to Rumsdale the

the granite rock I presume is the substrata, as the sand on the tract, and channel of the Loch, is siliceous sand.

18.—Set off this morning from Rumsdale to Morven. The granite, both red and grey, abounds the whole of the way. I find the bases of Morven to be white quartz rock. Ascended the Morven on the west side, computed to be 1929 feet above the level of the sea: find the sides covered with stones of all sizes, which time alone, I believe, has torn from the mountain. I now make use of my pick hammer, to find what these stones are composed of. I find every stone I break to be what is called plum-pudding-stone. Ascended to see from the summit of the mountain the shattered remains that time has much defaced. At the top I find the rock to be the same as those stones that cover the mountain's side, as might be expected. This plum-pudding-stone is made of rounded white quartz, and rounded pieces of red granite; all is cemented together, with a brownish matter, which has some appearance of being a part of decomposed granite, &c.

I can find no spar vein, or veins of metal in this mountain. From its summit I have an extensive view over a large extent of country, the day being clear. I first turn my eye to the north-west; the dreary road I have just got over. I look to Sandside, and am surprized I can not behold the hills of Binroy, Kenmore, and Bengow. I find, from my present elevation, that these hills are level with the dreary wastes of Caithness; and nothing appears to me to deserve the name of hills, but those stupendous chains which unite Caithness and Sutherland.

I now turn gradually round from the West to the South, and behold many high mountains. I behold the Ord of Caithness as the southernmost point of my present survey. I see the Pap of Caithness, a little to the east of where I stand, and the other lesser hills. I now turn round, and at one glance see the whole of Caithness, which to my view forms a figure similar to a half moon. I see the numerous lochs (lakes) that are interspersed over the level country, much of which is uncultivated. From information that plenty of trout is to be found in these lochs, I cannot entertain a doubt, but that shell-marl must likewise abound in them.

Though much of the country I saw, lies at present in a state of nature, and totally uncultivated, yet, in process of time, much of it may be brought into culture, by the application of good husbandry, and the shell-marl with which these lochs contain.

Descending on the south-side of the mountain, continue my route down the side of a burn to a Shepherd's house. The rock is stratified, and resembles the rock at Glendoning, in the county of Dumfries, where is the antimonial mine. The strata is very much upon edge, stretching in all directions, much intersected with veins of spar. This strata is much the same all the way down the water to Oldibae.

19.—Marked out a place to make a well at Achastle. I do not think there is any great chance of success. Examined the lime-quarry a little from the bridge of Berriedale; it appears to be about ten or twelve feet thick.

I intend to plan out the way to find the crop at the surface, if time will permit. Surveyed both sides of the river of Berriedale, to its confluence with the sea: the strata in general calcareous; very hard blue and reddish, dipping to the sea.

20.—Surveyed above Trafield; the strata is much the same as the above. From thence surveyed to the Ord of

Caithness;

Caithness; found the Ord to consist chiefly of red granite, with several large veins of the spar of lime, the crystallizations is thomboid bevellio.

21.—Surveyed with a guide to Longreen; found some small buckies. Bored for shell-marl by the burn side. Surveyed to Oldibae, and found, by the side of a burn, a specimen of small grained lead. There has been a very faint scratching for copper at this place: I think there is a very good appearance of some kind of ore, most probably lead. I have annexed a sketch, to point out how this, or any other vein may be easily sought for. The stretch of the vein must be particularly observed, and taking straight lines agreeable thereto, at the extremity there must be dug to the solids a ditch, right angles to the line A, B, at the end of the straight line, which is supposed to be upon the stretch of the vein A, B, at C, is the appearance found. When these right angle ditches are dug, which D, E, and F, G, represent, and the appearance found, then it is certain that the vein extends. Then cut a small ditch from A to B, upon the vein; turn into this ditch a burn or stream of water, which will cut up the earth to the vein, and carry off all the incumbent earth that covers the vein. This is called flooding, or hushing the vein. This plan can only be effected where there is a declivity, and plenty of water above the vein.

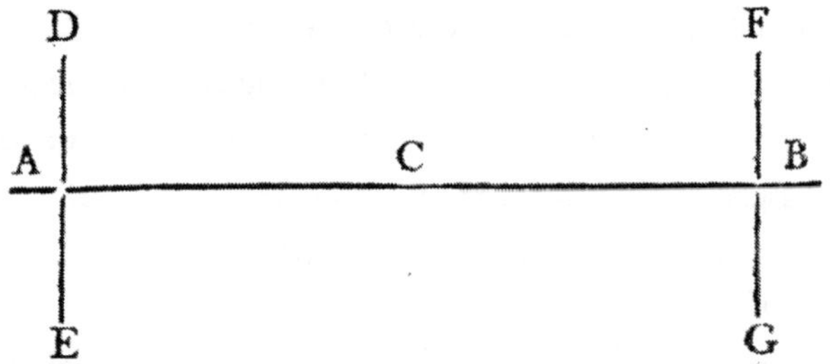

Surveyed down the water of Berriedale: found at Ionel rock, a plum-pudding-stone similar to what has been already

ready described; this stone is overlapping the strata, which strata is similar to that described at the confluence within the sea, below the bridge of Berriedale. I could not observe any stratification in the plum-pudding-stone, but found in many places large blocks of it lying upon the solid mass. This plum-pudding-stone appears upon all the hills in this place in blocks, &c.

23.—Went with Mr. Morison to survey the lime-rock at the foot of the old castle; found it dip south-east. This strata appears to be the same as that described in the 19th instant; only it is by a large dyke depressed below the line of elevation. This owes its situation to the same cause, namely, the dykes and slips at this place, which has distorted and divided the strata very much. The three places where the strata is found, are not three different stratas, but one strata, about nine feet thick. The above rock is good in quality, but great care must be taken in sorting this stone for burning, as it differs much in quality. Some of it requires more fire and more time to burn it than others; except this precaution be taken, great part of it will be unburnt.

I have marked out the most likely place to find this rock near the New Inver.

I have marked out a place for a new well to be made near the same place.

Bored for marl near Lowndow, at Achnacraig. The red granite comes in contact with the secondary strata; here only I have found the blue whinstone, and stratified stone in contact with each other.

The red granite appears to be the basis of the whin, and the whin to be the basis of a blue marlish strata. The summit of the Ord, and northward, is composed of a plum-pudding-stone; its chief component parts are red granite, and must be of a later formation. It appears to

be

be made up from the destruction of granite and other earths of a previous formation; it is much harder when in contact with each other than at a little distance.

24.—Waited the most part of this day for a boat to carry me round the rock of Berriedale, but no boat could set out, for the violent surge upon the sea. I then set off for Latheron, the property of Mr. Traill.

25.—Surveyed up the burn of Latheron, and thence to the barns, and found a fine lime-rock, presented dipping north-east. Found the lime-quarry above the house dipping one in five, and thickness from three to four feet. Surveyed from the march on the estate of John Campbell Sutherland Esq. of Forse, to the march on the estate of Sir Benjamin Dunbar, of Hempriggs, Bart. Here I found a very large dyke made up, and consisting of a heterogeneous mass, chiefly indurated brown clay, intermixed with rounded argillaceous stones, with spar veins of lime intersecting each other. In one of these veins I found a small vein of lead. This dyke stretches north-west and south-east; the strata in contact with the dyke, and by the coast is bluish and brown colour, dips south-west, and is calcareous.

26.—Dimbrey. Bored and sunk for limestone, and found a similar limestone to that stone which covers the lime rock at the farm-house. I advise a farther trial to be made at this place; the dips south-east one in two. Surveyed up this burn for limestone; the dip is south-east. Bored for shell-marl in Bigbaine Gallic of Benlore.

27.—Set off this morning from Latheron: Called upon Mr. Sutherland of Forse; thence to Clyth, the property of Sir John Sinclair. Mr. Henderson sent a guide with me to the several places I had to survey. Came to Rigou; found a large vein of the sulphat of barytes. This vein I consider as worthy the particular notice of any

any mining company that may be established in Caithness. A burn of water may be conveniently got to flood or hush away the incumbent earth that covers the spar; the water may be directed as in page 89. The above vein stretches north-east. On the coast, a little from this, found a fine lime-rock two feet thick, dipping south-west. The strata here in general is calcareous, thick, and of a blue colour, dipping to the south-west from one in three to one in seven, in general very regular.

28.—Set out from Clyth to Ulbster; went from Ulbster to Thrumster; found a lime-quarry, the rock dipping north-west one in four. This rock has the appearance of the lime-rock at Latheron. The roof and thickness are much the same.

30.—At Borrowston found a lime-quarry dipping north-west one in three and a half; thickness five feet, colour blue. Bored for shell-marl in the meadows and below Thrumster; found shell-marl and moss in a mixed state, of no great extent. Bored for shell-marl at Ulliquay. Bored for shell-marl at the Loch of Yarrows. Bored for shell-marl at the Loch of Buckego, and found, as computed, about 30 or 40 acres of shell-marl. I found a large vein of the spar of lime on the side of the above Loch. Up the lime-burn, found another large vein of the spar of lime, and some quagmires; some of it, from exposure to the air, petrified.

From this I surveyed to the farm of Major Innes at Tannach: the strata is much the same kind as that on the coast in that neighbourhood, hard, thick, calcareous and of a blue colour. At Tuonbeck found a slate-quarry, similar to that in the neighbourhood of Westfield.

31.—Set out this morning to survey the coast-side, near Ulbster: found the strata dipping in general north-west, one in two. Confining our route eastward, nearly

opposite

opposite the house of Ulbster, found a good vein of the sulphat of barytes, some places nearly three feet thick, stretching south-west and north-east.

From this place went with Mr. Brodie to ascertain the extent of shell-marl in the Loch of Buckego: bored in many places, and found shell-marl fourteen and sixteen feet thick. Bored near the house of Ulbster, and found marl.

September 1.—Bored this morning near the house of Ulbster, to ascertain the quantity of shell-marl discovered last night, and found it to be five and six feet thick. The extent is computed to be four or five acres. This moss was three times bored before, but no marl found.

Set off with Mr. Brodie to East-Clyth, to bore for shell-marl; from thence to Middle-Clyth: bored for shell-marl, and found at Warse three and a half feet thick. Bored for shell-marl at West-Clyth.

8.—Set off for Bilbster, the estate of Mr. Sinclair of Forss.

9.—Surveyed the burn of Bilbster, and found a very large dyke, composed of the spar of lime, intermixed with martial pyrites, and some crystals of lead. Bored for shell-marl in the moss in the Dam Park. Bored on the north side of the water of Wick, on the hill of Reagh, to ascertain the depth of moss above the good soil; and the depth of the soil from thence to the water of Wick, to search for a foundation for a new bridge. Found the rock; it is a bastard limestone, &c.

10.—Bored for a stone quarry at Nether Bilbster; found a quick-sand in the bore, with a spring of water. Bored for marl in Huberston mire.

11.—Employed this day in going over the grounds I have been exploring for the last two days.

13.—Set

13.—Set off this morning for Keiss, the property of Sir John Sinclair, by the way of Hopeville, the property of Mr. Brodie. Bored for shell-marl in the Fudyess; the rock dips south and south-west one in three; the strata consist of a hard calcareous freestone; soft blue slate, and some coal blue, &c. Near to the water of Wick, on the above farm, is bituminated blues. From thence proceeded to Keiss, and surveyed by the coast to the house: found the strata in general very hard, dipping south-east, south-west, and to the north; it consists of a bluish and reddish calcareous freestone. Found by the coast, east from the house, some veins of the spar of lime.

14.—Bored a little above the house of Keiss, and ascertained the quantity of quagmire shell-marl; some of it is petrified by exposure to the air; the quantity is not very considerable. Bored in many places in the large Moss of Keiss, for shell-marl, and found three feet thick of shell-marl. The above is about one mile from the house of Keiss. About a mile and a half farther, towards Mr. Sinclair of Barrock's estate, bored for shell-marl, and found two feet thick. Near this place is a large quagmire of shell-marl, and several smaller ones.

15.—Surveyed down the burn of Freswick: found the bank of the burn to be clay-marl, mixed with marine shells. At the house the strata dip north-east. Met with George Brodie, grieve at Lochend, who conducted me to Huna. Found at the commencement of Duncansbay the strata dipping north-east. Farther on, to John O' Groat's house, found the dip south-east, in general much distorted, and consisting of hard freestone, blue bastard limestone, and red calcareous stone, very hard. Here the marine shells are in great plenty.

16.—Began this morning at John O'Groat's house: found the strata chiefly of a reddish calcareous freestone.

At

At turning the point, found a rock of porphyry, from which I got some pebbles. From this to Duncansbay the strata dip east and north-west. Here also the strata are much distorted, and in some places nearly on edge. To the southernmost side of Duncansbay, found the strata dipping south-west, consisting chiefly of blue bastard limestone. Bored for marl in the moss of Duncansbay. Turning round the Head, the strata seem to be much the same as the above. Near the rock of Duncansbay, the strata are mostly red, and dip north-west. From this to Fasgow, I find a large vein of the spar of lime intermixed with iron ore. The vein stretches east and west.

Set out this morning from Huna to Wisegore. Bored for marl on the way to John O'Groat's house. Left Wisegore, and returned north; bored in several places, and found a thin stratum of limestone at Stempster. Set off for Lochend, and bored for marl at the farm of Warse.

18.—Bored for shell-marl at Lochend, above the Loch of Syster. Found bastard limestone at the edge, dipping north-east. Bored in Collin's moss in many places for marl; from thence to the moss of Cures, bored for marl. Found in the red bog a small quantity of shell-marl, not very good. From thence to the hills of Greenland bored for marl. From thence to the moss south from the house bored for marl. Bored for marl in the park of Powshaw, and found one foot thick of good shell-marl. Bored for marl in the moss of Wassance, and found 15 inches thick of good shell-marl; some of it is uncovered. Went round and down the north-east side of the Loch Halagh; found small shells, which give a good prospect of shell-marl being in the Loch. Found the strata much the same at Syster, dipping also to the north-east.

21.—Set

21.—Set off from Mey, the property of the Earl of Caithness, to the burn of Leaster: bored for shell-marl; found in one place four and a half feet thick; in another two feet six inches thick. Bored for shell-marl above the house of Leaster; found from six to fifteen inches of shell-marl in several places.

22.—Bored for shell-marl in the common above Scotlands-Haven; found four feet thick in one place. Surveyed the East Burn of Gills: found limestone in two places, about nine inches thick, of a blue colour. Bored for shell-marl in the moss and morasses, of great extent, on the way to the hill of Rigoyboll. Bored for shell-marl between Milster and Brabster. Bored for shell-marl in Crakestear.

23.—Returned to the above place, and bored for shell-marl. Bored for shell-marl in many places in the Black Girne. Returned by Holland Mey. Bored for shell-marl in several places. Bored for shell-marl in the white moss, not of great extent.

24.—Explored the rocks from the Broad Haven of Mey: the general depth found to be south-east, one in three, and in some places one in seven; the strata is very hard in general; it all effervesces with acids; is of a bluish colour eastward for more than a mile, and of a reddish colour. Near this place found blue limestone in several places, not exceeding ten inches thick, of a good quality; a good deal of it is lying bare within sea-mark. Bored for shell-marl in the moss of Mey: the shell-sand is of great plenty. East from Barrogil Castle, within sea-mark, is presented bituminated black strata; it burns to a white slate; it is often found in the coal-field, and is worked as one of the concomitants of coal. The strata in general at Mey, however, is not flattering for coal.

25.—Bored

25.—Bored for marl west from the castle, and found four feet thick of it, the extent not great.

27.—Set off this morning for Ratter, the property of Mr. Traill. Surveyed some of the rocks on the coast; found the dip south-east in general; from Ham westward, found two large dykes, one of them wholly composed of reddish common freestone in a mass, not in the least stratified. Found at Scarvill a vein of lime.

28.—Surveyed eastward by the coast, as far as the march with the Mey estate; in general, found the strata in great confusion, and much upon edge, consisting of thick and thin strata, some places bluish, and at others of a brownish red colour. Bored for shell-marl in the broad lane, as far as Gotisloft.

29.—Surveyed Mr. Traill's property at Greenland. At Loch Park found a vein of lead stretching north-west and south-east; the matrix is an argillaceous earth-stone, which by exposure to the air for a short time decomposes, and moulders down to a reddish brown earth, similar to the rocks at Lead Hills, where they are in contact with the lead. I would recommend this place for a particular investigation. Bored for shell-marl in the Stoups of Reister, and found one foot thick of it in the above field. Examined a lime-quarry, consisting of two strata, three and a half feet thick, dip north-east. Bored for shell-marl in Reister Park, and found it in one place three feet thick. Bored for shell-marl in the black moss of Haster. Bored for shell-marl over all the moss of Reister, and along the south side of the burn, as far as the Loch of Atterwall. Bored for shell-marl in Meersay Moss, and also in the meadows below.

30.—Bored for shell-marl in the Loch of Duren, and ascertained it to be in some places fifteen feet thick.

October 1.—Explored the above, which is computed to be thirty or forty acres of shell-marl, varying in thickness from the above to the thickness of two feet. Bored for shell-marl in Dreys moss, and found eight and nine feet thick over many acres. Bored in the moss of Wester for shell-marl, and found it three feet thick. Bored for shell-marl in the moss of Tain.

2.—Bored for limestone in the Park of Rothy Myre, and found some thin strata of limestone, which freely slackened when burned.

4.—Was directed to attend to-morrow at Thurso Castle, to get directions for the survey of both sides of the river of Thurso, &c.

5.—Attended at Thurso Castle, and was desired to attend to-morrow at Thurso, to receive the necessary directions, and to attend Mr. Forbes in searching for clay, to make bricks, tiles, and pottery ware.

6.—This morning was directed to survey with Mr. Forbes for clay, &c. Explored up the west side of the river Thurso; from thence to the Dam of Ormly, and bored for clay. Found shell-marl. Explored down to Scrabster: found clay in the burn, fit for common brick.

7.—Set out this morning for Geise. Bored for shell-marl in the Dam of Geise; ascertained in one place seven feet thick of it; the extent small. Bored for shell-marl up the burn of Geise, and found two feet thick of shell-marl. Bored for shell-marl in the moss of Geise. Surveyed the strata up the burn of Geise; the strata is much the same as the strata in the Crown Lands of Scrabster, namely, coal, metals, &c. dip south-east, all regular. Surveyed southward to Buckies, and bored for shell-marl in some places along the side of the hill. Examined the quarry at Buckies, which I think will turn out a good slate quarry; the slate is much the same kind as is common in many places in the low parts of Caithness. These slates are argillaceous, mixed with bitumen, which gives them the blue colour; but by exposure to the air the bitumen is volatilized, and the slate appears grey. The only cement or menstruum that preserves it from decomposition is calcareous. This ingredient also in the course of twenty or thirty years, is gradually decomposed, according as the fixed air is repelled by the action of the sun's rays. Although there is no slate in Caithness like the Eisdale slate, yet that of Caithness will be preferred to tile, for common use, as they can be had much cheaper than tile, and their durability is at least equal to the best tile. Dip south-east one in seven. A little east from the above bored for shell-marl: found a fine blue clay three and a half feet thick. South from this bored at a mill dam for clay. Surveyed down the river of Thurso to Geise: found blue clay-marl intermixed with marine shells, in great abundance.

8.—This morning surveyed from Aimster, up the river Thurso, half a mile. On the west side, found a yellowish clay, fit for bricks or tile, three feet thick. Surveyed upwards to Gerston. Surveyed the ditches: found blaes and bituminated slate. Surveyed the burn of Sixpenny; found some veins of the sulphat of barytes, and some small veins of the spar of lime, all of which are favourable for ores. From this went to the Castle of Brawll, and surveyed up the water to Gerston. Bored for clay at the bridge-end of Halkirk: the strata is much the same as it is in the burn of Geise, but much intermixed with veins of spar of lime. Dip south-east; the lime-rock at Gerston is from ten to twelve inches of good quality.

9.—Bored for marl in the Suchans of Gerston, and found one foot thick of shell-marl. Set off to Dale, on the south side of the river of Thurso. The flood is so considerable I cannot see the bed of the river.

12.—Set off this morning to Dalemore. Bored for shell-marl in the Grass Park; found it in one of the quagmires, but of no great extent. Bored for shell-marl in the Horse-Park. Surveyed by the side of the river, and found blue clay marl in great plenty, intermixed with marine shells, such as those at Geise. This place is supposed to be about twenty miles from the sea; and is one instance among many in Caithness, of the ocean's covering the inland country at some former period of time. Examined the lime rock of Cattach; found it in contact with a red granite rock on the north side of the lime rock, and in contact with the strata on the south side of it. It appears to be a lime-stone dyke without stratifications, stretching east and west. The best plan to find this rock to the east and west, is to follow the plan as in page 89, for finding the vein of lead. The lime rock is of very good quality; the strata in contact, but much intersected with spar veins, which will make it ill to work with; it is calcareous, dipping to the north. This place is said to be nearly the centre of the county. The above rock is very well worth a proper kiln, as there is plenty of peats to burn the stone.

12.—Set out this morning from Dale. Bored for marl in the lower parts of Harpsdale. Came to Halkirk, by the water side; found clay marl in several places, with marine shells as above intermixed. From Halkirk surveyed down to Thurso, on the south-east side of the river; found in some places good clay for brick or tile.

13.—Set off this morning to Auchingils. Explored the moss for marl. Bored in one place, and found shell-marl twelve feet thick. The greatest part of this shell-marl lies on the south-west side of the moss, the general thickness of the marl is from four to eight feet. Bored for shell-marl in the moss of Wydale: found from one to two feet thick, of inferior quality, and of small extent. Bored for shell-marl at the dam of Stainland; found it two feet thick; the extent is small, and quality inferior.

14.—Explored the clay I discovered yesterday near Mr. Campbell's farm of Carsgo, and found the clay to extend 100 yards along the river, and 100 yards right angles with the river. A little below the above bored, and found the yellowish blue clay extend down the river about 100 yards, and right angles to the river, about 30 yards. Found clay like the above in the ditch nearer to Mr. Campbell's, but of little extent.

15.—Set off this morning to explore the north-west side of the river: bored in many places opposite to the clay on the other side of the river: bored more to the house on the side of the river at Skinnet. On the north side of the house found fine blue clay from four to two feet thick, the extent seems to be about four or five acres.

16.—Set off this morning to follow out the clay discovered yesterday. Bored for it in many places, and found it in them all, down by the river for more than a mile, and particularly at Thurstan, where I found it greater in thickness; in one place it is six feet thick; the extent several acres.

18.—Set off this morning for Banniskirk. Bored for shell-marl on the east side of Spittle-house, by Knockloughby; found it in a quagmire. Bored for shell-marl, in Blacklass moss; in one place found it one foot thick. Bored for shell-marl in several small marshes in Lock Backless; found in one place, shell-marl seven inches thick. Bored for shell-marl in the Houstry of Dun, and found a little. Saw the quarry at which a fine vein of lead was

 found:

found: the lead in one place was four inches thick. I was sorry I could not, owing to water, explore any farther in it; the matrix is a similar rock to that already described at Greenland, with this difference, that it does not decompose by being exposed to the air; it is bluish in colour, &c. stretching south-east and north-west. This is certainly a vein that deserves investigation by a mining company. Bored for shell-marl in North Dun: found shell-marl eight feet depth. Bored for shell-marl in another moss in North Dun, and found it one foot thick.

19.—Bored and explored the Loch of Stempster, the joint property of Col. Williamson and Mr. Henderson of Stempster. In one place bored in shell-marl fifteen feet thick, and was not at the bottom of the shell-marl, as the boat would not bear the weight of drawing up the irons. Bored in all places, through and through the Loch, and on the sides of it found the shell-marl vary in thickness, covering an extent of surface computed at 200 acres, except about twenty acres in the Loch which is rocky, with very little marl on it. The medium thickness of this inexhaustible source of shell-marl may safely be computed at six feet depth.

21.—Set out this morning for Lynigar, the property of Mrs. M'Leod. Surveyed the north side of the Loch partly belonging to the estate of Lynigar: found some blocks of limestone, which it is probable were driven from a stratum of limestone seen within water-mark in dry weather. Unless I saw the lie of the stratum, I can give no direction where it may be found in the land. This Loch, in my opinion, contains shell-marl, as the small fresh-water shells, or *Buckies*, are in great plenty on the shore of the Loch.

22.—Bored

22.—Bored for shell-marl in the Girne of Lynigar, and found five feet thick of shell-marl. Bored for shell-marl in the white moss.

23.—Went to Holburnhead: searched for limestone, and found some thin stratums near the head.

25.—Set out this morning from the Castle of Dunbeath, and surveyed the shore. Found at Postosmance a large vein of calcareous spar, stretching south-east and north-west, nearly in the direction where I found the vein of lead on the Latheron estate by the shore. Surveyed up the burn by Leid Hay, from thence to Achavioll, at the upper end of which found a limestone dyke in contact with a whinstone ridge, stretching north-west and south-east. A little distance eastward from this, found a thin stratum of limestone: both the dyke and the thin stratum seem of good quality.

From this proceeded to Badnagow, and to the burn of Growdary: here the strata dip in all directions, and some of it are coal-metals. Proceeding down the burn, found a little of the black oxyde of manganese. The banks of the burn downwards, consist of a blue clay-marl, intermixed with marine shells. From the burn along the north-side of the river to the sea, dip north-east is blue, and effervesces with acids. Surveyed the south side upwards to Miltown, and from thence by Balacastle: here the strata are very regular, dipping to the sea. From this to Ramscraigs, and the burn of Borgea, the strata are much the same as the above. From thence to the Castle, by the sea bank, the strata are in many places much distorted, and chiefly of a reddish colour. The rock is steep, and there is no access.

Set out this morning to Bednagree, and from thence to the top of the burn. Bored for marl at Houstrey: the dip of the strata is north-east, in many places much distorted.

 From

From thence crossed the hill to the burn of Brackachy, the hills of which consist of a plum-pudding-stone, similar to that of Morven. Bored for marl in the quay, and thence returned by Redfairn, boring for marl on the way to the Castle.

30.—Went this morning with Mr. Manson to Buckies. Mr. Davidson accompanied us to see the place where I found the clay. I pointed out to them the places described in pages 101, and 102. Their joint computation was ten acres of clay.

November 3.—Set out this day for Ackergill, to bore for shell-marl.

4.—Arrived at Ackergill this morning, and was directed to the moss, where a person I had employed had gone before, to bore for shell-marl. Bored, and ascertained a small quantity of shell-marl: at one place four feet thick.

5.—Set out this morning from the Manse of Bower, to sail on board a sloop, (The Fisher), for Leith, but could not sail for contrary winds, until the 10th.

It is impossible for me to accurately state the enormous quantity of shell-marl that I have found in the county of Caithness, but I think it may safely be relied upon, that not less than the surface extent of four hundred acres is discovered. The limestone is also in great quantities. Of lead I have discovered five veins, besides the veins formerly known; of black oxyde of manganese two veins; of zinc one vein; and many good appearances of ores, in the course of my Survey.

No. VI.

No. VI.

The Sheep-Shearing Festival held on the 1st July, 1791.

As this was the origin of the Sheep-shearing Festivals, which have since promoted such a spirit of improvement in the country, it was thought proper to preserve an account of it in this Appendix.

A Sheep-shearing Festival was held at Newhall's Inn, on Friday, the 1st July, 1791. About 50 ladies and 70 gentlemen of rank and distinction were present, who were received, as they arrived, by Sir John Sinclair, the Chairman of the Society for the Improvement of British Wool. The company began to assemble about one o'clock, and were conducted to a grass plot, in a garden belonging to Mr. Dundas of Duddingston, adjoining to the inn. In the centre of the green, a pole was erected, with cross branches, on which were suspended specimens of various kinds of wool; and in particular some dressed skins of the Shetland breed of sheep, with the wool adhering, which were greatly admired. Latin inscriptions, appeared on a tablet fixed at the top of the pole, applicable to the occasion of the meeting. There were sheep of various breeds and countries collected in the garden, and on the neighbouring banks, viz. Spanish, English, Scots, and Shetland; and to add to this groupe, Mr. Dundas of Dundas, sent there some sheep from Abyssinia. The sheep-shearing began about two o'clock, and the dexterity and neatness with which Mr. Cully's clipper performed, was much praised. The wool of the various breeds was exhibited with labels denoting the kind, and peculiarities of its

texture.

texture. During the sheep-shearing a band of music attended, and played a great variety of favourite Scots airs adapted to the occasion.

The Ladies were in general dressed in white muslin, with flowers, and various coloured ribbons; and each bore a Shepherdess's Crook, decorated with taste and fancy. The day being favourable, the appearance on the green, of so much beauty and elegance, afforded a spectacle at once pleasing and interesting. And here none was more distinguished than the venerable patriotic Countess Dowager of Dundonald, whose hat was decorated with a bandeau of wool from her own flock, and dyed by herself of various beautiful vivid colours, which had a fine effect. Several of the Gentlemen were presented by her Ladyhsip with cockades, and other ornaments of this material. The Gentlemen were dressed variously, as taste and fancy suggested. Some of them appeared in cloth made from their own flocks, with crooks on their buttons, &c. and some of the Ladies in gowns of their own spinning.

A little after four o'clock the company left the garden, and sat down to an elegant entertainment in a large room adjoining to the inn. The first toast given by Sir John Sinclair, the President, or Chairman, was, "*The Royal Shepherd of Great Britain, and success to his Flock.*" A signal was then made to the Hind Frigate, which lay at anchor at a little distance, and a round of 21 guns was fired in honour of so popular a sentiment. A number of other loyal and patriotic toasts were afterwards given, and the *amor patriæ* appeared to glow so much in every breast, that no assemblage could have exhibited more harmony and happiness than appeared on this occasion. After tea and coffee, the ball was opened by the Countess of Hope-

toun

toun and Sir John Sinclair, and continued till near twelve, when the company separated, highly pleased with the day's entertainment.

Their country is much indebted to the Noblemen and Gentlemen who have established a Society for promoting such important objects; and, in this instance of the Festival, they have pleasantly united the *dulce cum utile*.

It is impossible to give the names of all the respectable and distinguished characters who were present upon the occasion; but we may mention a few, viz. the Marquis of Huntly, the Earls of Morton and Buchan, the Dowager Countess of Dundonald, Earl and Countess of Hopetoun, Lady Hopes, Lord and Lady Elibank, Lord Macdonald, and the Hon. Mr. Macdonald, the Hon. Capt. and Mrs. Cochrane, Hon. Capt. and Mrs. Napier, Mr. Heron, Lady Elizabeth Heron, Hon. Lieut. Murray, the Lord Chief Baron, his Lady and family, the Lord Provost of Edinburgh, Sir Thomas Blackett and family, Sir Gilbert Elliot, Sir John Inglis and family, Sir Michael Malcolm, Sir John Henderson, Sir James and Lady Foulis, Sir William Ramsay, Sir John and Lady Sinclair, Lady Clerk, Mark Pringle, Esq. M. P. Mr. and Mrs. Belsches, Capt. and Mrs. Mackay, Mr. Ramsay of Barnton, Mr. Bruce of Kinnaird, Mr. Askew of Pallinsburn, &c.

Sir Thomas Blackett, Mr. Askew, &c. came from England to attend this memorable Festival, which gave universal satisfaction to those who had the pleasure of attending it.

No. VII.

No. VII.

Letters regarding the Mermaid which was seen on the Coast of Caithness, in North Britain, Anno 1809, and one seen on the same Coast some years preceding.

FROM MISS. MACKAY, DAUGHTER OF THE REV. DAVID MACKAY, MINISTER OF REAY, TO MRS. INNES, DOWAGER OF SANDSIDE.

Reay Manse, May 25th, 1809.

MADAM,

To establish the truth of what has been hitherto considered improbable and fabulous, must be at all times a difficult task, and I have not the vanity to think, that my testimony alone would be sufficient for this purpose; but when to this is added that of four others, I hope it will have some effect in removing the doubts of those who may suppose that the wonderful appearance, I reported having seen in the sea on the 12th of January, was not a Mermaid, but some other uncommon, though less remarkable inhabitant of the deep.

As I would willingly contribute to remove the doubts of the sceptical on this subject, I beg leave to state to you the following account, after premising that my cousin, whose name is affixed along with mine, was one of the four witnesses, who beheld, with me, this uncommon spectacle.

While she and I were walking by the sea-shore on the 12th of January, about noon, our attention was attracted by seeing three people, who were at some distance, showing signs of terror and astonishment at something they saw in the water. On approaching them, we discovered that the object of their wonder, was a face resembling

sembling the human countenance, which appeared floating on the waves: at that time nothing but the face was visible:—it may not be improper to observe before I proceed, that the face, throat and arms, are all I can attempt to describe; all our endeavours to discover the appearance and position of the body being unavailing. The sea at that time ran very high, and as the waves advanced, the Mermaid gently sunk under them, and afterwards reappeared. The face seemed plump and round, the eyes and nose were small, the former were of a light grey colour, and the mouth was large; from the shape of the jaw bone, which seemed straight, the face looked short; as to the inside of the mouth I can say nothing, not having attended to it, though sometimes open. The forehead, nose, and chin, were white; the whole side face of a bright pink colour. The head was exceedingly round, the hair thick and long, of a green and oily cast, and appeared troublesome to it, the waves generally throwing it down over the face; it seemed to feel the annoyance, and as the waves retreated, with both its hands frequently threw back the hair and rubbed its throat, as if to remove any soiling it might have received from it. The throat was slender, smooth, and white; we did not think of observing whether it had elbows, but from the manner in which it used its arms, I must conclude that it had. The arms were long and slender, as were the hands and fingers: the latter were not webbed. The arms, (one of them at least), were frequently extended over its head, as if to frighten a bird that hovered over it, and seemed to distress it much. When this had no effect, it sometimes turned quite round several times successively. At a little distance we observed a seal. It sometimes laid its right hand under its cheek, and in this position floated for some time. We saw nothing like

hair

hair or scales on any part of it; indeed the smoothness of the skin particularly caught our attention.

The time it was discernible to us was about an hour. The sun was shining clearly at the time. It was from us a few yards only.

These are the few observations made by us during the appearance made by this phenomenon. If they afford you any satisfaction, I shall be particularly happy. I have stated nothing but what I clearly recollect. As my Cousin and I had frequently, previous to this period, combated an assertion which is very common among the lower class here, that Mermaids had been frequently seen on this coast, our evidence cannot be thought biassed by any former prejudice in favour of the existence of this wonderful creature.

To contribute in any degree to your pleasure or amusement, will add to the happiness of,

MADAM,

Your greatly obliged

(Signed) ELIZA MACKAY.
C. MACKENZIE.

Letter from Mr. William Munro, Schoolmaster of Thurso, to Dr. Torrence, regarding a Mermaid seen by him some years preceding.

Thurso, 9th June, 1809.

DEAR SIR,

Your queries respecting the Mermaid are before me. From the general scepticism which prevails among the learned and intelligent, about the existence of such a phenomenon, had not your character, and real desire for investigation, been too well known to me, for supposing that

you

you wished to have a fertile imagination indulged by a subject of merriment, I would have been disposed to have concluded, that in this instance, you aimed at being ranked among the laughing philosophers at my expense. Sensible, however, that this is not the case, and taking it for granted that you are sincere, I shall endeavour to answer your queries, though there is little probability that any testimony which I can give respecting the Mermaid, will operate towards convincing those, who have not been hitherto convinced by repeated testimonies adduced in support of the existence of such an appearance.

About twelve years ago, when I was Parochial Schoolmaster at Reay, in the course of my walking on the shore of Sandside-bay, being a fine warm day in summer, I was induced to extend my walk towards Sandside-head, when my attention was arrested by the appearance of a figure resembling an unclothed female, sitting upon a rock extended into the sea, and apparently in the action of combing its hair, which flowed around its shoulders, and of a light brown colour. The resemblance which the figure bore to its Prototype, in all its visible parts, was so striking, that had not the rock on which it was sitting been dangerous for bathing, I would have been constrained to have regarded it as really an human form, and to any eye unaccustomed to the situation, it must have undoubtedly appeared as such.

The head was covered with hair, of the colour above mentioned, and shaded on the crown. The forehead round, the face plump, the cheeks ruddy; the eyes blue, the mouth and lips of a natural form, resembling those of a man; the teeth I could not discover, as the mouth was shut. The breasts and abdomen, the arms and fingers, of the size of a full grown body of the human species. The fingers, from the action in which the hands were employed,

ployed, did not appear to be webbed; but as to this I am not positive.

It remained on the rock three or four minutes after I observed it, and was exercised during that period in combing its hair, which was long and thick, and of which it seemed proud; and then dropped into the sea, which was level with the abdomen, from whence it did not reappear to me.

I had a distinct view of its features, being at no great distance, on an eminence above the rock on which it was sitting, and the sun brightly shining. Immediately before its getting into its natural element, it seemed to have observed me, as the eyes were directed towards the eminence on which I stood.

It may be necessary to remark, that previous to the period I beheld this object, I had heard it reported frequently by several persons, and some of them persons whose veracity I never heard disputed, that they had seen such a phenomenon as I have described, though then, like many others, I was not disposed to credit their testimonies on this subject. I can say of a truth, that it was only by seeing the phenomenon, I was fully convinced of its existence.

If the above narrative can in any degree be subservient towards establishing the existence of a phenomenon, hitherto almost incredible to naturalists, or to remove the scepticism of others, who are ready to dispute every thing which they cannot fully comprehend, you are welcome to it from,

DEAR SIR,

Your much obliged and humble Servant,

(Signed) WILLIAM MUNRO.

To Dr. Torrence, Thurso.

It

It was thought proper to preserve these letters, in this Appendix, as they regard a curious subject in Natural History. The existence of Mermaids is largely treated of, in a book entitled "Telliamed, ou Entretiens d'un Philosophe Indien," par M. de Maillet, in 2 vols. 8vo. printed anno 1755, vol. 2, p. 181; also in the Works of George Waldron, Gent. 1 vol. folio, printed in 1731, in a description which he gives of the Isle of Man—p. 160, &c.

No. VIII.

Account of the Island of Stroma, the Pentland Frith, and Pentland Skerries.

[From the Statistical Account of Scotland, vol. 8, p. 164.]

THE island of Stroma is situated in the Pentland Frith, about a league from the shore of Cannisbay. It is a mile long, and half a mile in breadth. It contains 30 families, 97 females and 73 males, and rents at about 120*l.* sterling *per annum.* It is very productive in corn; but the inhabitants are obliged to supply themselves with fuel, from the mosses on the main land. The tenth sheaf was heretofore taken in part payment of the rent. This, with all other customs and services, has of late been converted, by the present proprietor, at the desire of the people, into money. There are few discriminating features in the character of the Stromareans from the other inhabitants of the parish. They speak the same language, wear the same apparel, and observe the same customs. The sea is one of their principal sources of support. They are dabbling in salt water from their childhood upwards. From their political situation, and the simplicity, sobriety and industry natural to them, there are perhaps, few islanders on earth happier than those of Stroma. They have a Society School in the island, and they come very regularly by sea to church, when the weather allows them to cross the Sound.

On the west of the island, there is a vast cavern, (or *Glupe*, as it is called,) at about 30 yards from the beach. It stretches down to a level with the sea, whose waves are seen pouring into it, by a narrow opening at the bottom. The sea is often exceedingly tempestuous, around the island, in the winter months. The coast on the west is exceedingly bold. The tremendous elevation of the billows, that beat against it during a storm, from that quarter, exceeds all power of description. Although the rocks are only inferior to those of Duncansbay Head, the spray is tossed above their loftiest summits, and falls in such profusion, as to run in rills to the opposite shore. A reservoir, in a commodious situation, is made to receive it, together with the rain which the clouds impart; and hence, a mill is kept going in the winter months, for grinding the grain of the island. The agitation of the spray is often so great, that the water in the spring wells becomes brakish, and a salt taste prevails in the air. The tide is supposed to rise to the height of six fathoms from the lowest ebb. During a storm from the west, the rise of the sea, on that side, is more than two fathoms higher, than on the east of the island. From the antiseptic influence of the salt particles, perpetually floating in the air, mummies were preserved for a great period of years, and were wont to be exhibited as curiosities, in a chapel situated in the island. The mummies are now destroyed, and the chapel is unroofed and mouldering into ruin.

Pentland

Pentland Frith, and Skerries.—The Pentland Frith is reckoned 24 miles in length, and varies from 4 to 5 leagues in breadth. It has the Orkney Isles on the N. and the coasts of Caithness on the S., and forms a communication between the German and the Atlantic Oceans. In the mouth of the Frith, and nearly half way between Duncansbay Head and the Orkneys, are situated the Pentland *Skerries.* These are two small uninhabited islands, the one considerably larger than the other, and stretching a little eastward of Duncansbay Head, the island of Stroma lying about two leagues to the west. The parts of the frith, most dangerous to navigation, are two currents, stretching from Duncansbay Head and St. John's Head, to a considerable distance from land. The former is called the *Boars of Duncansbay*, and the latter, the *Main of Mey.* The billows in them are often swollen to a monstrous size, even in the finest summer day. They seem to arise from the collision of the tides in opposite directions, and recoiling with increased impetuosity from the head-lands above mentioned.—Without the aid of skilful pilotage, they are hazardous even in the calmest weather. The tides in every part of the frith are various and irregular, and of course, the navigation dangerous, especially in the night, where a very small deviation from the proper course may be attended with fatal consequences.

No. IX.

Account of John O'Groat's House.

[From the Statistical Account of Scotland, vol. 8, p. 167.]

It may be proper to give an account of the most memorable place in the parish of Cannisbay, which has often been visited, by travellers from very distant countries, who, it is believed, have rarely been made acquainted with the peculiar circumstance, which first gave rise to its celebrity; its fame having been in general erroneously attributed, to its mere local situation, at the northern extremity of the island; whereas, it originated in an event not unpleasing to relate, and which furnishes a useful lesson of morality.

In the reign of James IV. of Scotland, *Malcolm*, *Gavin*, and *John de Groat*, (supposed to have been brothers, and originally from Holland), arrived in Caithness, from the south of Scotland, bringing with them, a letter written in Latin, by that prince, recommending them to the countenance and protection of his loving subjects, in the county of Caithness. They purchased, or got possession of, the lands of Warse and Duncansbay, lying in the parish of Cannisbay, on the side of the Pentland Frith; and each of them obtained an equal share of the property they acquired. In process of time, their families increased, and there came to be eight different proprietors of the name of *Groat*, who possessed these lands amongst them; but, whether the three original settlers split their property among their children, or whether they purchased for them, small possessions from one another, does not appear.

These eight families, having lived peaceably and comfortably in their small possessions, for a number of years, established an annual meeting, to celebrate the anniver-

sary

sary of the arrival of their ancestors on that coast. In the course of their festivity, on one of these occasions, a question arose, respecting the right of taking the door, and sitting at the head of the table, and such like points of precedency, (each contending for the seniority and chieftainship of the clan), which increased to a height, that would probably have proved fatal in its consequences to some, if not to all of them, had not John de Groat, who was proprietor of the ferry, interposed. He having acquired more knowledge of mankind, by his constant intercourse with strangers passing the Pentland Frith, saw the danger of such disputes; and having had address enough to procure silence, he began with expatiating on the comfort and happiness they had hitherto enjoyed, since their arrival in that remote corner, owing to the harmony which had subsisted among them. He assured them, that, as soon as they appeared to split and quarrel among themselves, their neighbours, who till then had treated them with respect, would fall upon them, take their property from them, and expel them from the country. He therefore conjured them, by the ties of blood, and their mutual safety, to return quietly, that night, to their several homes; and he pledged himself, that he would satisfy them all with respect to precedency, and prevent the possibility of such disputes among them, at their future anniversary meetings. They all acquiesced, and departed in peace. In due time time, John de Groat, to fulfil his engagement, built a room, distinct by itself, of an octagon shape, with eight doors and windows in it, and having placed in the middle, a table of oak, of the same shape, when the next anniversary meeting took place, he desired each of them to enter at his own door, and to sit at the head of the table; he taking himself the seat that was left unoccupied. By this ingenious contrivance, any dispute, in regard to rank, was prevented, as they all found themselves on a footing of equality, and their former harmony and good humour were restored. That building was then named John O'Groat's House, and though the house is totally gone, the place where it stood still retains the name, and deserves to be remembered, as long as good intentions, and good sense, are estimable in a country.*

* The particulars above mentioned, were communicated to John Sutherland, Esq. of Wester, above 50 years ago, by his father, who was then advanced in life, and who had seen the letter wrote by James IV. in the possession of George Groat of Warse. The remains of the oak table have been seen by many now living, who have inscribed their names on it. On the sea-shore in the neighbourhood, the celebrated John O'Groat's Buckies, or shells, are found in considerable quantities.

APPENDIX.

(A)

Observations on Inclosures.

THE following observations were transmitted from a number of intelligent quarters, for the Caithness Report, on the subject of Inclosures.

The questions asked were—"What are the best sorts of Inclosure for the County of Caithness?" And, "What the expense of making them, per yard or rood?" To which the following answers were returned.

---

1. *Sir Robert Anstruther*, Bart. Proprietor of the Estate of Wattin.—I took into my hand the Mains of Wattin, and other contiguous lands, containing about 220 acres in all, which I inclosed with a ditch, hedge, and snap dyke, at a yard high; a most complete fence. Thorns throve as well as any I ever saw, on all the dry grounds: where drains were not brought up before planting, they were not so good; nor in one place, where there was such a distance between the dyke and hedge, that calves got between, and spoilt the thorns; but cutting over would recover them. My object being to lay the land down in grass, and let for pasture, I paid little attention to rotation of crops, farther than to get each field in good order for grass-seeds, which I cut once, and rented for pasture annually, and got tolerable rents for each.

2. Mr. *Mackid*, Farmer at Wattin.—My farm is altogether inclosed with stone dykes and hedges, and divided into twenty-two inclosures; the largest twenty-three acres, and the smallest eight acres. The hedges on my farm, which were planted by Sir Robert Anstruther, thrive as well as upon any farm I have seen in the more southern parts of Scotland.

3. *General Sinclair*, of Lybster.—The inclosure which soonest answers some of the purposes of the best fence is, dyke and ditch, with a whin hedging, which thrives best in

the worst soil, and, in the winter, affords some nourishment for cattle as well as shelter. It stands for a long time, if not trespassed on. In 1770, that kind of fence was made for $1\frac{1}{2}d.$ per yard; it could not be done now under 4*d.* per yard. It was well banked by earth, from a ditch six feet wide and three deep.

4. *John Sinclair*, Esq. of Barrack.—I am of opinion, that the best sort of inclosure for this county, is a dry stone dyke, three feet high, and a coping of stones on level ground. The expense per rood of three feet, is 1*l.* 16*s.* per rood, allowing 12*s.* for building, 12*s.* for leading, and 12*s.* for quarrying, besides 2*s.* per rood for clearing the quarry of rubbish; and where the low ends of fields are wet, sunk fences faced up with stone, which will be, as to building, half the expense of stone fences as above: the leading, quarrying, and clearing the quarry, being also the same.

5. *Major Innes*, of Sandside.—The best inclosure is a double stone dyke, four feet high, and coping. The expense, 2*l.* 10*s.* per rood of thirty-six yards. A great part of the estate of Sandside is inclosed, and there is a stone fence between the arable and sheep-pasture, and partly subdivided.

6. *Alexander Henderson*, Esq. of Stemster.—In my opinion, a snap-dyke of two feet and a half or three feet, and a ditch, is the fittest mode of inclosing for this country, as the ditch carries off the surface-water, and the dyke, though low, is a sufficient fence, from the ruggedness of its top. The lands, in general, require to be as much intersected as possible with ditches; and slate-stone, which is the fittest for such inclosures, is to be found almost in every part of the country, at a very small distance below the surface. The expense may be from 20*s.* to 25*s.* per rood, including the ditch. I have made within these six years about 200 chain of such fences, and have inclosed about 100 acres since I came here.

7. *George Sutherland*, Esq. of Brabster.—The best sort of inclosure is a good stone wall; and, if its durability is considered, it is in the end the cheapest. The expense per rood, depends much on the facility or difficulty of procuring materials; in most parts of this county, it will not exceed 30*s.* or 35*s.* Turf-built dykes, if preserved from sheep, and cattle are not permitted to graze on their sides, will continue good for several years: the rearing them, however, lays waste, or considerably injures, a large proportion of ground, and should not, if possible, be resorted to. Upon decaying through age, they should be conveyed to the place whence the turf was originally

ginally dug. From 200 to 300 acres, as nearly as I can judge at present, is the utmost quantity of land inclosed by me.

8. *Alexander Sinclair*, Esq. of Achingale.—Stone fences unquestionably are the best: a four-foot dyke, including coping, generally costs 36*s.* per rood. All surface-water should be drained by an open ditch: the expense may be from $\frac{1}{2}$*d.* to 1*d.* Spouts and springs should be cut so deep, as effectually to catch the springs, then covered; the expense must depend upon the labour. I have made no stone inclosures, but have made many thousand yards of five-feet ditches, with a view to ring fences, and subdividing fields into ten or eleven acres, as suited the ground. The importance of draining is so obvious, that it would be presumptuous to mention it.

9. *Major Williamson.*—I give it as my decided opinion, that in Caithness, there should be no dyke without a ditch at the bottom of it: this for the purpose of draining. The field ought not to exceed eight chains in length. This for the rapidly draining off surface, or rain and snow water. Without respect to uniformity, the top ditch should have a declivity sufficient to carry off water, and no more. In arable lands, three feet deep by two is sufficient: price 1$\frac{1}{2}$*d.* per yard. Upon the bank, a dyke of two feet and a half high, with a heckle of not less than a foot: the expense of this depends upon the quarry, and its distance from the work.

10. *Captain Robertson*, of Warse.--The best inclosure is stone, which is done, including all expenses, at 1*s.* the yard, or 36*s.* the rood. Another (perhaps not inferior) method, is, by a ditch topped with stone on the side thrown up, after the earth is consolidated.

11. Mr. *William Henderson*, Wester Ormly.—I have always been against any more inclosing of a farm than a surrounding fence, (where winter herding has not been established), and two inclosures for pasture, suited to the size of the farm; because the interest of the expense of inclosing is too heavy a burden on the best land in this county, and does not afford an adequate benefit. Upon this principle, I have only inclosed five acres, in two divisions, for pasture. I prefer draining to any more inclosing; and have expended as much in draining, as would nearly inclose all my farm.

12. Dr. *Henderson*, Clyth.—I presume the best sort of inclosure for this county, where draining is so generally necessary, will be found to be, a ditch of proper size, and eighteen to twenty inches of stone dyke, with stone coping, built on the top of the earth thrown out of the ditch. Expense per rood

rood must vary according to the nature of the ground to be cut, and the distance of materials for building.

13. Mr. *George Miller*, Whitefield.—The sort of inclosure must, in a great measure, depend, upon the nature of the soil and subsoil. Where drains are necessary, ditches, which are made five feet broad and three feet deep, at 9*s*. per rood; but which, without a coping of stone, will not be found a sufficient fence, and even with a stone coping, ditches are very apt to fall in, and fill up; for which reason, where drains are not necessary, I would prefer stone dykes, even at three times the expense of ditches, which take up about double the ground that dykes do. I have inclosed about 230 acres, mostly with ditches, except two fields with stone dykes.

14. Mr. *Donald Miller*, East Noss.—The best inclosures for this county is a stone dyke and ditch: the country being too wet, ditch is absolutely necessary to carry off as much as possible of the surface-water, which will be a mean of warming the soil. I commonly inclose with a ditch of six feet broad, and three feet deep, and a stone dyke, (built on the earth thrown out of the ditch), of two feet and a half high, with stone coping, or snap. There were no inclosures on this farm at the time of my entry to it. I have inclosed with a ditch of six feet by three, and double feal dykes of about four feet high, one park of 81 acres, one of 39, one of 51, and one of 37 acres, with a ditch of six feet by three; one park of 16 acres, one of 14, one of 30, one of 15, one of 32, one of 14, one of 12, one of 9, and one of 18 acres, with a stone dyke and ditch; one park of 40 acres, with a ditch six by three in the middle of it; one of 23, one of 20, and one of 31 acres, inclosed on two sides by a stone dyke and ditch; on the other two sides by a stone dyke of four feet and a half high. Two inclosures are on each side of the house, of about two acres each; a garden of about one acre, and cow-yard about two acres. A ditch, of six by three feet, will cost from 3*d*. to 5*d*. per ell in length; stone dyke, of two feet and a half, with snap, from 1*s*. 1*d*. to 1*s*. 2*d*. per ell.

15. Mr. *Cumming*, Ratter.—A ditch, and snap stone fence, is the best kind of inclosure for Caithness. The expense must depend on the circumstances of the ground, and the nature of the materials. The advantage is great.

16. Mr. *John Manson*, Thurso East.—Stone fences are to be preferred, if such can be had, as they are most durable, and most secure for keeping stock. The expense per yard varies, less or more, in every place, in proportion as the distance

tance may be for driving the stones, and the workable nature of the quarry; 1*s*. per square yard is a tolerable correct estimate, in these times, for stone dykes. Ditches are much adopted at present, and are of use to the laying ground dry, which is a very essential thing in this country; but unless water continues to run in them, or that they are cleaned once in five or six years, they will crumble down in the space of fifteen or sixteen years, so as to be of no use as a fence; whereas, stone dykes, if substantially done, may, with some attention paid to them, last sixty years.

17. Mr. *Trotter*, Duncansbay.—The best inclosures for a bare cold country, like Caithness, is that which affords most shelter; I therefore think, a thorn-hedge the best, if it could be made to grow; and on good soil, lying to the south or south-east, or, (which is the same thing), sheltered from the north and north-west, if well taken care of, I have no doubt of its growing, and, with a ditch six feet wide and three feet deep, would be the cheapest fence. On all dry ground round the country, or along the shore-side, stone-dykes, four feet high, with a coping, are surely the most durable; but on wet soils, ditch and dyke are the best. A ditch six feet wide, three feet and a half deep, and two feet six inches of coping, would make both a fence and a drain. I cannot say with any certainty, at what prices they could be made at present, as I have not done any thing in that way for some time; but the price will differ, in proportion to the goodness of the materials used, and the distance from which they must be carried.

18. Mr. *James Anderson*, Ausdale.—The best sort of inclosures for this country, (where stones generally are to be found), are surely stone dykes, of (where sheep interfere) four feet and a half in height, and thirty-six by eighteen inches in thickness, exclusive of a raggling, or scasement, of four inches extra thickness, on each side, in the foundation course, and finished with a cover of loose earth on the top, raised considerably in the middle, and over which, two course of strong feal, which gives at least an additional foot of height, and the ends of the uppermost feal projecting considerably over the under ones, tends very much to prevent the sheep from jumping over, or even attempting it. I say such a dyke is found a sufficient fence against the Cheviot breed, particularly if the ground be a little cleared off about two feet distance from the foundation; but in respect to the black-faced, or mountain sheep, no dry stone dyke will turn them, when they are strong, or in good condition.—For dykes of the above description, I have paid not less than $5\frac{1}{2}d.$ for building, since I came to this place, and

and this year I have been obliged to pay 6*d*. per lineal yard. —The expense of carting the stones varies, in proportion to distance, quality of the road, and whether up or down hill; but valuing the labour, tear and wear of a man, horse, cart, harness, &c. at 2*s*. 7½*d*. per day, my outlays in that branch, have been exactly 7*d*. per yard. I have no other quarry, but that of picking up surface-stones, where they can be found, which, with breaking them, consumes much time, and I find the average expense thereof, stands me about 6*d*. per yard. The feal coping, I am sometimes obliged to cast, a considerable distance, and the operation in whole cannot be valued at less than 1*d*. per yard. So I conclude, that every lineal yard of finished dyke, costs me 1*s*. 8*d*., exclusive of quarry tools, &c.—The arable part of my farm is, with a very little exception, all inclosed, and three-fourths of it subdivided with stone dykes of the above description, being in quantity, as before observed, about thirty-one Scotch acres.

(B)

Rotation of Crops.

THE Questions asked were, "What do you consider to be the best Rotation of Crops, for the County of Caithness?" And, "What the average produce of each?"

1. The *Earl of Caithness*.—The following is the rotation adopted on the farm of Mey: 1. Turnips; 2. Bear and grass-seeds; 3. Hay; 4. Pasture; 5. Oats; the crop of which is always excellent from ley. The hay crop is a good one, from 200 to 250 stones, and sometimes more.

Lord Caithness tried an experiment some years ago, with English barley. The first year it produced fifteen returns; the second was inferior, both in respect to quantity and quality; and, the third year, it was inferior as to quantity and quality, to the common bear of the county. The first crop was as early as the bear crop, but the succeeding years it ripened much later.

2. *John Sinclair*, Esq. of Barrack.—Bear and oats the best crops; grass-seeds may be sown with either: wheat may likewise be cultivated to great advantage; also pease, beans, and turnips. I have generally had about four or five returns of oats, and four of bear. I have had ten returns of winter wheat;

wheat; and about 150 stone of sown-grass per acre, and sometimes 200 stone per acre. Red oats some years will weigh 16 stone; at other times half a stone more or less; but oftener 15 stone. Bear in general with me, 17, 17½, and 18 stone per boll; and one year, I had barley 19½ stone per boll.

3. *George Sutherland*, Esq. of Brabster.—The extent of arable land presently occupied by me, does not exceed 100 acres; in the course of another year, however, I intend making considerable additions to it. The rotation of crops, which I wish to adopt on my own farm, and consequently deem best, is the following: 1. Turnips, or potatoes, well manured: 2. Bear or oats, with grass-seeds; 3. Hay; 4. Ditto, or Pasture.

3. *Alexander Henderson*, Esq. of Stemster.—Although the farm occupied by me, consists of upwards of 300 acres, yet I cannot call above one-half of it arable; a good deal more of it has been occasionally under the plough; and about the year 1740, a considerable part of the low grounds was torn up and burnt by the then possessor, who having taken several successive crops of white oats, allowed the ground to run out, without any preparation, or grass-seeds being sown in it. This makes it now naturally in a much worse state than before it was touched. As to the rotation of crops, I have not had such experience as to enable me to say what is best: I have now gone over a part of my grounds with a six-years' shift, viz. 1. Turnips; 2. Bear, with grass-seeds; 3. Grass, cut; 4. Grass, pastured; 5. Oats; 6. Oats. This I consider as too hard for the land, which is rather light; and, therefore, I have this year altered my plan, and intend in future to adopt a four-years' shift on the best of the land, and to labour the rest in the best manner I can. From six to eight bolls of bear, from seven to nine bolls potatoe oats, and from four to seven bolls black or grey oats, I have found to be about the general return.

4. *Major Innes*, of Sandside.—About 200 acres are occupied in the farm of Sandside. The best rotation of crops is, first turnips; then bear or potatoe oats, with red and white clover, rye-grass, &c.; then let lay for one or two years, as the proprietor pleases, (but one year the most valuable for the farmer); spring-wheat may be sown after turnips; then the grass-land to be taken up for winter wheat, bear, or oats, then turnips, &c. The produce of bear, on an average, 14 bolls per acre; of oats, 12 bolls; the turnip and hay crops generally good, and what might be considered worth 10*l.* an acre.

5. *Alexander Sinclair*, Esq. of Achingale.—When manure is had

to be had in abundance, I would prefer the four-course shift as the most profitable, viz. oats, turnips, potatoes, bear with seeds, grass for one year. When manure is not to be had, but what is made by the cattle, the rotation must be considerably varied. Beans will not answer without dung, but pease may be tried; and if they do not ripen for a crop, they may be ploughed down, and will make an excellent preparation for the next crop, which may be oats. With that I would begin the second year's course, followed with turnips, potatoes, pease, bear and grass-seeds, grass, and two years' pasture. After these rotations, the average corn crops may be calculated at from 10 to 12 returns, in a good season. The average produce of turnips will, under proper management, equal that of any in Scotland. I have seen turnips which weighed 29 lb. Dutch, tops included. The average of hay may be from 150 stone to 200; and if annual rye-grass is substituted for perennial, it will exceed that quantity per acre.

6. *Major Williamson.*—The variety of soil and local circumstances are such, that any thing like a general rotation of crops cannot be fixed upon. The county, for that purpose, must be divided, I think, into three classes: the shores of the county, (having access to sea-weed), the midlands, and highlands. I confine my observations to the first class. The access to sea-weed gives the farmer so great a command of manure, that he is enabled to return the more frequently to corn, but not by the ordinary mode of application (fresh); sea-weed I consider the very best material for compost, and well-prepared compost the best enricher of the soil. I would, therefore, in all cases, begin with a thorough fallow, dunged, and would only have that portion in turnips necessary for keeping stock fresh; 2. Potatoe oats, with grass-seeds; 3. Hay, or pasture; 4. Oats. Conceiving that one fallow is insufficient to clean the land thoroughly, I would the fifth year, fallow and dung again; and in this stage sow potatoes and turnips upon a larger scale. Potatoes, could the land be cleared of them, I consider as the most valuable crop; admitting of being early carried off the ground, and enabling the farmer to lay the soil comfortably up for the winter. Turnips can only be carried off during the winter, which subjects the soil to the worst of injuries, to wit, poaching. Not feeling myself qualified by experience, to state what rotation is best to follow next, I leave it to the discretion of the farmer, to adopt what he considers the best, according to his situation and soil; satisfied that, until after a second well-wrought fallow, as already mentioned, the farmer will not have his lands in a husbandman-like condition.

7. Mr.

7. Mr. *William Henderson*, Wester Ormly.—I have 40 Scotch acres of arable land in my occupation, 24 of which I have in four fields, under the rotation of, 1. Turnips; 2. Bear or bigg; 3. Grass; 4. Oats; commonly called the four-crop shift. I have the other 16 acres, of very inferior land, under the rotation of, 1. Naked fallow; 2. Oats; 3. Grass; 4. Grass; 5. Oats; or the five-crop shift. These I judge the best for the land on my farm; and I conceive, that the rotation ought always to be suited to the nature of the land, and command of manure, and that no fixed rule, for all soils, can be applied with success.

8. Dr. *Manson*.—The rotation which appears to me best adapted for this county, on what is called old stock land, is the following, viz. turnips, or red fallow, bear, grass, oats. By this management, manure is only required once in four years, and the land kept constantly in a state to yield good crops. On light lands, I think an additional year under grass for pasturage, would be advisable. From stock land, under the above management, I think of bear and oats, eight bolls per acre might be expected; about 200 stones of hay; and as good turnips as can be raised in Scotland. I mention the above as a general plan, as I do not think our county so well adapted to other crops.

9. Mr. *Mathers*, Spring-Park.—In my opinion, the best rotation of crops for Caithness, is to begin with summer-fallow, or green crops, if dung can be got, and lay the field down the next year in common bear or bigg, with clover and rye-grass; after the first crop of grass, take two crops of oats, first red and the second black; a second crop of white oats reduces the ground too much, and proves not to be so valuable as the black. Many are of opinion, that the loss of a second crop, or a second year's crop of grass, is great; but I do not find, nor do I see it in any part of the country, excepting in particular places, where the ground is uncommonly good, that a second crop will pay in feeding cows, or in making hay; the corn, in general, is of more value than all the cattle are worth, if they were sold. Soiling is far the cheapest mode for feeding cows, and making dung. Too many cattle are kept, and the greater part starved.—The average produce of Caithness may be, of bear, five and a half returns; oats, say red or white, five returns; black oats, four and a half. Many of the great farmers have more; the smaller ones have a great deal less: I take the above average to be near the truth.

10. Mr. *Paton*.—The best rotation is, turnips, or clean fallow, bear and grass, grass, oats; but when the land is not in

in good heart, two crops of grass are necessary. When this rotation is done justice to, on a good soil, the average is, ten bolls of bear, twelve of oats; and on ordinary soil, eight of bear, and nine of oats; but I have reason to believe, that the general average of the county, where green crops are not attended to, is four bolls of bear, and five of oats, of inferior quality.

11. Mr. *Donald Miller*, East Noss.—When I entered to the possession of my farm, there might be about 150 acres arable land on it. The best rotation of crops I should suppose to be, first turnips after fallow; next, bear or oats, with grass-seeds, (I mean rye-grass and clover). If to be left under pasture, perennial rye-grass, with red and white clover, there being two pounds of white to each pound of red; if not intended for pasture, annual rye-grass and red clover alone. When ploughed up, one crop of oats, then fallow, turnips, &c. Produce, if bear, nine bolls per acre; if potatoe oats, six and a half; if Poland, seven and a half to eight bolls per acre. First year's crop of hay, 250 to 300 stone; second year, if perennial, 100 to 150; if annual, no hay. This, supposing the land in good heart, and a good soil.

12. Mr. *George Miller*, Whitefield.—I have found the best rotation to be, 1. Turnips; 2. Bear or oats laid down with grass-seeds; and then grass, cut the first year, eaten the second, and sometimes the third year; then broke up, and sown with red oats, and if in good heart, sown next year with black native oats. Never tried what weight an acre would produce of turnips: an average crop of red oats, say seven seeds; black, nearly so; and bear the same.

13. Mr. *Cumming*, Ratter.—The farm of Ratter consists of 190 acres of arable land, laid out as follows:

36 acres turnips, potatoes, pease, and beans;
36 acres bear and grass-seeds;
36 acres red clover and rye-grass—one crop only to be taken;
36 acres oats—at all times observing, only one crop of white corn to be taken:
46 acres for pasture, to be laid down in great order, and sown with such perennial grass, as will best sward the ground for four years pasturage.

190

The produce per acre, of ground under the above management, is from eight to nine, and even ten bolls per acre. If turnips

turnips are well managed, their produce will be equal to any in Scotland; and hay crops, from artificial grasses, will produce from 250 to even 400 stones per acre.

14. Dr. *Henderson*, Clyth.—My experience does not lead me to talk with any degree of confidence, as to the best rotation of crops for the county of Caithness. I presume, first turnips, or pease, or tares, or beans, and even potatoes, each uniformly sown in drills, as a green crop; followed by, second, bear or bigg, barley (early sown) or oats, (potatoe oats to have the preference in good land, sown down with annual rye-grass and red clover; third, grass; and fourth, potatoe oats, as the rotation best suited for all well-managed land, even in Caithness: in other places, such a rotation has been tried with great advantage. The average produce per acre, as far as I am enabled to say, is, on poor land, two seeds and a half; in richer land, four to six seeds; *in the hands of tenantry*, who say they sow about one boll of bear or oats per Scotch acre. On this farm, twelve to fourteen pecks of seed are sown per acre; the return from six to eight bolls per acre on the best land.

15. Mr. *John Manson*, Thurso East.—The arable land of this farm, consists of different soils; partly a good loam, the remainder a thin light soil. The loamy soil consists of 120 acres, which may answer a five-years' rotation, viz. 1. A green crop, turnips, and potatoes; 2. Bear, with perennial rye-grass, and red and white clover seeds; 3. Hay; 4. Pasture; 5. Potatoe oats. The thin light soil, 90 acres, a nine-years' rotation of, 1. Turnips and potatoes; 2. Red oats, with perennial rye-grass, and red and white clover seeds; 3. Hay; 4. Pasture; 5. Pasture, with a dressing of shelly sand; 6. Pasture; 7. Red oats; 8. Sown with pease, and ploughed in about the beginning of August; 9. Red oats.

The average produce of each crop may be as follows:

First, on the field of five-years' rotation: 1. The turnip crop, if well dunged and cleaned, may be worth, on an average, 8*l.* per acre; 2. Bear crop, eight seeds and a half; 3. The hay crop, from 200 to 250 stone; 4. The pasture will scarcely pay, say 25*s.* per acre; 5. Or potatoe oats, eight seeds.

Secondly, the fields of nine-years' rotation: 1. Turnip crop, 7*l.* per acre; 2. Red oats, six seeds; 3. Hay, 180 stones; 4, 5, and 6 years, Pasture, 12*s.* 6*d.* per acre; 7. Red oats, six seeds; 8. A fallow, and the pease ploughed in, to answer as dung; 9. Red oats, five seeds.

16. Mr. *Trotter*, Duncansbay.—In Wydale, I have about thirty-five acres of arable land, most of which is outfield, or what has never got any dung. At Duncansbay, I have fifty-

two acres of old arable. In my opinion, different modes of rotation must be adopted in this, as well as in every other county, according to the different sorts of soil, and other circumstances. Having two farms very opposite in soil and situation, I shall give the rotations I have adopted, and my reasons for so doing. First, in regard to Duncansbay, one half of the old arable land on that farm, is *overlaid*, (if I may use the expression), with shell-sand, so much so, that it will give no kind of oats but the small grey, and even of these the returns are not great. I have there a command of manure from the sea-weed, the mosses, and the natural pasture grass in my possession. That farm gives good bear, and every sort of green crops. The rotation there is, 1. Turnips or potatoes; 2. Bear, with grass-seeds; 3. Hay; 4. Oats; 5. Pease; 6. Bear. By this mode, I have twice bear, and three green crops. Both crops of bear get a coat of fresh sea-weed; the turnips or potatoes, a good dose of dung, and for the oats I top-dress on the sward with the heaviest earth I can get from the ditches; and for the pease I give a light coat of dung. This plan I follow with the six fields nearest the shore. But I have four fields, most of which I have taken in from very bad waste land, and at some distance from the shore. On these, there were neither shell-sand nor sea-weed; nor have they such a dry bottom as those on the shore-side. The rotation for them, is, 1. Summer-fallow, turnips or potatoes, if dry, with a good dose of dung mixed with shell-sand; 2. Bear or oats, for there is such a mixture of wet and dry, that I do not risk bear, on a wet or cold bottomed soil; 3. Grass, either pastured or cut; and, 4. Oats. I may afterwards change this mode, but it is fit for no other as yet.

The farm of Wydale, and all in the same situation, and under similar circumstances, would do better under a longer rotation; because it is more adapted for grass than corn crops, being of a cold, thin, wet nature, and having no great command of manure. I think the best rotation for such land is, 1. Fallow, or a few turnips, or potatoes on the dry places, may answer; 2. Oats, or bear if dry; 3. Hay; 4. Pasture; 5. Pasture; 6. Pasture; 7. Oats, after a top-dressing of marl on the sward. This I suppose may do for the first round of rotation; but in the second round, when the soil may be found more fertile, I should think it may not be necessary to continue it so long in pasture.

It is not an easy matter to give the average of each crop, nor the average produce of each rotation. But let us suppose meal and bear, at 20*s.* per boll, and the pease at the same price; the hay one shilling per stone; an acre of potatoes at seven pounds, and an acre of turnips at five—then the produce

of

of the whole six years' shift, per acre, will be thirty-five pounds, which divide by six, will give *5l.* 16*s.* 8*d.* The four years' shift, supposing the first year fallow, six returns of oats, one hundred and fifty stone of hay, at 1*s.* per stone; the whole produce in the four years is 19*l.* 10*s.*, which divide by four, gives 4*l.* 17*s.* 6*d.* And the seven years' shift, on the cold bottomed land in the middle of the county, with one year summer fallow, the two crops of oats, one of hay, and three years pasture, will amount to 21*l.* 10*s.* which divide by seven, the number of years in the shift, gives 3*l.* 1*s.* 5*d.*

17. *Hints for Rotations to introduce the Culture of Wheat.*—If the land is not perfectly clean, and in good heart, begin with a fallow, and adopt the following rotation: 1. Fallow; 2. Wheat; 3. Hay; 4. Oats; 5. Turnips; 6. Bear; 7. Hay; 8. Wheat, on one furrow, then either fallow or grass-seeds. The fallow should have four furrows, beginning early in May, or the first week of June at farthest. It will require thirty cubical yards of good dung per Scotch acre, and thirty bolls, or 120 English bushels, of Sunderland lime. The lime and dung to be laid on with the last furrow; the seed, which should be the best that can be had, to be sown in August, or September; and red wheat, being the hardiest, to be preferred to the white. The best sort, is the *creeping* wheat, as it is called, to be had from East Lothian, "which possesses a quality that no other wheat has, that of not being liable to be thrown out of the ground during the winter by frost, even on a high exposure, and a thin soil." In April, harrow and roll, and sow the grass-seeds. The produce will be from eight to ten bolls per acre. The quantity of seed should be three bushels per Scotch acre, if sown early; but more, if later.

On strong land the rotation to be, 1. Fallow; 2. Wheat; 3. Hay; 4. Pasture; 5. Oats. The fallow should get five furrows. The seed to be sown early; about the end of August, or the beginning of September. A greater quantity of manure will be necessary, than for light land; from 30 to 40 cubical yards of dung, and 150 bushels of lime. As grass-seeds do not answer with wheat, on strong land, unless when drilled, beans, if possible, should be tried, then bear and grass-seeds.

(C)

Waste Lands.

THE best means of improving the Waste Lands of the kingdom, is a subject that cannot be too frequently discussed, nor any important facts or observations regarding it, too carefully collected. The following communications, therefore, regarding that interesting branch of husbandry, are submitted to the reader's consideration.

1. The *Earl of Caithness*—Paring and burning answers well, but on the whole, it is considered to be a surer mode, to adopt the plan of constant ploughing for two or three years, and to plough the land three or four times each summer. It is said, that this plan has answered well at Reiss and Hempriggs.

Lord Caithness has brought the following extent of waste land, mixed with some arable, into a state of improvement.

	Acres.
1. Rossieburn Farm, ...	77
2. New land inclosed, and let to tenants, ...	79
3. Nisiter, ...	100
	256

2. *General Sinclair*, of Lybster.—The only attempt to improve waste land, has been confined to a moorish soil, which did not afford peat-fuel, by converting it into a better kind of pasture for the cattle of the fishermen. No advantage can compensate the loss of a deep peat-moss, near to the coast-side, (which is generally abused). Some commons may be, (and are here), more useful in their natural state, than in breaking up and dividing them.

3. *Major Innes*, of Sandside.—On an average, I have improved about ten acres of waste land yearly. The first year fallow; then lime is applied, or use some other manure. (Lord Meadowbank's compost very good). Then I sow it with rape or turnips; next, bear or oats, with grass-seeds; the crop of turnip or rape is eaten off by sheep; expense about 5*l.* exclusive of dyking. Mossy land ought to be pared and burnt, and used in the same way. In this northern climate, the paring spade is preferable to the paring plough. Sea-ware answers mossy

mossy ground when dry, or lime is good. We are not acquainted with marl at Sandside.

4. *John Sinclair*, Esq. of Barrack.—I have taken in and inclosed, since 1796, upwards of 500 acres of waste land, about 100 of which are generally under corn, and the rest rough hill-grass. It is all at present in the hands of tenants at a low rent, but yearly diminishing in rent, as hill ground cannot be kept in corn, and is therefore better inclosed, and kept for pasture. The best mode of improving the commons of Caithness, is by inclosing them, keeping them in grass, and cutting cross drains, until improved under the cattle's feet, and fit for cropping. The expense cannot be stated on an average at less than 5*l.* per acre, which will not be repaid; so that the safest method is to give small parcels of ground to cottagers for five, seven, or nine years, upon their paying articles in kind, as fowls, &c. which they can easily furnish instead of money. At the end of the term agreed upon, the land to be valued by two intelligent neighbouring farmers, and not measured by the chain, or *iron tether*, which the country people say, will be the ruin of Caithness.

5. *Alexander Henderson*, Esq. of Stemster.—From 20 to 30 acres is perhaps all I can be said to have improved, and even that, not in so sufficient a manner as I could have wished. This year I have sowed out a field of 15 acres, (new ground), with oats and grass-seeds, after being well marled, and some of it upwards of four years under the plough: I put from 140 to 180 barrels per acre. The oats looks tolerable, and the grass promises to be good pasture; but I am confident the best and cheapest way of improving our commons, is by giving small lots to cottagers, free of rent for some time, afterwards at a very low rent, for a 19 or 31 years lease, according to the situation and value of the ground. When commons are near the sea, or well accommodated with fuel, they will be quickly taken; and this I am certain will be found the cheapest and most effectual way of improving them, besides the advantage of accommodating a number of poor people, driven from their homes by the present rage for sheep-walks, and extensive farms, and who, though hitherto they have spent their time in sloth and idleness, in consequence of having held the little ground they occupied, in a manner for nothing, and being tenants at will, or liable to be turned off at the year's end, yet when they get a permanent residence, which they can call their own, and cannot be removed at the arbitrary will of any one, they will soon acquire habits of industry, application, and cleanliness, and be a source of riches to the

landed interest, the manufacturer, and the fisherman. Although my mind expands with the idea, yet I conceive it would be presumptuous in me, to pretend to point out the advantages resulting from such a plan to this country, in the present prosperous appearance of fisheries on the coast, as there are others, so much more capable, and interested in doing it.

Lime I have never had occasion to use as a manure, the price being so high, the roads so bad, and distance so great, as to make it almost impossible to get the little we require for building; but marl I have of the very best quality, and in the greatest abundance, both in the low grounds, and loch adjoining; indeed we have so much of it in the low grounds, where it is got with the greatest ease, from three to six feet deep, by pitting, that we seldom think of going to the lake for it, where it may be got to the depth of twenty-four feet and upwards, as proved by Mr. Busby, who, in surveying it, with the view of ascertaining the quantity, went in many parts to that depth, without finding the bottom. It is evident from the grounds it is now dug out of, that it has been long used in this country, far indeed beyond the memory of any now living. From the very imperfect means of conveyance in those times, they having nothing but creels, or caisies, to carry it in, on horses' backs, they were not able to take it any distance, in any considerable quantity; of course, it was only those lands which lay nearest the place where it was found, that received any advantage from it; marl has, therefore, in a manner, now lost its effects on those lands, and does not answer so well as it does upon new lands, or those more distant, and where it has not been used before: there it acts in a most powerful manner. It is to be got in many parts of this country, and is daily coming into more repute, as the promiscuous use of the commons is prevented. If the loch here, were drained, which might be done at a very small expense, (as there is not, at this moment above two feet water on any part of it, and a fall of upwards of ten feet in half a mile), there would be a fund sufficient to supply a great part of the interior of the county. I should, however, have to regret, besides the prospect of a fine sheet of water immediately before my door, the loss of exceeding fine trout and eels, which it contains in abundance, and wild fowl, which, in the season, supply me with the greatest profusion of delicious eggs, to the extent at least of 100 dozen a week; and I conceive, I should experience a greater loss in the birds themselves being driven away, as it is to them I attribute the lands in the neighbourhood, being more exempt from the destructive attacks of the grub, so prevalent in some parts: the birds, which are very numerous, sweep over the fields in vast flocks, during the months of May and

and June, the whole night, and pick up vast numbers of that most pernicious insect, both in the grub state, and after they take wing.

6. *George Sutherland*, Esq. of Brabster.—To one so well acquainted with the extent of waste ground, improved by individuals, in the other parts of the island to which we belong, as the President of the Board of Agriculture, the quantity brought into cultivation by most Caithness improvers, will appear comparatively small. On my farm, about 200 acres have been partially improved, by draining, inclosing, &c.; and from 20 to 30 have been rendered arable. Before requesting a plan for improving the commons of Caithness, it would have been deserving well of his fellow proprietors, had Sir John Sinclair suggested a quick, equitable, and cheap mode of dividing them; supposing a division to have taken place, the following seems the most obvious method of improvement. As much as possible of the commons should be parcelled out to the occupiers of farms in the immediate neighbourhood. The mode of melioration should, in this case, however, be fixed upon, and the party bound, under a penalty, to carry it into execution; every encouragement should likewise be given to small settlers: neither rent, customs, or services of any kind, ought to be exacted during the infant state of the improvement; but the colonist should be allowed to devote all his time and earnings, to the cultivation of the ground assigned him. In the rotation of crops for commons, potatoes, if the soil is in any degree favourable to their production, should take the lead, as furnishing to the settler a great quantity of food, and at an early period after his settlement. If the ground pulverises well, oats might, in the next stage of the rotation, be sown without a spring furrow, and by this saving of labour in one case, time would be afforded for bringing into tillage a considerable proportion of new ground. Where the soil of the common is strong, lime may be used with much advantage; in all cases, however, it is a forcing and exhausting manure. It calls forth the powers of the soil, (if I may be allowed the expression), without enriching it. Where the soil inclines to sand or moss, marl is preferable to lime; it does not act so forcibly; its effects continue longer; and being generally compounded with other substances, it possesses some enriching qualities.

7. *Alexander Sinclair*, Esq. of Achingale.—One hundred acres of new ground, have been rendered fit to receive manure by me. About fifty acres have been so improved, as to give tolerable crops, both white and green; and I have no doubt will do

 well

well upon being taken up again. This last ground was repeatedly ploughed, cross-ploughed, and harrowed, for two years. All the coarse pieces that could not be got reduced, were carried off, together with the grass, roots, and stones, and the land dunged with a compost of earth and cattle dung, and then ploughed up in the harvest of the second year. In the spring following, it was sown with oats, rye-grass, rib-grass, and white clover, for pasture. The crops pretty good; that of corn, about six returns; but had the manure not been laid on until the spring, and then another ploughing given to it, the different crops would have been much better, as was evident from two ridges of it, which were so used. The soil was stiff, cold, and poor naturally, but the corn crop averaged, as I have already said, about six returns. Grass-seeds never answer on Martinmas ploughing.—The expense of improving an acre of new ground, has been explained in a late treatise; but I think it is cheapest and most effectually done by crofters, properly situated as to fuel and water, and whose spots are regularly and properly laid out to them. In a rotation of crops on new ground, bear or barley can hardly be ventured upon, but oats, turnips, and the coarser kinds of artificial grasses, do very well. The effects of lime as a manure, must be very great on a new soil, and it is better calculated than marl, for creating a speedy return; but as a top-dressing, I would prefer marl.

8. *Major Williamson.*—I made an attempt to improve some waste-lands upon my farm, and, after reducing it thoroughly, laid on 80 cart-loads of Wick dung. I laid it down with bear and grass-seeds. I had about four bolls per acre of light bear; next year, about 90 stone of hay; and the third year, about five bolls of oats, with an abundant crop of sorrel. I considered my labour lost, and abandoned it; and until farmers can say, that their lands are in the highest possible state of culture, and every weed eradicated, I assert, that every attempt to cultivate waste-grounds is an abuse of labour.

9. Mr. *James Anderson.*—I do not believe that the commons of Caithness can be brought into culture, on a large scale, and with that advantage that would be deemed adequate by people of capital, without the aid of lime, to a certain extent, and judiciously applied.

10. Dr. *Henderson,* Clyth.—The best possible mode, in my opinion, for improving the commons of Caithness, is by increasing the population, and by enabling such increased population, where aid is necessary, to bring in these commons, by planting potatoes thereon, in what are called *lazy-beds,* than

than which no crop pays so soon, nor fits the land better for a luxuriant corn-crop, various proofs of which are to be met with in this country. The increased population will require wood, and other aid, to build houses for them; some fodder, during harvest and winter, to enable them to prepare manure for the spring, to be mixed with moss-earth, as directed by Lord Meadowbank; a plan which doubtless has been practised, in a rough and imperfect way, by many of the farmers of this county, for many years, especially the lower class, and who raise very heavy crops on their small lots of ground, by such mode. They will also require, in the spring, to be furnished with a sufficient quantity of potatoes, of a good quality, for seed.

11. Mr. *Cumming*, Ratter.—The best mode of improving the Caithness commons, or waste-ground, is, to make them mellow with ploughing. When ready to be cropped, manure well, with proper compost dung, if a loamy thin soil; if strong clay, apply 70 bolls of unslacked lime per acre. The ground to be sown with bear, if a strong soil; if a weak soil, sown with oats, both along with grass seeds, such as are the best suited to the soil. The first grass crop to be eaten by light cattle, and that only in dry weather. Early in the following spring, to be top-dressed with 100 bolls of marl per acre. If a strong clay soil, short manure will answer better than marl.

12. Mr. *Sinclair Gun*, Deal.—I have improved about 30 acres. The best plan of improving the commons of Caithness would be, to let the adjoining farms, to active tenants, with long leases: stipulations in a lease have little effect; reducing the sward does little good, unless attended to afterwards. Interest in the soil, and the view of a little profit, is the greatest spur a tenant can be touched with. The expenses of improving waste-ground, would be from 10*l.* to 16*l.* per acre, depending on the ground to work on.

The best rotation of crops for new-improved land, is four years round: fallow, oats, grass for pasture, then oats. If new land is left above one year in grass, it generally inclines much to its original state. It should always, therefore, be top-dressed with dung the second year in grass.

13. Mr. *Donald Miller*, East Noss.—I have improved 135 acres, on my farm. The best plan of improving commons, or waste-land, in my opinion, is, to plough up at Martinmas; let it lie, and rot till next fall, then cross-plough, so as to have the benefit of the winter frosts; when dry in spring, put on common harrows, so as to flatten it a little; then the brake-harrow; after which, plough; and continue ploughing and harrowing,

barrowing, till properly fallowed, or reduced; then plough up in ridges for the winter; next season, lay down with turnip, with a good deal of manure; next season, with oats, perennial rye-grass, and clover-seeds. After the first crop of hay, no beast should be allowed to go on the field that season, but the foggage, or second crop, should be allowed to lie, to keep the soil warm during winter; and no cattle should be suffered on it the following season, until the grass get some strength, and never but in dry weather, as, where the ground is wet, they will poach, and destroy it with their feet. It should remain under pasture as long as it keeps a sward.

In order to improve waste lands, long leases are absolutely necessary for a tenant, but which the Proprietors in general, in this county, are very averse to grant; owing to which, tenants cannot, with any degree of propriety, do much to the improvement of commons. There being neither lime nor marl on my farm, I cannot speak as to their effects, having never used any.

14. Mr. *William Henderson*, Wester Ormly.—The plan I followed in improving this land was, to plough it thin, in winter, and to let it lie in that state till the following winter, and then, immediately upon the thaw of an intense frost, when the ground is open and soft to a great depth, I put four horses to a strong plough, and ploughed it across, as deep as the plough could go, thereby generally turning six inches, in addition to the first furrow; which was thereby turned down, and rotted, and reduced much sooner than any other way I could devise. In this state I allowed it to lie till the third spring, after the first ploughing, and then I ploughed up the whole, and sowed it with oats; which was generally a good crop. The following year, I naked fallowed the wet ground, and put turnip in the dry ground, manuring all well; and laid it down afterwards with bear, or oats, according to the soil, with grass-seeds. I took only one crop of grass, after finding that taking more made the ground again cold and sour. But I found, that after the new ground is thoroughly reduced, and a crop taken, after the first crop of grass, it requires triple the quantity of manure per acre, that old arable land of the worst sort does, to produce a decent crop; and that it yields its whole substance so rapidly, that hardly any grass will grow, after the corn-crop laid down with it, unless manured on the surface, after reaping the corn. How long this weakness in the new soil continues, I have not yet ascertained; though it is now ten years since I first began the ploughing up of the new ground; but I suspect, that a farmer, having a lease much shorter than 31 years, will find it his interest, after the first three

three crops he takes of his new land, to let it alone, unless he has access to lime or marl at a cheap rate.

15. Mr. *George Miller*, Whitefield.—I have put fully 140 acres of waste land in a state of improvement, which, including houses, and ditches, and stocking, has cost me above 1700*l*. About 120 acres I have cropped mostly with oats, after burning and ploughing four times, which, in my opinion, is a ruinous system. Average crop 3½ seeds. I never had it in my power, to make experiments on the best plan for improving waste commons, except about one acre, on which I laid a little marl, and a little compost manure. The good effects of the marl are yet very visible, it being now two years under grass. The ground was never burned.

16. Mr. *Mackid*, Wattin.—In my opinion, the best mode of improving waste lands, is to grant long leases to cottagers, say 21 years, for a trifling acknowledgment, if it were only a shilling a-year, for five to ten acres each, to be improved by potatoes, turnips, and small patches of grass, laid down as the improvement by potatoes, &c. is carried on. I have had no experience in improving commons in Caithness, and therefore cannot say what the expense may be per acre. The effect of lime and marl is, to make the soil more active. Under good management, they strengthen the soil, and without lime or marl, grass will never come to perfection for pasture. Not having lime within a reasonable distance of me, I am preparing apparatus for raising marl out of the Loch of Wattin, which I have no doubt will be attended with the happiest effects in producing corn and grass. As a top-dressing, it ranks first; as a permanent manure, it cannot be exceeded. I have often tried winter wheat, but found it to throw out in the months of April and May. I have not tried spring wheat.

17. Mr. *Robert Ryrie*.—I have improved 25 acres of waste land. Being wet clay ground, have done it mostly all by red fallow for two years. I have tried turnip and potatoes in some spots, and in wet seasons have lost both crops. I always dung the ground after potatoes and turnip, and then sow bear and grass-seeds. From this mode, I have had 20 bolls of bear from two acres, when it was not touched by the grub-worm; and of grass, 200 stone per acre; and in general, when not destroyed by the grub, have nearly averaged five bolls per acre, and of hay 150 stone. I prefer red fallow to burning; as, after burning, the ground throws up a great quantity of sorrel. I have tried marl, and found it to answer well on dry black soil. Never tried lime.

Expense

Expense of Improving an Acre of Waste Land.

				£	s.	d.
To ploughing it five times, at 12*s*. per acre				3	0	0
Harrowing five times, at 12*s*.				3	0	0
Digging, and taking off stones				0	15	0
80 cart-loads of earth and dung, at 6*d*.				2	0	0
Eight days driving, at the rate of 10 carts a-day, at 12*s*.				4	16	0
				£13	11	0
To laying the dung on the ground before seed-furrow				0	12	0
Spreading an acre				0	1	6
Ploughing it down				0	12	0
Harrowing and rolling				0	6	0
Taking off grass and small stones				0	5	0
				£15	7	6
To 1 boll bear, for seed	1	0	0			
3 bushels rye-grass, at 5*s*. 6*d*.	0	16	6			
16 lb. clover-seed, at 1*s*. 3*d*.	1	0	0			
3 years rent, at 20*s*. per acre	3	0	0			
				5	16	6
				£21	4	0
Returns of bear, 5 bolls, at 20*s*.	5	0	0			
First crop of grass, 150 stone, at 1*s*. ..	8	0	0			
Third year, value per acre	2	0	0			
				15	0	0
				£6	4	0

The above statement is what I have actually paid. Having no provender, was obliged to hire carts and ploughs, and paid as stated.

I am certain, that those who have farms of old arable land, cannot improve waste land, in the cheapest way, and to do it any justice, under 8*l*. sterling per acre.

The best oat is the potatoe, which answers well on a deep loamy soil, if dry; and after grass, or fallow, the dun oat I think the next best; on thin, sharp soils, it gives more straw than the red or black, but the red is the earliest.

18. Mr. *Paton*, Bleachfield.—Commons must be improved according to their various qualities and situations. Where there is depth of soil, frequent ploughings for the first two years,

years, at least three furrows each year, and using the break-harrow to reduce it, lay a good foundation. After giving it two ploughings the third year, clean the surface, and drill it for turnip or potatoes. If near the shore, sea-ware, mixed with earth, and properly fermented, will make excellent manure, or laid plentifully on the surface, and instantly covered up. The land then to be sown with bear and grass, the grass crop to lie three years, and be pastured the last two; to be sown with a good proportion of white clover. Where the soil is thin, and in any measure dry, lime, or marl, may be used. After two years ploughing and cleaning the surface, oats and grass sown, principally white clover, to be pastured three or four years with sheep; then two crops of oats; then begin the rotation of five, viz. turnip, bear and grass, grass, grass, oats. The expense must vary according to the nature of soil or situation; the expenses laid out by those, who have little arable or stock land to keep their horses or cattle, while they are improving, is no just criterion to judge of the expense of improving commons or waste lands. I believe it may cost in some cases 15*l.* per acre, where the distance is great from lime, marl, or sea-ware. But I am persuaded, that when proper means are used, with judgment, 10*l.* per acre would be sufficient.

19. Dr. *Menson.*—The mere inclosure of wastes, seems to me the best mode of improvement. By it the natural grasses are allowed to make such progress, as to afford pasturage for sheep, or even Highland cattle. This is the only plan of improvement I would recommend, unless on particular spots, whose contiguity to manure might induce one to have recourse to the plough. Even this should be done with caution, as new lands require to be supplied with manure every year, and then, the farmer will be often disappointed, from the wetness of the ground in seed time, or from its being baked by the drought of summer, almost to the hardness of bricks.

Trenching in many situations would answer, but the great price of this operation precludes its adoption in our climate, where the returns would never repay the outlay. Trenching, draining, dunging, and clearing the ground, would, I think, cost twenty pounds per acre. This would be improvement with a vengeance! Lime and marl would no doubt be useful, but the price of the former, in many situations, and the distance from the latter, present an insurmountable obstacle to the use of them; and I think the advantage gained by them, in other places, greater than could be obtained here, from the wetness of our soil.

20. Mr. *Mathers,* Spring-Park.—In Dixon-Field I have four

four parks, containing 70 acres of hill ground, and about ten or twelve acres of moss, all of which I have ploughed several times; taken out large quantities of rocks and stones, and made a number of open and sunk drains on the farm, in the course of the eight years I have occupied it; but this is only the beginning of the operation, for though it were ploughed twenty times, and reduced like a garden, it will, in the course of two years, return to its original state, if strong dung is not immediately applied, in a reduced state, and then it will produce a good crop of oats or bear, with sown grass, and never will again retain its former adherence, but becomes pliable and fertile like old land, when broken up; however, it will always require a great deal of good dung, to keep it in heart, and to take the cold nature out of it. All hill ground is natually wet and spongy, some more so than others; whilst it is in that state, lime or marl will not operate, until it is first dunged as above mentioned, and made dry; the lime or marl would otherwise be lost. I tried marl when the land was in a wet state, and it did no good. The only plan I can think of, and the most profitable to the proprietor, as tenants are out of the question, is to give a proportion of hill ground to each farmer near the common, at a very low rate, and to take them bound, that they will improve a certain number of acres of new land, in a given time, during the lease. If he fails in making the hill ground equal to what is agreed on, at different periods of his lease, let him be removed, and let the farm be given to another, who may be more skilful and active. It is the old land that must work up the new; it never will be wrought up by itself, if it were given for nothing, even to a person of skill and property; I know this will be said to be selfish, but I assert it to be true, let people say what they will. Owing to the smallness of Caithness farms in general, the people are never able to get their circumstances improved; and as long as that mode is continued, things cannot alter much for the better. I know this is not sound doctrine, in the opinion of some people, but it is no less true.

21. Mr. *Alexander Trotter*, Duncansbay.—On the farm of Wydale, I have about 70 acres, all of which have been ploughed, and under corn crops, but the deep moss was only ploughed and burnt, and then sown with grass-seeds. The firm or hard ground was all summer-fallowed, and top-dressed with moss, earth and marl, mixed together in a compost, laid on after the third ploughing, and harrowed in with the seed. The expense of this mode, I suppose might be about four pound or four guineas per Scotch acre; allowing three ploughings, three double tines of harrowing, and 40 carts of manure,

manure, marl, and moss, in compost. The ploughing and burning the moss, might cost from 25*s*. to 30*s*. per acre. But I do not think this the best mode, although I was obliged to practise it at that time, for want of better workmen.

I think the following the best mode of improving all wastes, that can be ploughed with propriety. They should first get a complete dose of lime, shell-sand or marl, on the surface, before the sward is broke; let it lie in this state for nine or twelve months, then give it a good dunging, and plant potatoes in drills, if the land is wet, but in every second furrow if dry. This is the easiest way of reducing waste land; and if one crop doth not do it, keep it two years in potatoe or turnips. Thus the land is reduced, and we have a crop of potatoes, which will be in proportion to the dung laid on. The expense of lime, shell-sand, or marl, will be in proportion to the distance from them. Deep mosses, with an even surface, can be improved in the same way. But where the soil is thin and hard, and of a high elevation, it is better to top-dress it with such manure as can be easiest got after inclosing, and laying it dry, and to keep it in grass.

On the farm of Duncansbay, I have taken in about thirty, or thirty-five acres of waste land. On some of this, I have the best potatoe oats, ever grown in Duncansbay. The mode was, a good top-dressing of shell-sand, at the rate of forty-five carts per acre. This lay fifteen months; then a good coat of earth and dung mixed together; it was then ploughed in winter, indeed it was so hard and bare, having been all skinned for feal, (sods or turf), that the plough could make nothing of it at any other time. It was sown with grey oats, which were not good. I afterwards ploughed it deeper by an inch or two every time, and this is the second, and the best crop of potatoe oats.

The expense of top-dressing with shell-sand, cost me about 20*s*. per acre, and the dunging about 50*s*. As to the rotation for waste land, I do not see there can be much difference between it and arable. I think it depends on the situation for manure, and the distance from markets. I have always observed, that the effect of lime or marl is in proportion to the quantity, and dryness of the soil.

22. Mr. *John Manson*, Thurso East.—In regard to the question, whether paring and burning, or ploughing for several years, is the best mode of improving waste lands, I prefer ploughing, for the following reasons: When ground is pared and burned, though it is a quick process, and gives a good crop; yet when that crop is taken from the ground, it still requires to undergo a process nearly equal in expense, to what it might have cost from its original state by ploughing; for by taking a crop in this way, the vegetative part of the soil is pared,

pared, burned, and exhausted, in the first crop; and until new soil is raised up by the plough, and pulverized by the air, and enlivened by manure, suited for such soil, it cannot be said that it is in an improved state; whereas, if improved by the plough, say to lie eighteen months, after having got the first ploughing, and in the course of other eighteen months to be properly reduced by the plough and harrow, and a competency of dung laid on, it will yield good crops, and may be kept under a rotation of corn and grass, much better than fields of a similar soil, which have been pared and burnt. The above remarks refer to moor, not to mossy lands.

Comparison of the Two Plans.—Paring and Burning—The expenses of paring and burning an acre, and spreading the ashes, is £2 0 0
Once ploughing 12*s.* 6*d.*, one harrowing 2*s.* 6*d.* .. 0 15 6

This expense of................ £2 15 0

per acre is laid out for one crop, and recourse must be had to fallow, or rather turnips, with a good dose of dung, before it gives another crop of any value, which expense will be at least equal to the above account of paring and burning, exclusive of the dung, which, from the distance we have to drive it, makes the expense come very high. Six *rake* a day is all we can drive to our improving fields; hence six cart-loads being a day's work to a man and a pair of horses, cannot be valued at less than 10*s.*; and each cart-load of dung sells in Thurso at 6*d.* per cart-load. These 50 cart-loads per acre, cost 4*l.* 3*s.* 4*d.*; and the expense for two years, would come to 9*l.* 13*s.* 4*d.*, after which expense, there has not been returned to the soil what was unjustly taken from it by paring and burning. The crop of turnips will not exceed in value the expenses of the seed, and that of cleaning, taking the earth from, and putting it to the turnips.

2. *Ploughing, without Paring and Burning.*—Improving an acre of moor by the plough and harrow, may be thus stated:

	£	s.	d.
Expenses of the first ploughing, ...	£0	15	0
Cross-ploughing with a deep furrow, ...	0	12	6
The break-harrow, ...	0	5	0
A third ploughing, ...	0	10	0
A second harrowing, ...	0	2	6
Fifty cart-loads of dung, at 2*s.* 2*d.*	5	8	4
Spreading the dung, ...	0	2	6
Giving the seed-furrow, ...	0	10	0
Harrowing in the seed with grass-seeds, ..	0	2	6
	£8	8	4

In regard to the best rotation, after it is free from the first corn crop, it is best to pasture it for the first year, rather than to make hay of it. Next year pasture; but as new ground continues spongy and wet in the surface, for a long time, then break it up again. If the soil is somewhat good and deep, sow black oats; if thin shallow ground, a clean fallow, small ridges, and gathered to some height; give a good dose of strong compost dung; sow black oats with grass-seeds; and, if the gathering the ridges to some height, shall have the effect of preventing the water from getting away through the surface, it may be pastured for some time, to more advantage than by any other mode. As the soil of this country lies on a close and horizontal rock, where the soil is thin, it must be spongy, and wet in the surface. This was the reason why they had such high and large ridges in Caithness, under the old system of farming.

As to the best manure for improved wastes, if the field can be laid perfectly dry, marl or lime may be applied, to be followed up the next season with strong compost, or dung from the stable-yard. If the field is a poor, thin, wettish soil, strong compost is to be preferred.

(D)

Draining.

THE following Communications, on the subject of Draining, have been received for the Caithness Report.

---

1. *General Sinclair*, of Lybster.—The best sort of drains for the county, must be such as most effectually carry off superabundant moisture. The same method of draining that would succeed at Sandside or Dunnet, might not answer in the parish of Latheron, which is craggy, hilly, and much intersected with wet spongy veins of bad cold clay, impregnated with iron mould. The drain, of two feet deep in solid clay, at 2*d.* per yard, filled one foot deep, at least, with small stones, has answered best at Lybster: where the ground was spongy, three feet, and sometimes more, was required. When rock is the conductor for the water, the elevation of the highest part of it must be attended to, and the rock itself freed from water, however distant it may be from the field draining. The

greater declivity the field may have, the greater necessity there will be, for guarding against every the least obstruction to the passage of water, by giving it some new and repeated incisions, and by a careful attention to the progress of the ditcher.

The first expense attending this operation of ditching and draining, is considerable; but as the drains receive the stones so readily, with which our fields in this parish are incumbered, great abatement may be made in the calculation. The advantages of draining land which could not, in some places, bear the weight of a plough in summer, and rendering it fit for tillage in winter, are evident.

2. *John Sinclair*, Esq. of Barrack.—Open drains round fields, when wet, with covered drains in the field, if covered properly, and heather between the stones and the covering of earth, are to be preferred. The expense of the drains, when open, from 2½*d.* to 4*d.* and often 6*d.* per yard; and 4*d.* to 6*d.* if covered.

3. *Major Innes*, of Sandside.– Draining is of the first importance, and, in almost all cases, equal to a year's rent. A great deal of draining has been done at Sandside, but generally at too high a rate, for want of skill. The kind, and price, must depend on the nature of the soil; the leading drains built and flagged over, the cross drains filled with small stones, but where stones are not to be had, a particular kind of spade is necessary, and a sod, green side downwards, is made use of instead of flags.

4. *Alexander Henderson*, Esq. of Stemster.—Covered drains, I conceive to be the best, and the opener the conveyance for the water is, the better. They may be made from 2½*d.* to 3*d.* per yard.

5. *George Sutherland*, Esq. of Brabster.—Where the form can be regular, the common ditch, from the facility of making and cleaning it, seems preferable to every other sort of drain. Where covered ones are necessary, the open drain, flagged at bottom, faced with stones, and well secured at top, is perhaps the best. The difficulty attendant upon cleaning is, however, very great. The close drain, (denominated in this county *rumbling sewer*), answers well at first forming, but is apt to choke. Pit draining should be tried, when the other sorts fail of producing the desired effect. The expense, from a variety of circumstances, differs with the situation.

6. *Major Williamson*.—Having paid some attention to Mr. Johnstone's book, I made some attempts at draining with a boring-rod, in some of which I succeeded. Draining is certainly

tainly a very precarious operation in Caithness; for being mostly on an impervious bottom, it is difficult to ascertain the direction of the spring: I have been so often disappointed, that I now take the shortest direction to the bog, following the workmen with the rod, and piercing the bottom. I have often raised the water by this means, from the depth of four feet below the bottom of the drain, or six feet from the surface. These I fill with stones gathered from the land, and cover them up. I have not known any of these bores fill up.

7. Dr. *Henderson*, Clyth.—The best sort of drains are those which are filled up with small stones, covered with heather, and then with the earth taken out of them. Their advantages must be great, where the soil is naturally so wet, as is the case in Caithness.

8. Mr. *Donald Miller*, East Noss.—The nature of the drains to be preferred, depends much on situation: if open drains, four feet by three, and twelve inches in the bottom; if covered, the ditch to be opened four feet broad at top and bottom, and three feet deep, laid in the bottom with flat stones, built at each side about ten inches high, (leaving a space of ten inches betwixt the buildings; lay flat stones across the buildings, and then close up with earth. All drains ought to be made as straight as possible, (particularly covered ones), as they will be apt to choke at turns; they ought also to be deep, on account of drawing the water, and letting ploughs go over them.—For cutting such drains, from $2\frac{1}{2}d.$ to $3\frac{1}{2}d.$; covering, about $3d.$ per ell.

9. *Major Innes*, Keiss.—Open drains I consider as the best, at least to leave them open for a year or two; you will then know if they answer your purpose; and if they do, you can fill them up with useless stones, and cover them over with heather, &c. and then with the earth taken out of the drain.

10. Mr. *Sinclair Gun*, Deal.—Drains are of the greatest advantage, where a firm level bottom can be got. A water-run ought to be left open, *lintelled*, (covered with flags), of six inches square, or more, according to the quantity of water in the place. When a good bottom cannot be had, the drain ought to be made deeper, and about two foot deep of stones put in it, and carefully covered with heather, (if to be had), if not, with straw, before the earth is put on it.

11. Mr. *William Henderson*, Wester Ormly.—The drains I have adopted, from a belief of their being the most effectual, are those having six inches of building on each side, and

 a cover

a cover of stones over them; and another sort made, by placing a row of thick stones, about six inches diameter, on the middle the drain, and setting thin stones to the sides of them, with the upper end resting on the thick stones; thus leaving a triangular aperture, or drain, on each side of the row of stones. This last sort can be done at half the expense of the other, but having had them partly done by the labour of my farm-servants and cattle, I have not ascertained the exact expense of either. The advantages of draining, in this county, *are so very incalculable*, that I should be thought extravagant in my ideas on that subject; I will therefore avoid touching upon it, and leave it to people of more experience.

12. Mr. *Mackid*, Wattin.—This county being of a shallow soil, open drains are best adapted for it, particularly when the ground is subject to surface-water. Spouts and springs should be carried away by the drains commonly called rumbling drains, being made with stones thrown in promiscuously from the cart or the hand. The drain must be sunk to a proper depth, filled and convexed, first with flags or sods, or heather, and then with the soil. From the spongy nature of the soil in Caithness, drains are absolutely necessary, and no improvement can be carried on with advantage, without them.

13. Mr. *Mathers*, Spring-Park.—The first work a farmer should do, is to drain his ground; nothing can be done to perfection without it. In many cases, where the field lies level, and where the water does not run freely, an open drain is surely best; if the ground has a declivity, sunk ones are best; if filled with round stones, and covered up, laying heather above the stones, and then earth, it will be the driest part of the field. Either of these can be made for 1½*d.* or 2*d.* per yard: they require to be pretty deep, to receive the stones and the earth.

14. Mr. *George Miller*, Whitefield.—The sort of drain to be recommended, depends upon the nature of the soil, and the lie of the ground. Springs, and all sorts of under-water, may be taken off by hurling drains, (as they are called), but surface-water by open drains or ditches. Hurling drains will cost about 7*s.* 6*d.* per rood, and open drains, according to their size, from 1*s.* to 9*d.* per rood.

15. Mr. *Paton*, Bleachfield.—I believe open drains of two feet the best; the expense will be about 2*d.* per yard. The utility of drains, in this wet country, is so obvious, that it requires no explanation.

16. Mr. *John Manson*, Thurso-East.—A covered drain is the

the most secure of any. Suppose one to have an opening of eight inches square, it may cost $4\frac{1}{2}d.$ per yard, for digging, building, and filling it up again.

17. Mr. *James Anderson.*—Drains must be of different kinds, to suit the porpose for which they are intended; for instance, a catch-water drain, of which I have several, must be open; and its breadth, and depth, suited to the quantity of water which it is to receive; some of these cost me only 1*d.* per yard; others more, where the ground was hard to work. I have also a good many hundred yards of covered drains in my fields, and which answer the purpose most effectually; these, two feet wide, by nearly the same depth, cost me 1*d.* per yard in cutting, owing to the hardness of the subsoil. I found enough of small stones on the fields to fill them, at the rate of 12 inches perpendicular height.

The stone work was carefully and closely covered, with long heather, on which the soil was laid, and levelled; and it is surprising what quantity of water these drains discharge, almost every season of the year.

I here think it necessary to observe, that in so draining the only boggy part of this farm, I found one particular spot, where the drains had not the desired effect; it still continued wet, and the horses could not plough it. I therefore digged a pit, in the apparently uppermost side of this spot, to a considerable depth, and from thence, opened a communication with the drain nearest thereto: these I filled with stones, covered with heather, and earth, and the cure was *most complete.*

18. Mr. *Trotter*, Duncansbay.—Drains must differ according to the water they have to discharge. If intended for under-water, or springs, covered drains will be necessary; but if surface-water, open drains will do best. The way to clear ground of under-water is, cut for the drain a certain distance above the head of, the spring, or above where any of the water comes to the surface, and so deep, that no water can come below, the drain. The operator may, from the level of the ground, have some idea where the water comes from; and to cut the water, or bring it into the drain above the wet ground, is what is wanted. If the bottom of the drain be hard and firm, and not much water, the stones may be thrown in any way, only the largest undermost. But if there is a great run of water, the drain will need to be built on every side, and a large stone or flag laid on as a cover; or two stones set on edge, wide at bottom, and close at the top. But in this way, care must be taken, that the stones be laid firm on both sides, as well as above, or the stones next the water

 will

will be in danger of being removed. Which of these three ways is best, will depend on the kind of stones easiest got. If the ground be all, or any part of it, clay, the strongest clay must be laid first in, or next the stones; but if it be gravelly or loam, either divots or feal, (turf), must be laid next the stones, or whatever can be easiest got, to keep the loose earth from going down through the stones. If the bottom of the drain is loose sand, loam, or gravel, the stones must be well chosen, and sometimes it may be necessary to flag the bottom; but when the rock is the cause of water coming to the surface, then is the difficulty of finding the spring, and cutting the drain. I suppose indeed that nothing but boring, or digging pits, will do. It is hardly necessary to mention, that the uppermost stones must be laid low enough to be out of the reach of the plough, otherwise the surface-water will go down, and take sand or loose earth with it, into the water-run, which may stop the whole.

The best size of covered drains is, about four feet deep, and one and a half or two feet wide, and the expense of making and covering them, will depend on the soil and materials for filling them. All surface-water can be taken away with open drains, and ridges lying in a straight direction. Ridges 15 or 16 feet wide, and twice gathered, will generally keep any field dry; but in irregular lying fields, where the water does not run from the one end of the field to the other, it is often necessary, to have either an open drain, or one or two ridges drawn in the natural run of the water. When there is a hollow, and the water gathering to it from the sides, it is generally best to have an open drain, made with the plough, as it will be cheaper twice ploughed; or what we call two clearings, will in most cases be deep enough. Sometimes it is necessary to cast out some of the earth; for if it is left, the earth may be too high for the water to come over, out of the regular furrows. This is the kind of drain I use, when I think there will be a run of water all the winter; but if it is only occasional, or when a sudden fall of rain happens, that the regular furrows do not contain all the water, or the ridges may be too long, and the water gather too much force before it can get out, I gather a ridge or two in the natural run of the water. This eases every furrow, by discharging it at one of the sides, or in one furrow made larger for that purpose. There are not many fields, but what may be kept clear of surface-water in this way; and on wet soils, I keep the ridges of the same height, by ploughing always two and two, or four and four together. This is called casting out and in, and when well done, has a good appearance, as all the furrows are left

open

open and clear. Every person must know the necessity there is, for having all the cross-furrows or drains looked over twice a year, that is, after ploughing, and after harrowing. The advantage of laying ground dry, is the first, and one of the most material points in agriculture, even before dunging and cleaning; for who would lay manure among water, or on a wet soil? But if any one is obliged to put on manure, and bestow labour on soil not thoroughly dry, (which may be the case sometimes), whatever it may do in dry seasons, he will have but little benefit from it in wet ones. The expense of laying ground dry, cannot be accurately ascertained, as every field differs, in proportion to the hardness of the subsoil, its irregularity, and its distance from materials.

19. *General Remarks.*—As draining is so essential in Caithness, and its advantages are justly considered *to be incalculable,* one of the greatest improvements that could be made in the county is, to make the ridges, in all wet soils and situations, 30 feet broad, and proportionably high, with an open or covered ditch *in each furrow.* This would drain the land most effectually, and render it always accessible to the plough and the cart. This plan is found advantageous in Flanders, was recommended by the celebrated Arbuthnot, and has been successfully adopted by Mr. Andrew, a farmer at Tillylumb, near Perth. (See the Husbandry of Scotland, p. 50).

(E)

Manures.

The following Hints, regarding the important subject of Manure, were transmitted for the Caithness Report.

1. The *Earl of Caithness.*—Sea-ware is much used on the farm of Mey, but only answers for one crop. It is better calculated for bear than oats. Shell-sand answers well for bedding cattle. It kills weeds, when thus prepared, particularly sorrel. As good crops are got from shell-sand, after being bedded, as from dung.

2. *General Sinclair,* of Lybster.—Decayed moss, with a friable clay, and stable manure, are only used at Lybster, where some grounds are preparing for lime. The access to sea-

sea-ware is not convenient here. There is scarcely a vein of sand, or gravel, to be met with here, of any extent.

3. *Alexander Henderson*, Esq. of Stemster.—In this part of the country, we have no opportunity of trying sea-ware, or shell-sand. We prefer composts of dung, earth, moss, marl, or indeed, anything we can get. Formerly midding feal, (sods, or turfs), was our principal manure; and it being in general the surface of the very richest parts of the commons, little dung was necessary with it; and it always gave, if not a good crop of bear the first year, a good crop of oats the second; but as, from the laudable exertions of the principal Proprietors, this practice is now almost universally abolished, marl, and other substitutes, come to be more anxiously sought for.

4. *Major Innes*, of Sandside.—Sea-weed ought to be made use of *fresh*, and other dung should not be kept very long, otherwise it becomes a body of earth, rather than dung. Shell-sand is good for strong soils, or laid on grass, before ploughing up, without either breaking or burning. Lord Meadowbank's compost is a good manure: the best articles to use, must depend on the nature of the soil.

5. *George Sutherland*, Esq. of Brabster.—As a manure, dung takes the lead, and should form the principal part of every compost. It should not be used fresh, but kept. Sea-ware answers best when laid on in a rotten state, as may be now seen at my sea-coast farm. If the farmer wishes immediate, but short benefit, he ought to burn his shell-sand. Would he prefer many tolerable crops to a few great ones, he may content himself with breaking his sand.

6. *John Sinclair*, Esq. of Barrack.—A compost of black earth and dung, layer and layer, with some marl, or lime, intermixed, if it can be got, will answer dry land. The dung kept over winter in byres, by bedding the cattle or sheep, is the only proper manure for wet land. Lime answers best for hill ground, and marl for grass grounds that are to be ploughed. Lime for wheat and turnips.

7. *Alexander Sinclair*, Esq. of Achingale.—For light soils, a compost dunghill of good earth, stable-dung, and sea-ware, when it can be got, has been found to answer well. For clay and strong soils, Lord Meadowbank's compost deserves attention, and shell-sand with it, cannot fail producing good crops. Stable-dung, unquestionably, will be best, if taken alone, in a putrescent state. In compost, I presume it is always so, and if not, it should be so. Sea-ware laid on land during the winter,

ter, and early in the spring, seems not to require any preparation, but if laid on at seed-time, I should imagine it would be better to have it in a putrid state. Shell-sand, no doubt, will act the quicker, by being made into lime; but to break sand appears to me an useless operation. Shells may be broke to advantage, but the sand of shells, from what I have seen, is small enough for every purpose of manure.

8. *Major Innes*, Keiss.—As far as my experience and observation go, compost manure is by far the best for bear and oats. Dung, moss, and sea-weed, answer well; and if shell-sand could be got, so much the better. I believe the great secret of farming, is in preparing your manure properly. Lay on as much as your soil can bear, and never plough, harrow, or stir your ground in a bad day, or when the ground is wet. Rest your cattle in a bad day, and occupy the good day; and in general you will find, that by doing so, you will have a good crop.

9. *Major Williamson.*—Well prepared compost is the best enricher of the soil. Earth, dung, and decayed vegetables, are known to be the best articles for compost; but to incorporate these properly, a certain degree of fermentation is necessary. I have some reason to think, that a cart-load of fresh sea-weed will be sufficient to reduce three cart-loads of earth into a rich compost; or a load of dung and two of earth, if intimately mixed up during the summer, and left for the use of next year, will answer well. I have now a compost dung-heap, pretty nearly in these proportions, and that part of it which has been mixed, is now above a blood-heat. I collect the urine of cattle, and throw upon it; but I think the heap is injured by the pressure of the servants' feet in the operation. This compost I mean next year to apply to my turnip and fallow field, at the rate of 50 cart-loads per acre.

Sea-weed, applied fresh, will produce an abundant crop of bear, or oats; its effects last no longer. Shell-sand is a neglected jewel, that ought to be applied directly from the shore.

10. *Capt. Robertson*, Warse.--Sea-ware and dung, kept till putrid, make excellent manure for a single crop, and no more. Shell-sand, when burnt, has the speediest effect in fertilizing the soil, but will sooner exhaust its power. If laid on the land without being burnt, the duration of its influence is unknown, as it will continue for a great length of time.

As to the bank of shells at Duncansbay, which Mr. Sinclair of Freswick let on a short lease, some years ago, at, I think, a rent of 50*l.* a-year, to Mr. Traill, it is sufficiently certain, that, notwith-

notwithstanding what is annually taken away, it suffers no sensible diminution, but rather increases in the western direction of the shore, although the accumulation of the bank within the bay is not observed to become greater. No doubt the quantity taken away is replaced, at least in part; but in so large a bank, the quantity taken away is comparatively so inconsiderable, that it would require a long period of time to determine its diminution, or to mark its increase by the accession of new sand thrown in. The best mode of using them as a permanent manure, is undoubtedly in their natural state; but for an active stimulant, they must be burnt. They make excellent litter for horses and cattle, and answer well for houses, being the very best lime for plaster; but I believe the quantity burnt does not increase byslacking, as rock-lime does.

11. Mr. *William Henderson*, Wester Ormly.—I use all the year's farm-yard dung in making compost during the harvest, to be used on turnip and fallow the following spring and summer; and finding the quantity thus increased to be triple, and as it answers well, I intend to continue the practice. I use the sea-weed in layers, with garden-earth from Thurso, and find it an excellent compost.

12. Mr. *Mathers*, Spring-Park.—The best new mode of manuring, (Lord Meadowbank's), is a great improvement. It is a good plan to mix sea-ware with dung; for it makes the dung a great deal stronger, though the ware adds very little bulk to the dung when rotten. If sea-ware comes in fresh, it is a great advantage to lay it on the ground immediately. I should suppose, every kind of shell-sand would operate sooner when burnt. It will be years before unburnt shells will dissolve on the ground, and many of them never.

13. Dr. *Manson*.—All decomposed vegetable and animal matter, is supposed useful for the growth of plants. I cannot enter into the varieties of soils, or quantities necessary; but in general observe, that where plenty of such substances is laid on, the farmer is amply repaid, except, on light land, where much is thrown up, and nothing comes to maturity. Animal matter, and vegetable ashes, should be speedily applied, lest the one may lose by evaporation, and both by solution in water. Thus street dung is supposed to have twice the effect, if recently laid on, that it would have if kept for a year. I do not see any use in keeping dung, if not to decompose sufficiently the component parts of it; every day after is a loss.

Sea-ware I think should be applied fresh, when possible, but in either way, a crop of bear or oats may be obtained, from the use of it, in quantity and quality, equal to what is obtained from

from the use of dung only. As to oats, I think with sea-ware they would answer best on a clayey soil.

In a county like this, where the arable land is generally clayey, every addition of calcareous matter must be supposed useful, and I certainly prefer the shells burnt. Indeed it has surprised me, that this county has yielded grain for such a length of time, without the assistance of lime, knowing that there is a certain proportion of that substance in every *grain*. The application of broken shells, is no doubt useful, by opening the soil, but their usefulness as lime, must be very slow indeed, having only the action of the sun and weather to bring them into a state fit to nourish the plant. In tenaceous clayey soils, I think, peat-moss might be usefully employed, if used in sufficient quantity, for the purpose of keeping the soil open, and allowing the superfluous moisture to subside, independent of its use as a manure, when decomposed; perhaps if dried as for fuel; as in this state it would best answer the purpose I propose. I do not think marl is ever laid on in sufficient quantity, and the farmers seem wholly ignorant of the strength of the different parts of the same stratum.

14. Mr. *Donald Miller*, East Noss.—I prefer earth, shell-sand, sea-ware, and summer dung, covered over during winter with the winter dung; trenched early in spring, put upon land for turnips. Sea-ware, if got at Martinmas, or in winter, (if the land is dry), to be laid on the land pretty thick, and ploughed down; if the land is wet, to be put on the top of the midding. What shell-sand is got here, is quite small; the manner in which I use it is, for bedding cattle and horses, and compost middings.

15. Mr. *George Miller*, Whitefield.—It is a matter very much disputed, what is the best kind of manure; some preferring compost, to pure stable-yard dung; lime to marl, and so on. I prefer sea-ware made up with earth, and letting it lie in that state unused, for some months, to laying it on fresh.

When shells are burnt, they are no more shells, but lime. I never had it in my power to try shell-sand, but have been informed that it has been used to advantage.

16. Mr. *Leith*.—Of all the various sorts of manure for the purposes of Agriculture, there are none more in general use than compost, consisting of earth, lime, and dung. The glutinous, or oleaginous matter, found in the miry or muddy parts of natural, and sometimes of artificial woods, and the miry parts in other grounds, especially such as are frequented by snipes. This glutinous earth is dug from these mires, and after having lain some time exposed to the air, is then trenched over,

over, and carted to the compost dunghill, and mixed with the other ingredients that compose the compost. For clay soils, fresh dung is to be preferred. The shell-sand broken, is also proper for being spread upon the surface of clay-ground before it is ploughed down, as it contributes to keep the soil open. Kept dung, and burnt shells, may be laid upon loamy and gravelly soils, with good effect.

17. Mr. *Paton*, Bleachfield,—Thurso dung is the best manure; sea-ware, when properly mixed with earth, and allowed to putrify, makes excellent manure, much preferable to laying it on the land, except when immediately ploughed in. Mixing dung with earth, where it is to be laid on a deep soil, is lost labour. Straw is a much better substitute for preserving the urine of the cattle than earth: I am not acquainted with the effect of shell-sand, but certainly, when burnt, it must be the more instant, and when broken, the more durable.

Moss, when properly mixed with *but little* stable-dung, and allowed to ferment, makes good manure for a clay soil.

18. Mr. *Cumming*, Ratter*.—The best mode of using compost, is to spread it on the surface after pease or fallow, when the ground is to be laid down to bear and grass, observing at same time, that the manure be as little exposed to the air as possible.

Shell-sand ought not to be burnt or broken; it is good in compost, and answers well for bedding horses and cattle.

Sea-weed makes an excellent compost, but ought not to be applied in wet weather. When put on land fresh, it ought to be ploughed in, for if permitted to rot, it would lose its substance.

19. Mr. *James Anderson*,—The best manure I have, because the only kind I can procure, exclusive of what my sheep leave on the fields, while eating the turnips, and which is no small supplement, is as follows: in summer I lay about two feet thick of earth, on the place where my byre-dung is to be thrown, and when that first earth is well covered, new lay, or add another layer of earth, perhaps early in winter; on which the whole of the byre-dung is laid, till March; when nearly all this upper dung is carted off to the intended turnip field; and all the dung afterwards made, goes the same way, where it is mixed with what earth and rubbish can be

* William Earl of Caithness, who occupied the farm of Ratter, always kept his bear in bykes, made up with straw and simmons, and found that it might thus be kept extremely well. Each byke contained from ten to twenty bolls.

collected,

collected, and laid up in long dykes, of about four feet in height, by six or seven broad, narrow at top. About a month or five weeks before using, these composts, as well as the byre-midding, are carefully turned from top to bottom; and the turnip field gets the whole; a little for the garden, and potatoes, excepted. I should have observed, that my stable dung goes also to the compost.

Sea-ware is of such a fructifying nature, that I never knew it fail as a manure, whether applied by itself, or mixed with earth; such as have access to but little of it, will surely make the most of it by compost; and when plenty, I should think both ways best.

Shell-sand, such as I have seen in Buchan, is a powerful manure, used in its natural state; that found in the west country, about Loch Broom, is much richer, but difficult to be obtained in very large quantities; being, as far as I understand, generally under sea-mark. I have known it to work wonders, in cleaning and meliorating the soil; but never saw any of it burnt or broken, intentionally.

20. Mr. *Daniel Miller*, Skinnet.—Lime is too expensive to be used in this neighbourhood. Thirty cart-loads of marl to an acre, has a good effect on clover leys; marl also improves compost dunghills; say one cart of marl to six of black earth, or moss, with two carts of farm-yard dung.

21. Mr. *Robert Ryrie*.—The best manures certainly are, lime and marl to be used on fallows, or the marl on grass in autumn. Sea-ware answers best, when mixed with earth and dung. I never tried shell-sand, but should think it would operate sooner burnt than broken.

22. Mr. *Sinclair Gun*.—Manures should only be used for green crops, or to a fallow; if otherwise applied, (excepting as top-dressing for grass), weeds reap by far the greatest part of the benefit. I never had an opportunity of trying the value or effects of sea-weed, or shell-sand. Without lime, improvements must be slow and imperfect. The effect of lime, (especially on new ground), is very great: marl is a good substitute for lime, but a slow operator.

23. Mr. *Swanson*, Gerston.—Manures may be differently used, agreeably to the ground and quality. Lime or marl laid on the sward in autumn, with good earth, after the plough, always answers. I have found lime, with prepared earth, do well, and it keeps the ground 14, 18, or 20 years. Marl is an excellent substitute; but if either is not well supported, or the ground much rested, they soon impoverish it.

Earth,

Earth, and what is got from the stables and byres, are generally used; and when kept for a year, and trenched once or twice, makes excellent manure. Sea-ware I am told does well, either laid fresh on the land, or mixed with dung, &c. I believe the last is most productive. I think shell-sand would answer better to be a little burnt, before applying it as a manure.

24. Mr. *George Innes*, Isauld.—Compound dunghills, containing a mixture of earth, stable-dung, and sea-ware, with shell-sand, if properly mixed, are found to be the best manure, when neither lime or marl can be got.

25. Mr. *John Manson*, Thurso-East.—A well-mixed compost, is the best manure of any, in my opinion, as it may be made to answer every soil, and also adds to its staple. Shell-sand will answer well for bedding cattle, and may then be applied to fields under the five-shift course, as it gets a little of it often. When used for pasture ground, laying it on the surface is preferable. As to sea-ware, when rotted, it keeps the soil the longest; but to serve a field with rotted ware, requires six times the quantity that is necessary when applied fresh. Sea-ware, used by itself, gives only one good crop, the next one being very slight; of course, mixing it with earth is the best plan.

26. Mr. *Alexander Trotter*, Duncansbay.—The best manure about a farm, is that made by the cattle, when they are fed on green vegetables. Next to that, is a rich compost, which will depend on the situation of the place, in regard to materials. I make all my composts of dry moss, or the dry surface of bogs, for a foundation; then shell-sand; then sea-ware, or dung, always two or three times trenched over. The proportion of each, is just as I find it has a proper degree of moisture; if too dry, I add sea-ware and dung, and if too moist, dry moss. I bed all my horses and cattle with shell-sand and dry moss; but every one is not so well situated for shell-sand and sea-ware, as I am. Most of this county, however, is well supplied with moss and marl, and therefore there is no just ground to complain of want of manure.

The best way of using manure, in my opinion, is with green crops and summer-fallow. But in the long-shift rotation, there may be more dung than can be laid on the green crop, or summer-fallow; then top-dressing on the sward, in the end of summer, or beginning of harvest, will answer well both for grass and corn. I always approve of sea-ware being made into composts, with earth, moss, or horse-dung, unless by those who have very dry lands, a rough stubble, dry weather, and wish for a crop of bear. Sea-ware sometimes comes in such

such quantities, that those who are nearest, are glad to apply it every where, rather than to lose any.

Shell-sand is a very slow manure, and is of more benefit to the proprietor than the tenant, unless where there is a long lease. I have tried shells, burnt and broken: when burnt, the effect is immediate; but when broken, very slow.

27. *Sea-Shells.—Improved Mode of using them.*—As sea-shells abound so much at Duncansbay, the following plan, recommended by Mr. Mitchell, surgeon at Ayr, might be of considerable importance, by furnishing a cheap and valuable manure, to be obtained from that article, by an improved mode of preparation.

Take thirty-two Winchester bushels of lime, and slack it with sea-water, previously boiled to the saturated state, or to the state of brine, to the consistency of soaper's waste. This quantity is sufficient for an acre of land, and may be either thrown out of the carts with a shovel over the land, in the above state, or made into compost with forty carts of moss or earth, in which state it will be found to pay fully for the additional labour, and is sufficient for an acre of fallow ground, though ever so reduced before. Its component parts are muriate and sulphate of lime, mineral alkali in an uncombined state, also muriate and carbonate of soda. All the experiments have done well with it, but especially wheat and beans, and it has not been behind any manure with which it has been compared. There is one instance, in which it was tried in comparison with seventy-two cart-loads of soaper's waste and dung; and although this was an extraordinary dressing, nevertheless, that with the new manure, was fully above the average of the field. The experiments this year are more extensive, and, as far as the season has gone, look well, and promise a good crop*. This species of manure, however, could only be prepared near the sea, or in the neighbourhood of the salt springs in Cheshire; but as a sufficient dressing for an acre, can be transported in four single-horse carts, it may be carried twenty or thirty miles inland to advantage.

Mr. Mitchell calculates, that 3000 gallons of sea-water, boiled down to about 600 gallons, will slack 64 bushels of of lime shells; a quantity sufficient for two acres. The expense of carrying the water from the sea, the evaporation, and slacking, will cost 20*s.*; the 64 bushels of lime-shells, cost him 40*s.*; 3*l.* in all: hence the total price of this manure is only at the rate of 30*s.* per acre; and the expense of carriage must be trifling, owing to the smallness of the bulk. The price, however, must depend upon the strength of the sea-water, the

* Aiton's Ayrshire, p. 385.

price of the coals, and of lime-shells. In situations where the sea-water is strong, double the quantity of lime slackened at the sea-side, would answer the purpose equally well, and it is in the power of every one to make it. Indeed, brine might be prepared, by making pits in the neighbourhood of the sea, where the soil is retentive, or reservoirs in the rocks, filling them in the summer months with sea-water. The heat of the sun would soon make the water of the strength required, at very little expense*.

(F)

Live Stock.

ON this important subject, the following Communications were transmitted, to be inserted in the Caithness Report.

CATTLE.

1. *Col. Williamson.*—An ordinary country stot, at three years and a half old, (the common age at which they are brought to market), will weigh from 150lb. to 170lb., in the condition in which they are usually exposed for sale. Such could be bought this year, (1807), as low as 2*l.* 15*s.*, or thereabouts; but I have known them sell as high as 6*l.* He would, if well grazed, and put upon turnips early in November, with straw in the night, be ready for the butcher by the beginning of February, and weigh from 250lb. to 300lb.

An ordinary country cow, will, at five or six years old, weigh about 200lb. when in the same condition. Such could be bought this year as low as 3*l.*, but have been sold as high as 6*l.* or 7*l.* in former years. She would, if fed and grazed as above mentioned, increase in the same proportion, in the same space of time.

Stots are seldom brought to the butcher at the age mentioned; and cows never here, as far as I know, under five years old. Stots and queys, of three years and a half old, the produce of picked country cows, and Highland bulls, and properly fed during that period, seldom sell under 7*l.*; and I have sold my whole stock, of that age, as high as 11*l.* per head; and even this year, my stots of that age, sold to a drover at 8*l.*, which is higher than was given in this county, or in Suther-

* It is said, that shells might be reduced to powder, as bones are, by sprinkling them with urine. That would make an excellent manure.

land,

land, except for the Dunrobin stock. These stots, if fed as the former, would weigh above 400lb.

The above refers to the old breed of Caithness cattle only; and the variety is so great, that it is difficult to give an average. I have known cows, when full fat, not exceed 170lb. in weight.

As to the difference between the Caithness and Sutherland cattle, it is my opinion, that the Sutherland are the best, as they are nearly all of a Highland breed: whereas the variety of the Caithness, and the greater number being of bad kinds, makes them little sought after. Cattle of good kinds might certainly be reared, as well in Caithness, as in any other Lowland situation. As to a tendency to fatten, it is generally admitted, that the best cattle are easiest fed.

2. Mr. *John Macdonald*, Achascoriclett.—The number of the Caithness cattle annually sold, may be about 2000. The number of three years old stots sold, about 1500, from 28 to 30 stone, of 8lb. weight per stone. The number of heifers bred, is about 1500; of which 500, or thereabouts, are annually sold, the remainder kept for breeding: weight about 26 stone of 8lb. The number of cows in the county, about 8000, from the age of four to fifteen years. Their weight about 33 stone. The marks of distinction between them and the Skye breed, are, that they are narrower in the back, barer of hair, and a little longer in the leg. The best stocks may be valued this year, (1807), at from four guineas to 4*l.* 10*s.* per head. The second-best stocks, may fetch about 4*l.* The inferior, from 50*s.* to 52*s.*

They begin purchasing the Caithness cattle, for droving, about the latter end of April, or about the 14th of that month, and they continue to the end of September. The first market at which the North Country cattle is shown, is Amulrie, on the first Wednesday in May; then Cokehill, on the 16th of the same month; then Falkirk, Broughill, and Newcastle. The cattle are frequently bought on credit; but ready-money makes a difference of 7½ per cent. with the general run of the farmers. It would be possible to buy them half fat, but the price would be greatly higher; and, from the long journey, and bad keeping on the road, it would make little difference in the end. The best way to buy them is, in a travelling condition. The expense of driving cattle from the borders of the county of Caithness to Carlisle, is about 7*s.* 6*d.* per head. Driving them carefully, it takes, in the month of August, thirty-two days. The best sized drove, for driving cattle with safety, is about 250; or 500, if driven in two divisions.

The farmers would have no reluctance to sell their stots,

separate from their queys, about the same price, if no better in quality.

It will take, in this country, 18 months to fatten a stot properly. First, good pasture, and then turnip and oat-straw. They are known to weigh, when fat, from 50 to 60 stone of 8lb. They require more turnip, than a pound of green food, as turnip, for every stone they weigh; but not so much of green grass, or foggage. If properly kept, the cows make excellent milkers, and their milk is of a superior quality. Crossing the Caithness and the Low Country breeds, would improve the quantity of milk, but diminish the value of the breed for droving.

3. *Alexander Sinclair*, Esq. of Achingale.—Real Highland cattle, seem to be the best adapted for the climate and pasture of Caithness. Under proper treatment, and with half the attention paid to other cattle brought to this county, they will always improve in size and figure. Such other cattle as I have seen, with hardly an exception, are unfit for our cold, late springs, and rainy autumns, and we are not yet a land of soiling, nor is it likely will be for a length of time.

4. *Major Williamson.*—The dairy seems to be too much an object for the cattle stock of this county, and prevents their arriving at such perfection as to hold a respectable place in the Southern markets. The county is by nature calculated for breeding, or store-farming. In this respect, I look upon Caithness as much resembling Aberdeen-shire. In Aberdeenshire, the Lowland farmer keeps no more cows than are sufficient to supply his family with milk, butter, and cheese, and no calves, except from a favourite cow. Yet the Aberdeenshire cattle, hold the first place in the English market. Whence then their stock of cattle? They are purchased from the mountainous districts, fed upon the rich pastures in the Lowlands, and sent to market at three or four years old. In Aberdeenshire, the breed of cattle is founded upon the Highland breeds. Judiciously crossing, to increase the size, is pursued; but every attention possible is paid to preserve the symmetry of the parent stock. Caithness should follow the same system.

In the more fertile parts, let the farmer abandon keeping cattle. His grass is too valuable to pay in that mode. When his grass is eaten up, let him purchase that stock from the Highlander, which in April or May, is sent to the moors to starve. But to effect this, Sir John Sinclair must banish his Galloways, Mr. Traill his Dunlops, and Sandside his Northumbrians;—then the hardy Kylo will be cherished, and increase in size, beauty, and value. This arrangement will only require a few years to be in full operation.

5. Mr.

5. Mr. *Sinclair Gun*, Deal.—The kind of stock kept on a farm, should depend on the situation of the place. In the interior of Caithness, rearing of young cattle, of good quality, I think, would answer best. There can be no better cattle, or more weighty for their size, than the Skye breed; yet, by the time they are a year in Caithness, they completely lose their fine coat, and are not of the same value for driving to the South Country markets. I am of opinion, however, that Caithness might, by proper attention, bring as valuable cattle to market as Skye. A few good bulls from Argyle, or Skye, would be of the greatest use to this country; as an instance of this, in 1787, when the Caithness cattle were selling at 2*l.* a-piece, in the South markets, an acquaintance of mine sold his stock, then of three-year-olds, at 5*l.* sterling, although reared in Caithness; and this year, the same stock was sold as high as 9*l.* for three-year-olds in this county. The real Highland, and the Skye cattle, are the only breeds that ought to be reared in Caithness, considering the distance from markets, and the bad roads which they have to travel, where grass cannot be had.

6. Mr. *Mackid*, Wattin.—Cattle of the Argyleshire breed, upon stock land grass, well fed, when three or four years old, if stots, will weigh 20 stone, 16lb. to the stone. Cows, if fed on grass, will weigh about 19 stone, when slaughtered. From this, it is my opinion, they are the best breed for Caithness.

7. Mr. *Daniel Miller*, Skinnet.—The Galloway bull, with an English cow, will produce the best work cattle. The West Highland, or Skye bull, with any good cow, the best cattle for the drover. The Skye cattle are the best, and fittest of any I have seen, for this country. By giving them good pasture, they will yield from four to five pints of milk per day, and feed the calf besides. In a bad spring, they may be preserved with less provender than cattle of the same size, and will fetch a higher price at any market. The calves are small, and lively, and there is therefore little risk of accident in the calving. They are apt, however, to lose their native beauty, from the different manner of treatment they in general meet with in Caithness.

8. Mr. *Trotter*, Duncansbay.—The best kind of cattle, in my opinion, are those that can shift best for themselves in the winter; or, in other words, those that can be brought through on the least provender, and will find the readiest market. I suppose that the Isle of Skye, the Argyle, or any of the hardy Highland breeds, would answer this description best. The Galloway breed is easily fed, and makes good working cattle

 for

the farmer; but they cannot do without a full mouthful. I would therefore prefer the real Highlanders; and when the country is more improved, they can be crossed with larger bulls, and made large enough.

9. Mr. *Cumming*, Ratter.—Weighty oxen are best for ploughing; Argyle and Skye oxen best for carting. A number of Orkney cows come to Caithness. Their price is from 2*l.* 2*s.* to 5*l.* each. They will milk from two to five Scotch pints per day: cows of this description suit cottagers best.

10. Mr. *Mathers*, Spring-Park.—The country in general, within these some years past, have got into better cattle and horses, but still there is need of an improvement. There is hardly a milk cow in the country equal to the cows to be found in Aberdeenshire, Fife, &c. It would be a good plan, to collect a sum of money, say 200*l.* sterling: and to employ a proper person to purchase a good breed of young cows, and a few bulls; to keep an exact account of the price of each beast; lots to be drawn for the cows and bulls, and every one to pay what his lot cost. This would be to the country a general good, as well as promoting private interest.

11. Mr. *John Manson*, Thurso-East.—The Caithness cattle are hardiest for the road, but the Galloways carry most beef, and have by far the best hide. The choice of the Caithness cattle, crossed with the Galloways, make a good stock.

A cow on this farm, generally produces five guineas. Milk sells at Thurso at three pence warm, and three halfpence, if skimmed, per Scotch pint.

12. *On Beef for the Navy.*—The small sized Scotch, or Welsh cattle, are much better calculated for beef, for the *immediate service* of the Navy, than the large bony beef. The beef is sweeter and fleshier, and has proportionably less bone. When the great beef is cut up, the sailors are very often dissatisfied, as sometimes a large proportion of it consists of bone. Whereas the small beef, full of flesh, with small bone, is always received with pleasure. For long voyages, however, the large beef is preferable, taking the salt better; the grain is stronger, and better able to bear the effects of the salt and saltpetre.

Special care should be taken, not to admit into the Navy any beef fed with oilcake, as it does not stand the salt for foreign voyages; and when boiling, the fat parts from the beef, and turns into oil in coppers; owing to this, a 4lb. piece of beef, sometimes is reduced to 2lb. Whereas beef, when fattened with turnips or grass, swells, and becomes apparently larger.

SHEEP.

1. Mr. *James Hall*, Achastle—Is convinced, that there is not much difference in regard to grazing, between the Cheviot and black-faced breeds, and that the latter requires as much pasture as the former, when they are of the same weight. He is of opinion, that the Cheviot, when grown up, can bear more hardships, in regard to weather, than the black-faced breed, whose wool opens to every blast that blows. It must at the same time be admitted, that the lambs of the black-faced, are hardier when dropped, being covered with a thick coat of hair. The Cheviot are not liable to any disease worth mentioning, except the braxy; but the sheep farmers in Caithness, are liable to loss from foxes, eagles, &c. which are unknown to the farmers in the south. There is no specific cure for the braxy, only turnips, clover, and other green food, will prevent that disease coming on, and where the sheep are solely fed on that food, will in general cure it. Unless compelled by the braxy, however, turnips are more beneficial in February and March, than in November, or any of the winter months. Besides the Glut, Rumsdale, Dalganachy, and Sandside, the Cheviot sheep might be bred at the Breamore; if proper winterings could be had. Some small farms also, in the hills, in the neighbourhood of Wick, might answer, by judicious management, but the grounds have not been thoroughly examined, and they may be liable to the rot. In cases of extremity, he has known 20 sheep maintained on a stone of hay, per day; but if provender were plentiful, he would prefer giving a stone and a half, or even two stone, to 20 sheep, per day. On the Estate of Langwell, where there is no brushwood, eight fleeces will make a stone of 24 lb., but where the pasture is woody, it will require ten fleeces. The average weight of the Cheviot breed, reared in Caithness, when fat, will be about 14 lb. a quarter. It is probable, that salt would be of great use in preventing or curing the rot; for sheep tainted with the rot, fed on grass where the sea-spray comes, will recover.*

2. *Communication from* Mr. *Atkinson, of Larbottle, in Northumberland, of a Cure for the Braxy in Sheep.*—To prevent, or to cure this disorder, so fatal to young sheep, has long been most anxiously wished for by sheep farmers; and the following plan for that purpose, has been found to answer, by

* A few of the large quiet breed, might be kept on Lowland farms, to pasture with the cows.

by Mr. Atkinson of Larbottle, one of the most respectable and experienced farmers upon the borders.

Having about 540 lambs or hogs likely to be affected by that disorder, and having bought about eight acres of turnips, he resolved to try the following experiment.

The sheep, (some of them about the beginning of November, and others in December), were first put on an acre of the turnips, for two or three hours a day, to teach them to eat that food. The turnips may either be netted or hurdled, or the sheep may be herded by a careful shepherd, as may be most convenient. After that acre was consumed, the turnips were drawn, led out, and eaten upon an adjoining heath; and thus the pasture of a very barren heath, and from three to four double cart-loads of turnips per day, were found sufficient for the whole 540 sheep. The turnips were supposed worth from 6*l.* to 7*l.* per acre, and eight acres of such turnips were sufficient for 540 hogs for about four months, not only totally preventing the braxy, but the sheep were found in very good order at clipping time. Less turnips would have done, if the sheep had had moss or ling to go to, but they had nothing, excepting some very indifferent dry heath. The turnips prevents costiveness, and indigestion, which are the great causes of the braxy; and heath, with a very moderate proportion of turnips, is most excellent feeding for all sheep, even the Leicester. It is better to divide the sheep into lots of about 250 each, than to keep too many together.

Besides the other advantages of this practice, it is very important to teach sheep, when young, how to eat turnips. It makes them worth from 2*s.* to 5*s.* a piece more, when they are sold to be fattened off.

On the supposition that 500 lambs or hogs are kept on 50*l.* worth of turnips, with the liberty of pasture on the adjoining heath or common, the total expense would not exceed 2*s.* a piece; a small sum, considering the great advantages of the practice. On this plan also, husbandry and sheep-farming ought to be united, even in Highland districts.

HORSES.

1. Mr. *Mackid*, Wattin.—Horses may be reared to advantage in Caithness. The breed I found most profitable is the Angus-shire, which I brought into this county about eight years ago. It was the practice upon the farm of Wattin, before I occupied it, to let the young horses run out summer and winter. I have followed the same practice, and found it answer

answer well, until three years old. Their size is about fifteen hands, and they are of the real draught kind, broad and squat. To show the advantage of rearing horses of this breed, I have always sold them to advantage; and lately I sold a pair of three years old horses, then fit for work, which good judge thought worth one hundred guineas.

2. Mr. *John Manson*, Thurso-East.—As to horses, those reared on the farm of Thurso-East, seem to suit this county, as draught horses, better, in general, than any I see brought to it.

3. Dr. *Henderson*, Clyth.—I do not think work horses of a large size, advantageous for this county: those of a good bone, squat, and of a moderate size, I should consider best adapted for it.

4. Mr. *Mathers*, Spring-Park.—I think the middle sized horses, such as Sir John Sinclair's work-horses, and others resembling them, are the fittest for this country. They are easily kept, and are fit to work any common plough.

5. Mr. *Alexander Trotter*, Duncansbay.—I think the best stock of horses in the county are at Thurso-East, and as fit for work as any that can be brought into it. They are of the same kind with those in the upper ward of Lanarkshire. They are equally steady on good, and on bad roads; they are not delicate, nor easily hurt, with indifferent usage, or hard work. And when the roads are made better, and the servants fitter to take more care of them, and more handy, they can then be crossed with a half-bred stallion, which will give them mettle enough for any county.

HOGS.

1. Mr. *Mathers*, Spring-Park.—There is nothing more neglected, than in not getting a good breed of hogs. Those in the county at present, are of the very worst kind. It would be an easy matter to get a good breed from Fife. They might be had quite young, at from 10*s.* to 12*s.*, and I was informed they grew so large in the space of twelve months, that one would bring 3*l.* 10*s.* in the summer. They get nothing but weeds, from corn, or green crops. They have very short legs, a large body, and do not wander from the house where they are kept.

2. Dr. *Manson*.—I do not know which is the best kind of hog, but am confident, that *thousands* of pounds might be made, by a proper attention to rearing them, *in this county*,

Even some Highland districts, have the start of us in this respect.

3. Mr. *Alexander Trotter*, Duncansbay.—The Caithness breed of hogs, is the best for the table, I ever saw; but perhaps if they were crossed with the Sutherland hogs, a larger size would be got; and I am told, easily fed: that might be an improvement.

4. Mr. *Paton*, Bleachfield.—Since potatoes have become so abundant, hogs are no despicable kind of stock. They ought to be fed on the refuse of the kitchen, and not suffered to wander about the farm.

General Observations on the several Sorts of Live Stock in Caithness.

1. *General Sinclair*, of Lybster.—The small country breed of cattle and horses, answer best here. For a considerable time yet, we must work on the surface, to which our hardy little horses and oxen are sufficiently adequate. Sheep are entirely excluded here, on account of our unfenced small possessions for fishers. The people have a deep-rooted aversion to hogs.

2. *John Sinclair*, Esq. of Barrack.—Black cattle of the Isle of Skye breed, and white-faced sheep of the Cheviot breed, with Northumberland tups; Highland mares, with a half-bred stallion, with a few large horses and mares for the plough, and as many swine as may answer for hams for a family, are the sorts of stock to be recommended.

3. *Major Innes*, of Sandside.—The Northumberland breed of cattle is the best, if you keep them on arable land, and house them in winter. If your cattle must, at any season, be fed on hill ground, the West Highland kind is the most profitable.—The Cheviot sheep, on a large scale, are the best; but the black-faced sheep might be reared to good account, by many Highland tenants, on a more confined scale. The country is sadly defective in good horses, and it is doubtful to me, if there is one good horse in it. A good horse, for our Highland mares, would make a good breed.—South Country hogs are the best.

4. *George Sutherland*, Esq. of Brabster.—The best description of stock for a farm, is that which finds the readiest market, at a high price. No one kind is long valuable. Are cattle in demand? all rear cattle until the market is glutted.

—Do

—Do sheep sell well? whole districts are depopulated to introduce them, and in a short series of years, wool and mutton are "things of no value." When any one species is cultivated, further than seems necessary to supply the wants of mankind, the farmer possessed of sagacity, will turn his attention to the propagation of a different sort.

5. Mr. *Swanson*, Gerston.—In my opinion, the farmers in this county, from the wretched situation of the roads, should use part cattle and part horses, for the labouring of their farms. Sheep seldom answer well in the inland. Hogs are only to be reared by distillers or brewers, otherwise they are reared at a very great expense.

6. *Captain Robertson*, Warse.—The Argyleshire cattle would probably answer best. Sheep of a good breed could scarce be expected to answer, at least not in the northern part of the county. The Galloway breed of horses, and the native swine of the country, would surely, of their respective kinds, be the best stock: no pork is equal to Caithness pork.

(G)

On the Culture of Bees.

In a Letter to Sir John Sinclair, Bart. President of the Board of Agriculture, from James Bonner.

SIR,

I BEG leave to lay the following observations before you, in regard to the great improvements which may be made in this country, in the rearing and management of bees. And permit me to give some account of myself, that I may not be thought altogether unqualified to form a plan, for rearing these useful insects, on a larger scale than perhaps they have ever yet been done in Britain.

My father had bees for sixty years, and when I was a boy of six or eight years old, I considered it the greatest happiness to be sent into the garden to watch them in swarming time. When I was sixteen, I had three hives of my own, and in a few years after, I had forty. In the year 1772 I purchased Wildman and Maxwell's treatise on bees; after reading which, I was so anxious to see Mr. Wildman, that I took ship at Berwick for London, in order to hold a conversation with that

that gentleman, upon my favourite subject. After two days of unsuccessful inquiry, I learned that he had gone to France. I then made search after other treatises on bees, and though I visited many booksellers shops, could only find Thorley's and White's, both of which I purchased. I next went to the Adelphi, and informed the Society of Arts what number of hives I had. They said I deserved a premium, and had I lived south of the Tweed, I certainly would have got it.

Having returned home, I purchased all the books, magazines, &c. that could give me the least information on the subject. I have reared as many bees as I could, and supported a wife and ten children by their produce. My number of stock hives at present amounts to eighty.

In the year 1789 I published a treatise on the generation and management of bees, which has met the approbation of many noblemen and gentlemen in this country. I have now in readiness, and have got a good many subscribers, for another impression, with the addition of many new and valuable discoveries, which I hope will please the philosopher and practical bee-master, and be useful to society at large; for I can say without vanity, that no expense has been spared, and that I have studied them unweariedly, and with delight, for thirty years; and shall think my time and application well bestowed, could I by my example or advice, stir up my countrymen, to set about with cheerfulness, such a pleasing and profitable branch of science.

After having said so much, I have only to observe, that forty years experience, and undivided attention, should surely, in some degree, qualify me to form a plan for increasing the quantity of bees, and of consequence, honey and wax, in this country, in a greater degree than they have ever yet been done.

It is well known, that there is a very considerable sum of money sent yearly from this country, to purchase honey and wax from Russia, Poland, Spain, Minorca, &c. which in general is of a far inferior quality to home produce: whereas, were as many bees kept in Scotland, (which might easily be done), we could not only amply supply ourselves with honey and wax of the best quality, but have a surplus to sell to our neighbours; for it has been my opinion, these twenty years, and I speak it with the greatest confidence, that there might be at least ten, if not twenty times more bee-hives in Britain than are kept at present. There is not, I believe, at an average, more than thirty kept in each parish, and that only in particular parts of the country; whereas there might be three hundred with great ease. By the above computation, reckoning 873 country parishes, that number multiplied by 30, would not produce more than 26,190 hives for all Scotland;

whereas,

whereas, if each parish kept three hundred, there would 261,900 stock hives be kept yearly, which, with proper management, would double their stock every year; and by valuing each to be taken for use at 1*l.* there would be 261,900*l.* of annual wealth to the country from that article, still leaving the stock good.

An objection perhaps may be started by some, saying, where is all the pasture for this vast number of bees to feed on? and that a field may be overstocked with bees, as with sheep or cattle. I own there is a possibility, but scarcely a probability of this, for were we to consider the vast number of flowers bees feed on, particularly wild, and garden mustard, clover, and heath, (from all which, but particularly heath, in which Scotland so much abounds, bees collect honey amazingly fast), without dwelling on the various kinds of flowers with which our gardens, meadows, corn-fields and pasture land abound, we may justly say, the harvest is great, but the labourers few. For example, one acre of fine clover, mustard, or heath, in a good day, will afford more honey than two bee-hives can collect; and if there be, according to the common computation, 27,794 square miles, or 17,788,160 acres, in Scotland, how much honey might not be collected from such an immense tract of country!

In very bad seasons, they would not double their stock, but if the weather is as favourable, as it has been this year, and the last, they would do it twice over. This season I have sold hives for two guineas, some for three guineas, and even some for four guineas. There are also people, who, in spring, had only two hives, whose stock is increased to six, seven, and eight.

I shall now proceed shortly to state, how bees may very speedily be increased to the number above-mentioned. Would gentlemen set about rearing with spirit, they should begin with employing persons skilled in hives, to purchase six or eight for a beginning, taking care they do not suffer by hunger, cold, or robbing bees, the three capital enemies which ruin bees in this country; whose attacks, however, with very little trouble, may easily be prevented. Were gentlemen, I say, to set such an example, the tenants and cottagers in their neighbourhood would soon imitate their example; and should, (as has been done in England), premiums be given to people, to encourage them to keep a good number of hives, such as 10*s.* to those having ten living hives in May; 2*l.* to those having twenty; 4*l.* to those having forty; 6*l.* to those having sixty, &c. &c., additional attention and success might be expected. A qualified person might also be appointed, to superintend the bees of a certain district; one person, indeed, might

oversee

oversee several counties, he being bound and obliged to visit and examine all the hives in his district twice or thrice a-year, doing, or causing to be done to them, what he sees necessary, he being allowed a small compensation for his trouble, until the proper management were more properly known. There might also be a small treatise, containing a few plain and simple directions, published, and sold cheap, or given to the poor gratis, in order to instruct them in the proper management.

I have thus laid before you some hints, showing how easily bees might be increased in this country, and turn out of considerable advantage to it. Should you be pleased to take this letter into your consideration, and to use your influence with the Board of Trustees, the Highland Society, or any other public body, that this plan, or any other you may devise, may be adopted, you will do an important service to Scotland; and should any other hint of mine be wanting, in order to facilitate the business, I will count it my greatest honour to serve my country in so delightful and profitable a branch of science. Should I be permitted to take an active part in carrying the above plan into execution, I could undertake the survey of Berwickshire, the county of Peebles, the three Lothians, Clackmannanshire, and Fife, or any other district of similar extent, on being allowed the sum of 50*l*. a-year, and 1*s*. 6*d*. for each hive under my inspection, in order to enable me to keep a horse, and to defray the expense of travelling.

If it should be deemed proper that a few young men be instructed in the nature and proper management of bees, (which will require about two years each), I would willingly take them as apprentices, and instruct them, on being paid 10*l*. of apprentice fee, and 10*l*. for their yearly board. I shall immediately set about writing a paper of short directions, which will consist of about 50 pages, and will not cost above one shilling each copy.

I remain, with all due respect, Sir,

Your most obedient, and very humble Servant,

JAMES BONNER.

Edinburgh, 16*th Sept*. 1794.

Hints

(H).

Hints as to Watering Hilly Districts. By Sir John Sinclair, Bart.

HEAT and moisture seem to be the two principal sources of vegetation. In cold seasons, or in a bleak country, nothing thrives. If the soil be dry, and parched, the growth of every plant is retarded; but where the atmosphere is warm, and where the earth is not deficient in moisture, every thing prospers.

Heat cannot be commanded in any country; though by draining, inclosing, and rearing plantations, shelter may be obtained, and warmth augmented. But in all hilly countries, and particularly in many parts of England, Wales, and Scotland, there is a superabundance of moisture, which, under the management of the skilful husbandman, may, in many cases, make the hills as productive as the richest plains, and of almost equal value to the farmer, to the proprietor, and to the public.

Watering, it is well known, is an ancient practice, and at this period, it is in use, in many parts of Europe, with infinite advantage. In Switzerland, in Italy, and in many parts of England, it is carried on with spirit, and on a great scale. Even in Scotland, particularly in Aberdeen-shire, and in some parts of Angus * and Perthshire, it has been practised with much success. But in Pennsylvania, it has been brought to very great perfection indeed; for there, according to the testimony of Dr. Edwards, a very respectable and intelligent gentleman of that country, " hills so steep as not to be arable, are watered, and produce greater quantities of grass than flat grounds, without having ever had a forkful of manure put upon them, and are now richer than they were 30 years ago, after having had two crops of hay, and sometimes three, (though that is rather severe), annually taken from them."

The plan of watering high lands, as followed in America, Dr. Edwards has very obligingly communicated to me; and I think the knowledge of so valuable a practice, cannot be too much diffused in all the hilly districts of Great Britain.

The first object, certainly, is to secure a complete command of the spring, or stream, to be made use of. For that pur-

* See particularly the Statistical Account of the Parish of Tealing, Vol. iv. No. 12.

pose,

pose, a dam must be made, as near the source as the circumstances of the case may require, and the water must be then brought on the same level, by a canal, or ditch, all along the side of the hill.

In Leicestershire, the spirit level is made use of, for the purpose of finding out the proper line to conduct the water. But in America, what they call the rafter level, somewhat resembling the common mason's level, on a larger scale, is found to answer infinitely better, and is not only much truer, but can be made at a very trifling expense. Dr. Edwards recommends the span to be from 10 to 12 feet, the feet of the level to be about two inches broad, for the sake of lightness, and the cross bars to be three inches, as the strength of the instrument depends upon them.

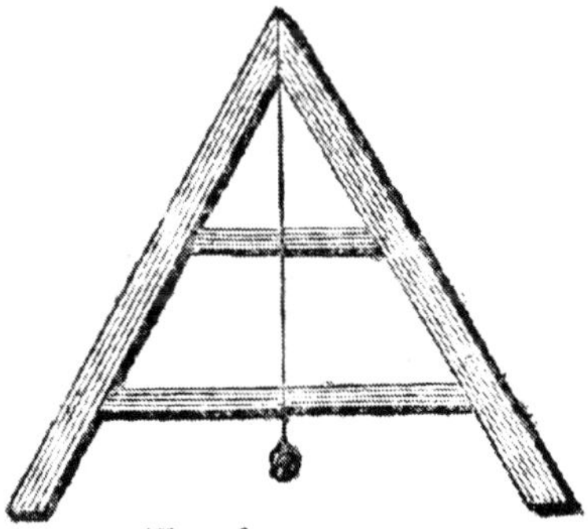

Ten feet span.

With this instrument, the line, or course, which the water ought to take, is very easily marked out. One foot of the level is put on the surface of the water, or on the place from which it is to be taken; and the other foot is put on the spot pointed out by the plummet standing exactly in the centre. The line, or course, is marked by small sticks, or pegs, by which the canal is afterwards conducted. To bring the water along with any degree of precision, the ground must be accurately marked out at small distances, not exceeding 10 or 12 feet; and the level must go all the zig-zag courses that the variation of the ground requires.

When the true level is found, and the canal made, the water should be turned into it, which, if stopped, either at the far end, or in any part of it, with a gate being shut down, it will flow over, and irrigate all the land below; or, what I think is a better way, the canal may be made so high on the bank, that the lower side of it shall be about six inches above the water, when standing on a level with its source. It is then let

let out by small gutters, about 10 or 15 feet from each other, which, (after allowing room for a foot-path by the side of the canal), are spread a little below, by arms each way, so as to meet one another, in such a manner as completely to throw all the ground under water. By this mode, if there is plenty of water, the whole ground may be irrigated, but if it is scarce, half of these gutters may be stopped, by small sods, one day, (or two days, if necessary), and the other half afterwards, when the first are taken up, so that the whole can be floated alternately every other day; a practice preferred by some, even where the water is abundant.

At a distance of near two rods below the first canal, another is made, to receive all the water that has flowed over the ground between the two, and again turned out as above.

The whole surface of the land to be irrigated, should be made so fair and smooth, that where the water is turned out, to produce its great effect, there should not, to have it complete, be a hillock, or a hollow in which a drop of water can stand, or over which it cannot flow.

Dr. Edwards concludes his observations upon this subject in the following words:—" I have sometimes, among gentlemen who make observations very judiciously, found a difference of sentiments about the value of watered meadows: many taking up an idea, that the expenses and trouble of obtaining them, were not sufficiently compensated, as they allege they could procure better grass by the ordinary course of cropping. But from all the observations I have ever been able to make, both in England and America, I cannot hesitate a moment, to pronounce water-meadows, by far the most valuable kind of property, that a man can possibly possess.

" A good meadow, with a fine large stream of water thrown over it, will certainly last as long as grass will continue to grow, that is, for ever; and all that I have ever seen, are better now, by the unanimous testimony of their owners, than they were when first made; and the burdens of hay they produce, are certainly equal, in point of quantity, (if not superior), to any other. If, therefore, this be the case, what a valuable property is land, that will always be produeing a crop equal to that of grain, (for such is hay estimated), without any considerable labour of hands, horses, or other expenses! And that this is the case, I will endeavour to evince, by such authorities as have made the deepest impression on my mind.

" I begin with Mr. Bakewell, because, in this case, like every thing he undertakes in the way of agriculture, &c. he has the good luck to merit the first rank on the list. If I recollect right, he possesses above an hundred acres of watered meadows,—his opinion is, that there is no other land in this country

country will bear any kind of comparison with them, in point of profit; and his reasoning on the subject is, though in a very few words, unanswerable—he says, clover in the fields ought by all means to be raised in its course; but then he also says, it is a crop produced by his labour, and at a certain expense per acre; whereas the watered meadows, after the first expense, are productive for ever, without scarcely any more being laid out on them.

"In the western parts of England, particularly in Somersetshire, and some of those counties which border on Wales, the floating of grass lands is in high repute, and the advantages are there well understood. To be sure, Nature has dealt very handsomely by that county—the falls of water are considerable, and the banks over which it can be conducted, are bold, by which means it must run off rapidly, and which is absolutely necessary to produce great effects.

"In some parts of England, they are at a considerable expense, in the first instance, to get the water over their grounds; they even throw it over that which is level by nature, but by art made unlevel. Mr. Bakewell has displayed much ingenuity in this:—it is done by ridging up all the land like a cornfield, but made very high in the middle; and on the top of those ridges a small canal is cut, proportioned to the size of each, and the quantity of water with which they are to be supplied from the principal canal. When all those small ones are filled, they being dammed up at the far end, the water must overflow, and run rapidly down, on each side of the ridge, to the furrows, by which it is carried off, and either again taken up, and collected into some other reservoir, to be used over more ground, or conducted entirely away, as circumstances require. Those ridges have from the roads a very beautiful appearance, for on their tops are seen the full, overflowing canals, and in their furrows, lively, brisk running rivulets.

"I conclude my observations, with respect to England, by remarking, that I have heard some practical farmers say, that, with good land to till, they can make three rents, and must do so to live; but that with the same quantity of watered meadows, at the same price per acre, they can easily make five rents, with less than half the trouble.

"The remarks I have been able to make in America, coincide precisely with those I have made here; they have in that country carried the watering of meadows to a very considerable pitch of perfection, especially in some parts of Pennsylvania. I have seen one estate there, owned by a man who possessed in all from 220 to 230 acres, near 200 of which are watered meadows; the rest was occupied by buildings, orchards,

chards, some arable lots round the house, &c.; and this man, I am well informed, made, and put out more money to interest, than any man in the same county, with twice his quantity of land, could ever make out to do by the common mode of farming; and the reason is obvious—he had in a manner nothing to do all the year round, except at the time of cutting, making, and gathering in his hay; at least this is the only season of hurry, or great expense to him. It is true, he had a dairy, which required care and industry; but this being managed by women, it was attended with not much above half the expense of business conducted by the labour of men. This circumstance alone, is a great bounty on having all the ground a man can, in meadows of this kind, especially where manure is scarce, and capitals small.

"The only plausible objection I have ever heard to those meadows, (for every thing will be opposed), is, that the hay is not quite so good as hay growing on drier ground; this, if true, should be taken into the account, as being a reason of some weight. I do not know this to be the case, but let us for a moment admit it, then I would estimate, or compare it thus: Suppose a field with good cultivation, and well manured, should always produce thirty bushels of wheat per acre; and supposing the adjoining field, would for ever produce thirty bushels of rye per acre, without any cultivation, I certainly would not hesitate a single moment, in preferring the rye-field to become my property, in preference to that of the wheat; but this comparison is too much to the prejudice of the watered meadow; because as yet it remains a dispute, whether the hay it produces, is in any respect inferior to that which grows on upland, or in common fields."

Thus far Dr. Edwards, whose judicious observations upon the subject, cannot be too strongly recommended to the attention of the reader.

I shall conclude with a few short remarks, on the advantages to be derived from watering land.

1. It is by far the easiest, the cheapest, and the most certain mode of improving poor land.

2. The land, when once improved, is put in a state of perpetual and increasing fertility, without any occasion for manure, or any additional expense.

3. The land is not only made fertile, but becomes extremely productive, being capable of producing an immense quantity of hay, besides pasture, every year.

4. The land is not only extremely productive, but, under proper management, produces grass early in the year, when it is doubly valuable, at least for sheep, especially ewes and lambs,

lambs, coming before any other spring growth, and when one ton is probably worth two at any other season.

5. Not only is the land thus improved without the necessity of manure, but it produces food for animals, which is converted into manure, with which other land may be enriched.

Lastly, not only is the manure arising from the produce of the water-meadows a new acquisition, but also all the manure acquired from the land that would otherwise have required dung from other parts of the farm.

It is not, therefore, too high a calculation to state, that an acre of water-meadow, either directly, or indirectly, produces as much manure as may be sufficient for an acre of arable land; consequently, a million acres more of water-meadow would be the means of improving another million of acres, of arable land, or two millions of acres in all; and calling the produce of each acre five pounds, it would consequently add ten millions per annum, to the general income of the nation.

(I)

Hints for the Improvement of the Northern Counties and Islands of Scotland. By Sir John Sinclair, Bart.

THE state of that great extent of country, comprehended in the Northern Counties and Islands of Scotland, is undoubtedly, at present, far from being such as could be wished for, by any friend to the prosperity of these kingdoms. At the same time there is no reason for despair. When we consider the disadvantages to which Holland was by nature subject,* we

* The celebrated de Witt thus states the natural burdens and hindrances of his native country. "Holland lying in the latitude of 51 to 53 degrees North, upon the sea, having many inland rivers, and being besides a low and plain country, is thereby subject to many inconveniences.

"1. There are sharp and very long winters, so that there is need of more light, firing, clothing, and food, than in warmer countries: besides which, all the cattle of our pasture land must then be housed, though thereby we bestow more cost and pains, and yet reap less profit of milk meats, than in summer, or in other adjacent lands, where the cattle remain longer, or perhaps are all the winter in the fields.

"2. The seasons are here so short, that they must be very punctually observed, to return us any profit by our ploughed lands; for the seed in this moist country, being rotted and consumed in the earth, cannot be sowed again conveniently.

"3. By

we shall soon perceive what obstacles may be surmounted by industry and perseverance.

The means that might be pointed out, which, in a greater or lesser degree, would tend to the improvement of these extensive districts, are extremely numerous. The Author will endeavour shortly to state some of the most important; attempting no more, than merely to throw out such hints as may occur, without endeavouring to observe any particular order.

1. *Climate.*—It is certain that the wetness and coldness of the climate, in the Northern Highlands and Islands of Scotland, are among the greatest disadvantages of that part of the kingdom. Though they cannot be totally removed, yet they may be consderably palliated by industry and exertion. The rain will fall from the heavens, nor can it be prevented by any human ability; but when it does fall, it may be carried off by drains properly laid out, so as to do but little injury. Cold blasts will blow, but their force may be weakened by plantations, judiciously formed, under whose genial influence our domestic animals may be sheltered from the inclemency of the seasons. The snow will descend, but it will disappear much sooner, if the rigour of the climate is corrected, and the nature of the soil improved by a better system of cultivation.

2. *Soil.*—In a considerable part of these northern regions, the soil, naturally, either is not unproductive, or it is capable of being made sufficiently fertile for the common purposes of agriculture. The greater part of the wastes also abound in peat, which, it is now sufficiently ascertained, when drained, limed, and properly treated, may become extremely useful as soil, or a valuable article as a manure.

3. *Ancient System of Husbandry.*—The manner in which this county was formerly possessed, cannot be better described than it is by an intelligent Clergyman, in the Statistical Account of his parish. A proprietor formerly let a certain moderate extent of land to his tenants, for which he received a trifling acknowledgment in money, (specie being then very rare in the country), the rent being principally paid in grain, or *victual*, that is, bear and oatmeal. In addition to the rent, the tenants of that description were bound to pay the following services: namely, tilling, dunging, sowing, and harrowing a part of an

" 3. By the vicinity of the sea, and plainness of the land, it is subject, in spring and autumn, not only to unwholesome weather for the inhabitants, but in the spring, the sharp cold winds blast most of the blossoms of the fruit trees, and about autumn much unripe fruit is blown down by our usual storms of wind."

extensive farm in the proprietor's possession—providing a certain quantity of peats for his fuel—thatching a part of his houses—furnishing *simmons*, or ropes of straw, or heath, for that purpose, and for securing his corn in the barn-yard—weeding the land—leading a certain quantity of turf from the common, for manuring the farm—mowing—making, and ingathering the hay, the spontaneous produce of the meadow and marshy grounds—cutting down, harvesting, thrashing out, manufacturing, and carrying to the market, or sea-port, a part of the produce of the farm. Besides these services, the tenants paid in kind the following articles, under the name of Customs, namely, *straw-cazzies*, (a sort of bag made of straw, used as sacks for carrying grain or meal) ropes made of hair, for drawing the plough—*floss*, or reeds, used for these and similar purposes—*tethers*, or ropes made of hair, which being fixed in the ground by a peg, or small stake, and the cattle tied to them, prevented them from wandering over the open country—straw for thatching, &c. The tenants also, according to the extent of their possessions, kept a certain number of cattle during the winter season; paid vicarage, or the smaller tithes, as of lamb, wool, &c. a certain number of fowls and eggs; in the Highlands, veal, kid, butter, and cheese; and on the sea coast, the tithe of their fish and oil, besides assisting in carrying sea-ware for manuring the proprietor's farm. In some parts of the country, the tenth sheaf of the produce, or tithe, was exacted by the proprietor in kind. Sometimes, also, a certain quantity of lint was spun for the lady of the house, and a certain quantity of woollen yarn annually exacted. Such were the various sorts of payments, which almost universally prevailed in the County of Caithness, about 40 or 50 years ago; but of late they have been converted, by the generality of landlords, either into grain or money, or have fallen into disuse*.

4. *Productions.*—It is certain, that the grain of this part of the kingdom is inferior, in point of quality, to that produced in the more southern districts. But that is principally owing to defective husbandry, and the crops will necessarily improve in quality as the agriculture is amended. It is also proper to remark, that any change of seed, that has as yet taken place, is by means of importations from a more southern climate; whereas the plan had much better been reversed. Seed from Sweden or Norway is more likely to thrive there, than from Kent or Sussex, or even the Lothians.

* Statistical Account of Scotland, vol. vii. p. 524. Parish of Bower, by the Rev. Mr. William Smith.

One

One production from the more northern parts of Europe, has been strongly recommended for the district under review. The celebrated Linnæus discovered in Sweden, a species of lucerne, which, in compliment to him, is known in that country under the name of *Linnean hay*. It is stated to be fit for any soil, particularly wet clay, and if sown two inches asunder, in the middle of April, will soon produce an abundant crop. It is supposed, that in the works of this great naturalist, there are many other hints, which might be of the utmost service in the improvement of these Northern Counties, and a knowledge of which ought, if possible, to be obtained. Many of those hints are contained in some parts of his works which remain untranslated from the Swedish.

There is another production, which merits to be particularly attended to in the district under review, namely, the *Swedish turnip*. There is no article of that sort that seems to thrive better in the Northern parts of Scotland. The information received upon that subject from Mr. Robertson, landlord of Dalwhinnie, who resides in the situation the wildest, and most inland of any in the Highlands, is on that head particularly satisfactory. He first tried them in 1790, and found them to answer remarkably well. He sows the seed in a b d, between the 20th of April and the 10th of May, and transplants them about the middle of July, when they are from eight to ten weeks old, nearly the size of cabbage plants. It is necessary to transplant them in damp weather. They grow best in coarse, heavy, and wet land. They grow, though buried under ten feet of snow, which is not unusual at this place. They are transplanted into drills; each plant is from seven to nine inches asunder, and the drills about a foot. Dung is of use, though not absolutely necessary, if the ground is in good heart. The tops may be cut from August till April, without injury to the turnips, and they make excellent greens for the table. The turnips themselves are always good, even after they have seeded. It is probable, that this plant will be found one of the most valuable ever imported into this country. I understand, on very respectable authority, that working horses have been fed upon it during the winter season, without any other food, and have thriven as well, with a good deal of work, as if they had had the usual quantity of hay and corn.

The culture of winter, and even spring rye, which are found to answer so well in Denmark and Sweden, and without which, indeed, the inhabitants of those kingdoms could not exist, is also strongly to be recommended.

5. *Stock.*—The species of stock, in which the greatest im-

 provements

provements is to be effected in this country, is that of sheep and the experiments which have been tried with the Cheviot breed, have put it beyond all doubt, that they are well calculated for this part of the kingdom.

There are still in some of the Northern Counties, a good number of goats in particular parishes. Upon examining lately, some goat-skins from the interior Highlands of Scotland, I found that they had, under their coarse hair, the same kind of fine down, for which the shawl-goat of the East is so celebrated. There is every reason to believe, therefore, that the shawl-goat itself would thrive in these counties; or perhaps the native goat, if properly attended to, might produce as fine shawl-wool or down, and in as great quantity, as those of the East. It is singular, that this circumstance, notwithstanding the frequent discussions which have taken place respecting shawl-wool, should never have been formerly observed.

It is probable that the Highland hog might be much improved by a cross with the Chinese, whose disposition to fatten on scanty fare is well known.

6. *Implements.*—It is certain, that the greater part of the implements of husbandry used in the North, might be much improved, and where extensive farms in tillage are to be found, there is no instrument that can be more advantageously adopted, than the thrashing-mill. The Rev. Mr. Mackay of Reay, has transmitted to the Board, the model of an ingenious instrument of this sort, of his own invention, and another is promised by Mr. Munro of Delny. The importance of this discovery to the public, has never yet been sufficiently explained. According to an experiment made by Mr. Beatson of Kilrie, in Fife, there is an addition of one in twelve, when grain is thrashed in a mill properly constructed, instead of being done by the flail. What an object in a national point of view! It was supposed that we could not supply ourselves with bread, without the harvests of America, and behold! we have nothing to do, but to thrash the grain we now raise, thoroughly, and the business will in a great measure be accomplished.

It may be proper to add, that besides the loss of grain, thrashing with the flail is a very unwholesome occupation, (from the quantity of dust perpetually flying about), and that those who make thrashing a constant occupation, are never healthy, and seldom live long. What an object therefore is it, not only to increase the quantity of grain, but to render an unhealthy occupation unnecessary! Some intelligent persons imagine, that the same machinery might be made use of for grinding

grinding, as well as thrashing corn. In that event, there would be sufficient occupation for those now employed in thrashing, in other branches connected with the manufacture of grain.

7. *Size of Farms.*—This is one of the most difficult subjects connected with the improvement of the country. The following general principles are applicable to all farms without exception; namely, 1. That the farmer should have no useless time either for himself or servants; 2. No useless stock; and 3. No useless or unproductive territory. It is particularly necessary, that the business of the farm should be so arranged, (which must depend upon its being of a proper size,) that the farmer, his servants, and the cattle kept upon it, should have full employment during the whole year, without any occasion, or indeed opportunity, for idleness. Every day unemployed, or for which there is no work, deprives the husbandman of so much additional profit, which otherwise he might have gained. The size of tillage farms ought to depend upon the number of ploughs, whether one, two, or more, which the farmer can afford to keep, and the extent of ground necessary for each plough; much depends upon the nature of the stock, the soil that is cultivated, and the system of husbandry that is adopted. In regard to grazing farms, there is hardly any bounds to them, but the capital of the grazier.

8. *Rotation of Crops.*—The generality of ground in the Highlands is of a light nature, and consequently well adapted for turnips, and other green crops. Where the country is fit for tillage, the following rotation is recommended: 1. Turnips well limed, or dunged; 2. Either barley, or oats, with grass-seeds; 3. Hay; 4. Oats. Then recommence the rotation, if the land is of tolerable quality; if not, when laid down with grass the third year, pasture it for three or four years.

9. *Infield and Outfield.*—The distinction between infield and outfield land is well known. The one is land that has been perpetually tilled for ages, and has received all the manure of the farm. The other receives no dung, but after laying waste for a few years, is ploughed up, and cropt with oats, as long as it will produce any thing. This is done, not from any expectation of a crop of corn, but merely for the sake of the straw, to enable the farmer to maintain his cattle during the winter season, and raise more dung for his infield land. This distinction of infield and outfield ought to be abolished, and the best plan for cultivating outfield land, seems to be the one adopted by Sir George Suttie, as stated in Mr. Buchan Hepburn's very intelligent Report of the Agriculture of East Lothian

thian. His system was alternate crops of oats and clover, beginning with a fallow to clean the land, and repeating it occasionally when the land got foul again.

10. *Run-Rigg.*—Wherever the system of run-rigg, known in England under the name of the common-field system, is established, no improvement can possibly take place.

11. *Leases.*—In the course of the inquiries carried on by the Board of Agriculture, much light has been thrown upon the subject of leases, and when the General Report is drawn up, every point in dispute respecting the duration of leases, and the clauses that ought to be inserted in them, will, it is hoped, be finally determined. Short leases are certainly contrary to the improvement of the country; but when a farm is in a tolerable state of cultivation, there is every reason to believe, that a lease for 21 years, is the one that is the most likely to be the basis of a fair bargain between the landlord and the tenant.

12. *Services.*—The abolition of personal services, is a subject that ought certainly to come under the most serious consideration of the Board, and a recommendation from that respectable institution, would probably be sufficient to effect it.

13. *Tacksmen.*—The mode of letting great tracts of land to *tacksmen*, as they are here called, or middle men, according to the appellation they receive in Ireland, is a subject entitled to very serious discussion, a practice that ought to be prohibited, as injurious to the public interest. There are doubtless, many instances, and several are on my own property, where the tacksman behaves as kindly to the people under him, as it is possible for any landlord to do. But on the whole, it is a bad system, and which ought not to be continued.

14. *Turf Houses.*—This mode of constructing habitations ought to be prohibited, as in every point of view exceptionable. In the first place, it destroys a considerable space of valuable ground, (for the best part of the surface is always taken for that purpose); in the second place, a house built of such an article cannot last long; and, in the third place, it is much damper, and consequently more unwholesome, than if it were formed of harder and better materials.

15. *Feal.*—The practice of taking off the surface of the ground, in order to increase the dunghill, and also that of paring *divots*, or thin turf, for the purpose of covering the roofs of houses, are also pernicious customs, which ought to be put an end to. The absurdity, and destructive consequences

quences of both having long been foreseen, as appears from the following anecdote. It is well known, that the Treaty of Union, (an event which has proved so beneficial to both kingdoms), was violently opposed in the Scotch Parliament; some members of which were constantly exclaiming, that it would be the ruin of Scotland. "The ruin of Scotland!" said an intelligent Laird, "I'll tell you what will be more destructive to Scotland, the *flaughter spade*." The instrument commonly made use of for cutting turf, is known by that name. It is inconceivable how many acres of land have been destroyed by this instrument since the Union.

16. *Peat.*—In such parts of the North, as are situated at a distance from the coast, peat must be the fuel of the country, and it certainly is, in many instances, of so good a quality, as to be little inferior to coal, and superior to wood. Mr. Marshall, in his very intelligent Report of the Agricultural State of the Central Highlands, has very properly suggested, that the making of peats should be a distinct profession, in which case the fuel would become much less expensive, whilst, at the same time, it would obviate every objection arising from the system at present adopted, by which every individual, being obliged to prepare his own peat, is compelled to waste the best part of the summer in that manufacture. It has occurred to some persons, who have thought much upon this subject, that the manufacture of peat might be much improved, by employing presses, such as are used in the manufacture of cyder, which would expel at once all humidity or wet, and make the peat much sooner fit for being used. This is an idea which may require investigation and experiment, its utility being extremely obvious.

17. *Heather Hay.*—The Northern parts of Scotland might maintain, during the summer season, perhaps, five times as much stock as they do at present; but the difficulty is, how to support them during the winter. Among other suggestions for that purpose, the use of hay, made of heath, has been recommended, and it has been proposed to inclose a piece of heath ground with turf walls, to burn the heather, or ling, and when it was two years old, to cut it with a scythe for hay*.

* The late Mr. Bradfute, Minister of Dunsyre, in Scotland, transmitted the following anecdote to the author. Some years ago, he stated, that a mason who lived in his neighbourhood, near a verge of Scotch fir, recently planted among heather, which, from being inclosed, grew luxuriantly, being much in want of fodder for the cattle he kept, went out every day, and topped the heather with a hook, and gave it to the cattle, who ate it greedily. Mr. Bradfute visited them in April, and found them in as good condition as any black cattle in the country.

Upon

Upon mentioning this idea to a gentleman from Sweden, he stated, that it was a common practice in some parts of that kingdom, and that there could be no doubt of the beneficial consequences that would result from it. The introduction of other kinds of heath, also, might be of use. Some excellent sorts might be procured from the Mediterranean, but there is reason to believe, that some still more valuable might be got from Canada.

18. *Plantations*,—It is unnecessary to dwell long on the advantages that would result from increasing the plantations in this part of the kingdom, not only on account of the shelter they would afford, of the advantages that would thence arise for improving the habitations of the people, and indeed in many other respects, too numerous now to enter into. It will be sufficient, at present, to allude to two circumstances, namely, 1. That planting is the best mode of improving and rendering land of indifferent quality valuable; and 2. That the branches and leaves of trees have been found in Sweden, and other countries, an excellent food for cattle and sheep, during the winter season. I understand, from the most unquestionable authority, that sheep have been fed on the branches of the Scotch fir, for several weeks, during a heavy fall of snow, and, without any other sustenance, have been kept in an excellent condition*.

19. *Inclosing*.—The advantages of inclosures need hardly here be dwelt on. First, they ornament the country. 2. They tend to increase the value of the property, both to the landlord and the tenant, by giving a complete command of the ground that is inclosed; so that any species of crop, for which the soil is best calculated, may be cultivated in it. 3. It prevents the necessity of herding, and, the cattle not being disturbed, they thrive infinitely better. 4. Nothing is more desirable, in a cold climate, than shelter. It is commonly observed, that the grass nearest the wall is always the best, and most luxuriant; and hence it is evident, that a well inclosed country must always be the most productive, at least of that article. From the shelter also of inclosures, cattle are maintained on less food than where they are more exposed to the inclemency of the seasons.

When land is to be inclosed, the following particulars ought to be attended to. 1. That uniformity of soil is to be preferred to regularity of figure. It is perfectly absurd to put

* See the Annals of Agriculture, vol. v. p 138, Lord Townshend's account of his feeding about 600 deer, sheep, and other animals, for several days, on the trimmings of Scotch fir.

wet

wet and dry land within the same fence. 2. The best means of securing a supply of water ought to be attended to, as that is a very material object for the cattle, particularly if they are dairy cows. One pond, however, may be so situated as to be equally accessible to several inclosures, if placed in any particular spot or corner where they all unite. 3. The size of the inclosures ought to be various. Inclosures, when too small, certainly take up a good deal of ground; besides, they keep the land moister, and consequently it is more easily poached. Large ones yield little shelter, and it is difficult to give the land rest from the treading of the cattle, so as to enable the grass to recover itself; but when there are many inclosures of different sizes, not a particle of grass may be lost. The cattle may be taken from the one to the other, so as to enable each of them, in their turn, to get into a state of good pasturage, and, in favourable seasons, some of them may be kept up entirely for hay, or foggage, in the manner so well described in the Pembrokeshire Report*.

It is imagined by some, in forming inclosures, that a part of the fence ought to go through the lower grounds, in order that the land may not only be inclosed, but rendered dry by the ditches. This, however, is a mistaken idea; at least the plan adopted by the late Lord Galloway, for making the verge on the higher part of the field, seems to be infinitely preferable. In that case, the cattle, for the sake of shelter, keep above, and the manure that falls, washed down by the rain, enriches the whole field, instead of being carried at once into a ditch, where its beneficial effects are lost for ever.

20. *Flax.*—The culture of flax ought to be particularly attended to in this part of the kingdom. It has in general been considered as an exhausting crop, because, it is said, it returns nothing to the soil. But this is altogether owing to mismanagement. It appears from Mr. Billingsley's excellent Report of Somersetshire†, that the water in which flax is steeped, is a most excellent manure; and in Lincolnshire, the sediment found at the bottom of the pits used for that purpose, is accounted extremely valuable. These are facts entitled to the particular attention of every district, where flax or hemp are cultivated.

The hazard attending the watering is another objection, and undoubtedly it requires a good deal of skill to manage that branch of the culture. But there can be no doubt, that as good flax might be obtained by keeping the flax until the

* Page 36.

† Page 147.

ensuing summer after it grew, and watering it then, when the season is most favourable to that operation, as if it were watered when first separated from off the ground.

A third objection is the difficulty of procuring good seed. There is reason, however, to believe, that by delaying rippling the flax intended for seed, until the season of sowing, the seed of Scotland would be intrinsically as good as that of foreign growth. Perhaps a change of seed, from one country or climate to another, may be of service; so that old foreign seed, in consequence of that circumstance, may answer as well as fresh native. But if native seed is to be used at all, it is certainly desirable, that it should be sown in as much perfection as possible; the best mode of having it in perfection, seems to be that of keeping it, as seed corn ought to be, unseparated from the stalk, as shortly as possible previous to its being sown. Perhaps also the crop might be much improved by mixing the seed with salt, as is the practice in America*.

The profit arising from the culture of flax, has been variously stated. In Atholl, the common tenants sow two pecks of seed per acre, which produces eight stone of lint, at an average, worth 10*s.* per stone, so that the produce is, at an average, worth only 4*l.* per acre. The following, however, is the produce of an English acre, upon Mr. Traill's farm at Castle-hill, in the County of Caithness, including the spinning, &c. It produced, of scutched flax, 43 stone, which yielded the following quantities of yarn:

85 lb. of five-hank lint, worth 1*s.* 3*d.* per pound,	£5	6	3
43 lb. of three-hank ditto, worth 1*s.* ditto.......	2	3	0
72 lb. of two-hank ditto, worth 9*d.* ditto, ...	2	14	0
	£10	3	3
25 stone of tow, worth 5*s.* per stone, ...	6	5	0
Total produce of an acre is, ...	£16	8	3

On this occasion, (anno 1793), an experiment was tried, which merits to be particularly attended to. Some part of the crop being likely to be spoiled when spread out to dry, after being watered, Mr. Traill put it on a kiln, where he dried it gradually, and the experiment was found to be of great advantage, in regard both to the quantity and quality of the lint and tow.

* This practice is chiefly confined to the Eastern States of America, but is found to answer. Mr. Jay has been so good as to promise me a particular account of it. They mix fine dry salt with the seed, in the proportion of about one-sixteenth, and sow them together.

From

From the moistness of the climate, and other advantages, the North of Scotland seems to be well calculated for the culture of flax; and were it to be encouraged by the Board of Trustees, whose funds are specially appropriated for that purpose, no doubt can be entertained of its success. So remote a part of the kingdom, however, lies under so many disadvantages of every sort, that nothing but public attention and encouragement can enable it to prosper. The wealth of the country naturally flows with attractive force to the capital, and ought to be sent back again to the extremities, in order that the whole body politic may be kept in a due state of health and vigour. The sums given on such occasions, are seldom, in themselves, of much consequence; and indeed, would be of little avail, were it not that money goes much farther in a remote corner, than in the neighbourhood of the metropolis. But the sum itself is nothing, compared to that degree of animation and energy, which is excited by the idea of being attended to and encouraged. A spirit of industry is thus roused, which would otherwise lie dormant; but which, once put in motion, is not easily laid aside.

21. *Commons.*—Some improvements might be made in the laws, respecting the division of commons in Scotland, that would be of considerable moment. It is particularly desirable to shorten and to simplify the business as much as possible, by empowering the Court of Session to appoint Commissioners, with full authority to divide the commons, instead of the Court itself going through all the tedious forms at present necessary on that occasion. The power of dividing commons also, in which the King, or any Royal Borough is interested, (which they cannot excercise by the Act 1 William, cap. 37), ought to be given.

22. *Thirlage.*—The abolition of thirlage, giving a fair compensation to the proprietor of the mill, seems to be indispensably necessary for promoting the improvement of many districts in Scotland, to which the exercise of that right, or apprehension of its being abused, is at present a considerable hindrance. A fair equivalent ought certainly to be secured to any one possessing a legal right. It is contrary, however, to all wise policy, that any individual should continue in the possession of a right, for which he can receive a compensation, if the exercise of it is hostile to the interest or the improvement of the country; and if this principle is a just one, which can hardly be questioned, its application to claims of thirlage is pretty evident.

23. *Entails.*—Estates under strict entail, seem to be doomed

doomed to perpetual sterility. It is a common saying, "Who would be fool enough to lay out money on the improvement of an entailed estate!" An act was passed some years ago, which does great credit to the learned and respectable character (the Chief Baron Montgomery) by whom it was introduced, and which went as far, as perhaps could be ventured on at the time. But as the consequences resulting from it have not been so beneficial as could have been wished, it is well entitled to consideration, whether an extension of the law is not desirable, if not necessary,

Two measures for that purpose, have been suggested, namely, to give power to the heir in possession, either, first, to grant longer leases; or secondly, to feu out his lands, particularly all waste ground, at its present value, those around the mansion house to be excepted. If the feu-duty were equal to the full value of the lands at the time, and payable not in money, but in grain, or the average *fiar* price, it is impossible for the heirs of entail to suffer any material loss; and the gain to the public, were such a source of improvement laid open, would be immense.

24. *Want of Capital.*—Among the many disadvantages to which this part of the kingdom is subject, the want of capital, for carrying on its improvement, is undoubtedly among the first. It is not easy, however, to point out how this circumstance can well be remedied, unless by the establishment of a bank. At the same time it is to be observed, that a small capital, if employed with industry and economy, and, if it has no obstructions to contend with, has worked wonders. Where, indeed, there is a disposition to do well, it is very seldom that any want of pecuniary assistance is experienced. At any rate, when a country is opened by easy access, good roads, and good harbours, capital will flow from the centre of a kingdom to its extremities; and contribute to their improvement.

25. *Distance of Conveyance.*—It is impossible for any person who has not experienced it, to judge of the great disadvantage, in an agricultural, as well as commercial light, from the distance of conveyance. If any improvement is attempted, by the introduction either of new sorts of grain, or other productions, of new kinds of stock, or by endeavouring to prevail on intelligent men, from other districts, to settle in a country, the more remote and inaccessible it is, it becomes the more difficult to effect it.

In regard to grain or grass seeds in particular, the very worst generally goes to the North. Edinburgh is often supplied from the refuse of London; and Caithness or Orkney from the

the refuse of Edinburgh. Hence experiments are tried, and improvements carried on, under such disadvantages, as cannot easily be overcome, and which the most ardent spirit cannot always surmount.

26. *Harbours.*—Along the Eastern Coast of Scotland, from the Bay of Cromarty to Duncansbay Head, there is a miserable want of harbours, for supplying which, some public assistance would be laid out with the utmost propriety. The harbour at Wick, which is at last completed, is not only of the utmost importance to the fisheries in general, and to the inhabitants of the neighbourhood, but to that valuable branch of the commerce of the kingdom, that is obliged to range along that coast, without a place for shelter, though too often necessary. The harbour at Thurso, is the next that ought to be undertaken.

27. *Roads.*—Unless so remote a district is rendered accessible by good roads, no great improvement can be expected; for nothing else will open this remote but valuable part of the kingdom, to the enterprising and the industrious. The roads that are necessary, should not all be made at the public expense; at the same time it is certain, that the greater part of them must have the assistance of Government, if they are at all to be made.

28. *Tax on Clover-Seed.*—Among the bars to the improvement of the more northern part of the kingdom, is the tax on clover-seed imported. As the sowing of artificial grasses is one of the greatest means of its improvement, it should not be impeded by any financial regulations, and it cannot be doubted, when this subject comes before Parliament, that it will be repealed, at least in so far as regards a part of the kingdom, where the importation of clover-seed, at a cheap rate, and if possible from the best market, ought to meet with the greatest encouragement. There is reason to believe that seed might be procured from America, perhaps superior in quality to what has yet been imported from Holland or Flanders.

29. *Police.*—Some regulations for the destruction of foxes, and other vermin, would be extremely desirable, as a means of improvement, without which that great object, the establishment of sheep farms in the Highlands, cannot be effected. A bill might be brought in, empowering the Justices at their Quarter Sessions, to make regulations to that effect, binding all those who could possibly be benefited by such regulations.

30. *Corn.*

30. *Corn Laws.*—A revisal of the corn system, at least in so far as respects the exportation and importation of oats, seems to be necessary; and I have no hesitation to assert, that if the price of oats on importation were raised to 30*s.* per quarter, that the Northern Districts alone would supply the London market, with all that it now procures of that article from foreign states. At present, the importation price is so low, that there is no encouragement to grow that species of corn, and still less to send it to the London market, where it is not likely to enter *into a fair competition*, considering our taxes and expense of cultivation, with grain of foreign growth.

31. *Beneficial Practices.*—There are but two particulars connected with the agricultural state of the more northern part of the kingdom, which seems to be entitled to the attention of other districts, namely, 1st, the mode of thatching with clay and straw; and 2dly, some practices in the dairy.

The mode of thatching may be thus described: The straw must be thrashed whole in the sheaf, that is, without untying the band which keeps it together. After the corn is thrashed, put four sheaves into one bundle, and make as many bundles of the same size, as may contain a quantity of straw necessary for your purpose. The thatcher then puts up his ladder, within three feet of the right-hand gable, and spreads out one of the bundles on the lower part of the roof, between the ladder and the gable. If the roof is covered with *divots*, or thin turf, the thatcher must twist the upper part of the straw into a knot, then with a stick, prepared for the purpose, force the knot thus formed, either under, or through the divots, so that it may have a firm hold of the roof; then spread the lower part of the bundle of straw nicely on the roof. Continue thus to the very top of the roof, then clay it all over, and begin another tier, or row.

Wheat then is by far the best for the purpose; next, rye straw; strong barley straw is preferable to oat. The thatch should not be thinner than six inches, and when it is eight inches thick, it is the more durable. Divots, or thin turf, were originally thought the best foundation, but it is now found by experience, that it rots the straw, and that straw alone, stitched with rope-yarn, lasts infinitely longer. The thatcher gets 6*s.* per rood, and pays his assistant out of that allowance. He must be supplied, however, with the straw. If straw alone, stitched with rope-yarn, is used, it will last 20 years, but the straw must be laid on two inches thicker than when clay is added.

A roof thatched with divots, straw, and clay, in the common way, will last from 17 to 20 years; it can be mended also

also, without raising any part of the roof that is entire. This kind of roof is much less liable to catch fire, than straw roofs, without clay. The clay that answers the purpose best, is that which has a due proportion of sand. If stiff clay is used, there must be added one cart-load of sand, to every two cart-loads of clay.

Slated roofs are undoubtedly preferable to any other; but where they cannot be afforded, or where straw roofs are constructed, the addition of clay, on the plan above described, seems to be extremely useful.

As the Highlands was a grazing country, I expected to have found there some dairy practices that might be of use. The only information which I think it necessary to take notice of here, relates to the rennet they make use of, which is not confined to the stomach of the calf, but extends to other animals. Some have tried the stomach of lambs, of hares, and of deer, and found them to answer. It is said, that the rennet from the stomach of a sow, improves much the richness and quality of the cheese. Where other articles are wanted, the gizzard of a fowl, properly prepared, will coagulate the milk.

They have in the Highlands a species of cheese, called *caise tennal*, or gathered curd, which some are particularly fond of. It is made as follows:—The curd is freed from whey as much as possible, and put, without the smallest particle of salt, into a plate or dish, and kept in a dark and damp place for 14 or 20 days; it is then broken down, and mixed with salt in the usual proportion, and put into the cheese-press. It is ripe in six or eight months. It is commonly made of sweet milk, but some put cream into it, when the curd is mixed with salt.

32. *Spirit of Improvement.*—The only means, by which a nation that depends upon its agricultural exertions, can be raised to great prosperity, is by exciting a general spirit of improvement. This can easily be effected, when the Government will take the trouble of doing it, by good example, and by a proper share of perseverance. When once excited, such a spirit soon becomes universally prevalent. The fashion of doing good, of improving an estate, of being skilled in agriculture, and the like, quickly spreads, like any other one. Even the young are then early trained, in the course of their academical studies, to become good husbandmen, and the old become ashamed of their ancient prejudices, and unable to withstand the torrent of improvement.

I embrace this opportunity with pleasure, of doing justice to Dr. Drury, the very intelligent Master of Harrow School, whose example, if followed by other persons in the same situation,

situation, would be attended with the best of consequences. The establishment of the Board of Agriculture, he justly perceived, might be the means of impressing his pupils with new ideas, which might be of the utmost consequence to them, in their progress through life. Formerly, in reading the Georgics with his young people, he had remarked, that they were more captivated with the beauty and arrangement of the language, than with the subject treated of; but since they were informed that these matters had become the immediate concern of the Legislature; that they were now investigated by the first characters in their country, and must prove the most certain source of opulence and prosperity to themselves and their fellow-citizens, he had no doubt that they would feel themselves more deeply interested in such investigations, and would go forth into life, not merely satisfied with their utility, but studiously disposed to encourage and promote inquiries, that could only result from the purest patriotism, and the truest philanthropy.

Conclusion to the Report of the Northern Districts of Scotland, as originally drawn up by Sir John Sinclair.

The Report, when completed, will close the General View of the Agriculture of Great Britain, an undertaking which, whether we consider the greatness of the object, the rapidity with which it has been executed, or the manner in which, in general, it has been drawn up, will probably stand unrivalled in any other age or country. From the foundation which is now laid, little doubt can be entertained, that both the theory and practice of Agriculture must soon be brought to a degree of perfection, which they would not otherwise have attained; and indeed, by following the same plan, (that of combining the information and experience of great bodies of people, the practicability of which is now sufficiently proved), every other useful art may be brought to the same desirable state of improvement. And this is an object, in which Great Britain alone is not interested; the advantages of such inquiries are not confined to this particular territory, or that particular age, but in them are involved the most valuable interests of society, and, indeed, the real prosperity and happiness of the human race.*

Account

---

* That truly great and respectable character, General Washington, lately stated in a letter to the Author, his idea of the consequences which may be expected from the establishment of the Board of Agriculture. "I have read with peculiar pleasure and approbation, the work you patronise,

(K)

Account of the Settlement of the British Society for Fisheries, &c. at Pulteney Town, near Wick, in the County of Caithness.

SIR JOHN SINCLAIR, contemplating the great national benefit which would result from prosecuting the Herring and other Fisheries on the Coast of Caithness, recommended many years ago to the British Society for extending the Fisheries, and improving the Sea Coasts of the Kingdom, incorporated by Act of Parliament in 1786, to form a Settlement at an eligible situation in that county. The many shipwrecks, and consequent loss of lives, to which the Baltic traders, and the Coasting vessels resorting to, and passing along that part of Scotland, were exposed, from the want of a Harbour, or place of safety between the Bay of Cromarty and the Pentland Firth, urged Sir John's perseverance, until he prevailed on Sir Benjamin Dunbar, Bart. of Hempriggs, in 1801, to grant a feu to the Society of about 400 Scotch acres of land, on the Southside of the River of Wick, at 62*l.* per annum. In 1803 the purchase was completed.

---

tronise, so much to your own honour, and the utility of the public. Such a General View of the Agriculture in the several Counties of Great Britain is extremely interesting, and cannot fail of being very beneficial to the agricultural concerns of your country, and to those of every other wherein they are read, and must entitle you to their warmest thanks, for having set such a plan on foot, and for prosecuting it with the zeal and intelligence you do.

"I am so much pleased with the plan and execution myself, as to pray you to have the goodness to direct your bookseller to continue to forward them to me, accompanied with the cost, which shall be paid to his order, or remitted so soon as the amount is made known to me; when the whole are received, I will promote, as far as in me lies, the reprinting of them here.

"I know of no pursuit in which more real and important service can be rendered to any country, than by improving its agriculture, its breed of useful animals, and other branches of a husbandman's cares; nor can I conceive any plan more conducive to this end, than the one you have introduced, for bringing to view the actual state of them in all parts of the kingdom, by which good and bad habits are exhibited in a manner too plain to be misconceived. For the accounts given to the British Board of Agriculture appear in general to be drawn up in a masterly manner, so as fully to answer the expectations formed in the excellent Plan which produced them, affording, at the same time, a fund of information, useful in political economy, and serviceable in all countries."

The Government, viewing the public utility which would arise from the formation of a suitable Harbour on the Coast of Caithness, directed Mr. Telford, in 1802, to make a survey and estimates. The result was, that the situation recommended by Sir John Sinclair, and purchased by the British Society, was deemed the most eligible.

The expense of the proposed Harbour having been estimated at 14,000*l.*, the public granted 7500*l.* from the balances of the Forfeited Estates in Scotland, for its construction, in addition to 1000*l.* previously appropriated for that purpose, in aid of the funds of the Society.

The Harbour is now nearly completed, and by the Custom-house returns, 15,000 tons of shipping landed and cleared out with cargoes between the 10th October 1810, and the 10th October 1811. The Harbour is sufficiently capacious for the accommodation of 100 decked vessels at one time.

At the head of the Harbour several curing-houses have been erected, and a piece of ground is to be shortly inclosed, for the building and repair of ships and smaller vessels.

From one to two hundred settlers are building houses on lots of land feued to them by the Society, at 15*s.* 20*s.* and 25*s.* each, according to the elegibility of the situation. These lots are 50 feet long in front, by 100 feet in depth backward. The plan of the Town and Harbour has been laid down by Mr. Telford the Engineer, and it has been named *Pulteney Town*, as a mark of respect to the late Sir William Pulteney, who was Governor of the Society at the time of the purchase.

The land belonging to the Society has been lately subdivided into allotments, and instructions are preparing for the agricultural improvements of which it is most susceptible.

The Society have made a Canal from the Loch of Hempriggs, about two miles distant from their property, to supply water for a Corn-mill already erected, and for such other machinery as shall be found necessary. Sir Benjamin Dunbar has erected a thrashing-mill on the head of that Canal. It is intended also, by one or more Canals, to bring water from the Loch for irrigating the land, for scouring out the Harbour, and for supplying, by means of pipes introduced into their houses, the settlers with water for domestic purposes.

The Improvements already made by the Society, have not only doubled the former rental of that tract of ground, but have had a beneficial effect on the adjacent country. Mr. Burn, the Architect of the Harbour, has converted a small piece of land attached to his house, which was formerly a barren sand, into a rich corn-field. Mr. John Macleay is levelling five acres of hitherto unproductive rugged ground, into a beautiful lawn, on which he is building a house, that will be

an

an ornament to the neighbourhood. Other improvements of a similar nature are carrying on.

The Society's land abounds with lime, and with stone quarries, and from its advantageous situation, and other circumstances, presents great encouragement to persons disposed to prosecute the herring, cod, and ling fishery, for which the Coast of Caithness is peculiarly adapted.

(L)

Linnean Names of the Plants used as Medicines for Sheep and Horses in Caithness.

It appears, that the Linnean name of the small *wild myrtle*, mentioned in p. 218 of the Caithness Report, is, *myrica gale;*—of the *creeping bur*, mentioned in page 219, is, *lycopodium clavatum;* and of the *upright bur*, which grows in flat bogs, and is much more powerful than the creeping bur, is *lycopodium selago.* The uses of these plants in medicine, have been already explained in the Report.

INDEX.

O 4 Bruisers,

Draining,

Houses

Peter-

Rents

Sheep,

Watten,

INDEX TO APPENDIX.

Coal,

Henderson,

Ord

Ryrie,

London: Printed by B. M'Millan, Bow Street, Covent Garden.

LIST OF PUBLICATIONS
OF
THE BOARD OF AGRICULTURE,
Which may be had of the Publishers of this Volume.

ENGLAND.

	£.	s.	d.
A General View of the Agriculture of Bedfordshire, by THOS. BATCHELOR, Farmer, 8vo. - - -	0	14	0
——— of Berkshire, by Dr. MAVOR, 8vo. -	0	18	0
——— of Buckinghamshire, by the Rev. ST. JOHN PRIEST, 8vo. - - - - - -	0	12	0
——— of Cambridgeshire, by the Rev Mr. GOOCH, 8vo.	0	9	0
——— of Cheshire, by HENRY HOLLAND, Esq. 8vo.	0	10	0
——— of Cornwall, by G. B. WORGAN, 8vo. -	0	12	0
——— of Derbyshire, by JOHN FAREY, Sen. Mineral Surveyor, 8vo. Vol. I. - - - -	1	1	0
——— of Devonshire, by CHARLES VANCOUVER, 8vo.	0	15	0
——— of Durham, by Mr. BAILEY, 8vo. - -	0	10	6
——— of Essex, by the SECRETARY of the BOARD, 2 vols. 8vo. - - - - - - -	1	1	0
——— of Gloucestershire, by Mr. RUDGE, 8vo. -	0	9	0
——— of Hampshire, by CHARLES VANCOUVER, 8vo.	0	16	0
——— of Hertfordshire, by the SECRETARY of the BOARD, 8vo. - - - - - - -	0	7	0
——— of Herefordshire, by JOHN DUNCUMBE, A. M. 8vo. - - - - - - - -	0	6	0
——— of Huntingdonshire, by Mr. R PARKINSON, 8vo.	0	9	0
——— of Kent, by JOHN BOYS, of Betshanger, Farmer, 8vo. Second Edition, - - - - -	0	7	0
——— of Lancashire, by Mr. JOHN HOLT, of Walton, near Liverpool, 8vo. - - - - -	0	6	0
——— of Leicestershire and Rutland, by WM. PITT, of Pendeford, near Wolverhampton, and Mr. R. PARKINSON,	0	14	0
——— of Lincolnshire, by the SECRETARY of the BOARD, 8vo. Second Edition, - - - - -	0	12	0
——— of Middlesex, by JOHN MIDDLETON, Esq. of West Barns Farm, Merton, and of Lambeth, Surrey, Land Surveyor, 8vo. Second Edition, - -	0	14	0
——— of the County of Norfolk, by the SECRETARY of the BOARD, 8vo. - - - - - -	0	9	0
——— of the County of Norfolk, by NATHANIEL KENT, Esq. of Fulham, Middlesex, 8vo. - -	0	6	0
——— of Northampton, by W. PITT, of Pendeford, near Wolverhampton, 8vo. - - - - -	0	8	0
——— of Northumberland, Cumberland, and Westmorland, by Messrs. BAILEY, CULLEY and PRINGLE, 8vo.	0	9	0
——— of North Wales, by WALTER DAVIES, A. M. Rector of Manafon, in Montgomeryshire, 8vo. - -	0	12	0
——— of Nottinghamshire, by ROBERT LOWE, Esq. of Oxton, 8vo. - - - - - - - -	0	5	0
——— of Oxfordshire, by the SECRETARY of the BOARD, 8vo. - - - - - - -	0	12	0
——— of Salop, by the Rev. JOSEPH PLYMLEY, M. A. Archdeacon of Salop, in the Diocese of Hereford, and Honorary Member of the Board, 8vo. - -	0	9	0
——— of Somerset, by JOHN BILLINGSLEY, Esq. of Ashwick Grove, near Shepton Mallet, 8vo. - -	0	7	0

	£.	s.	d.
A General View of the Agriculture of Stafford, by Wm. Pitt, of Pendeford, near Wolverhampton, 8vo. Second Edition,	0	9	0
——— of Suffolk, by the Secretary of the Board, 8vo. Second Edition, - - - - -	0	8	0
——— of Surrey, by William Stevenson, 8vo.	0	15	0
——— of Sussex, by the Rev. Arthur Young, 8vo.	0	14	0
——— of Wiltshire, by Thos. Davis, 8vo. -	0	9	0
——— of Worcestershire, by Wm. Pitt, of Pendeford, near Wolverhampton, 8vo. - - -	0	10	6
——— of Yorkshire (the West Riding), by Robert Brown, Farmer at Markle, near Haddington, Scotland, 8vo.	0	9	0
——— of Yorkshire (the North Riding), by John Tuke, Land Surveyor, 8vo. - - -	0	9	0

SCOTLAND.

A General View of the Agriculture of the County of Aberdeen, by George Skene Keith, D.D. Minister of Keith-Hall and Kinkell, 8vo. - - - -	0	15	0
——— of Argyle, by John Smith, D.D. one of the Ministers of Campbelton, 8vo. Second Edition, -	0	9	0
——— of Berwickshire, by Robert Kerr, 8vo.	0	13	0
——— of Caithness, by Capt. J. Henderson, 8vo.	0	15	0
——— of Clydesdale, by John Naismith, 8vo. Second Edition, - - - - - - -	0	7	0
——— of East-Lothian, from the Papers of the late R. Somerville, Esq. 8vo. - - - - -	0	6	0
——— of Fife, by John Thomson, D.D. Minister at Markinch, 8vo. - - - - - -	0	7	0
——— of Galloway, by the Rev. S. Smith, 8vo. -	0	9	0
——— of The Hebrides, by Mr. M'Donald, 8vo.	1	1	0
——— of Inverness-shire, by James Robertson, D.D. Minister at Callander, 8vo. - - - - -	0	14	0
——— of Kincardineshire, by Mr. Robertson, 8vo.	0	10	6
——— of Mid-Lothian, by George Robertson, Farmer at Granton, near Edinburgh, 8vo. - -	0	7	0
——— of Nairne and Moray, by Mr. Naismith, 8vo.	0	14	0
——— of Perth, by James Robertson, D.D. Minister at Callander, 8vo. - - - - - -	0	7	0
——— of Ross and Cromarty, by Sir G. S. Mackenzie,	0	9	0
——— of Roxburgh and Selkirk, by the Rev. Robert Douglas, D.D. Minister at Galashiels, 8vo. -	0	7	0
——— of Sutherland, by Capt. J. Henderson, 8vo.	0	12	0
Communications to the Board of Agriculture, on Subjects relative to the Husbandry and internal Improvement of the Country. Vol. I. 4to. - - - -	1	1	0
Ditto, Vol. II. - - - - - - - -	1	1	0
Ditto, Vol. III. - - - - - -	0	18	0
Ditto, Vol. IV. - - - - - -	0	18	0
Ditto, Vol. V. - - - - - - -	1	1	0
Ditto, Vol. VI. - - - - -	1	10	0
Ditto, Vol. VII. Part I. - - - - - -	0	14	0
Report of the Committee of the Board of Agriculture on the Culture and Use of Potatoes, 4to. - - - -	0	7	6
Account of Experiments tried by the Board of Agriculture on the Composition of various Sorts of Bread, 4to. -	0	1	0
Letter from the Earl of Winchilsea, on the Advantages of Cottagers renting Land, 4to. - - - - -	0	1	0
Elkington's Mode of Draining, by Johnstone, 8vo.	0	12	0

A CATALOGUE

OF

AGRICULTURAL SEEDS, &c.

SOLD BY

THOMAS GIBBS AND Co.

Seedsmen and Nurserymen to the Board of Agriculture,

Corner of Half-Moon-Street, Piccadilly, London :

Who also Sell every Article in the Nursery and Seed Line; and with whom Bailiffs, wanting Places, leave their Address, and particulars of Situations in which they have previously been.

Barley. Isle of Thanet.
—— Norfolk.
—— Naked.
—— Winter.
Beans. Small Essex.
—— Tick.
—— Mazagan.
Broom. Common yellow.
Buck, or French wheat.
Burnet.

Cabbage. Gibbs' true drum-head, for cattle.
—— Scotch.
—— American.
—— Large red.
—— Long-sided.
—— White turnip above ground.
—— Purple ditto ditto, or kohl rabi.
—— White turnip under ground.
—— Tall green borecole.
—— Tall purple ditto.
—— Siberian hardy sprouting.
Carrot. Large thick orange, for cattle.
—— Large thick red, ditto.
Canary.
Chicory.
Clover. Common red.
—— Perennial, or cow-grass.
—— White Dutch.
—— Yellow, trefoil, non-such, or black grass.

Clover. Malta.
—— Providential.

Flax, or linseed.
Furze.

Grass. Meadow foxtail.
—— Meadow fescue.
—— Sheep's fescue.
—— Hardish fescue.
—— Purple ditto.
—— Float ditto.
—— Crested dogstail.
—— Rough cocksfoot.
—— Tall oat-grass.
—— Yellow ditto.
—— Meadow ditto.
—— Sweet vernal.
—— Great meadow.
—— Common ditto.
—— Marsh ditto.
—— Compressed ditto.
—— Annual ditto.
—— Common ray-grass.
—— Peacey ditto.
—— Improved perennial do
—— Timothy.
—— Yorkshire.
With many other sorts.

Hemp. Russian.
—— English.
Honeysuckle. French.

Lettuce. Large Coss.
Lentils. Small.
—— Large.

Lucerne.

Mangel wurzel.
Maw-seed.
Medicago, various sorts.
Millet. Red.
—— White.
Mustard. Brown.

Oats. Early Essex.
—— Dutch brew.
—— Tartarian.
—— Poland.
—— Potatoe.
—— Flanders.
—— Caspian.
—— Black.

Parsley. Plain.
Parsnip. Large thick.
Pea. Marlborough grey.
— Large grey rouncival.
— Early white.
— White boiling.
— Pearl.
— Blue Prussian.
— Maple.
Potatoes. Ox-noble.
—— Late champion.
—— Large red.
—— Nicholson seedling.
—— Bomb-shell.

Rib-grass. Lambs-tongue, or
—— Upright plantain.
Rape, or coleseed.
Rye.

Sainfoin.
Saridella.

Tares. Spring.
—— Winter.
—— White.
—— Perennial.
Trefoil. Birdsfoot.
—— Common, various sorts.
Turnip. Early stone.
—— White Norfolk.
—— Norfolk bell.
—— Stubble.
—— Green top.

Turnip. Red top.
—— Large yellow.
—— Globe.
—— White tankard.
—— Green ditto.
—— Red-top ditto.
—— Large Dutch.
—— True yellow Swedish, or ruta baga.
—— White Swedish.

Vetch. Kidney.
—— Chickling.
—— Pale-flowered.
—— Everlasting.
—— Great wood.
—— Six-flowered.
—— Tufted.
—— Bush.
—— Hoary.
—— Sainfoin.
—— Red-flowered.
—— Biennial.
—— Bastard.
—— Broad-podded.
—— Rough.
—— Single-flowered.
—— Narbonne.
—— Flat-podded.
—— Hairy ditto.
—— Narrow-leaved.
—— Streaked.
—— White-flowered.
—— White-seeded.
—— Horse-shoe.
—— Milk.
—— Liquorice.

Weld.
Wheat. Red Lammas.
—— Common white.
—— White hedge.
—— White Siberian.
—— Egyptian.
—— Sicilian.
—— Round African.
—— Zealand.
—— Cape.
—— Dantzick.
Woad.

Yarrow.

Printed by B. M'Millan,
Bow-Street, Covent-Garden.

Lightning Source UK Ltd.
Milton Keynes UK
UKHW050702201221
395957UK00004B/233

9 781241 526597